The Diary and Letters of
Madame D'Arblay

by

Frances Burney

VOL. I

The Echo Library 2006

Published by
The Echo Library
Echo Library

131 High St.
Teddington

Middlesex TW11 8HH
www.echolibrary.com

ISBN 1-40680-092-9

CONTENTS

before the King and Queen—Dr. Burney is Disappointed of a Place—A Visit to Warren Hastings and his Wife—A Proposal from the Queen—Miss Burney accepts the Queen's Offer.

Confidences—The Queen tired of Her Gewgaws—A Holiday at last—Tea Room Gambols—A dreadful Mishap—"Is it Permitted?"— The Plump Provost and his Lady—The Equerries Violate the Rules—Mr. Turbulent on Court Routine—An Equerry on the Court Concert—Dr, Herschel's Large Telescope—Illness, and some Reflections it gave rise to.

PREFACE

"THE Diary and Letters of Madame D'Arblay," edited by her niece, Mrs. Barrett, were originally published in seven volumes, during the years 1842-1846. The work comprised but a portion of the diary and voluminous correspondence of its gifted writer, for the selection of which Madame D'Arblay, herself in part, and in part Mrs. Barrett, were responsible. From this selection the present one has been made, which, it is believed, will be found to include all the most valuable and interesting passages of the original. We can at least claim for this, the first popular edition of the Diary, that we have scrupulously fulfilled Madame D'Arblay's injunction to her former editor, "that whatever might be effaced or Omitted, nothing should in anywise be altered or added to her records."

Of the Diary itself it is hardly necessary here to say anything in praise. It has long been acknowledged a classic; it is indubitably the most entertaining, in Some respects the most valuable, work of its kind in the English language, Regarded as a series of pictures of the society of the time, the Diary is unsurpassed for vivid Colouring and truthful delineation. As such alone it would possess a strong claim upon our attention, but how largely is our interest increased, when we find that the figures which fill the most prominent positions in the foreground of these pictures, are those of the most noble, most gifted, and Most distinguished men of the day! To mention but a few

FRANCES Burney was descended from a family which bore the name of Macburney, and which, though probably of Irish origin, had been long settled in Shropshire and was possessed of considerable estates in that county. Unhappily, many years before her birth, the Macburneys began, as if of set purpose and in a spirit of determined rivalry, to expose and ruin themselves. The heir apparent, Mr. James Macburney offended his father by making a runaway rnatch with an actress from Goodman's -fields - The old gentleman could devise no more judicious mode of wreaking vengeance on his undutiful boy than by marrying the cook. The cook gave birth to a son, named Joseph, who succeeded to all the lands of the family, while James was cut off with a shilling. The favourite son, however, was so extravagant that he soon became as poor as his disinherited brother. Both were forced to earn their bread by their labour. Joseph turned dancing-master and settled in Norfolk. James struck off the Mac from the beginning of his name and set up as a portrait painter at Chester. Here he had a son, named Charles, well known as the author of the "History of Music" and as the father of two remarkable children, of a son distinguished by learning and of a daughter still more honourably distinguished by genius.

Charles early showed a taste for that art of which, at a later period, he became the historian. He was apprenticed to a celebrated musician[1] in London, and He applied himself to study with vigour and success. He early found a kind and munificent Patron in Fulk Greville, a highborn and highbred man, who seems to have had in large measure all the accomplishments and all the follies, all the virtues and all the vices, which, a hundred years ago, were considered as making up the character of a fine gentleman. Under such protection, the young artist had every prospect of a brilliant career in the capital. But -his health failed. It became necessary for him to retreat from the smoke and river fog of London to the pure air of the coast. He accepted the place of organist at Lynn, and settled at that town with a young lady who had recently become his wife. [2]

At Lynn, in June, 1752, Frances Burney was born. [3]Nothing in her childhood indicated that she would, while still a young woman, have secured for herself an honourable and permanent place among English writers. She was shy and silent. Her brothers and sisters called her a dunce, and not altogether without some show of reason ; for at eight years old she did not know her letters.

In 1760, Mr. Burney quitted Lynn for London, and took a house in Poland-street; a situation which had been fashionable in the reign of Queen Anne, but which, since that time, had been deserted by most of its wealthy and noble inhabitants. He afterwards resided in St. Martin's- street, on the south side of Leicestersquare. His house there is still well known, and will continue to be well known as long as our island retains any trace of civilisation ; for it was the dwelling of Newton, and the square turret which distinguishes it from all the surrounding buildings was Newton's observatory,

Mr. Burney at once obtained as many pupils of the most respectable description as he had time to attend, and was thus enabled to support his family, modestly indeed, and frugally, but in comfort and independence. His professional merit obtained for him the degree of Doctor of Music from the

University of Oxford; [4] and his works on subjects connected with art gained for him a place, respectable, though certainly not eminent, among men of letters.

The progress of the mind of Frances Burney, from her ninth to her twenty-fifth year, well deserves to be recorded, When her education had proceeded no further than the hornbook, she lost her mother, and thenceforward she educated herself. Her father appears to have been as bad a father as a very honest, affectionate and sweet-tempered man can well be. He loved his daughter dearly ; but it never seems to have occurred to him that a parent has other duties to perform to children than that of fondling them. It would indeed have been impossible for him to superintend their education himself. His professional engagements occupied him all day. At seven in the morning, he began to attend his pupils, and, when London was full, was sometimes employed in teaching till eleven at night. He was often forced to carry in his pocket a tin box of sandwiches and a bottle of wine and water, on which he dined in a hackney coach while hurrying from one scholar to another. Two of his daughters he sent to a seminary at Paris; but he imagined that Frances would run some risk of being perverted from the Protestant faith if she were educated in a Catholic country, and he therefore kept her at home. No governess, no teacher of any art or of any language was provided for her. But one of her sisters showed her how to write ; and, before she was fourteen, she began to find pleasure in reading.

it was not, however, by reading that her intellect was formed. Indeed, when her best novels were produced, her knowledge of books was very small. When at the height of her fame, she was unacquainted with the most celebrated works of Voltaire and Moli6re ; and, what seems still more extraordinary, had never heard or seen a line of Churchill, who, when she was a girl, was the most popular of living poets. It is particularly deserving of observation that she appears to have been by no means a novel reader. Her father's library was large, and he had admitted into it so many books which rigid moralists generally exclude that he felt uneasy, as he afterwards owned, when Johnson began to examine the shelves. But in the whole collection there was only a single novel, Fielding's "Amelia." [5]

An education, however, which to most girls would have been useless, but which suited Fanny's mind better than elaborate culture, was in constant progress during her passage from childhood to womanhood. The great book of human nature was turned over before her. Her father's social position was very peculiar. He belonged in fortune and station to the middle class. His daughters seemed to have been suffered to mix freely with those whom butlers and waiting-maids call vulgar. We are told that they were in the habit of playing with the children of a wigmaker who lived in the adjoining house. Yet few nobles could assemble in the most stately mansions of Grosvenor-square or St. James's-square a society so various and so brilliant as was sometimes to be found in Dr. Burney's cabin. His mind, though not very powerful or capacious, was restlessly active ; and, in the intervals of his professional pursuits, he had contrived to lay up much miscellaneous information. His attainments, the suavity of his temper and the general simplicity of his manners had obtained for him ready admission to the first literary circles. While he was still at Lynn, he had won Johnson's heart by sounding with honest zeal the praises of the "English Dictionary." In London, the two friends met frequently and agreed most harmoniously. One tie, indeed, was wanting to their mutual attachment. Burney loved his own art passionately, and Johnson just knew the bell of St. Clement's church from the organ. Theyhad, however, many topics in common; and on winter nights their conversations were sometimes prolonged till the fire had gone out and the candles had burned away to the wicks. Burney'sadmiration of the powers which had produced "Rasselas" and "The Rambler" bordered on idolatry. He gave a singular proof of this at his first visit to Johnson's ill-furnished garret. The master of the apartment was not at home. The enthusiastic visitor looked about for some relic which he could carry away, but he could see nothing lighter than the chairs and the fireirons. At last he discovered an old broom, tore some bristles from the stump, wrapped them in silver paper, and departed as happy as Louis IX. when the holy nail of St. Denis was found. [6]Johnson, on the other hand, condescended to growl out that Burney was an honest fellow, a man whom it was impossible not to like.

Garrick, too, was a frequent visitor in Poland-street and St. Martin's-street. That wonderful actor loved the society of children, partly from good nature and partly from vanity. The ecstasies of mirth and terror, which his gestures and play of countenance never failed to produce in a nursery, flattered him quite as much as the applause of mature critics. He often exhibited all his powers of mimicry for the amusement of the little Burneys, awed them by shuddering and crouching as if he saw a ghost, scared them by raving like a maniac in St. Luke's, and then at once became an auctioneer, a chimney-sweeper or an old woman, and made them laugh till the tears ran down their cheeks.

But it would be tedious to recount the names of all the men of letters and artists whom Frances Burney had an opportunity of seeing and hearing. Colman, Twining, Harris, Baretti, Hawkesworth, Reynolds, Barry, were among those who occasionally surrounded the tea table and supper tray at her father's modest dwelling. This was not all. The distinction which Dr. Burney had acquired as a musician and as the historian of music, attracted to his house the most eminent musical performers of that age. The greatest Italian singers who visited England regarded him as the dispenser of fame in their art, and exerted themselves to obtain his suffrage. Pacchierotti became his intimate friend. The rapacious Agujari, who sang for nobody else under fifty pounds an air, sang her best for Dr. Burney without a fee; and in the company of Dr. Burney even the haughty and eccentric Gabrielli constrained herself to behave with civility. It was thus in his power to give, with scarcely any expense, concerts equal to those of the aristocracy. On such occasions, the quiet street in which he lived was blocked up by coroneted chariots, and his little drawing-room was crowded with peers, peeresses, ministers and ambassadors. On one evening, of which we happen to have a full account, there were present Lord Mulgrave, Lord Bruce, Lord and Lady Edgecumbe, Lord Barrington from the War office, Lord Sandwich from the Admiralty, Lord Ashburnham, with his gold key dangling from his pocket, and the French ambassador, M. De Guignes, renowned for his fine person and for his success in gallantry. But the great show of the night was the Russian ambassador, Count Orloff, whose gigantic figure was all in a blaze with jewels, and in whose demeanour the untamed ferocity of the Scythian might be discerned through a thin varnish of French Politeness. As he stalked about the small parlour, brushing the ceiling with his toupee, the girls whispered to each other, with mingled admiration and borror, that he was the favoured lover of his august mistress; that be had borne the chief part in the revolution to which she owed her throne; and that his huge hands, now glittering with diamond rings, had given the last squeeze to the windpipe of her unfortunate husband.

With such illustrious guests as these were mingled all the most remarkable specimens of the race of lions, a kind of game which is hunted in London every spring with more than Meltonian ardour and perseverance. Bruce, who had washed down steaks cut from living oxen with water from the fountains of the Nile, came to swagger and talk about his travels. Ornai lisped broken English, and made all the assembled musicians hold their ears by howling Otaheitean love-songs, such as those with which Oberea charmed her Opano.

With the literary and fashionable society which occasionally met under Dr. Burney's roof, Frances can scarcely be said to have mingled. [7]She was not a musician, and could therefore bear no part in the concerts. She was shy almost to awkwardness, and she scarcely ever joined in the conversation. The slightest remark from a stranger disconcerted her, and even the old friends of her father who tried to draw her out could seldom extract more than a Yes or a No. Her figure was small, her face not distinguished by beauty. She was therefore suffered to withdraw quietly to the background, and, unobserved herself, to observe all that passed. Her nearest relations were aware that she had good sense, but seem not to have suspected that under her demure and bashful deportment were concealed a fertile invention and a keen sense of the ridiculous. She had not, it is true, an eye for the fine shades of character. But every marked peculiarity instantly caught her notice and remained engraven on her imagination. Thus while still a girl she had laid up such a store of materials for fiction as few of those who mix much in the world are able to accumulate during a long life. She had watched and listened to people of every class, from princes and great officers of state down to artists living in garrets and poets familiar with subterranean cookshops. Hundreds of remarkable persons had passed in review before her, English, French, German, Italian, lords and fiddlers, deans of cathedrals and managers of theatres, travellers leading about newly caught savages, and singing women escorted by deputy husbands.

So strong was the impression made on the mind of Frances by the society which she was in the habit of seeing and hearing, that she began to write little fictitious narratives as soon as she could use her pen with ease, which, as we have said, was not very early. Her sisters were amused by her stories. But Dr. Burney knew nothing of their existence ; and in another quarter her literary propensities met with serious discouragement. When she was fifteen, her father took a second wife. [8]The new Mrs. Burney soon found out that her daughter-in-law was fond of scribbling, and delivered several good-natured lectures on the subject. The advice no doubt was well meant, and might have been given by the most judicious friend ; for at that time, from causes to which we may hereafter advert, nothing could be more disadvantageous to a young lady than to be known as a novel writer. Frances yielded, relinquished her favourite pursuit, and made a bonfire of all her manuscripts. [9]

She now hemmed and stitched from breakfast to dinner with scrupulous regularity. But the dinners of that time were early ; and the afternoon was her own. Though she had given up novelwriting, she was still fond of using her pen. She began to keep a diary, and she corresponded largely with a person who seems to have had the chief share in the formation of her mind. This was Samuel Crisp, an old friend of her father. His name, well known, near a century ago, in the most splendid circles of London, has long been forgotten. His history is, however, so interesting and instructive, that it tempts us to venture on a digression. Long before Frances Burney was born, Mr. Crisp had made his entrance into the world, with every advantage. He was well connected and well educated. His face and figure were conspicuously handsome; his manners were polished; his fortune was easy; his character was without stain ; he lived in the best society; he had read much ; he talked well; his taste in literature, music, painting, architecture, sculpture, was held in high esteem. Nothing that the world can give seemed to be wanting to his happiness and respectability, except that he should understand the limits of his powers, and should not throw away distinctions which were within his reach in the pursuit of distinctions which were unattainable. " It is an uncontrolled truth," says Swift, "that no man ever made an ill figure who understood his own talents, nor a good one who mistook them." Every day brings with it fresh illustrations of this weighty saying ; but the best commentary that we remember is the history of Samuel Crisp. Men like him have their proper place, and it is a most important one, in the Commonwealth of Letters. It is by the judgment of such men that the rank of authors is finally determined. It is neither to the multitude, nor to the few who are gifted with great creative genius, that we are to look for sound critical decisions. The multitude, unacquainted with the best models, are captivated by whatever stuns and dazzles them. They deserted Mrs. Siddons to run after Master Betty; and they now prefer, we have no doubt, Jack Sheppard to Van Artevelde. A man of great original genius, on the other hand, a man who has attained to mastery in some high walk of art, is by no means to be implicitly trusted as a judge of the performances of others. The erroneous decisions pronounced by such men are without number. It is commonly supposed that jealousy makes them unjust. But a more creditable explanation may easily be found. The very excellence of a work shows that some of the faculties of the author have been developed at the expense of the rest - for it is not given to the human intellect to expand itself widely in all directions at once and to be at the same time gigantic and well-proportioned. Whoever becomes pre-eminent in any art, nay, in any style of art, generally does so by devoting himself with intense and exclusive enthusiasm to the pursuit of one kind of excellence. His perception of other kinds of excellence is too often impaired. Out of his own department, he blames at random, and is far less to be trusted than the mere connoisseur, who produces nothing, and whose business is only to judge and enjoy. One painter is distinguished by his exquisite finishing. He toils day after day to bring the veins of a cabbage leaf, the folds of a lace veil, the wrinkles of an old woman's face, nearer and nearer to perfection. In the time which he employs on a square foot of canvas, a master of a different order covers the walls of a palace with gods burying giants under mountains, or makes the cupola of a church alive with seraphim and martyrs. The more fervent the passion of each of these artists for his art, the higher the !merit of each in his own line, the more unlikely it is that they will justly appreciate each other. Many persons, who never handled a pencil, probably do far more justice to Michael Angelo than would have been done by Gerard Douw, and far more justice to Gerard Douw than would have been done by Michael Angelo.

It is the same with literature. Thousands, who have no spark of the genius of Dryden or Wordsworth, do to Dryden the justice which has never been done by Wordsworth, and to Wordsworth the justice which, we suspect, would never have been done by Dryden. Gray, Johnson, Richardson, Fielding, are all highly esteemed by the great body of intelligent and well informed men. But Gray could see no merit in "Rasselas," and Johnson could see no merit in "The Bard." Fielding thought Richardson a solemn prig, and Richardson perpetually expressed contempt and disgust for Fielding's lowness.

Mr. Crisp seems, as far as we can judge, to have been a man eminently qualified for the useful office of a connoisseur. His talents and knowledge fitted him to appreciate justly almost every species of intellectual superiority. As an adviser he was inestimable. Nay, he might probably have held a respectable rank as a writer if he would have confined himself to some department of literature in which nothing more than sense, taste, and reading was required. Unhappily, he set his heart on being a great poet, wrote a tragedy in five acts on the death of Virginia, and offered it to Garrick, who was his personal friend. Garrick read, shook his head, and expressed a doubt whether it would be wise in Mr. Crisp to stake a reputation, which stood high, on the success of such a piece. But the author, blinded by self-love, set in motion a machinery such as none could long resist. His intercessors were the most eloquent man and the most lovely woman of that generation. Pitt was induced to read "Virginia" and to pronounce it excellent. Lady Coventry, with fingers which might have furnished a model to sculptors, forced the manuscript into the reluctant hand of the manager; and, in the year 1754, the play was brought forward.

Nothing that skill or friendship could do was omitted. Garrick wrote both prologue and epilogue. The zealous friends of the author filled every box ; and, by their strenuous exertions, the life of the play was prolonged during ten nights. But though there was no clamorous reprobation, it was universally felt that the attempt had failed. When "Virginia" was printed, the pub lic disappointment was even greater than at the representation. The critics, the Monthly Reviewers in particular, fell on plot ,characters, and diction without mercy, but, we fear, not without justice. We have never met with a copy of the play; but if we mayjudge from the lines which are extracted in the "Gentleman's Magazine," and which do not appear to have been malevolently selected, we should say that nothing but the acting of Garrick and the partiality of the audience could have saved so feeble and unnatural a drama from instant damnation. The ambition of the poet was still unsubdued.. When the London season closed, he applied himself vigorously to the work of removing blemishes. He does not seem to have suspected, what we are strongly inclined to suspect, that the whole piece was one blemish, and that the passages which were meant to be fine were, in truth, bursts of that tame extravagance into which writers fall when they set themselves to be sublime and pathetic in spite of nature. He omitted, added, retouched, and flattered himself with hopes of a complete success in the following year; but, in the following year, Garrick showed no disposition to bring the amended tragedy on the stage. Solicitation and remonstrance were tried in vain. Lady Coventry, drooping under that malady which seems ever to select what is loveliest for its prey, could render no assistance. The manager's language was civilly evasive; but his resolution was inflexible. Crisp had committed a great error ; but he had escaped with a very slight penance. His play had not been hooted from the boards. It had, on the contrary, been better received than many very estimable performances have been-than Johnson's "Irene," for example, or Goldsmith's "Good-natured Man." Had Crisp been wise, he would have thought himself happy in having purchased self-knowledge so cheap. He would have relinquished, without vain repinings, the hope of poetical distinction, and would have turned to the many sources of happiness which he still possessed. Had he been, on the other hand, an unfeeling and unblushing dunce, he would have gone on writing scores of bad tragedies in defiance of censure and derision. But he had too much sense to risk a second defeat, yet too little to bear his first defeat like a man. The fatal delusion that he was a great dramatist had taken firm possession of his mind. His failure he attributed to every cause except the true one. He complained of the ill-will of Garrick, who appears to have done everything that ability and zeal could do, and who, from selfish motives, would, of course, have been well pleased if "Virginia" had been as successful as "The Beggar's Opera." Nay, Crisp complained of the languor of the friends whose partiality had given him three benefit nights to which he had no claim. He complained of the injustice of the spectators, when, in truth, he ought to have been grateful for their unexampled patience. He lost his temper and spirits, and became a cynic and a hater of mankind. From London be retired to Hampton, and from Hampton to a solitary and long-deserted mansion, built on a common in one of the wildest tracts of Surrey. [10]No road, not even a sheepwalk, connected his lonely dwelling with the abodes of men. The place of his retreat was strictly concealed from his old associates. In the spring, he sometimes emerged, and was seen at exhibitions and concerts in London. But he soon disappeared and hid himself, with no society but his books, in his dreary hermitage. He survived his failure about thirty years. A new generation sprang up around him. No memory of his bad verses remained among men. His very name was forgotten. How completely the world had lost sight of him will appear from a single circumstance. We looked for his name in a copious Dictionary of Dramatic Authors published while he was still alive, and we found only that Mr. Samuel Crisp, of the Custom-house, had written a play called "Virginia," acted in 1754. To the last, however, the unhappy man continued to brood over the injustice of the manager and the pit, and tried to convince himself and others that he had missed the highest literary honours only because he had omitted some fine passages in compliance with Garrick's judgment. Alas for human nature, that the wounds of vanity should smart and bleed so much longer than the wounds of affection! Few people, we believe, whose nearest friends and relations died in 1754, had any acute feeling of the loss in 1782. Dear sisters, and favourite daughters, and brides snatched away before the honeymoon was passed, had been forgotten, or were remembered only with a tranquil regret. But Samuel Crisp was still mourning for his tragedy, like Rachel weeping for her children, and would not be comforted. "Never," such was his language twenty-eight years after his disaster, "never give up or alter a tittle unless it perfectly coincides with your inward feelings. I can say this to my sorrow and my cost. But mum!" Soon after these words were written, his life—a life which might have been eminently useful and happy—ended in the same gloom in which, during more than a quarter of a century, it had been passed. We have thought it worth while to rescue from oblivion this curious fragment of literary history. It seems to us at once ludicrous, melancholy, and full of instruction. [11]

Crisp was an old and very intimate friend of the Burneys. To them alone was confided the name of the desolate old hall in which he hid himself like a wild beast in a den. For them were reserved such remains of his humanity as had survived the failure of his play. Frances Burney he regarded as his daughter. He called her his Fannikin; and she in return called him her dear Daddy. In truth, he seems to have done much more than her real father for the development of her intellect ; for though he was a bad poet, he was a scholar, a thinker, and an excellent counsellor. He was particularly fond of Dr. Burney's concerts. They had indeed, been commenced at his suggestion, and when he visited London he constantly attended them. But when he grew old, and when gout, brought on partly by mental irritation, confined him to his retreat, he was desirous of having a glimpse of that gay and brilliant world from which he was exiled, and he pressed Fannikin to send him full accounts of her father's evening parties. A few of her letters to him have been published; and it is impossible to read them without discerning in them all the powers which afterwards produced "Evelina" and "Cecilia"; the quickness in catching every odd peculiarity of character and manner; the skill in grouping; the humour, often richly comic, sometimes even farcical.

Fanny's propensity to novel-writing had for a time been kept down. It now rose up stronger than ever. The heroes and heroines of the tales which had perished in the flames were still present to the eye of her mind. One favourite story, in particular, haunted her imagination. It was about a certain Caroline Evelyn, a beautiful damsel who made an unfortunate love match and died, leaving an infant daughter. Frances began to image to herself the various scenes, tragic and comic, through which the poor motherless girl, highly connected on one side, meanly connected on the other, might have to pass. A crowd of unreal beings, good and bad, grave and ludicrous, surrounded the pretty, timid young orphan ; a coarse sea captain ; an ugly, insolent fop, blazing in a superb court dress ; another fop, as ugly and as insolent, but lodged on Snow-hill and tricked out in second-hand finery for the Hampstead ball; an old woman, wrinkles and rouge, flirting her fan with the air of a miss of seventeen and screaming in a dialect made up of vulgar French and vulgar English; a poet, lean and ragged, with a broad Scotch accent. By degrees these shadows acquired stronger and stronger consistence ; the impulse which urged Frances to write became irresistible; and the result was the "History of Evelina."

Then came, naturally enough, a wish, mingled with many fears, to appear before the public ; for, timid as Frances was, and bashful, and altogether unaccustomed to hear her own praises, it is clear that she wanted neither a strong passion for distinction, nor a just confidence in her own powers. Her scheme was to become, if possible, a candidate for fame without running any risk of disgrace. She had not money to bear the expense of printing. It was therefore necessary that some bookseller should be induced to take the risk; and such a bookseller was not readily found. Dodsley refused even to look at the manuscript unless he were intrusted with the name of the author. A publisher in Fleet-street, named Lowndes, was more complaisant. Some correspondence took place between this person and Miss Burney, who took the name of Grafton, and desired that the letters addressed to her might be left at the Orange Coffee-house. But, before the bargain was finally struck, Fanny thought it her duty to obtain her father's consent. She told him that she had written a book, that she wished to have his permission to publish it anonymously, but that she hoped that he would not insist upon seeing it. What followed may serve to illustrate what we meant when we said that Dr. Burney was as bad a father as so goodhearted a man could possibly be. It never seems to have crossed his mind that Fanny was about to take a step on which the whole happiness of her life might depend, a step which might raise her to an honourable eminence or cover her with ridicule and contempt. Several people had already been trusted, and strict concealment was therefore not to be expected. On so grave an occasion, it was surely his duty to give his best counsel to his daughter, to win her confidence, to prevent her from exposing herself if her book were a bad one, and, if it were a good one, to see that the terms which she made with the publisher were likely to be beneficial to her. Instead of this, he only stared, burst out a-laughing, kissed her, gave her leave to do as she liked, and never even asked the name of her work. The contract with Lowndes was speedily concluded. Twenty pounds were given for the copyright, and were accepted by Fanny with delight. Her father's inexcusable neglect of his duty happily caused her no worse evil than the loss of twelve or fifteen hundred pounds. [12]

After many delays, "Evelina" appeared in January, 1778.

Poor Fanny was sick with terror, and durst hardly stir out of doors. Some days passed before anything was heard of the book. It had, indeed, nothing but its own merits to push it into public favour. Its author was unknown. The house by which it was published, was not, we believe, held high in estimation. No body of partisans had been engaged to applaud. The better class of readers expected little from a novel about a young lady's entrance into the world. There was, indeed, at that time a disposition among the most respectable people to condemn novels generally: nor was this disposition by any means without excuse; for works of that sort were then almost always silly and very frequently wicked.

Soon, however, the first faint accents of praise began to be heard: The keepers of the circulating libraries reported that everybody was asking for "Evelina," and that some person had guessed Anstey [13]to be the author. Then came a favourable notice in the "London Review"; then another still more favourable in the "Monthly." And now the book found its way to tables which had seldom been polluted by marble-covered volumes. Scholars and statesmen, who contemptuously abandoned the crowd of romances to Miss Lydia Languish and Miss Sukey Saunter, were not ashamed to own that they could not tear themselves away from "Evelina." Fine carriages and rich liveries, not often seen east of Temple-bar, were attracted to the publisher's shop in Fleet-street. Lowndes was daily questioned about the author, but was himself as much in the dark as any of the questioners. The mystery, however, could not remain a mystery long. It was known to brothers and sisters, aunts and cousins: and they were far too proud and too happy to be discreet. Dr. Burney wept over the book in rapture. Daddy Crisp shook his fist at his Fannikin in affectionate anger at not having been admitted to her confidence. The truth was whispered to Mrs. Thrale: and then it began to spread fast.

The book had been admired while it had been ascribed to men of letters long conversant with the world and accustomed to composition. But when it was known that a reserved, silent young woman had produced the best work of fiction that had appeared since' the death of Smollett, the acclamations were redoubled. What she had done was, indeed, extraordinary. But, as usual, various reports improved the story till it became miraculous. "Evelina," it was said, was the work of a girl of seventeen. Incredible as this tale was, it continued to be repeated down to our own time. Frances was too honest to confirm it. Probably she Was too much a woman to contradict it; and it was long before any of her detractors thought of this mode of annoyance. Yet there was no want of low minds and bad hearts in the generation which witnessed her first appearance. There was the envious Kenrick and the savage Wolcot, the asp George Steevens and the polecat John Williams. It did not, however, occur to them to search the parish register of Lynn, in order that they might be able to twit a lady with having concealed her age. That truly chivalrous exploit was reserved for a bad writer [14]of our own time, whose spite she had provoked by not furnishing him with materials for a worthless edition of Boswell's "Life of Johnson," some sheets of which our readers have doubtless seen round parcels of better books.

But we must return to our story. The triumph was complete. The timid and obscure girl found herself on the highest pinnacle of fame. Great men, on whom she had gazed at a distance with humble reverence, addressed her with admiration, tempered by the tenderness due to her sex and age. Burke, Windham, Gibbon, Reynolds, Sheridan, were among her most ardent eulogists. Cumberland[15]acknowledged her merit, after his fashion, by biting his lips and wriggling in his chair whenever her name was mentioned. But it was at Streatham that she tasted, in the highest perfection, the sweets of flattery mingled with the sweets of friendship. Mrs. Thrale, then at the height of prosperity and popularity-with gay spirits, quick wit, showy, though superficial, acquirements, pleasing, though not refined, manners, a singularly amiable temper and a loving heart-felt towards Fanny as towards a younger sister. With the Thrales, Johnson was domesticated. He was an old friend of Dr. Burney; but he had probably taken little notice of Dr. Burney's daughters ; and Fanny, we imagine, had never in her life dared to speak to him, unless to ask whether he wanted a nineteenth or a twentieth cup of tea. He was charmed by her tale, and preferred it to the novels of Fielding, to whom, indeed, he had always been grossly unjust. He did not, indeed, carry his partiality so far as to place "Evelina" by the side of "Clarissa" and "Sir Charles Grandison"; yet he said that his little favourite had done enough to have made even Richardson feel uneasy. With Johnson's cordial approbation of the book was mingled a fondness, half gallant, half paternal, for the writer; and this fondness his age and character entitled him to show without restraint. He began by putting her hand to his lips. But he soon clasped her in his huge arms, and immediately implored her to be a good girl. She was his pet, his dear love, his dear little Burney, his little character-monger. At one time, he broke forth in praise of the good taste of her caps. At another time, he insisted on teaching her Latin. That, with all his coarseness and irritability, he was a man of sterling benevolence, has long been acknowledged. But how gentle and endearing his deportment could be, was not known till the recollections of Madame.D'Arblay were published.

We have mentioned a few of the most eminent of those who paid their homage to the author of " Evelina." The crowd of inferior admirers would require a catalogue as long as that in the second book of the " Iliad." In that catalogue would be Mrs. Cholmondeley, the sayer of odd things; and Seward, much given to yawning; and Baretti, who slew the man in the Haymarket ; and Paoli, talking broken English; and Langton, taller by the head than any other member of the club; and Lady Millar, who kept a vase wherein fools were wont to put bad verses ; and Jerningham, who wrote verses fit to be put into the vase of Lady Millar; and Dr. Franklin-not, as some have dreamed, the great Pennsylvanian Dr. Franklin, who could not then have paid his respects to Miss Burney without much risk of being hanged, drawn, and quartered, but Dr. Franklin the less.

A'tag ,uEiwv, ort r6aroC yE 6aoc TEXap6vtoC Atag, i1XX,i rOV JLEi&V.

It would not have been surprising if such success had turned even a strong head and corrupted even a generous and affectionate nature. But in the "Diary," we can find no trace of any feeling inconsistent with a truly modest and amiable disposition. There is, indeed, abundant proof that Frances enjoyed with an intense, though a troubled, joy, the honours which her genius had won ; but it is equally clear that her happiness sprang from the happiness of her father, her sister, and her dear Daddy Crisp. While flattered by the great, the opulent and the learned, while followed along the Steyne at Brighton and the Pantiles at Tunbridge Wells by the gaze of admiring crowds, her heart seems to have been still with the little domestic circle in St. Martin'sstreet. If she recorded with minute diligence all the compliments, delicate and coarse, which she heard wherever she turned, she recorded them for the eyes of two or three persons who had loved her from infancy, who had loved her in obscurity, and to whom her fame gave the purest and most exquisite delight. Nothing can be more unjust than to confound these outpourings of a kind heart, sure of perfect sympathy, with the egotism of a bluestocking who prates to all who come near her about her own novel or her own volume of sonnets.

It was natural that the triumphant issue of Miss Burney's first venture should tempt her to try a second. "Evelina," though it had raised her fame, had added nothing to her fortune. Some of her friends urged her to write for the stage. Johnson promised to give her his advice as to the composition. Murphy, who was supposed to understand the temper of the pit as well as any man of his time, undertook to instruct her as to stage effect. Sheridan declared that he would accept a play from her without even reading it. Thus encouraged, she wrote a comedy named "The Witlings." Fortunately, it was never acted or printed. We can, we think, easily perceive, from the little which is said on the subject in the "Diary," that "The Witlings" would have been damned, and that Murpby and Sheridan thought so, though they were too polite to say so. Happily Frances had a friend who was not afraid to give her pain. Crisp, wiser for her than he had been for himself, read the manuscript in his lonely retreat and manfully told her that she had failed, and that to remove blemishes here and there would be useless; that the piece had abundance of wit but no interest, that it was bad as a whole ; that it would remind every reader of the "Femmes Savantes," which, strange to say, she had never read, and that she could not sustain so close a comparison with Moli6re. This opinion, in which Dr. Burney concurred, was sent to Frances in what she called "a hissing, groaning, catcalling epistle." But she had too much sense not to know that it was better to be hissed and catcalled by her Daddy than by a whole sea of heads in the pit of Drury-lane theatre ; and she had too good a heart not to be grateful for so rare an act of friendship. She returned an answer which shows how well she deserved to have a judicious, faithful, and affectionate adviser. "I intend," she wrote, "to console myself for your censure by this greatest proof I have received of the sincerity, candour, and, let me add, esteem of my dear daddy. And, as I happen to love myself more than my play, this consolation is not a very trifling one. This, however, seriously I do believe, that when my two daddies put their heads together to concert that hissing, groaning, catcalling epistle they sent me, they felt as sorry for poor little Miss Bayes as she could possibly do for herself. You see I do not attempt to repay your frankness with an air of pretended carelessness. But, though somewhat disconcerted just now, I will promise not to let my vexation live out another day. Adieu, my dear daddy; I won't be mortified and I won't be downed;

but I will be proud to find I have, out of my own family, as well as in it, a friend who loves me well enough to speak plain truth to me."

Frances now turned from her dramatic schemes to an undertaking far better suited to her talents. She determined to write a new tale on a plan excellently contrived for the display of the powers in which her superiority to other writers lay. It was, in truth, a grand and various picture gallery, which presented to the eye a long series of men and women, each marked by some strong peculiar feature. There were avarice and prodigality, the pride of blood and the pride of money, morbid restlessness and morbid apathy, frivolous garrulity, supercilious silence, a Democritus to laugh at everything and a Heraclitus to lament over everything. The work proceeded fast, and in twelve months was completed,

It wanted something of the simplicity which had been among the most attractive charms of "Evelina"; but it furnished ample proof that the four years, which had elapsed since "Evelina" appeared, had not been unprofitably spent. Those who saw "Cecilia" in manuscript pronounced it the best novel of the age. Mrs. Thrale laughed and wept over it. Crisp was even vehement in applause, and offered to insure the rapid and complete success of the book for half-a-crown. What Miss Burney received for the copyright is not mentioned in the " Diary "; but we have observed several expressions from which we infer that the sum was considerable. That the sale would be great, nobody could doubt; and Frances now had shrewd and experienced advisers, who would not suffer her to wrong herself. We have been told that the publishers gave her two thousand pounds, and we have no doubt that they might have given a still larger sum without being losers. [16]

"Cecilia" was published in the summer of 1782. The curiosity of the town was intense. We have been informed by persons who remember those days, that no romance of Sir Walter Scott was more impatiently awaited or more eagerly snatched from the counters of the booksellers. High as public expectation was, it was amply satisfied; and "Cecilia" was placed, by general acclamation, among the classical novels of England.

Miss Burney was now thirty. Her youth had been singularly prosperous; but clouds soon began to gather over that clear and radiant dawn. Events deeply painful to a heart so kind as that of Frances followed each other in rapid succession. She was first called upon to attend the deathbed of her best friend, Samuel Crisp. When she returned to St. Martin's-street after performing this melancholy duty, she was appalled by hearing that Johnson had been struck with paralysis, and, not many months Later, she parted from him for the last time with solemn tenderness. He wished to look on her once more; and on the day before his death she long remained in tears on the stairs leading to his bedroom, in the hope that she might be called in to receive his blessing. But he was then sinking fast, and, though he sent her an affectionate message, was unable to see her. But this was not the worst. There are separations far more cruel than those which are made by death. Frances might weep with proud affection for Crisp and Johnson. She had to blush as well as to weep for Mrs. Thrale.

Life, however, still smiled upon her. Domestic happiness, friendship, independence, leisure, letters, all these things were hers; and she flung them all away.

Among the distinguished persons to whom Miss Burney had been introduced, none appears to have stood higher in her regard than Mrs. Delany. This lady was an interesting and venerablerelic of a past age. She was the niece of George Granville, Lord Lansdowne, who, in his youth, exchanged verses and compliments with Edmun Waller, and who was among the first to applaud the opening talents of Pope. She had married Dr. Delany, a man known to his contemporaries as a profound scholar and eloquent preacher, but remembered in our time chiefly as one of that small circle in which the fierce spirit of Swift, tortured by disappointed ambition, by remorse, and by the approaches of madness, sought for amusement and repose. Dr. Delany had long been dead. His widow, nobly descended, eminently accomplished, and retaining, in spite of the infirmities of advanced age, the vigour of her faculties, and the serenity of her temper, enjoyed and deserved the favour of the royal family. She had a pension of three hundred a-year; and a house at Windsor, belonging to the crown, had been fitted up for her accommodation. At this house, the king and queen sometimes called, and found a very natural pleasure in thus catching an occasional glimpse of the private life of English families.

In December, 1785, Miss Burney was on a visit to Mrs. Delany at Windsor. The dinner was over. The old lady was taking a nap. Her grandniece, a little girl of seven, was playing at some Christmas game with the visitors, when the door opened, and a stout gentleman entered unannounced, with a star on his breast, and "What? what? what?" in his mouth. A cry of "The king!" was set up. A general scampering followed. Miss Burney owns that she could not have been more terrified if she had seen a ghost. But Mrs. Delany came forward to pay her duty to her royal friend, and the disturbance was quieted. Frances was then presented, and underwent a long examination and crossexamination about all that she had written, and all that she meant to write. The queen soon made her appearance, and his majesty repeated, for the benefit of his consort, the information which he had extracted from Miss Burney. The good nature of the royal pair might have softened even the authors of the "Probationary Odes," [17]and could not but be delightful to a young lady who had been brought up a Tory. In a few days the visit was repeated. Miss Burney was more at ease than before. His majesty, instead of seeking for information, condescended to impart it, and passed sentence on many great writers, English and foreign. Voltairehe pronounced a monster. Rousseau he liked rather better. "But was there ever," he cried, " such stuff as great part of Shakspeare? Only one must not say so. But what think you? What? Is there not sad stuff? What? What?"

The next day Frances enjoyed the privilege of listening to some equally valuable criticism uttered by the queen touching Goethe ,

And Klopstock, and might have learned an important lesson of economy from the mode in which her majesty's library had been formed. "1 picked the book up on a stall," said the queen. "Oh, it is amazing what good books there are on stalls!" Mrs. Delany, who seems to have understood from these words that her majesty was in the habit of exploring the booths of Moorfields and

Holywell-street in person, could not suppress an exclamation of surprise. "Why," said the queen, "I don't pick them up myself. I have a servant very clever; and if they are not to be had at the booksellers, they are not for me more than for another." Miss Burney describes this conversation as delightful; and, indeed, we cannot wonder that, with her literary tastes, she should be delighted at hearing in how magnificent a manner the greatest lady in the land encouraged literature.

The truth is, that Frances was fascinated by the condescending kindness of the two great personages to whom she had been presented. Her father was even more infatuated than herself. The result was a step of which we cannot think with patience, but recorded as it is with all its consequences in these volumes deserves at least this praise, that it has furnished a most impressive warning.

A German lady of the name of Haggerdorn, one of the keepers of the queen's robes, retired about this time, and her majesty offered the vacant post to Miss Burney. When we consider that Miss Burney was decidedly the most popular writer of fictitious narrative then living, that competence, if not opulence, was within her reach, and that she was more than usually happy in her domestic circle, and when we compare the sacrifice which she was invited to make with the remuneration which was held out to her, we are divided between laughter and indignation.

What was demanded of her was that she should consent to be almost as completely separated from her family and friends as if she had gone to Calcutta, and almost as close a prisoner as if she had been sent to gaol for a libel; that with talents which had instructed and delighted the highest living minds, she should now be employed only in mixing snuff and sticking pins; that she should be summoned by a waiting-woman's bell to a waiting-woman's duties; that she should pass her whole life under the restraints of a paltry etiquette, should sometimes fast till she was ready to swoon with hunger, should sometimes stand till her knees have way with fatigue; that she should not dare to speak or move without considering how her mistress might like her words and gestures. Instead of those distinguished men and women, the flower of all political parties, with whom she had been in the habit of mixing on terms of equal friendship, she was to have for her perpetual companion the chief keeper of the robes, an old hag from Germany, of mean understanding, of insolent manners, and of temper which, naturally savage, had now been exasperated by disease. Now and then, indeed, poor Frances might console herself for the loss of Burke's and Windham's society by joining in the "celestial colloquy sublime" of his majesty's equerries.

And what was the consideration for which she was to sell herself to this slavery? A peerage in her own right? A pension of two thousand a-year for life? A seventy-four for her brother in the navy? A deanery for her brother in the church? Not so. The price at which she was valued was her board, her lodging, the attendance of a man-servant, and two hundred pounds a-year.

The man who, even when hard pressed by hunger, sells his birthright for a mess of pottage, is unwise. But what shall we say of him who parts with his birthright and does not get even the pottage in return ? It is not necessary to inquire whether opulence be an adequate compensation for the sacrifice of bodily and mental freedom ; for Frances Burney paid for leave to be a prisoner and a menial. It was evidently understood as one of the terms of her engagement, that, while she was a member of the royal household, she was not to appear before the public as an author; and, even had there been no such understanding, her avocations were such as left her no leisure for any considerable intellectual effort. That her place was incompatible with her literary pursuits was indeed frankly acknowledged by the king when she resigned. "She had given up," he said, "five years of her pen." That during those five years she might, without painful exertion, without any exertion that would not have been a pleasure, have earned enough to buy an annuity for life much larger than the precarious salary which she received at Court, is quite certain. The same income, too, which in St. Martin'sstreet would have afforded her every comfort, must have been found scanty at St. James's. We cannot venture to speak confidently of the price of millinery and jewellery; but we are greatly deceived if a lady, who had to attend Queen Charlotte on many public occasions, could possibly save a farthing out of a salary of two hundred a-year. The principle of the arrangement was, in short, simply this, that Frances Burney should become a slave, and should be rewarded by being made a beggar.

With what object their majesties brought her to their palace, we must own ourselves unable to conceive. Their object could not be to encourage her literary exertions; for they took her from a situation in which it was almost certain that she would write and put her into a situation in which it was impossible for her to write. Their object could not be to promote her pecuniary interest for they took her from a situation where she was likely to becom rich, and put her into a situation in which she could not but continue poor. Their object could not be to obtain an eminentl useful waiting-maid; for it is clear that, though Miss Burney was the only woman of her time who could have described the death of Harrel, [18]thousands might have been found more expert in tying ribbons and filling snuff-boxes. To grant her a pension on the civil list would have been an act of judicious liberality honourable to the Court. If this was impracticable, the next best thing was to let her alone. That the king and queen meant her nothing but kindness, we do not in the least doubt. But their kindness was the kindness of persons raised high above the mass of mankind, accustomed to be addressed with profound deference, accustomed to see all who approach them mortified by their coldness and elated by their smiles. They fancied that to be noticed by them, to be near them, to serve them, was in itself a kind of happiness ; and that Frances Burney ought to be full of gratitude for being permitted to purchase, by the surrender of health, wealth, freedom, domestic affection and literary fame, the privilege of standing behind a royal chair and holding a pair of royal gloves.

And who can blame them ? Who can wonder that princes should be under such a delusion when they are encouraged in it by the very persons who suffer from it most cruelly ? Was it to be expected that George III. and Queen Charlotte should understand the interest of Frances Burney better, or promote it with more zeal, than herself and her father ? No deception was practised. The conditions of the house of bondage were set forth with all simplicity. The hook was presented without a bait ; the net was spread in sight of the bird, and the naked hook was greedily swallowed, and the silly bird made haste to entangle herself in the net.

It is not strange indeed that an invitation to Court should have caused a fluttering in the bosom of an inexperienced woman. But it was the duty of the parent to watch over the child, and to show her, that on one side were only infantine vanities and chimerical hopes, on the other, liberty, peace of mind, affluence, social enjoyments, honourable distinctions. Strange to say, the only hesitation was on the part of Frances. Dr. Burney was transported out of himself with delight. Not such are the raptures of a Circassian father who has sold his pretty daughter well to a Turkish slave merchant. Yet Dr. Burney was an amiable man a man of good abilities, a man who had seen much of the world. But he seems to have thought that going to Court was like going to heaven ; that to see princes and princesses was a kind of beatific vision ; that the exquisite felicity enjoyed by royal persons Was not confined to themselves, but was communicated by some mysterious efflux or reflection to all who were suffered to stand at their toilettes or to bear their trains. He overruled all his daughter's objections, and himself escorted her to prison. The door closed. The key was turned. She, looking back with tender regret on all she had left, and forward with anxiety and terror to the new life On which she was entering, was unable to speak or stand; and he went on his way homeward rejoicing in her marvellous prosperity.

And now began a slavery of five years, of five years taken from the best part of life, and wasted in menial drudgery or in recreations duller than menial drudgery, under galling restraints and amidst unfriendly or uninteresting companions. The history of an ordinary day was this: Miss Burney had to rise and dress herself early, that she might be ready to answer the royal bell, which rang at half after seven. Till about eight she attended in the queen's dressing-room, and had the honour of lacing her august mistress's stays, and of putting on the hoop, gown, and neckhandkerchief. The morning was chiefly spent in rummaging drawers, and laying fine clothes in their proper places. Then the queen was to be powdered and dressed for the day. Twice a week her majesty's hair was curled and craped; and this operation appears to have added a full hour to the business of the toilette. It was generally three before Miss Burney was at liberty. Then she had two hours at her own disposal. To these hours we owe great Part of her "Diary." At five she had to attend her colleague, Madame Schwellenberg, a hateful old toadeater, as illiterate as a chambermaid, as proud as a Whole German Chapter, rude, peevish, unable to bear solitude, unable to conduct herself with common decency in society. With this delightful associate, Frances Burney had to dine and pass the evening. The pair generally remained together from five to eleven, and often had no other company the whole time, except during the hour from eight to nine, when the equerries came to tea. If poor Frances attempted to escape to her own apartment, and to forget her wretchedness over a book, the execrable old woman railed and stormed, and complained that she was neglected. Yet, When Frances stayed, she was constantly assailed with insolent reproaches. Literary fame was, in the eyes of the

German crone, a blemish, a proof that the person -who enjoyed it was meanly born, and out of the pale of good society. All her scanty stock of broken English was employed to express the contempt with 'which she regarded the author of "Evelina" and "Cecilia." Frances detested cards, and indeed knew nothing about them; but she soon found that the least miserable Way of passing an evening with Madame Schwellenberg Was at the card-table, and consented, with patient sadness, to give hours which might have called forth the laughter and tears of many generations to the king of clubs and the knave of spades. Between eleven and twelve, the bell rang again. Miss Burney had to pass twenty minutes or half an hour in undressing the queen, and was then at liberty to retire and to dream that she was chatting with her brother by the quiet hearth in St, Martin's- street, that she was the centre of an admiring assembly at Mrs. Crewe's, that Burke was calling her the first woman of the age, or that Dilly was giving her a cheque for two thousand guineas.

Men, we must suppose, are less patient than women ; for we are utterly at a loss to conceive how any human being could endure such a life while there remained a vacant garret in Grub-street, a crossing in want of a sweeper, a parish workhouse or a parish vault. And it was for such a life that Frances Burney had given up liberty and peace, a happy fireside, attached friends, a -wide and splendid circle of acquaintance, intellectual pursuits, in which she was qualified to excel, and the sure hope of what to her would have been affluence.

There is nothing new under the sun. The last great master of Attic eloquence and Attic wit has left us a forcible and touching description of the misery of a man of letters, who, lulled by hopes similar to those of Frances, had entered the service of one of the magnates of Rome. "Unhappy that I am," cries the victim of his own childish ambition: "would nothing content me but that I must leave mine old pursuits and mine old companions, and the life which was without care, and the sleep which had no limit save mine own pleasure, and the walks which I was free to take where I listed, and fling myself into the lowest pit of a dungeon like this? And, O God! for what? Is this the bait which enticed me? Was there no way by which I might have enjoyed in freedom comforts even greater than those which I now earn by servitude? Like a lion which has been made so tame that men may lead him about by a thread, I am dragged up and down, with broken and humbled spirit, at the beels of those to whom, in my own domain, I should have been an object of awe and wonder. And, worst of all, I feel that here I gain no credit, that here I give no pleasure. The talents and accomplishments, which charmed a far different circle, are here out of place. I am rude in the arts of palaces, and can ill bear comparison with those whose calling from their youth up has been to flatter and to sue. Have I, then, two lives, that, after I have wasted one in the service of others, there may yet remain to me a second, which I may live unto myself?"

Now and then, indeed, events occurred which disturbed the ,wretched monotony of Francis Burney's life. The Court moved from Kew to Windsor, and from Windsor back to Kew. One dull colonel went out of waiting, and another dull colonel came into waiting. An impertinent servant made a blunder about tea, and caused a misunderstanding between the gentlemen and the ladies. A half-witted French Protestant minister talked oddly about conjugal fidelity. An unlucky member of the household mentioned a passage in the " Morning Herald " reflecting on the queen ; and forthwith Madame Schwellenberg, began to storm in bad English, and told him that he had made her "what you call perspire!"

A more important occurrence was the royal visit to Oxford. Miss Burney went in the queen's train to Nuneham, was utterly neglected there in the crowd, and could with difficulty find a ,servant to show the way to her bedroom or a hairdresser to arrange her curls. She had the honour of entering Oxford in the last of a long string of carriages which formed the royal procession, of walking after the queen all day through refectories and chapels and of standing, half dead with fatigue and hunqer, while her august mistress was seated at an excellent cold collation. At Magdalene college, Frances was left for a moment in a parlour, where she sank down on a chair. A good-natured equerry saw that she was exhausted, and shared with her some apricots and bread which he had wisely put into his pockets. At that moment the door opened; the queen entered; the wearied attendants sprang up ; the bread and fruit were hastily concealed. "I found," says poor Miss Burney, "that our appetites were to be supposed annihilated at the same moment that our strength was to be invincible."

Yet Oxford, seen even under such disadvantages, " revived in her," to use her own words, a "consciousness to pleasure which had long lain nearly dormant." She forgot, during one moment, that she was a waiting-maid, and felt as a woman of true genius might be expected to feel amidst venerable remains of antiquity, beautiful works of art, vast repositories of knowledge, and memorials of the illustrious dead. Had she still been what she was before her father induced her to take the most fatal step of her life, we can easily imagine what pleasure she would have derived from a visit to the noblest of English cities. She might, indeed, have been forced to ride in a hack chaise, and might not have worn so fine a gown of Chambery gauze as that in which she tottered after the royal party; but with what delight would she have then paced the cloisters of Magdalene, compared the antique gloom of Merton with the splendour of Christchurch, and looked down from the dome of the Radcliffe library on the magnificent sea of turrets and battlements below! How gladly should learned men have laid aside for a few hours Pindar's "Odes" and Aristotle's "Ethics," to escort the author of "Cecilia" from college to college! What neat little banquets would she have found set out in their monastic cells! With what eagerness would pictures, medals, and illuminated missals have been brought forth from the most mysterious cabinets for her amusement! How much she would have had to hear and to tell about Johnson, as she walked over Pembroke, and about Reynolds, in the antechapel of New college. But these indulgences were not for one who had sold herself into bondage.

About eighteen months after the visit to Oxford, another event diversified the wearisome life which Frances led at Court. Warren Hastings was brought to the bar of the House of Peers. The queen and princesses were present when the trial commenced, and Miss Burney was permitted to attend. During the subsequent proceedings, a day rule for the same purpose was occasionally granted to her; for the queen took the strongest interest in the trial, and, when she could not go herself to Westminster-hall, liked to receive a report of what passed from a person who had singular powers of observation, and who was, moreover, personally acquainted with some of the most distinguished managers. The portion of the "Diary" which relates to this celebrated proceeding is lively and Picturesque. Yet we read it, we own, with pain; for it seems to us to prove that the fine understanding of Frances Burney was beginning to feel the pernicious influence of a mode of life which is as incompatible with health of mind as the air of the Pomptine marshes with health of body. From the first day, she espouses the cause of Hastings with a presumptuous vehemence and acrimony quite inconsistent with the modesty and suavity of her ordinary deportment. She shudders when Burke enters the Hall at the head of the Commons. She pronounces him the cruel oppressor of an innocent man. She is at a loss to conceive how the managers can look at the defendant and not blush. Windham comes to her from the managers' box, to offer her refreshment. "But," says she, "I could not break bread with him." Then again, she exclaims, "Ah, Mr. Windham, how come you ever engaged in so cruel, so unjust a cause?" "Mr. Burke saw me," she says, "and he bowed with the most marked civility of manner." This, be it observed, was just after his opening speech, a speech which had produced a mighty effect, and which certainly, no other orator that ever lived could have made. "My curtsy," she continues, "was the most ungrateful, distant and cold; I could not do otherwise; so hurt I felt to see him the head of such a cause." Now, not only had Burke treated her with constant kindness, but the very last act which he performed on the day on which he was turned out of the Pay office, about four years before this trial, was to make Dr. Burney organist of Chelsea hospital. When, at the Westminster election, Dr. Burney was divided between his gratitude for this favour and his Tory opinions, Burke in the noblest manner disclaimed all right to exact a sacrifice of principle. "You have little or no obligations to me," he wrote; "but if you had as many as I really wish it were in my power, as it is certainly in my desire, to lay on you, I hope you do not think me capable of conferring them in order to subject your mind or your affairs to a painful and mischievous servitude." Was this a man to be uncivilly treated by a daughter of Dr. Burney because she chose to differ from him respecting a vast and most complicated question which he had studied deeply guring many years and which she had never studied at all? It Is clear, from Miss Burney's own statement, that when she behaved so unkindly to Mr. Burke, she did not even know of what Hastings was accused. One thing, however, she must have known, that Burke had been able to convince a House of Commons, bitterly prejudiced against him, that the charges were well founded, and that Pitt and Dundas had concurred with Fox and Sheridan in supporting the impeachment. Surely a woman Of far inferior abilities to Miss Burney might have been expected to see that this never could have happened unless there had been a strong case against the late Governor-general. And there was, as all reasonable men now admit, a strong case against him. That there were great public services to be set off against his great crimes is perfectly true. But his services and his crimes were equally unknown to the lady who so confidently asserted his perfect innocence, and imputed to his accusers—that is to say, to all the greatest men of all parties in the state-not merely error, but gross injustice and barbarity.

She had, it is true, occasionally seen Mr. Hastings, and had found his manners and conversation agreeable. But surely she could not be so weak as to infer from the gentleness of his deportment in a drawing-room that he was incapable of committing a great state crime under the influence of ambition and revenge. A silly Miss, fresh from a boarding- school, might fall into such a mistake ; but the woman who had drawn the character of Mr. Monckton[19]should have known better.

The truth is that she had been too long at Court. She was sinking into a slavery worse than that of the body. The iron was beginning to enter into the soul. Accustomed during many months to watch the eye of a mistress, to receive with boundless gratitude the slightest mark of royal condescension, to feel wretched at every symptom of royal displeasure, to associate only with spirits long tamed and broken in, she was degeneratin- into something fit for her place. Queen Charlotte was a violent partisan of Hastings, had received presents from him, and had so far departed from the severity of her virtue as to lend her countenance to his wife, whose conduct had certainly been as reprehensible as that of any of the frail beauties who were then rigidly excluded from the English Court. The king, it was well known, took the same side. To the king and queen, all the members of the household looked submissively for guidance. The impeachment, therefore, was an atrocious persecution ; the managers were rascals ; the defendant was the most deserving and the worst used man in the kingdom. This was the cant of the whole palace, from gold stick in waiting down to the tabledeckers and yeomen of the silver scullery; and Miss Burney canted like the rest, though in livelier tones and with less bitter feelings.

The account which she has given of the king's illness contains much excellent narrative and description, and will, we think, be more valued by the historians of a future age than any equal portion of Pepys' or Evelyn's " Diaries." That account shows also how affectionate and compassionate her nature was, But it shows also, we must say, that her way of life was rapidly impairing her powers of reasoning and her sense of justice. We do not mean to discuss, in this place, the question whether the views of Mr. Pitt or those of 'Mr. Fox respecting the regency were the more correct. It is, indeed, quite needless to discuss that question ; for the censure of Miss Burney falls alike on Pitt and Fox, on majority and minority. She is angry with the House of Commons for presuming to inquire whether the king was mad or not and whether there was a chance of his recovering his senses. "melancholy day," she writes; "news bad both at home and abroad. At home the dear unhappy king still worse ; abroad new examinations voted of the physicians. Good heavens! what an insult does this seem from Parliamentary power, to investigate and bring forth to the world every circumstance of such a malady as is ever held sacred to secrecy in the most private families! How indignant we all feel here, no words can say." It is proper to observe that the motion which roused the indignation at Kew was made by Mr. Pitt himself, and that if withstood by Mr. Pitt, it would certainly have been rejected. We see therefore, that the loyalty of the minister, who was then generally regarded as the most heroic champion of his prince, was lukewarm indeed when compared with the boiling zeal which filled the pages of the backstairs and the women of the bedchamber. Of the Regency bill, Pitt's own bill, Miss Burney speaks with horror. "I shuddered," she says, "to hear it named." And again, "Oh, how dreadful will be the day when that unhappy bill takes place ! I cannot approve the plan of it." The truth is that Mr. Pitt, whether a wise and upright statesman or not, was a statesman, and, whatever motives he might have for imposing restrictions on the regent, felt that in some way or other there must be some provision made for the execution of some part of the kingly office, or that no government would be left in the country. But this was a matter of which the household never thought. It never occurred, as far as we can see, to the exons and keepers of the robes that it was necessary that there should be somewhere or other a power in the state to pass laws, to observe order, to pardon criminals, to fill up offices, to negotiate with foreign governments, to command the army and navy. Nay, these enlightened politicians, and Miss Burney among the rest, seem to have thought that any person who considered the subject with reference to the public interest showed himself to be a bad-hearted man. Nobody wonders at this in a gentleman usher, but it is melancholy to see genius sinking into such debasement.

During more than two years after the king's recovery, Frances dragged on a miserable existence at the palace. The consolations which had for a time mitigated the wretchedness of servitude were one by one withdrawn. Mrs. Delany, whose society had been a great resource when the Court was at Windsor, was now dead. One of the gentlemen of the royal establishment, [20]Colonel Digby, appears to have been a man of sense, of taste, of some reading, and of prepossessing manners. Agreeable associates were scarce in the prison house, and he and Miss Burney therefore naturally were attached to each other. She owns that she valued him as a friend, and it would not have been strange if his attentions had led her to entertain for him a sentiment warmer than friendship. He quitted the Court, and married in a way which astonished Miss Burney greatly, and which evidently wounded her feelings and lowered him in her esteem. The palace grew duller and duller; Madame Schwellenberg became more and more savage and insolent; and now the health of poor Frances began to give way; and all who saw her pale face, and emaciated figure and herfeeble walk predicted that her sufferings would soon be over.

Frances uniformly speaks of her royal mistress and of the princesses with respect and affection. The princesses seem to have well'deserved all the praise which is bestowed on them in the "Diary." They were, we doubt not, most amiable women. But "the sweet queen," as she is constantly called in these volumes, is not by any means an object of admiration to us. She had, undoubtedly, sense enough to know what kind of deportment suited her high station, and self-command enough to maintain that deportment invariably. She was, in her intercourse. with Miss Burney, generally gracious and affable, sometimes, when displeased, cold and reserved, but never, under any circumstances, rude, peevish or violent. She knew how to dispense, gracefully and skilfully, those little civilities which, when paid by a sovereign, are prized at many times their intrinsic value; how to pay a compliment; how to lend a book; how to ask after a relation. But she seems to have been utterly regardless of the comfort, the health, the life of her attendants, when her own convenience was concerned. Weak, feverish, hardly able to stand, Frances had still to rise before seven, in order to dress "the sweet queen," and to sit up till midnight, in order to undress "the sweet queen." The indisposition of the handmaid could not, and did not, escape the notice of her royal mistress. But the established doctrine of the Court was that all sickness was to be considered as a pretence until it proved fatal. The only way in which the invalid could clear herself from the suspicion of malingering, as it is called in the army, was to go on lacing and unlacing, till she fell down dead at the royal feet. "This," Miss Burney wrote, when she was suffering cruelly from sickness, watching and labour, "is by no means from hardness of heart; far otherwise. There is no hardness of heart in any one of them but it is prejudice and want of personal experience."

Many strangers sympathised with the bodily and mental sufferings of this distinguished woman. All who saw her saw that her frame was sinking, that her heart was breaking. The last, it should seem, to observe the change was her father. At length, in spite of himself, his eyes were opened. In May, 1790, his daughter had an interview of three hours with him, the only long interview which they had had since he took her to Windsor in 1786. She told him that she was miserable, that she was worn with attendance and want of sleep, that she had no comfort in life, nothing to love, nothing to hope, that her family and friends were to her as though they were not, and were remembered by her as men remember the dead. From daybreak to midnight the same killing labour, the same recreations, more hateful than labour itself, followed each other without variety, without any interval of liberty and repose.

The doctor was greatly dejected by this news; but was too good- natured a man not to say that, if she wished to resign, his house and arms were open to her. Still, however, he could not bear to remove her from the Court. His veneration for royalty amounted in truth to idolatry. It can be compared only to the grovelling superstition of those Syrian devotees who made their children pass through the fire to Moloch. When he induced his daughter to accept the place of keeper of the robes, he entertained, as she tells us, a hope that some worldly advantage or other, not set down in the contract of service, would be the result of her connection with the Court. What advantage he expected we do not know, nor did he probably know himself. But, whatever he expected, he certainly got nothing. Miss Burney had been hired for board, lodging and two hundred a-year. Board, lodging and two hundred a-year she had duly received. We have looked carefully through the " Diary" in the hope of finding some trace of those extraordinary benefactions on which the doctor reckoned. But we can discover only a promise, never performed, of a gown: [21]and for this promise Miss Burney was expected to return thanks, such as might have suited the beggar with whom Saint Martin, in the legend, divided his cloak. The experience of four years was, however, insufficient to dispel the illusion which had taken possession of the doctor's mind ; and between the dear father and "the sweet queen" there seemed to be little doubt that some day or other Frances would drop down a corpse. Six months had elapsed since the interview between the parent and the daughter. The resignation was not sent in. The sufferer grew worse and worse. She took bark, but it soon ceased to produce a beneficial effect. She was stimulated with wine ; she was soothed with opium; but in vain. Her breath began to fail. The whisper that she was in a decline spread through the Court. The pains in her side became so severe that she was forced to crawl from the card-table of the old Fury to whom she was tethered three or four times in an evening for the purpose of taking hartshorn. Had she been a negrQslave, a humane planter would have excused her fromwork. But her majesty showed no mercy. Thrice a day the accursed bell still rang ; the queen was still to be dressed for the morning at seven, and to be dressed for the day at noon, and to be undressed at eleven at night.

But there had arisen, in literary and fashionable society, a general feeling of compassion for Miss Burney, and of indignation against both her father and the queen. "Is it possible," said a great French lady to the doctor "that your daughter is in A situation where she is never allowed a holiday?" HoraceWalpole wrote to Frances to express his sympathy. Boswell, boiling over with good-natured rage, almost forced an entrance into the palace to see her. "My dear ma'am, why do you stay? It won't do, ma'am - you must resign. We can put up with it no longer. Some very violent measures, I assure you, will be taken. We shall address Dr. Burney in a body." Burke and Reynolds, though less noisy, were zealous in the same cause. Windham spoke to Dr. Burney, but found him still irresolute. "I will set the club upon him," cried Windham; "Miss Burney has some very true admirers there, and I am sure they will eagerly assist." Indeed, the Burney family seem to have been apprehensive that some public affront, such as the doctor's unpardonable folly, to use the mildest term had richly deserved, would be put upon'him. The medical men spoke out, and plainly told him that his daughter must resign or die.

At last paternal affection, medical authority, and the voice of all London crying shame, triumphed over Dr. Burney's love of courts. He determined that Frances should write a letter of resignation. It was with difficulty that, though her life was at stake, she mustered spirit to put the paper into the queen's hands. "I could not," so runs the "Diary "summon courage to present my memorial-my heart always failed me from seeing the queen's entire freedom from such an expectation. For though I was frequently so ill in her presence that I could hardly stand, I saw she concluded me, while life remained, inevitably hers."

At last, with a trembling hand, the paper was delivered. Then came the storm. Juno, as in the A_neid, delegated the work of vengeance to Alecto. The queen was calm and gentle, but Madame Schwellenberg raved like a maniac in the incurable ward of Bedlam ! Such insolence! Such ingratitude! Such folly ! Would Miss Burneybring utter destruction on herself and her family ? Would she throw away the inestimable advantages of royal protection ? Would she part with privileges which, once relinquished, could never be regained " It was idle to talk of health and life. If people could not live in the palace, the best thing that could befall them was to die in it. The resignation was not accepted. The language of the medical men became stronger and stronger. Dr. Burney's parental fears were fully roused; and he explicitly declared, in a letter meant to be shown to the queen, that his daughter must retire. The Schwellenberg raged like a wild cat. "A scene almost horrible ensued," says Miss Burney. "She was too much enraged for disguise, and uttered the most furious expressions of indignant contempt at our proceedings. I am sure she would gladly have confined us both in the Bastille, had England such a misery, as a fit place to bring us to ourselves, from a daring so outrageous against imperial wishes." This passage deserves notice, as being the only one in in her "Diary," as far as we have observed, which shows Miss Burney to have been aware that she was a native of a free country, and she could not be pressed for a waiting-maid against her will, that she had just as good a right to live, if she chose, in St.-Martin's-street as Queen Charlotte had to live at St. James's.

The queen promised that, after the next birthday, Miss Burney would be set at liberty. But the promise was ill kept; and her Majesty showed displeasure at being reminded of it. At length Frances was informed that in a fortnight her attendance should Cease. "I heard this," she says, "with a fearful presentiment I should surely never go through another fortnight in so weak and languishing and painful a state of health. . . . As the time of separation approached, the queen's cordiality rather diminished, and traces of internal displeasure appeared sometimes, arising from an opinion I ought rather to have struggled on, live or die, than to quit her. Yet I am sure she saw how poor was my own chance, except by a change in the mode of life, and at least ceased to wonder, though she could not approve." Sweetqueen! What noble candour, to admit that the undutifulness of people who did not think the honour of adjusting her tuckers worth the sacrifice of their own lives, was, though highly criminal, not altogether unnatural!

We perfectly understand her majesty's contempt for the lives of others where her own pleasure was concerned. But what pleasure she can have found in having Miss Burney about her, it is not so easy to comprehend. That Miss Burney was an eminently skilful keeper of the robes is not very probable. Few women, indeed, had paid less attention to dress. Now and then, in the course of five years, she had been asked to read aloud or to write a copy of verses. But better readers might easily have been found: and her verses were worse than even the Poet Laureate's Birthday odes. Perhaps that economy, which was among her majesty's most conspicuous virtues, had something to do with her conduct on this occasion. Miss Burney had never hinted that she expected a retiring pension ; and, indeed, would gladly have given the little that she had for freedom. But her majesty knew what the public thought, and what became her own dignity. She could not for very shame suffer a woman of distinguished genius, who had quitted a lucrative career to wait on her, who had served her faithfully for a pittance during five years, and whose constitution had been impaired by labour and watching, to leave the Court without some mark of royal liberality. George III., Who, on all occasions where Miss Burney was concerned, seems to have behaved like an honest, good-natured gentleman, felt this, and said plainly that she was entitled to a provision. At length, in return for all the miserywhich she had undergone, and for the health which she had sacrificed, an annuity of one hundred Pounds was granted to her, dependent on the queen's pleasure.

Then the prison was opened, and Frances was free once more.

Johnson, as Burke observed, might have added a striking page to his "the Vanity of Human Wishes, if he had lived to see his little Burney as she went into the palace andas she came out of it.

The pleasures, so long untasted, of liberty, of friendship, of domestic affection, were almost too acute forher shattered frame. But happy days and tranquil nights soon restored the health which the queen's toilette and Madame Schwellenberg's cardtable had impaired. Kind and anxious faces surrounded the invalid. Conversation the most polished and brilliant revived her spirits. Travelling was recommended to her; and she rambled by easy journeys from cathedral to cathedral, and from watering place to watering place. She crossed the New forest, and visited Stonehenge and Wilton, the cliffs of Lyme, and the beautiful valley of Sidmouth. Thence she journeyed by Powderham castle, and by the ruins of Glastonbury abbey to Bath, and from Bath, when the winter was approaching, returned well and cheerful to London. There she visited her old dungeon, and found her successor already far on the way to the grave, and kept to strict duty, from morning till midnight, with a sprained ankle and a nervous fever.

At this time England swarmed with French exiles, driven from their country by the Revolution. A colony of these refugees settled at juniper hall, in Surrey, not far from Norbury park, where Mr. Locke, an intimate friend of the Burney family, resided. Frances visited Norbury, and was introduced to the strangers. She had strong prejudices against them ; for her Toryism was far beyond, we do not say that of Mr. Pitt, but that of Mr. Reeves ; and the inmates of juniper hall were all attached to the constitution of 1791, and were, therefore, more detested by the royalists of the first emigration than Petion or Marat. But such a woman as Miss Burney could not long resist the fascination of that remarkable society. She had lived with Johnson and Windham, with Mrs. Montague and Mrs. Thrale. Yet she was forced to own that she had never heard conversation before. The most animated eloquence, the keenest observation, the most sparkling wit, the most courtly grace, were united to charm her. For Madame de Stal was there, and M. de Talleyrand. There, too, was M. de Narbonne, a noble representative of French aristocracy ; and with M.de Narbonne was his friend and follower General D'Arblay, an honourable and amiable man, with a handsome person, frank soldierlike manners, and some taste for letters.

The prejudices which Frances had conceived against the constitutional royalists of France rapidly vanished. She listened with rapture to Talleyrand and

Madame de Stal, joined with M. D'Arblay in execrating the Jacobins and in weeping for the unhappy Bourbons, took French lessons from him, fell in love with him, and married him on no better provision than a precarious annuity of one hundred pounds.

Here the "Diary" stops for the present. [22]We will, therefore, bring our narrative to a speedy close, by rapidly recounting the most important events which we know to have befallen Madame d'Arblay during the latter part of her life.

M. D'Arblay's fortune had perished in the general wreck of the French Revolution ; -and in a foreign country his talents, whatever they may have been, could scarcely make him rich. The task of providing for the family devolved on his wife. In the year 1796, she published by subscription her third novel, "Camilla." It was impatiently expected by the public; and the sum which she obtained for it was, we believe, greater than had ever at that time been received for a novel.

We have heard that she had cleared more than three thousand guineas. But we give this merely as a rumour. [23]"Camilla," however, never attained popularity like that which "Evelina" and "Cecilia" had enjoyed; and it must be allowed that there was a perceptible falling off, not, indeed, in humour or in power of portraying character, but in grace and in purity of style.

We have heard that, about this time, a tragedy by Madame D'Arblay was performed without success. We do not know whether it was ever printed ; nor, indeed, have we had time to make any researches into its history or merits. [24]

During the short truce which followed the treaty of Amiens, M. D'Arblay visited France. Lauriston and La Fayette represented his claims to the French government, and obtained a 'Promise that he should be reinstated in his military rank. M. D'Arblay, however, insisted that he should never be 'required to serve against the countrymen of his wife. The First Consul, of course, would not hear of such a condition, and ordered the general's commission to be instantly revoked.

Madame D'Arblayjoined her husband at Paris, a short time before the war of 1803 broke out, and remained in France ten years, cut off from almost all intercourse with the land of her birth. At length, when Napoleon was on his march to Moscow, she with great difficulty obtained from his ministers permission to visit her own country, in company with her son, who was a native of England. She returned in time to receive the last blessing of her father, who died in his eighty-seventh year. In 1814 she published her last novel, "The Wanderer," a book which no judicious friend to her memory will attempt to draw from the oblivion into which it has justly fallen. [25]In the same year her son Alexander was sent to Cambridge. He obtained an honourable place among the wranglers of his year, and was elected a fellow of Christ's college. But his reputation at the University was higher than might be inferred from his success in academical contests. His French education had not fitted him for the examinations of the Senate house; but, in pure mathematics, we have been assured by some of his competitors that he had very few equals. He went into the Church, and it was thought likely that he would attain high eminence as a preacher; but he died before his mother, All that we have heard of him leads us to believe that he was such a son as such a mother deserved to have.' In 1831, Madame D'Arblay published the memoirs of her father; and on the sixth of January, 1840, she died in her eighty-eighth year.

We now turn from the life of Madame D'Arblay to her writings. There can, we apprehend, be little difference of opinion as to the nature of her merit, whatever differences may exist as to its degree. She was emphatically what Johnson called her, a character-monger. It was in the exhibition of human passions and whims that her strength lay; and in this department of art she had, we think-, very distinguished skill. But, in order that we may, according to our duty as kings at arms, versed inthe laws of literary precedence, marshal her to the exact seat to which she is entitled, we must carry our examination somewhat further.

There is, in one respect, a remarkable analogy between the faces and the minds of men. No two faces are alike ; and yet very few faces deviate very widely from the common standard. Among the eighteen hundred thousand human beings who inhabit London, there is not one who could be taken by his acquaintance for another; yet we may walk from Paddington to Mile-end without seeing one person in whom any feature is so overcharged that we turn round to stare at it. An infinite number of varieties lies between limits which are not very far asunder. The specimens which pass those limits on either side, form a very small minority.

It is the same with the characters of men. Here, too, the variety passes all enumeration. But the cases in which the deviation from the common standard is striking and grotesque, are very few. In one mind avarice predominates ; in another pride ; in a third, love of pleasure-just as in one countenance the nose is the most marked feature, while in others the chief expression lies in the brow, or in the lines of the mouth. But there are very few countenances in which nose, brow, and mouth do not contri. bute, though in unequal degrees, to the general effect ; and so there are very few characters in which one overgrown propensity makes all others utterly insignificant.

It is evident that a portrait painter, who was able only to represent faces and figures such as those -which we pay money to see at fairs, would not, however spirited his execution might be, take rank among the highest artists. He must always be placed below those who have skill to seize peculiarities which do not amount to deformity. The slighter those peculiarities, the greater is the merit of the limner who can catch them and transfer them to his canvas. To paint Daniel Lambert or the living skeleton, the pig-faced lady or the Siamese twins, so that nobody can mistake them, is an exploit within the reach of a sign painter. A thirdrate artist might give us the squint of Wilkes, and the depressed nose and protuberant cheeks of Gibbon. It would require a much higher degree of skill to paint two such men as Mr. Canning and Sir Thomas Lawrence, so that nobody who had ever seen them could for a moment hesitate to assign each picture to its original. Here the mere caricaturist would be quite at fault. He would find in neither face anything on which he could lay hold for the Purpose of making a distinction. Two ample bald foreheads, two reg ular profiles, two full faces of the same oval form, would baffle his art ; and he would be reduced to the miserable shift of writing their names at the foot of his picture. Yet there was a great difference ; and a person who had seen them once would no more have mistaken one of them for the other than he would have mistaken Mr. Pitt for Mr. Fox. But the difference lay in delicate lineaments and shades, reserved for pencils of a rare order,

This distinction runs through all the imitative arts. Foote's mimicry was exquisitely ludicrous, but it was all caricature. He could take off only some strange peculiarity, a stammer or a lisp, a Northumbrian burr or an Irish brogue, a stoop or a shuffle. "If a man," said Johnson, "hops on one leg, Foote can hop on one leg." Garrick, on the other hand, could seize those differences of manner and pronunciation, which, though highly characteristic, are yet too slight to be described, Foote, we have no doubt, could have made the Haymarket theatre shake with laughter by imitating a conversation between a Scotchman and a Somersetshire man. But Garrick could have imitated a dialogue between two fashionable men both models of the best breeding, Lord Chesterfield, for example, and Lord Albemarle, so that no person could doubt which was which, although no person could say that, in any point, either Lord Chesterfield or Lord Albemarle spoke or moved otherwise than in conformity with the usages of the best society.

The same distinction is found in the drama, and in fictitious narrative. Highest among those who have exhibited human nature by means of dialogue, stands Shakspeare. His variety is like the variety of nature, endless diversity, scarcely any monstrosity. The characters of which he has given us an impression as vivid as that which we receive from the characters of our own associates, are to be reckoned by scores. Yet in all these scores hardly one character is to be found which deviates widely from the common standard, and which we should call very eccentric if we met it in real life. The silly notion that every man has one ruling passion, and that this clue, once known, unravels all the mysteries of his conduct, finds no countenance in the plays of Shakspeare. There man appears as he is, made up of a crowd of passions, which contend for the mastery over him, and govern him in turn. What is Hamlet's ruling passion? Or Othello's? Or Harry the Fifth's? Or Wolsey's? Or Lear's? Or Shylock's? Or Benedick's? Or Macbeth's? Or that of Cassius? Or that of Falconbridge? But we might go on for ever. Take a single example-Shylock. Is he so eager for money as to be indifferent to revenge? Or so eager for revenge as to be indifferent to money? Or so bent on both together as to be indifferent to the honour of his nation and the law of Moses? All his propensities are mingled with each other, so that, in trying to apportion to each its proper part, we find the same difficulty which constantly meets us in real life. A superficial critic may say that hatred is Shylock's ruling passion. But how many passions have amalgamated to form that hatred? It is partly the result of wounded pride: Antonio has called him dog. It is partly the result of covetousness: Antonio has hindered him of half a million; and when Antonio is gone, there will be no limit to the gains of usury. It is partly the result of national and religious feeling: Antonio has spit on the Jewish gaberdine; and the oath of revenge has been sworn by the Jewish Sabbath. We might go through all the characters which we have mentioned, and through fifty more in the same way; for it is the constant manner of Shakspeare to represent the human mind as lying, not under the absolute dominion of one despotic propensity, but under a mixed government in which a hundred powers balance each other. Admirable as he was in all parts of his art, we most admire him for this, that while he has left us a greater number of striking portraits than all other dramatists Put together, he has scarcely left us a single caricature.

Shakspeare has had neither equal nor second. But among the writers who, in the point which we have noticed, have approached nearest to the manner of the great master, we have no hesitation in placing Jane Austen, a woman of whom England is justly proud. She has given us a multitude of characters, all, in a certain sense, common-place, all such as we meet every day. yet they are all as perfectly discriminated from each other as if they were the most eccentric of human beings. There are, for example, four clergymen, none of whom we should be surprised to find in any parsonage in the kingdom—Mr. Edward Ferrers, Mr. Henry Tilney, Mr. Edmund Bertram, and Mr. Elton. They are all specimens of the upper part of the middle class. They have been liberally educated. They all lie under the restraints of the same sacred profession. They are all young. They are all in love. Not one of them has any hobbyhorse, to use the phrase of Sterne. Not one has a ruling passion, such as we read of in Pope. Who would not have expected them to be insipid likenesses of each other? No such thing. Harpagon is not more unlike to Jourdain, Joseph Surface is not more unlike to Sir Lucius O'Trigger, than every one of Miss Austen's young divines to all his reverend -brethren. And almost all this is done by touches so delicate that they elude analysis, that they defy the powers of description, and that we know them to exist only by the general effect to which they have contributed.

A line must be drawn, we conceive, between artists of this class -and those poets and novelists whose skill lies in the exhibiting of what Ben Jonson called humours. The words of Ben are so much to the purpose that we will quote them :-

"When some one peculiar quality Doth so possess a man, that it doth draw All his affects, his spirits and his powers, In their confluxions all to run one way, This may be truly said to be a humour."

There are undoubtedly persons in whom humours such as Ben describes have attained a complete ascendancy. The avarice of Elwes, the insane desire of Sir Egerton Brydges for a barony, to which he had no more right than to the crown of Spain, the malevolence which long meditation on imaginary wrongs generated in the gloomy mind of Bellingham, are instances. The feeling which animated Clarkson and other virtuous men against the slave trade and slavery, is an instance of a more honourable kind.

Seeing that such humours exist, we cannot deny that they are proper subjects for the imitations of art. But we conceive that the imitation of such humours, however skilful and amusing, is not an achievement of the highest order ; and, as such humours are rare in real life, they ought, we conceive, to be sparingly introduced into works which profess to be pictures of real life. Nevertheless, a writer may show so much genius in the exhibition of these humours as to be fairly entitled to a distinguished and permanent rank among classics. The chief seats of all, however, the places on the dais and under the canopy, are reserved for the few who have excelled in the difficult art of portraying characters in which no single feature is extravagantly over-charged.

If we have expounded the law soundly, we can have no difficulty in applying it to the particular case before us. Madame D'Arblay has left us scarcely anything but humours. Almost every one of her men and women has some one propensity developed to a morbid degree. In "Cecilia," for example, Mr. Delville never opens his lips without some allusion to his own birth and station ; or Mr. Briggs, without some allusion to the hoarding of money; or Mr. Hobson, without betraying the self-indulgence and self-importance of a purseproud upstart; or Mr. Simkins, without uttering some sneaking remark for the purpose of currying favour with his customers; or Mr. Meadows, without expressing apathy and weariness of life; or Mr. Albany, without declaiming about the vices of the rich and the misery of the poor; or Mrs. Belfield, without some-indelicate eulogy on her son ; or Lady Margaret, without indicating jealousy of her husband. Morrice is all skipping, officious impertinence, Mr. Gosport all sarcasm, Lady Honoria all lively prattle, Miss Larolles all silly prattle. If ever Madame D'Arblay aimed at more, as in the character of Monckton, we do not think that she succeeded well. [26]We are, therefore, forced to refuse to Madame D'Arblay a place in the highest rank of art; but we cannot deny that, in the rank to which she belonged, she had few equals and scarcely any superior. The variety of humours which is to be found in her novels is immense ; and though the talk of each person separately is monotonous, the general effect is not monotony, but a very lively and agreeable diversity. Her plots are rudely constructed and improbable, if we consider them in themselves. But they are admirably framed for the purpose of exhibiting striking groups of eccentric characters, each governed by his own peculiar whim, each talking his own peculiar jargon, and each bringing out by opposition the oddities of all the rest. We will give one example out of many which occur to us. All probability is violated in order to bring Mr. Delville, Mr. Briggs, Mr. Hobson, and Mr. Albany into a room together. But when we have them there, we soon forget probability in the exquisitely ludicrous effect which is produced by the conflict of four old fools, each raging with a monomania of his own, each talking a dialect of his own, and each inflaming all the others anew every time he opens his mouth. Madame D'Arblay was most successful in comedy, and, indeed, in comedy which bordered on farce. But we are inclined to infer from some passages, both in "Cecilia" and "Camilla," that she might have attained equal distinction in the pathetic. We have formed this judgment less from those ambitious'scenes of distress which lie near the catastrophe of each of those novels, than from some exquisite strokes of natural tenderness which take us, here and there, by surprise. We would mention as examples, Mrs. Hill's account of her little boy's death in "Cecilia," and the parting of Sir Hugh Tyrold and Camilla, when the honest baronet thinks himself dying.

It is melancholy to think that the whole fame of Madame D'Arblay rests on what she did during the earlier part of her life, and that everything which she published during the forty-three years which preceded her death lowered her reputation. Yet we have no reason to think that at the time when her faculties ought to have been in their maturity, they were smitten with any blight. In "The Wanderer," we catch now and then a gleam of her genius. Even in the memoirs of her father, there is no trace of dotage. They are very bad; but they are so, as it seems to us, not from a decay of power, but from a total perversion of power. The truth is, that Madame D'Arblay's style underwent a gradual and most pernicious change-a change which, in degree at least, we believe to be unexampled in literary history, and of which it may be useful to trace the progress. When she wrote her letters to Mr. Crisp, her early journals and her'first novel, her style was not, indeed, brilliant or energetic ; but it was easy, clear, and free from all offensive thoughts. When she wrote "Cecilia" she aimed higher. She had then lived much in a circle of which Johnson was the centre; and she was herself one of his most submissive worshippers. It seems never to have crossed her mind that the style even of his best writings was by no means faultless and that even had it been faultless, it might not be wise in her to imitate it. Phraseology which is proper in a disguisition on the Unities or in a preface to a dictionary, may be quite out of place in a tale of fashionable life. Old gentlemen do not criticise the reigning modes, nor do young gentlemen make love, with the balanced epithets and sonorous cadences which, on occasions of great dignity, a skilful writer may use with happy effect.

In an evil hour the author of "Evelina," took "The Rambler" for her model. This would not have been wise even if she could have imitated her pattern as well as Hawkesworth did. But such imitation was beyond her power. She had her own style. It was a tolerably good one; and might, without any violent change, have been improved into a very good one. She determined to throw it away, and to adopt a style in which she could attain excellence only by achieving an almost miraculous victory over nature and over habit. She could cease to be Fanny Burney; it was not so easy to become Samuel Johnson.

In "Cecilia" the change of manner began to appear. But in "Cecilia" the imitation of Johnson, though not always in the best taste, is sometimes eminently happy; and the passages which are so verbose as to be positively offensive, are few. There were people who whispered that Johnson had assisted his young friend, and that the novel owed all its finest passages to his hand. This was merely the fabrication of envy. Miss Burney's real excellences were as much beyond the reach of Johnson as his real excellences were beyond her reach, He could no more have written the Masquerade scene or the Vauxhall scene, than she could have written the life of Cowley or the review of Soame jenyns. But we have not the smallest doubt that he revised "Cecilia," and that he re-touched the style of many passages. [27]We know that he was in the habit of giving assistance of this kind most freely. Goldsmith, Hawkesworth, Boswell, Lord Hailes, Mrs. Williams, were among those who obtained his help. Nay, he even corrected the poetry of Mr. Crabbe, whom, we believe, he had never seen. When Miss Burney thought of writing a comedy, he promised to give her his best counsel, though he owned that he was not particularly well qualified to advise on matters relating to the stage, We therefore think it in the highest degree improbable that his little Fanny, when living in habits of the most affectionate intercourse with him, would have brought out an important work without consulting him; and, when we look into "Cecilia," we see such traces of his hand in the grave and elevated passages as it is impossible to mistake. Before we conclude this article, we will give two or three examples.

When next Madame D'Arblay appeared before the world as a writer, she was in a very different situation. She would not content herself with the simple English in which "Evelina" had been written. She had no longer the friend who, we are confident, had polished and strengthened the style of "Cecilia." Shehad to write in Johnson's manner without Johnson's aid. The consequence was, that in "Camilla" every passage which she meant to be fine is detestable; and that the book has been saved from condemnation only by the admirable spirit and force of those scenes in which she was content to be familiar.

But there was to be a still deeper descent. After the publication of "Camilla" Madame D'Arblay resided ten years at Paris. During these years there was scarcely any intercourse between France and England. It was with difficulty that a short letter could occasionally be transmitted. All Madame D'Arblay's companions were French. She must have written spoken, thought in French. Ovid expressed his fear that a shorter exile might have affected the purity of his Latin. During a shorter exile Gibbon unlearned his native English. Madame D'Arblay had carried a bad style to France. She brought back a style which we are really at a loss to describe. It is a sort of broken Johnsonese, a barbarous, patois, bearing the same relation to the language of "Rasselas" which the gibberish of the negroes of Jamaica bears to the English of the House of Lords. Sometimes it reminds us of the finest, that is to say the vilest, parts of Mr. Galt's novels; sometimes of the perorations of Exeter hall; sometimes of the leading articles of the "Morning Post." But it most resembles the puffs of Mr. Rowland and Dr. Goss. It matters not what ideas are clothed in such a style. The genius of Shakspeare and Bacon united would not save a work so written from general derision.

It is only by means of specimens that we can enable our readers to judge how widely Madame D'Arblay's three styles differed from each other.

The following passage was written before she became intimate with Johnson. It is from "Evelina."

"His son seems weaker in his understanding and more gay in his temper; but his gaiety is that of a foolish, overgrown schoolboy, whose mirth consists in noise and disturbance. He disdains his father for his close attention to business and love of money, though he seems himself to have no talents, spirit or generosity to make him superior to either. His chief delight appears to be in tormenting and ridiculing his sisters, who in return most cordially despise him. Miss Branghton, the eldest daughter, is by no means ugly; but looks proud, ill-tempered and conceited. She hates the city, though without knowing why; for it is easy to discover she has lived nowhere else. Miss Poly Branghton is rather pretty, very foolish, very ignorant, very giddy and, I believe, very good natured."

This is not a fine style, but simple, perspicuous, and agreeable. We now come to "Cecilia," written during Miss Burney's intimacy with Johnson - and we leave it to our readers to judge whether the following passage was not at least corrected by his hand.

"It is rather an imaginary than an actual evil and, though a deep wound to pride, no offence to morality. Thus have I laid open to you my whole heart, confessed my perplexities, acknowledged my vain glory and exposed, with equal sincerity, the sources of my doubts and the motives of my decision. But now, indeed, how to proceed I know not. The difficulties which are yet to encounter I fear to enumerate, and the petition I have to urge I have scarce courage to mention. My family, mistaking ambition for honour and rank for dignity, have long planned a splendid connection for me, to which, though my invariable repugnance has stopped any advances, their wishes and their views immoveably adhere. I am but too certain they will now listen to no other. I dread, therefore, to make a trial where I despair of success. I know not how to risk a prayer with those who may silence me by a command."

Take now a specimen of Madame D'Arblay's later style. This is the way in which she tells us that her father, on his journey back from the Continent, caught the rheumatism.

"He was assaulted, during his precipitated return, by the rudest fierceness of wintry elemental strife; through which, with bad accommodations and innumerable accidents, he became a prey to the merciless pangs of the acutest spasmodic rheumatism, which barely suffered him to reach his home ere, long and piteously, it confined him, a tortured prisoner, to his bed. Such was the check that almost instantly curbed, though it could not subdue, the rising pleasure of his hopes of entering upon a new species of existence-that of an approved man of letters ; for it was on the bed of sickness, exchanging the light wines of France, Italy and Germany, for the black and loathsome potions of the Apothecaries' hall, writhed by darting stitches and burning with fiery fever, that he felt the full force of that sublunary equipoise that seems evermore to hang suspended over the attainment of long-sought and uncommon felicity, just as it is ripening to burst forth with enjoyment!"

Here is a second passage from "Evelina."

"Mrs. Selwyn is very kind and attentive to me. She is extremely clever. Her understanding, indeed, may be called masculine; but unfortunately her manners deserve the same epithet, for, in studying to acquire the knowledge of the other sex, she has lost all the softness of her own. In regard to myself, however, as I have neither courage nor inclination to argue with her, I have never been personally hurt at her want of gentleness -a virtue which nevertheless seems so essential a part of the female character, that I find myselfmore awkward and less at ease with a woman who wants it than I do with a man."

This is a good style of its kind, and the following passage from "Cecilia" is also in a good style, though not in a faultless one. We say with confidence-either Sam Johnson or the devil.

"Even the imperious Mr. Delville was more supportable here than in London. Secure in his own castle, he looked round him with a pride of power and possession which softened while it swelled him. Hissuperiority was undisputed: his will was without control. He was not, as inthe the great capital of the kingdom, surrounded by competitors. No rivalry disturbed his peace; no equality mortified his greatness. All he saw were either vassals of his power, or guests bending to his pleasure. He abated, therefore, considerably the stern gloom of his haughtiness and soothed his proud mind by the courtesy of condescension."

We will stake our reputation for critical sagacity on this, that no such paragraph as that which we have last quoted can be found in any of Madame D'Arblay's works except "Cecilia." Compare with it the following sample of her later style.

"if beneficence be judged by the happiness which it diffuses, whose claim, by that proof, shall stand higher than that of Mrs. Montagu, from the munificence with which she celebrated her annual festival for those hapless Artificers who perform the most abject offices of any authorised calling in being the active guardians of our blazing hearths? Not to vain glory but to kindness of heart, should be adjudged the publicity of that superb charity which made its jetty objects, for one bright morning, cease to consider themselves as degraded outcasts from all society."

We add one or two short samples. Sheridan refused to permit his lovely wife to sing in.public, and was warmly praised on this account by Johnson.

"The last of men," says Madame D'Arblay "was Dr. Johnson to have abetted squandering the delicacy of integrity by nullifying the labours of talents."

The Club, Johnson's Club, did itself no honour by rejecting, on political grounds, two distinguished men-one a Tory, the other a Whig. Madame D'Arblay tells the story thus:—"A similar ebullition of political rancour with that which so difficultly had been conquered for Mr. Canning foamed over the ballot box to the exclusion of Mr. Rogers." .

An offence punishable with imprisonment is, in this language, an offence "which produces incarceration." To be starved to death is "to sink from inanition into nonentity." Sir Isaac Newton is "the developer of the skies in their embodied movements;" and Mrs. Thrale, when a party of clever people sat silent, is said to have been "provoked by the dullness of a Witurnity that, in the midst of such renowned interlocutors, produced as narcotic a torpor as could have been caused by a dearth the most barren of all human faculties."

In truth it is impossible to look at any page of Madame D'Arblay's later works without finding flowers of rhetoric like these Nothing in the language of those jargonists at whom Mr. Gosport laughed, nothing in the language of Sir Sedley Clarendel, approaches this new Euphuism. [28]

It is from no unfriendly feeling to Madame D'Arblay's memory that we have expressed ourselves, so strongly on the subject of her style. On the contrary, we conceive that we have really rendered a service to her reputation. That her later works were complete failures is a fact too notorious to be dissembled, and some persons, we believe, have consequently taken up a notion that she was from the first an overrated writer, and that she had not the powers which were necessary to maintain her on the eminence on which good luck and fashion had placed her. We believe, on the contrary, that her early popularity was no more than the just reward of distinguished merit, and would never have undergone an eclipse if she had only been content to go on writing in her mother tongue. If she failed when she quitted her own province and attempted to occupy one in which she had neither part nor lot, this reproach is common to her with a crowd of distinguished men. Newton failed when he turned from the courses of the stars and the ebb and flow of the ocean to apocalyptic seals and vials. Bentley failed when he turned from Homer and Aristophanes to edit the "Paradise Lost." Enigo failed when he attempted to rival the Gothic churches of the fourteenth century. Wilkie failed when he took it into his head that the "Blind Fiddler" and the "Rent Day" were unworthy of his powers, and challenged competition with Lawrence as a portrait painter. Such failures should be noted for the instruction of posterity, but they detract little from the permanent reputation of those who have really done great things.

Yet one word more. It is not only on account of the intrinsic merit of Madame D'Arblay's early works that she is entitled to honourable mention. Her appearance is an important epoch in our literary history. "Evelina" was the first tale written by a woman, and purporting to be a picture of life and manners, that lived or deserved to live. "The Female Quixote" is no exception. That work has undoubtedly great merit, when considered as a wild, satirical harlequinade; but if we consider it as a picture of life and manners, we must pronounce it more absurd than any of the romances which it was designed to ridicule. [29]

Indeed, most of the popular novels which preceded "Evelina" were such as no lady would have written; and many of them were such as no lady could without confusion own that she had read. The very name of novel was held in horror among religious people. In decent families, which did not profess extraordinary sanctity, there was a strong feeling against all such works. Sir Anthony Absolute, two or three years before "Evelina" appeared, spoke the sense of the great body of fathers and husbands when he pronounced the circulating library an evergreen tree of diabolical knowledge. This feeling on the part of the grave and reflecting increased the evil from which it had sprung. The novelist having little character to lose, and having few readers among serious people, took without scruple liberties which in our generation seem almost incredible.

Miss Burney did for the English novel what Jeremy Collier[30]did for the English drama; and she did it in a better way. She first showed that a tale might be written in which both the fashionable and the vulgar life of London might be exhibited with great force and with broad comic humour, and which yet should not contain a single line inconsistent with rigid morality or even with virgin delicacy. She took away the reproach which lay on a most useful and delightful species of composition. She vindicated the right of her sex to an equal share in a fair and noble province of letters. Several accomplished women have followed in her track. At present, the novels which we owe to English ladies form no small part of the literary glory of our Country. No class of works is more honourably distinguished by fine observation, by grace, by delicate wit, by pure moral feeling. Several among the successors of Madame D'Arblay have equalled her; two, we think, have surpassed her. But the fact that she has been surpassed gives her an additional claim to our respect and gratitude; for, in truth, we owe to her not only "Evelina," "Cecilia," and "Camilla," but also "Mansfield Park" and "The Absentee."

---

1   Dr. Arne.-ED.

2   The lady's maiden name was Esther Sheepe. She was, by the mother's side, of French extraction, from a family of the name of Dubois—a name which will be remembered as that of one of the characters in her daughter Fanny's first novel, "Evelina."-ED.

3   She was born on the 13th of June, 1752-ED.

4   This degree was conferred upon him on Friday, the 23rd of June, 1769.-ED.

5   The "Early Diary of Frances Burney, from 1768 to 1778," recently published, throws some new light upon her education. It is her own statement that her father's library contained but one novel-', Amelia " ; yet as a girl we find her acquainted with the works of Richardson and Sterne, of Marivaux and Prévost, with "Rasselas" and the "Vicar of Wakefield." in history and poetry, moreover, she appears to have been fairly well read, and she found constant literary employment as her father's amanuensis. As to Voltaire, she notes, on her twenty-first birthday, that she has just finished the "Heoriade"; but her remarks upon the book prove how little she was acquainted with the author. She thinks he "has made too free with religion in giving words to the Almighty. But M. Voltaire, I understand, is not a man of very rigid principles at least not in religion" ED.

6   This is not quite accurate. Burney secured the relic in the manner described, not, however, to gratify his own enthusiasm, but to comply with the request of his friend Mr. Bewley, of Massingham, Norfolk, that he would procure for him some memento of the great Dr. Johnson. The tuft of the Doctor's hearth-broom, which Burney sent him, half in jest, was preserved with the greatest care by its delighted recipient. "He thinks it more precious than pearls," wrote Fanny. ("Early Diary," vol. i, p. 169. This incident occurred in 1760.-ED.

7   The "Early Diary," however, proves that, in spite of her shyness, Fanny was very much at home in the brilliant society which congregated at her father's house, and occasionally took her full share in the conversation. Nor do we find her by any means avoiding the diversions common to young ladies of her age and station. She goes to dances, to the play, to the Opera, to Ranelagh, and even, on one memorable occasion, to a masquerade- -"a very private one," however."-ED.

8   Mrs. . Stephen Allen, a widow, of Lynn. She was married to Dr. Burney

(not yet Doctor, however) in October, 1767. His first wife died on the 28th of September, 1761.-ED.

9   There is some difficulty here as to the chronology. "This sacrifice," says the editor of "The Diary," "was made in the young authoress's fifteenth year." This could not be; for the sacrifice was the effect, according to the editor's own showing of the remonstrances of the second Mrs. Burney; and Frances was in her sixteenth year when her father's second marriage took place.

10   She now hemmed and stitched from breakfast to

11   The picture drawn by Macaulay of Mr. Crisp's wounded vanity and consequent misanthropy is absurdly overcharged. In the first place, bis play of "Virginia," which was first produced at Drury Lane on the 25th of February, 1754, actually achieved something like a suc`es d'estime. It ran eleven nights, no contemptible run for those days ; was revived both at Drury Lane and at Covent Garden; was printed and reprinted; and all this all in his own lifetime. It had, in fact, at least as much success as it deserved, though, doubtless, too little to satisfy the ambition of its author. In the second place, there is absolutely no evidence whatever that his life was long embittered by disappointment connected with his tragedy. It is clear, from Madame D'Arblay's "Memoirs of Dr. Burney," that Mr. Crisp's retirement to Chesington, many years after the production of "Virginia," was mainly due to a straitened income and the gout. Nor was his seclusion unenlivened by friendship. The Burneys, in particular, visited him from time to time; and Fanny has left us descriptions of scenes of almost uproarious gaiety, enacted at Chesington by this gloomy recluse and his young friends. But we shall hear more of Chesington and its inmates hereafter-ED.

12   Scarcely, we think; when her fame was at its height, Fanny Burney received no more than 250 pounds for her second novel, "Cecilia." See the "Early Diary," vol. ii. p. 307.-ED,

13   Christopher Anstey, the author of that amusing and witty poetical satire, the "New Bath Guide."-ED.

14   John Wilson Croker.-ED.

15   Richard Cumberland's fame as playwright and novelist can hardly be said to have survived to the present day. Sheridan caricatured him as Sir Fretful Plagiary, in the "Critic." We shall meet with him hereafter in "The Diary."-ED.

16   See note ante, p. xxiv.

17   "Probationary Odes for the Laureateship," a volume of lively satirical verse published after the appointment of Sir Thomas Warton to that office on the death of William Whitehead, in 1785.-ED.

18   See "Cecilia," Book V. chap. 6.-ED.

19   In "Cecilia."-ED.

20   The "Mr. Fairly" of "The Diary."-ED.

21   Macaulay is mistaken. Fanny did receive the gown, a "lilac tabby," and

wore it on the princess royal's birthday, September 29, 1786.-ED.

22   The fifth volume of " The "Diary" concludes with Fanny's marriage to
M. d'Arblay. The seven volumes of the original edition were published
at intervals, from 1842 to 1846. -ED.

23   The rumour was probably not far from correct. "Camilla" was
published by subscription, at one guinea the set, and the subscribers
numbered over eleven hundred. Four thousand copies were printed,
and three thousand five hundred were sold in three months. Within six
weeks of its pEublication, Dr. Burney told Lord Orford that about two
thousand pounds had already been realized.-ED.

24   Fanny's tragedy of "Edwy and Elgiva", written during the period of her
slavery at court, was produced by Sheridan at Drury-lane in March,
1795. It proved a failure, although the leading parts were plaved by
Kemble and Mrs. Siddons. This tragedy, which was never published, is
occasionally referred to in her letters of that year. See also an article by
Mr. E. S. Shuckburgh, in "Macmillan's Magazine" for February, 1896. -
ED.

25   We find it difficult to understand Macaulay's estimate of "The
Wanderer." Later critics appear, in general, to have echoed Macaulay
without being at the pains of reading the book. If it has not the naive
freshness of "Evelina," nor the sustained excellence of style of
"Cecilia," "The Wanderer" is inferior to neither in the "exhibition of
human passions and whims." The story is interesting and full of variety;
the characters live, as none but the greatest novelists have known how
to make them. In Juliet, Fanny has given us one of her most fascinating
heroines, while her pictures of the fashionable society of
Brighthelmstone are distinguished by a force and vivacity of satire
which she has rarely surpassed. it is true that in both "The Wanderer"
and "Camilla" we meet with occasional touches of that peculiar
extravagance of style which disfigure, the "Memoirs of Dr. Burney," but
these passages, in the novels, are SO comparatively inoffensive, and so
nearly forgotten in the general power and charm of the story that we
scarcely care to instance them as serious blemishes-ED.

26   This criticism of Madame D'Arblay appears to us somewhat too
sweeping. It must be remembered that the persons of "one propensity,"
instanced by Macaulay, are all to be found among the minor characters
in her novels. The circumstances, moreover, under which they are
introduced, are frequently such as to render the display of their
particular humours not only excusable, but natural. But surely in others
of her creations, in her heroines especially, she is justly entitled to the
praise of having portrayed "characters in which no single feature is
extravagantly overcharged."-ED.

27   this conjecture may be considered as finally disposed of by Dr.
Johnson's explicit declaration that he never saw one word of"Cecilia"
before it was printed.-ED.

28   The above "flowers of rhetoric" are taken from the "Memoirs of Dr. Burney," published in 1832; but it is scarcely just- -indeed, it is wholly unjust—to include "Camilla" and "The Wanderer" under the same censure with that book. The literary style of the "Memoirs" is the more amazing, since we find Madame D'Arblay, in 1815, correcting in her son the very fault which is there indulged to so unfortunate an extent. She writes to him - "I beg you, when you write to me, to let your pen paint Your thoughts as they rise, not as you seek or labour to embellish them. I remember you once wrote me a letter so very fine from Cambridge, that, if it had not made me laugh, it would have made me sick."-ED.

29   "The Female Quixote" is the title of a novel by Charlotte Lenox, published in 1752. It was written as a satire upon the Heroic Romances, so popular in England during the seventeenth century, and the early part of the eighteenth; and scarcely claims to be considered as a picture of life and manners. It is a delightful book however, and the character of the heroine, Arabella, is invested with a charm which never, even in the midst of her wildest extravagancies, fails to make itself felt.-ED.

30   Author of the famous "Short View of the Immorality and the Profaneness of the English Stage," published in 1698; a book which, no doubt, struck at a real evil, but which is written in a spirit of violence and bigotry productive rather of amusement than of conviction. It caused, however, a tremendous sensation at the time, and its effect upon the English drama was very considerable; not an unmixed blessing either.-ED.

SECTION 1 (1778.)

MISS BURNEY PUBLISHES HER FIRST NOVEL AND FINDS HERSELF FAMOUS.

[MISS Burney's first novel, " Evelina," had been submitted in manuscript to the great publisher, Dodsley, who refused to look at an anonymous work. It was then offered to Lowndes, who published it. The negotiations with the publisher were carried on by Fanny's brother Charles, and her cousin, Edward Burney. These two, with her sisters, and her aunts Anne and Rebecca (Dr. Burney's sisters), appear to have been the only persons entrusted with the secret. It will be most convenient here, at the commencement of - The Diary," to give a few necessary details respecting the Burney family. By his first*wife, Esther Sleepe, Dr. Burney became the father of seven children:—

1. Esther ("Hetty"), born 1749; married, in 1770, her cousin Charles Rousseau Burney, eldest son of Dr. Burney's elder brother, Richard Burney, of Worcester. Hetty's husband is always called "Mr. Burney" in the "Diary". He was a musician.

2. James, the sailor, afterwards Admiral Burney, known to readers of "Elia." He was born June 5, 1750; accompanied the great discoverer, Captain Cook, on his second and third voyages; served in the East Indies in 1783, after which he retired from active service. In 1785 he married Miss Sally Payne, and the rest of his life was devoted to literature and whist. His "History of the Discoveries in the South Sea or Pacific Ocean" is still a standard work. James died November 17, 1821.

3. Charles born June, 1751 ; died young.

4- Frances" our "Fanny," born June 13, 1752.

5. Susanna Elizabeth, the "peculiar darling of the whole house of Dr. Burney, as well as of his heart"—so Fanny writes of her favourite sister. She was born about 1755, and married, in the beginning Of 1781, Captain Molesworth Phillips, who, as Cook's lieutenant of marines, had seen the discoverer murdered by savages, in February, 1779, and narrowly escaped with his own life on that occasion. Susan died January 6, 1800.

6. Charles, afterwards Dr. Charles, the distinguished Greek scholar; born December 4, 1757. After his death, in 1817, his magnificent library was purchased for the British Museum, at a cost Of 13,500 pounds.

7. Charlotte Ann, born about 1759. She married Clement Francis, in February, 1786. He died in 1792, and she married again in 1798, Mrs. Barrett, the editress of the "Diary and Letters of Madame d'Arblay," was Charlotte's daughter by her first marriage.

By his second wife, Elizabeth Allen, whom he married in 1767, Dr. Burney had two children—a son, Richard Thomas, and a daughter, Sarah Harriet. The latter followed the career of her famous half-sister, and acquired some distinction as a novelist. Cousins Richard and Edward were younger sons of Uncle Richard Burney, of Worcester. Edward was successful as an artist, especially as a book-illustrator. He painted the portrait of Fanny Burney, a reproduction of which forms the frontispiece to the present volume. Some of his work may be seen in the South Kensington Museum.

Chesington, where we shall presently find Fanny on a visit to Mr. Crisp, was an old roomy mansion, standing in the midst of a lonely common in Surrey, between Kingston and Epsom. It had belonged to Mr. Crisp's friend, Christopher Hamilton, and on his death became the property of his unmarried sister, Mrs. Sarah Hamilton, who, being in poor circumstances, let part of the house to a farmer, and took boarders. Of the latter, Mr. Crisp was the most constant, boarding at Chesington for nearly twenty years, and dying there in 1783. Kitty Cooke, whose name occurs in the "Diary," was the niece of Mrs. Hamilton, and resided with her at Chesington. Mrs. Sophia Gast, whom we find a frequent visitor there, was the sister of Mr. Crisp, and resided at Burford, in Oxfordshire.

Chesington Hall, the name the old manor house goes by in the locality, is still standing, and is a plain brick building with a small bell turret in the roof, but in other respects it has been somewhat modernized since the days of Fanny Burney. The common has been parcelled out into fields, and a picturesque country road now gives access to the front entrance to the house. From the lawn at the back a narrow avenue of venerable trees, which throw out their long arms in strange grotesque fashion, leads directly to the little village church where Mr. Crisp is buried. -ED.]

"EVELINA" AND THE MYSTERY ATTENDING ITS PUBLICATION.

THIS year was ushered in by a grand and most important event! At the latter end of January, the literaryworld was favoured with the first publication of the ingenious, learned, and most profound Fanny Burney! I doubt not but this memorable affair will, in future times, mark the period whence chronologers will date the zenith of the polite arts in this island!

This admirable authoress has named her most elaborate performance, "Evelina; or, a Young Lady's Entrance into the World."

Perhaps this may seem a rather bold attempt and title, for a female whose knowledge of the world is very confined, and whose inclinations, as well as situation, incline her to a private and domestic life. All I can urge is, that I have only presumed to trace the accidents and adventures to which a "young woman" is liable; I have not pretended to show the world what it actually is, but what it appears to a girl of seventeen, and so far as that, surely any girl who is past seventeen may safely do? The motto of my excuse shall be taken from Pope's "Temple of Fame ":

In every work regard the writer's end None e'er can compass more than they intend.

About the middle of January, my cousin Edward brought me a parcel, under the name of Grafton. I had, some little time before, acquainted both my aunts of my frolic. They will, I am sure, be discreet ; indeed, I exacted a vow from them Of strict secrecy ; and they love me with such partial kindness, that I have a pleasure in reposing much confidence in them. I immediately conjectured what the parcel was, and found the following letter.

Fleet-street, Jan. 7, 1778.

Sir, I take the liberty to send you a novel, which a gentleman, your acquaintance, said you would hand to him. I beg with expedition, as 'tis time it should be published, and 'tis requisite he first revise it, or the reviewers may find a flaw.—I am, sir, your obedient servant, Thomas Lowndes.

To Mr. Grafton, To be left at the Orange Coffee-house.

My aunts, now, would take no denial to my reading it to them, in order to mark errata; and to cut the matter short, I was compelled to communicate the affair to my cousin Edward, and then to obey their commands.

Of course, they were all prodigiously charmed with it. My cousin now became my agent, as deputy to Charles, with Mr. Lowndes, and when I had made the errata, carried it to him.

The book, however, was not published till the latter end of the month. A thousand little odd incidents happened about this time, but I am not in a humour to recollect them; however, they were none of them productive of a discovery either to my father or mother.

My little book, I am told, is now at all the circulating libraries. I have an exceeding odd sensation,,when I consider that it is now in the power of any and every body to read what I so carefully hoarded even from my best friends, till this last month or two; and that a work which was so lately lodged, in all privacy, in my bureau, may now be seen by every butcher and baker, cobbler and tinker, throughout the three kingdoms, for the small tribute of threepence.

My aunt Anne and Miss Humphries being settled at this time at Brompton, I was going thither with Susan to tea, when Charlotte acquainted me that they were then employed in reading "Evelina" to the invalid, my cousin Richard. My sister had recommended it to Miss Humphries, and my aunts and Edward agreed that they would read it, but without mentioning anything of the author.

This intelligence gave me the utmost uneasiness-I foresaw a thousand dangers of a discovery-I dreaded the indiscreet warmth of all my confidants. In truth, I was quite sick with apprehension, and was too uncomfortable to go to Brompton, and Susan carried my excuses.

Upon her return, I was somewhat tranquillised, for she assured me that there was not the smallest suspicion of the author, and that they had concluded it to be the work of a man ! and Miss Humphries, who read it aloud to Richard said several things in its commendation, and concluded them by exclaiming, "It's a thousand pities the author should lie concealed!"

Finding myself more safe than I had apprehended, I ventured to go to Brompton next day. In my way up-stairs,[I heard Miss Humphries in the midst of Mr. Villars' letter of consolation upon Sir John Belmont's rejection of his daughter; and just as I entered the room, she cried out, "How pretty that is!"

How much in luck would she have thought herself, had she known who heard her! in a private confabulation which I had with my aunt Anne, she told me a thousand things that had been said in its praise, and assured me they had not for a moment doubted that the work was a man's.

Comforted and made easy by these assurances, I longed for the diversion of hearing their observations, and therefore (though rather mal `a propos) after I had been near two hours in the room, I told Miss Humphries that I was afraid I had interrupted her, and begged she would go on with what she was reading.

"Why," cried she, taking up the book, "we have been prodigiously entertained;" and very readily she continued.

I must own I suffered great difficulty in refraining from laughing upon several occasions,-and several times, when they praised what they read, I was upon the point of saying, "You'are very good!" and so forth, and I could scarcely keep myself from making acknowledgments, and bowing my head involuntarily. However, I got off perfectly safe.

Monday.—Susan and I went to tea at Brompton, We met Miss Humphries coming to town. She told us she had just finished "Evelina," and gave us to understand that she could not get away till she had done it. We heard afterwards from my aunt the most flattering praises; and Richard could talk Of nothing else. His encomiums gave me double pleasure, from being wholly unexpected: for I had prepared myself to hear that he held it extremely cheap. ' It Seems, to my utter amazement, Miss Humphries has guessed the author to be Anstey, who wrote the "Bath Guide"! How improbable and how extraordinary a supposition! But they have both of them done it so much honour that, but for Richard's anger at Evelina's bashfulness, I never Could believe they did not suspect me. I never went to Brompton without finding the third volume in Richard's hands; he speaks of all the characters as if they were his acquaintance, and Praises different parts perpetually: both he and Miss Humphries seem to have it by heart, for it is always `a propos to Whatever is the subject of discourse, and their whole conversation almost consists of quotations from it.

Chesington, June 18.—I came hither the first week in May. My recovery from that time to this, has been slow and sure ; but as I could walk hardly three yards in a day at first, I found so much time to spare, that I could not resist treating myself with a little private sport with "Evelina," a young lady whom I think I have some right to make free with. I had promised Hetty that she should read it to Mr. Crisp, at her own particular request ; but I wrote my excuses, and introduced it myself.

I told him it was a book which Hetty had taken to Brompton, to divert my cousin Richard during his confinement. He was so indifferent about it, that I thought he would not give himself the trouble to read it, and often embarrassed me by unlucky questions, such as, "If it was reckoned clever?" and "What I thought of it?" and "Whether folks laughed at it?" I always evaded any direct or satisfactory answer; but he was so totally free from any idea of suspicion, that my perplexity escaped his notice.

At length, he desired me to begin reading to him. I dared not trust my voice with the little introductory ode, for as that is no romance, but the sincere effusion of my heart, I could as soon read aloud my own letters, written in my own name and character : I therefore skipped it, and have so kept the book out of his sight, that, to this day, he knows not it is there. Indeed, I have, since, heartily repented that I read any of the book to him, for I found it a much more awkward thing than I had expected : my voice quite faltered when I began it, which, however, I passed off for the effect of remaining weakness of lungs; and, in short, from an invincible embarrassment, which I could not for a page together repress, the book, by my reading, lost all manner of spirit.

Nevertheless, though he has by no means treated it with the praise so lavishly bestowed upon it from other quarters, I had the satisfaction to observe that he was even greedily eager to go on with it ; so that I flatter myself the story caught his attention: and, indeed, allowing for my mauling reading, he gave it quite as much credit as I had any reason to expect. But, now that I was sensible of my error in being 'my own mistress of the ceremonies, I determined to leave to Hetty the third volume, and therefore pretended I had not brought it. He was in a delightful ill humour about it, and I enjoyed his impatience far more than I should have done his forbearance. Hetty, therefore, when she comes, has undertaken to bring it,

I have had a visit from my beloved Susy, who, with my mother[31]and little Sally, [32]spent a day here, to my no small satisfaction; and yet I was put into an embarrassment, of which I even yet know not what will be the end, during their short stay: for Mr. Crisp, before my mother, very innocently said, "O! Susan, pray Susette, do send me the third volume of "Evelina;" Fanny brought me the two first on purpose, I believe, to tantalize me."

I felt 'myself in a ferment ; and Susan, too, looked foolish, and knew.not what to answer. As I sat on the same sofa with him, I gave him a gentle shove, as a token, which he could not but understand, that he had said something wrong—though I believe he could not imagine what. Indeed, how should he?

My mother instantly darted forward, and repeated "Evelina,— what's that, pray?"

Again I jolted Mr. Crisp, who, very much perplexed, said, in a boggling manner, that it was a novel-he supposed from the circulating library—only a trumpery novel."

Ah, my dear daddy! thought I, you would have devised some other sort of speech, if you knew all! But he was really, as he well might be, quite at a loss for what I wanted him to say.

"You have had it here, then, have you?" continued my mother.

"Yes-two of the volumes," said Mr. Crisp.

"What, had you them from the library?" asked my mother.

"No, ma'am," answered I, horribly frightened, "from my sister."

The truth is, the books are Susan's, who bought them the first day of publication; but I did not dare own that, as it would have been almost an acknowledgment of all the rest.

She asked some further questions, to which we made the same sort of answers, and then the matter dropped. Whether itrests upon her mind, or not, I cannot tell.

Two days after, I received from Charlotte a letter the most intereiting that could be written to me, for it acquainted me that My dear father was, at length, reading my book, which has now been published six months. How this has come to pass, I am yet in the dark; but, it seems, that the very Moment almost that my mother and Susan and Sally left the house, he desired Charlotte to bring him the "Monthly Review;" she contrived to look over his shoulder as he opened it, which he did at the account of "Evelina; Or, a Young Lady's Entrance into the World." He read it with great earnestness, then put it down ; and presently after snatched it up, and read it again. Doubtless, his paternal heart felt some agitation for his girl, in reading a review of her publication! [33]how he got at the name, I cannot imagine.

Soon after he turned to Charlotte, and bidding her come close to him, he put his finger on the word " Evelina," and saying, she knew what it was, bade her -write down the name, and send the man to Lowndes, as if for herself. This she did, and away went William.

He then told Charlotte, that he had never known the name of it till the day before. 'Tis strange how he got at it! He added that I had come off vastly well in this review, except for "the Captain." Charlotte told him it had also been in "Kenrick's review, [34]and he desired her to copy out for him what was said in both of them. He asked her, too, whether I had mentioned the work was by a lady?

When William returned, he took the books from him, and the moment he was gone, opened the first volume-and opened it upon the Ode! How great must have been his astonishment, at seeing himself so addressed! [35]Indeed, Charlotte says he looked all amazement, read a line or two with great eagerness, and their, stopping short, he seemed quite affected, and the tears started into his eyes: dear soul! I am sure they did into mine, nay, I even sobbed, as I read the account.

I believe he was obliged to go out before he advanced much further. But the next day I had a letter from Susan, in which I heard that he had begun reading it with Lady Hales, and Miss Coussmaker, and that they liked it vastly! [36] "Lady Hales spoke of it very innocently, in the highest terms, declaring she was sure it was written by somebody in high life, And that it had all the marks of real genius! She added, "he must be a man of great abilities!"

How ridiculous! but Miss Coussmaker was a little nearer the truth, for she gave it as her opinion, that the writer was a woman, for she said there was such a remarkable delicacy in the conversations and descriptions, notwithstanding the grossness and vulgarity of some of the characters, and that all oaths and indelicate words were so carefully, yet naturally avoided, that she could not but suspect the writer was a female ; but, she added, notwithstanding the preface declared that the writer never would be known, she hoped, if the book circulated as she expected it would, he or she would be tempted to make a discovery.

Ha! ha! ha!-that's my answer. They little think how well they are already acquainted with the writer they so much honour! Susan begged to have, then, my father's real and final opinion;—and it is such that I almost blush to write, even for my own private reading ; but yet is such as I can by no means suffer to pass unrecorded, as my whole journal contains nothing so grateful to me. I will copy his own words, according to Susan's solemn declaration of their authenticity.

"Upon my word I think it the best novel I know, except Fielding's, and, in some respects, better than his! I have been excessively pleased with it; there are, perhaps a few things that might have been otherwise. Mirvan's trick upon Lovel is, I think, carried too far,-there is something even disgusting in it: however, this instance excepted, I protest I think it will scarce bear an improvement. The language is as good as anybody need write—I declare, as good as I would wish to read. Lord Orville's character is just what it should be - perfectly benevolent and upright; and there is a boldness in it that struck me mightily, for he is a man not ashamed of being better than the rest of mankind. Evelina is in a new style too, so perfectly innocent and natural ; and the scene between her and her father, Sir John Belmont, is a scene for a tragedy! I blubbered at it, and Lady Hales and Miss Coussmaker are not yet recovered from hearing it, it made them quite ill: indeed, it is wrought up in a most extraordinary manner."

This account delighted me more than I- can express. How little did I dream of ever being so much honoured! But the approbation of all the world put together, would not bear any competition, in my estimation, with that of my beloved father.

July 25.—Mrs. Cholmondeley has been reading and praising "Evelina," and my father Is quite delighted at her approbation, and told Susan that I could not have had a greater compliment than making two such women my friends as Mrs. Thrale[37]and Mrs. Cholmondeley. for they were severe and knowing, and afraid of praising `a tort et `a travers, as their opinions are liable to be quoted.

Mrs. Thrale said she had only to complain it was too short. She recommended it to my mother to read!—how droll!—and she told her she would be much entertained with it, for there was a great deal of human life in it, and of the manners of the present times, and added that it was written "by somebody

Who knows the top and the bottom, the highest and the lowest of mankind." She has even lent her set to my mother, who brought it home with her!

By the way, I have again resumed my correspondence with my friend Mr. Lowndes. When I sent the errata I desired to have a set directed to Mr. Grafton, at the Orange Coffee-house, for I had no copy but the one he sent tne to make the errata from, which Was incomplete and unbound. However, I heard nothing at all from him; and therefore, after some consideration, and much demure I determined to make an attempt once more; for my father told me it was a shame that I, the author, should not have even one set of my own work; I ought, he said, to have had six: and indeed, he is often enraged that Lowndes gave no more for the MS.—but I was satisfied,-and that sufficed. [38]

I therefore wrote him word, that I supposed, in the hurry of his business, and variety of his concerns, he had forgotten my request, which I now repeated. I also added, that if ever the book went through another edition, I should be glad to have timely notice, as I had some corrections and alterations to propose.

I received an immediate answer, and intelligence from my sisters, that he had sent a set of " Evelina " most elegantly bound. The answer I will copy.

Fleet-street, July 2, 1778.

Sir,—I bound up a set for you the first day I had them, and hoped by some means to hear from you. The Great World send hereto buy "Evelina." A polite lady said, Do, Mr. Lowndes, give me "Evelina," I am treated as unfashionable for not having read it. I think the impression will be sold by Christmas. If meantime, or about that time, you favour me with any commands, I shall be proud to observe them. Your obliged servant, J. Lowndes.

To Mr. Grafton.

(anny Burney to Miss S. Burney.

Chesington, Sunday, July 6.

Your letter, my dearest Susan, and the inclosed one from Lovirrides, have flung me into such a vehement perturbation, that i hardly can tell whether I wake or dream, and it is even With difficulty that I can fetch my breath. I have been strolling round the garden three or four times, in hopes of regaining a little quietness. However, I am not very angry at my inward disturbance, though it even exceeds what I experienced from the "Monthly Review."

My dear Susy, what a wonderful affair has this been, and how extraordinary is this torrent of success, which sweeps down all before it! I often think it too much, nay, almost wish it would happen to some other person, who had more ambition, whose hopes were more sanguine, and who could less have borne to be buried in the oblivion which I even sought. But though it might have been better bestowed, it could by no one be more gratefully received.

Indeed I can't help being grave upon the subject; for a success so really unexpected almost overpowers me. I wonder at myself that my spirits are not more elated. I believe half the flattery I have had would have made me madly merry; but all serves only to almost depress me by the fullness of heart it occasions. I have been serving Daddy Crisp a pretty trick this morning How he would rail if he found it all out ! I had a fancy to dive pretty deeply into the real rank in which he held my book; so I told him that your last letter acquainted me who was reported to be the author of "Evelina." I added that it was a profound secret, and he must by no means mention it to a human being. He bid me tell him directly, according to his usual style of command—but I insisted upon his guessing.

"I can't guess," said he - "may be it is you."

Oddso! thought I, what do you mean by that?

"Pooh, nonsense!" cried I," what should make you think of me?"

"Why, you look guilty," answered he.

This was a horrible home stroke. Deuce take my looks! thought I- -I shall owe them a grudge for this ! however I found it was a mere random shot, and, without much difficulty, I laughed it to scorn.

And who do you think he guessed next ?—My father!—there's for you!— and several questions he asked me, whether he had lately been shut up much- and so on. And this was not all—for he afterwards guessed Mrs. Thrale and Mrs. Greville. [39]

There's honour and glory for you!—I assure you I grinned prodigiously.

July 20.-I have had a letter from Susan. She informs me that my father, when he took the books back to Streatham, actually acquainted Mrs. Thrale with my secret. He took an opportunity, when they were alone together, of saying that Upon her recommendation, he had himself, as well as my mother; been reading "Evelina."

Well!" cried she, "and is it not a very pretty book? and a Very clever book? and a very comical book?

"Why,',' answered he. "'tis well enough; but I have something to tell you about it."

"Well? what?" cried she; "has Mrs. Cholmondeley found out the author?"

" No," returned he, " not that I know of, but I believe I have, though but very lately."

"Well, pray let's hear!" cried she, eagerly, "I want to know him of all things."

How my father must laugh at the him!—He then, however, undeceived her in regard to that particular, by telling her it was "our Fanny!" for she knows all about our family, as my father talks to'her of his domestic concerns without any reserve.

A hundred handsome things, of course, followed; and she afterwards read some of the comic parts to Dr. Johnson, Mr. Thrale, and whoever came near her. How I should have quivered had I been there ! but they tell me that Dr. Johnson laughed as heartily as my father himself did.

Nothing can be more ridiculous than the scenes in which I am almost perpetually engaged. Mr. Crisp, who is totally without suspicion, says, almost daily, something that has double the meaning he intends to convey; for, as I am often writing, either letters, Italian, or some of my own vagaries, he commonly calls me the scribe, and the authoress; asks when I shall print; says he will have all my works on royal paper, etc.; and the other day, Mrs. Gast, who frequently lectures me about studying too hard, and injuring my health, said-

'Pray, Miss Burney, now you write so much, when do you intend to publish?"

"Publish?" cried Mr. Crisp, "why, she has published; she brought out a book the other day that has made a great noise "Evelina"— and she bribed the reviewers to speak well of it, and set it a going."

I was almost ready to run out of the room; but, though the hit was so palpable in regard to the book, what he said of the reviewers was so much the contrary that it checked my alarm: indeed, had he the most remote idea of the truth, be would be the last man to have hinted at it before a room full of people.

"Oh!" cried I, as composedly as I could, "that is but a small part of my authorship—I shall give you a list of my folios Soon,"

They had all some jocularity upon the occasion, but I found I was perfectly safe ; indeed my best security is, that my daddy concludes the author to be a man, and all the rest follow as he leads.

Mr. Burney, [40]yesterday, after dinner, said—"Gentlemen and ladies, I'll propose a toast"; then filling his glass, he drank to The author of "Evelina!"

Had they known the author was present, they could not have more civilly accepted the toast; it was a bold kind of drollery in Mr. Burney, for I was fain to drink my own health in a bumper, which he filled for me, laughing heartily himself,

August 3—I have an immensity to write. Susan has copied me a letter which Mrs. Thrale has written to my father, upon the occasion of returning my mother two novels by Madame Riccoboni. [41]It is so honourable to me, and so sweet in her, that I must COPY it for my faithful journal.

Streatham, July 22.

Dear Sir, I forgot to give you the novels in your carriage, which I now send. "Evelina" certainly excels them far enough, both in probability of story, elegance of sentiment, and general power over the mind, whether exerted in humour or pathos; add to this, that Riccoboni is a veteran author, and all she ever can be; but I cannot tell what might not be expected from "Evelina," were she to try her genius at comedy.

So far had I written of my letter, when Mr. Johnson returned home, full of the praises of the book I had lent him, and protesting there Were passages in it which Might do honour to Richardson. We talk of it for ever, and he feels ardent after the d`enouement; hee "could not get rid of the rogue," he said. I lent him the second volume, and he is now busy with the other.

You must be more a philosopher, and less a father, than I wish you, not to be pleased with this letter ; and the giving such pleasure yields to nothing but receiving it. Long, my dear sir, may you live to enjoy the just praises of your children! and long may they live to deserve and delight such a parent! These are things that you would say in verse - but poetry implies fiction, and all this is naked truth. my compliments to Mrs. Burney, and kindest wishes to all your flock, etc.

How, sweet, how amiable in this charming woman is her desire of making my dear father satisfied with his scribbler's 'attempt! I do, indeed, feel the most grateful love for her. But Dr. Johnson's approbation!—It almost crazed me with agreeable surprise—it gave me such a flight of spirits that I danced a jig to Mr. Crisp, Without any preparation, music, or explanation;—to his no small amazement and diversion. I left him, however, to make his own comments upon my friskiness without affording him the smallest assistance.

Susan also writes me word, that when my father went last to Streatham, Dr. Johnson was not there, but Mrs. Thrale told him, that when he gave her the first volume of "Evelina," which she had lent him, he said, "Why, madam, why, what a charming book you lent me!" and eagerly inquired for the rest. He was particularly pleased with the Snow-hill scenes, and said that Mr. Smith's vulgar gentility was admirably portrayed; and when Sir Clement joins them, he said there was a shade of character prodigiously well marked. Well may it be said, that the greatest winds are ever the most candid to the inferior set! I think I should love Dr. Johnson for such lenity to a poor mere worm in literature, even if I were not myself the identical grub he has obliged.

I now come to last Saturday evening, when my beloved father came to Chesington, in full health, charming spirits, and all kindness, openness, and entertainment.

In his way hither he had stopped at Streatham, and he settled with Mrs. Thrale that he would call on her again in his way to town, and carry me with him ! and Mrs. Thrale said, "We all long to know her."

I have been in a kind of twitter ever since, for there seems something very formidable in the idea of appearing as an authoress ! I ever dreaded it, as it is a title which must raise more expectations than I have any chance of answering. Yet I am highly flattered by her invitation, and highly delighted in the prospect of being introduced to the Streatham society.

She sent me some very serious advice to write for the theatre, as, she says, I so naturally run into conversations, that "Evelina" absolutely and plainly points out that path to me; and she hinted how much she should be pleased to be honoured with my confidence."

My dear father communicated this intelligence, and a great deal more, with a pleasure that almost surpassed that with which I heard it, and he seems quite eager for me to make another attempt. He desired to take upon himself the communication to my daddy Crisp, and as it is now in so many hands that it is possible accident might discover it to him, I readily consented.

Sunday evening, as I was going into my father's room, I heard him say, "The variety of characters—the variety of scenes—and the language—why, she has had very little education but what she has given herself,-less than any of the others!" and Mr. Crisp exclaimed, "Wonderful!—it's wonderful!"

I now found what was going forward, and therefore deemed it most fitting to decamp. About an hour after, as I was passing through the hall, I met my daddy (CrispHis face was all animation and archness; he doubled his fist at me, and would have stopped me, but I ran past him into the parlour.

Before supper, however, I again met him, and he would not suffer me to escape ; he caught both my hands, and looked as if he would have looked me through, and then exclaimed, "Why you little hussy,—you young devil!—an't you ashamed to look me in the face, you Evelina, you! Why, what a dance have you led me about it! Young friend, indeed! O you little hussy, what tricks have you served me!"

I was obliged to allow of his running on with these gentle appellations for I know not how long, ere he could sufficiently compose himself after his great surprise, to ask or hear any particulars - and then, he broke out every three instants with exclamations of astonishment at how I had found time to write so much unsuspected, and how and where I had picked up such various materials; and not a few times did he, with me, as he had with my father, exclaim, "wonderful!"

He has, since, made me read him all my letters upon this subject. He said Lowndes would have made an estate had he given me one thousand pounds for it, and that he ought not to have given me less. "You have nothing to do now," continued he, "but to take your pen in hand, for your fame and reputation are made, and any bookseller will snap at what you write."

i then told him that I could not but really and unaffectedly regret that the affair was spread to Mrs. Williams and her friends.

"Pho," said he, "if those who are proper judges think it right, that it should be known, why should you trouble yourself about it? You have not spread it, there can be no imputation of vanity fall to your share, and it cannot come out more to your honour than through such a channel as Mrs. Thrale."

A FIRST VISIT TO MRS. THRALE AND ANINTRODUCTION To DR. JOHNSON.

(an introduction to Mrs. Thrale was practically an introduction into the most brilliant literary circle of the day. Literary lions of all sizes, from the monarch Johnson downwards, were wont to resort to Streatham, to eat Thrale's dinners, and to enjoy the conversation of his lively wife. At Streatham Dr. Burney had been a welcome guest since 1776, when he commenced his intimacy with the family by giving music lessons to the eldest daughter, Hester Thrale (Johnson's "Queenie" The head of the house, Henry Thrale, the wealthy brewer and member of Parliament for Southwark, was a sensible, unassuming man, whom Johnson loved and esteemed, and who returned Johnson's attachment with the sincerest regard. His acquirements, in Johnson's opinion were of a far more solid character than those Of his wife, whose wit and vivacity, however, gave her more distinction in those brilliant assemblies to which Fanny is now, for the first time, to be introduced. Mrs. Thrale was in her thirty-eighth year at the date of Fanny's first visit.-ED.] -411PSt-I have now to write

August.—I have now to write an account of the most consequential day I have spent since my birth: namely, my visit.

Our journey to Streatham, was the least pleasant part of the day.. for the roads were dreadfully dusty, and I was really in the fidgets from thinking what my reception might be, and from fearing they would expect a less awkward and backward kind of person than I was sure they would find.

Mr. Thrale's house is white, and very pleasantly situated, in a fine paddock. Mrs. Thrale was strolling about, and came to us as we got out of the chaise.

"Ah," cried she, "I hear Dr. Burney's voice! and you have brought your daughter?—well, now you are good!" She then received me, taking both my hands, and with mixed politeness and cordiality welcoming me to Streatham. She led me]Into the house, and addressed herself almost wholly for a few minutes to my father, as if to give me an assurance she did not mean to regard me as a show, or to distress or frighten me by drawing me out. Afterwards she took me upstairs, and showed me the house, [42]and said she had very much wished to see me at Streatham, and should always think herself much obliged to Dr. Burney for his goodness in bringing me, which she looked upon as a very great favour.

But though we were some time together, and though she was so very civil, she did not hint at my book, and I love her much more than ever for her delicacy in avoiding a subject which she could not but see would have greatly embarrassed me.

When we returned to the music-room, we found Miss Thrale was with my father. Miss Thrale is a very fine girl, about fourteen years of age, but cold and reserved, though full of knowledge and intelligence.

Soon after, Mrs. Thrale took me to the library ; she talked a little while upon common topics, and then, at last, she mentioned "Evelina."

" Yesterday at supper," said she, "we talked it all over, and discussed all your characters - but Dr. Johnson's favourite is Mr. Smith. He declares the fine gentleman manqué was never better drawn; and he acted him all the evening, saying he was 'all for the ladies!' He repeated whole scenes by heart. I declare I was astonished at him. O, you can't imagine how much he is pleased with the book; he 'could not get rid of the rogue,' he told me. But was it not droll," said she, "that I should recommend it to Dr. Burney? and tease him, so innocently, to read it?"

I now prevailed upon Mrs. Thrale to let me amuse myself, and she went to dress. I then prowled about to choose some book and I saw upon the reading-table, "Evelina."—I had just fixed upon a new translation of Cicero's "Laelius," when the library-door was opened, and Mr. Seward[43]entered. I instantly put away my book, because I dreaded being thought studious and affected. He offered his service to find anything for me, and then, in the same breath, ran on to speak of the work with which I had myself 'favoured the world!'

The exact words he began with I cannot recollect, for I was actually confounded by the attack; and his abrupt manner of letting me know he was au fait equally astonished and provoked me. How different from the delicacy of Mr. and Mrs. Thrale.

When we were summoned to dinner, Mrs. Thrale made my father and me sit on each side of her. I said that I hoped I did not take Dr. Johnson's place;—for he had not yet appeared.

"No," answered Mrs. Thrale, "he will sit by you, which I am sure will give him great pleasure."

Soon after we were seated, this great man entered. I have so true a veneration for him, that the very sight of him inspires me with delight and reverence, notwithstanding the cruel infirmities to which he is subject; for he has almost perpetual convulsive movements, either of his hands, lips, feet, or knees, and sometimes of all together.

Mrs. Thrale introduced me to him, and he took his place. We had a noble dinner, and a most elegant dessert. Dr. Johnson, in the middle of dinner, asked Mrs. Thrale what were some little pies that were near him.

"Mutton," answered she, "so I don't ask you to eat any, because I know you despise it."

"No, madam, no," cried he, "I despise nothing that is so good of its sort; but I am too proud now to eat of it. Sitting by Miss Burney makes me very proud to-day!"

"Miss Burney," said Mrs. Thrale, laughing, "you must take care of your heart if Dr. Johnson attacks it for I assure you he is not often successless."

"What's that you say, madam?" cried he; "are you Making mischief between the young lady and me already?"

A little while after he drank Miss Thrale's health and mine, and then added: "'Tis a terrible thing that we cannot wish young ladies well, without wishing them to become old women!"

"But some people," said Mr. Seward, "are old and young at the same time, for they wear so well that they never look old."

No, sir, no," cried the doctor, laughing; "that never yet was; you might as well say they are at the same time tall and short. I remember an epitaph to that purpose, which is in—"

(I have quite forgot what,—and also the name it was made upon, but the rest I recollect exactly:

"——lies buried here; So early wise, so lasting fair, That none, unless her years you told, Thought her a child, or thought her old."

We left Streatham at about eight o'clock, and Mr. Seward, who handed me into the chaise, added his interest to the rest, that my father would not fail to bring me next week. In short I was loaded with civilities from them all. And my ride home was equally happy with the rest of the day, for my kind and most beloved father was so happy in my happiness, and congratulated me so sweetly, that he could, like myself, think on no other subject: and he told me that, after passing through such a house as that, I could have nothing to fear-meaning for my book, my honoured book.

Yet my honours stopped not here ; for Hetty, who, with her sposo, was here to receive us, told me she had lately met Mrs. Reynolds, [44]sister of Sir Joshua; and that she talked very much and very highly of a new novel called "Evelina"; though without a shadow of suspicion as to the scribbler ; and not contented with her own praise, she said that Sir Joshua, who began it one day when he was too much engaged to go on with it, was so much caught, that he could think of nothing else, and was quite absent all the day, not knowing a word that was said to him : and, when he took it up again, found himself so much interested in it, that he sat up all night to finish it! Sir Joshua, it seems, vows he would give fifty pounds to know the author! I have also heard, by the means of Charles, [45]that other persons have declared they will find him out!

FANNY BURNEY INTERVIEWS HER PUBLISHER.

This intelligence determined me upon going myself to Mr. Lowndes, and discovering what sort of answers he made to such curious inquirers as I found were likely to address him. But as I did not dare trust myself to speak, for I felt that I should not be able to act my part well, I asked my mother to accompany me. We introduced ourselves by buying the book, for which I had a commission from Mrs. G—. Fortunately Mr. Lowndes himself was in the shop; as we found by his air of consequence and authority, as well as his age; for I never saw him before.

The moment he had given my mother the book, she asked him if he could tell her who wrote it.

"No," he answered; "I don't know myself."

"Pho, pho," said she, "you mayn't choose to tell, but you must know."

"I don't indeed, ma'am," answered he "I have no honour in keeping the secret, for I have never been trusted. All I know of the matter is, that it is a gentleman of the other end of the town."

MY mother made a thousand other inquiries, to which his answers were to the following effect: that for a great while, he did not know if it was a man or a woman; but now, he knew that much, and that he was a master of his subject, and well versed in the manners of the times.

"For some time," continued he, "I thought it had been Horace Walpole's; for he once published a book in this snug manner; but I don't think it is now. I have often people come to inquire of me who it is; but I suppose he will come Out soon, and then when the rest of the world knows it, I shall. Servants often come for it from the other end of the town, and I have asked them divers questions myself, to see if I could get at the author but I never got any satisfaction."

Just before we came away, upon my mother's still further pressing him, he said, with a most important face,

"Why, to tell you the truth, madam, I have been informed that it is a piece of real secret history ; and, in that case, it will never be known."

This was too much for me - I grinned irresistibly, and was obliged to look out at the shop-door till we came away.

How many ridiculous things have I heard upon this subject! I hope that next, some particular family will be fixed upon, to whom this secret history must belong! However, I am delighted to find myself so safe.

CONVERSATIONS WITH MRs. THRALE AND DR. JOHNSON.

Streatham, Sunday, Aug. 23—I know not how to express the fullness of my contentment at this sweet place. All my best expectations are exceeded, and you know they were not very moderate. If, when my dear father comes, Susan and Mr. Crisp were to come too, I believe it would require at least a day's pondering to enable me to form another wish.

Our journey was charming. The kind Mrs. Thrale would give courage to the most timid. She did not ask me questions, or catechise me upon what I knew, or use any means to draw me out, but made it her business to draw herself out that is, to start subjects, to support them herself, and to take all the weight of the conversation, as if it behoved her to find me entertainment. But I am so much in love with her, that I shall be obliged to run away from the subject, or shall write of nothing else.

When we arrived here, Mrs. Thrale showed me my room, which is an exceedingly pleasant one, and then conducted me to the library, there to divert myself while she dressed.

Miss Thrale soon joined me: and I begin to like her. Mr. Thrale was neither well nor in spirits all day. Indeed, he seems not to be a happy man, though he has every means of happiness in his power. But I think I have rarely seen a very rich man with a light heart and light spirits.

Dr. Johnson was in the utmost good humour.

There was no other company at the house all day.

After dinner, I had a delightful stroll with Mrs. Thrale, and she gave me a list of all her " good neighbours " in the town of Streatham, and said she was determined to take me to see Mr. T—, the clergyman, who was a character i could not but be diverted with, for he had so furious and so absurd a rage for building, that in his garden he had as many temples, and summer-houses, and statues as in the gardens of Stow, though he had so little room for them that they all seemed tumbling one upon another.

In short, she was all unaffected drollery and sweet good humour. At tea we all met again, and Dr. Johnson was gaily sociable. He gave a very droll account of the children of Mr. Langton. [46] "Who," he said, "might be very good children if they were let alone; but the father is never easy when he is not making them do something which they cannot do; they must repeat a fable, or a speech, or the Hebrew alphabet; and they might as well count twenty, for what they know of the matter: however, the father says half, for he prompts every other word. But he could not have chosen a man who would have been less entertained by such means."

"I believe not !" cried Mrs. Thrale: "nothing is more ridiculous than parents cramming their children's nonsense down other people's throats. I keep mine as much out of the way as I can."

"Yours, madam," answered he, "are in nobody's way - no children can be better managed or less troublesome; but your fault is, a too great perverseness in not allowing anybody to give them anything. Why Should they not have a cherry, or a gooseberry, as well as bigger children?"

"Because they are sure to return such gifts by wiping their hands upon the giver's gown or coat, and nothing makes children more offensive. People only make the offer to please the parents, and they wish the poor children at Jericho when they accept it."

"But, madam, it is a great deal more offensive to refuse them. Let those who make the offer look to their own gowns and coats, for when you interfere, they only wish you at Jericho."

"It is difficult," said Mrs. Thrale, "to please everybody." She then asked whether -Mr. Langton took any better care of his affairs than formerly?

"No, madam," cried the doctor, "and never will; he complains of the ill effects of habit, and rests contentedly upon a confessed indolence. He told his father himself that he had 'no turn to economy;' but a thief might as well plead that he had 'no turn to honesty.'"

Was not that excellent? At night, Mrs. Thrale asked if I would have anything ? I answered, "No," but Dr. Johnson said,

"Yes: she is used, madam, to suppers; she would like an egg or two, and a few slices of ham, or a rasher—a rasher, I believe, would please her better."

How ridiculous! However, nothing could persuade Mrs. Thrale not to have the cloth laid: and Dr. Johnson was so facetious, that he challenged Mr. Thrale to get drunk!

"I wish," said he, "my master[47]would say to me, Johnson, if you will oblige me, you will call for a bottle of Toulon, and then we will set to it, glass for glass, till it is done ; and after that, I will say, Thrale, if you will oblige me, you will call for another bottle of Toulon, and then we will set to it, glass for glass, till that is done : and by the time we should have drunk the two bottles, we should be so happy, and such good friends, that we should fly into each other's arms, and both together call for the third!"

Now for this morning's breakfast.

Dr. Johnson, as usual, came last into the library ; he was in high spirits, and full of mirth and sport. I had the honour of sitting next to him: and now, all at once, he flung aside his reserve, thinking, perhaps, that it was time I should fling aside mine.

Mrs. Thrale told him that she intended taking me to Mr. T—'s.

"So you ought, madam," cried he; "'tis your business to be Cicerone to her."

Then suddenly he snatched my hand, and kissing it, "Ah!" he added, "they will little think what a tartar you carry to them!"

"No, that they won't!" cried Mrs. Thrale; "Miss Burney looks so meek and so quiet, nobody would suspect what a comical girl she is - but I believe she has a great deal of malice at heart."

"Oh, she's a toad!" cried the doctor, laughing—"a sly young rogue! with her Smiths and her Branghtons!"

"Why, Dr. Johnson said Mrs. Thrale, "I hope you are well this morning! if one may judge by your spirits and good humour, the fever you threatened us with is gone off."

He had complained that he was going to be ill last night.

"Why no, madam, no," answered he, " "I am not yet well. I could not sleep at all; there I lay, restless and uneasy, and thinking all the time of Miss Burney.

Perhaps I have offended. her, thought I; perhaps she is angry - I have seen her but once and I talked to her of a rasher!—Were you angry?"

I think I need not tell you my answer.

"I have been endeavouring to find some excuse," continued he, "and, as I could not sleep, I got up, and looked for some authority for the word; and I find, madam, it is used by Dryden: in one of his prologues, he says—'And snatch a homely rasher from the coals.' So You must not mind me, madam; I say strange things, but I mean no harm."

I was almost afraid he thought I was really idiot enough to have taken him seriously; but, a few minutes after, he put his hand on my arm, and shaking his head, exclaimed, "Oh, you are a sly little rogue!—what a Holborn beau have you drawn!"

"Ay, Miss Burney," said Mrs, Thrale, "the Holborn beau is Dr Johnson's favourite ; and we have all your characters by heart, from Mr. Smith up to Lady Louisa."

"Oh, Mr. Smith, Mr. Smith is the man !" cried he, laughing violently. "Harry Fielding never drew so good a character!— such a fine varnish of low politeness!—such a struggle to appear a gentleman! Madam, there is no character better drawn anywhere—in any book or by any author."

I almost poked myself under the table. Never did I feel so delicious a confusion since I was born ! But he added a great deal more, only I cannot recollect his exact words, and I do not choose to give him mine.

About noon when I went into the library, book hunting, Mrs. Thrale came to me. We had a very nice confab about various books, and exchanged opinions and imitations of Baretti; she told me many excellent tales of him, and I, in return, related my stories.

She gave me a long and very entertaining account of Dr. Goldsmith, who was intimately known here; but in speaking of "The Good-natured Man," when I extolled my favourite 84 Croaker, I found that admirable character was a downright theft from Dr. Johnson. Look at "The Rambler," and you will find Suspirius is the man, and that not merely the idea, but the particulars of the character, are all stolen thence! [48]

While we were yet reading this "Rambler," Dr. Johnson came in: we told him what we were about.

"Ah, madam," cried he, "Goldsmith was not scrupulous but he would have been a great man had he known the real value of his own internal resources."

"Miss Burney," said Mrs. Thrale, "is fond of his 'Vicar of Wakefield.' and so am I;—don't you like it, sir?"

" No, madam, it is very faulty ; there is nothing of real life in it, and very little of nature. It is a mere fanciful performance."

He then seated himself upon a sofa, and calling to me, said Come,—Evelina,—come and sit by me."

I obeyed; and he took me almost in his arms,—that is, one of his arms, for one would go three times, at least, round me, -and, half laughing, half serious, he charged me to "be a good girl!"

"But, my dear," continued he with a very droll look, "what makes you so fond of the Scotch? I don't like you for that;—I hate these Scotch, and so must you. I wish Branghton had sent the dog to jail! That Scotch dog Macartney."

"Why, sir," said Mrs. Thrale, " don't you remember he says he would, but that he should get nothing by it?"

" Why, ay, true," cried the doctor, see-sawing very solemnly, "that, indeed, is some palliation for his forbearance. But I must not have you so fond of the Scotch, my little Burney; make your hero what you will but a Scotchman. Besides, you write Scotch—you say 'the one'—my dear, that's not English, Never use that phrase again."

"Perhaps," said Mrs. Thrale, "it may be used in Macartney's letter, and then it will be a propriety."

"No, madam, no!" cried he; "you can't make a beauty of it - it is in the third volume; put it in Macartney's letter, and welcome— that, or any thing that is nonsense."

"Why, surely," cried I, "the poor man is used ill enough by the Branghtons."

"But Branghton," said he, "only hates him because of his wretchedness— poor fellow!—But, my dear love, how should he ever have eaten a good dinner before he came to England? And then he laughed violently at young Branghton's idea.

"Well," said Mrs. Thrale, "I always liked Macartney; he is a very pretty character, and I took to him, as the folks say." " Why, madam," answered he, "I like Macartney myself. yes, poor fellow, I liked the man, but I love not the nation." And then he proceeded, in a dry manner, to make at once sarcastic reflections on the Scotch, and flattering speeches to me. [49]

DR. JOHNSON ON SOME "LADIES" OF HIS ACQUAINTANCE

Saturday.—Dr. Johnson was again all himself; and so civil to me!—even admiring how I dressed myself! Indeed, it is well I have so much of his favour - for it seems he always speaks his mind concerning the dress of ladies, and all ladies who are here obey his injunctions implicitly, and alter whatever he disapproves. This is a part of his character that much surprises me: but notwithstanding he is sometimes so absent, and always so near sighted, he scrutinizes into every part of almost everybody's appearance. They tell me of a Miss Brown, who often visits here, and who has a slovenly way of dressing. "And when she comes down in a morning," says Mrs. Thrale, "her hair will be all loose, and her cap half off; and then Dr. Johnson, who sees something is wrong, and does not know where the fault is, concludes it is in the cap, and says, "My dear, what do you wear such a vile cap for?" "I'll change it, Sir!" cries the poor girl, "if you don't like it." Ay, do,'he says; and away runs poor Miss Brown; but when she gets on another, it's the same thing, for the cap has nothing to do with the fault. And then she wonders Dr. Johnson should not like the cap, for she thinks it very pretty. And so on with her gown, which he also makes her change; but if the poor girl were to change through all her wardrobe, unless she could put her things on better, he would still find fault."

When Dr. Johnson was gone, she told me of my mother's[50]being obliged to change her dress.

"Now," said she " Mrs. Burney had on a very pretty linen jacket and coat, and was going to church; but Dr. Johnson, who, I suppose, did not like her in a jacket, saw something was the matter, and so found fault with the linen: and he looked and peered, and then said, 'Why, madam, this won't do! you must not go to church so!' So away went poor Mrs. Burney, and changed her gown! And when she had done so, he did not like it, but he did not know why, so he told her she should not wear a black hat and cloak in summer! "How he did bother poor Mrs. Burney! and himself too, for if the things had been put on to his mind, he would have taken no notice of them."

"Why," said Mr. Thrale, very drily, "I don't think Mrs. Burney a very good dresser."

"Last time she came," said Mrs. Thrale, "she was in a white cloak, and she told Dr. Johnson she had got her old white cloak scoured on purpose to oblige him! 'Scoured!' says he; 'ay, have you, madam?'—so he see-sawed, for he could not for shame find fault, but he did not seem to like the scouring.'

And now let me try to recollect an account he gave of certain celebrated ladies of his acquaintance: an account in which, had you heard it from himself, would have made you die with laughing, his manner is so peculiar, and enforces his humour so originally. It was begun by Mrs. Thrale's apologising to him for troubling him with some question she thought trifling—O, I remember! We had been talking of colours, and of the fantastic names given to them, and why the palest lilac should b called a soupir `etouff`e; and when Dr. Johnson came in, she applied to him.

"Why, madam," said he, with wonderful readiness, "it is called a stifled sigh because it is checked in its progress, and only half a colour."

I could not help expressing my amazement at his universal readiness upon all subjects, and Mrs. Thrale said to him, "Sir, Miss Burney wonders at your patience with such stuff, but I tell her you are used to me, for I believe I torment you with more foolish questions than anybody else dares do."

"No, madam," said he; 'you don't torment me;—you teaze me, indeed, sometimes."

"Ay, so I do, Dr. Johnson, and I wonder you bear with my nonsense."

No, madam, you never talk nonsense; you have as much sense and more wit, than any woman I know."

"Oh," cried Mrs. Thrale, blushing, "it is my turn to go under the table this morning, Miss Burney!"

"And yet," continued the doctor, with the most comical look, "I have known all the wits, from Mrs. Montagu down to Bet Flint."

"Bet Flint cried Mrs. Thrale -pray, who is she?"

"Such a fine character, madam! She was habitually a slut and a drunkard, and occasionally a thief and a harlot."

"And, for heaven's sake, how came you to know her?"

"Why, madam, she figured in the literary world, too! Bet Flint wrote her own life, and called herself Cassandra, and it was in verse;—it began:

'When Nature first ordained my birth,
A diminutive I was born on earth:
And then I came from a dark abode,
Into a gay and gaudy world.' [51]

So Bet brought me her verses to correct; but I gave her half-a-crown, and she liked it as well. Bet had a fine spirit;— she advertised for a husband, but she had no success, for she told me no man aspired to her! Then she hired very handsome lodgings and a footboy; and she got a harpsichord, but Bet could not play; however, she put herself in fine attitudes, and drummed."

Then he gave an account of another of these geniuses, who called herself by some fine name, I have forgotten what.

"She had not quite the same stock of virtue," continued he, "nor the same stock of honesty as Bet Flint; but I suppose she envied her accomplishments, for she was so little moved by the power of harmony, that while Bet Flint thought she was drumming very divinely, the other jade had her indicted for a nuisance!"

"And pray what became of her, sir?

"Why, madam, she stole a quilt from the man of the house, and he had her taken up: but Bet Flint had a spirit not to be subdued; so when she found herself obliged to go to jail, she ordered a sedan chair, and bid her footboy walk before her. However, the boy proved refractory, for he was ashamed, though his mistress was not.""

"And did she ever get out of jail again, sir?" "Yes, madam; when she came to her trial the judge acquitted her. 'So now,' she said to me, 'the quilt is MY own, and now I'll make a petticoat of it.' Oh, I loved Bet Flint!" [52]

Oh, how we all laughed! Then he gave an account of another lady, who called herself Laurinda, and who also wrote verses and stole furniture; but he had not the same affection for her, he said, though she too "was a lady who had high notions of honour."

Then followed the history of another, who called herself Hortensia, and who walked up and down the park repeating a book of Virgil. But," said he " "though I know her story, I never had the good fortune to see her."

After this he gave us an account of the famous Mrs. Pinkethman: "And she," he said, "told me she owed all her misfortunes to her wit; for she was so unhappy as to marry a man who thought himself also a wit, though I believe she gave him not implicit credit for it, but it occasioned much contradiction and ill-will."

"Bless me, sir," cried Mrs. Thrale, "how can all these vagabonds contrive to get at you, of all people?"

"O the dear creatures!" cried he, laughing heartily, "I can't but be glad to see them."

"Why, I wonder, sir, you never went to see Mrs. Rudd, [53]among the rest."

"Why, madam, I believe I should," said he, "if it was not for the newspapers; but I am prevented many frolics that I should like very well, since I am become such a theme for the papers."

Now, would you ever have imagined this? Bet Flint, it seems, took Kitty Fisher[54]to see him, but to his no little regret he was not at home. "And Mrs. Williams," [55]he added, "did not love Bet Flint, but Bet Flint made herself very easy about that."

A LEARNED MAN ON "EVELINA."

When we were dressed for dinner, and went into the parlour, we had the agreeable surprise of seeing Mr. Seward. There was also Mr. Lort, [56]who is reckoned one of the most learned men alive, and is also a collector of curiosities,, alike in literature and natural history. His manners are somewhat blunt and odd, and he is altogether out of the common road, without having chosen a better path.

The day was passed most agreeably. In the evening we had, as usual, a literary conversation. Mr. Lort produced several curious MSS. of the famous Bristol Chatterton; among others, his will, and divers verses written against Dr. Johnson, as a placeman and pensioner; all of which he read aloud, with a steady voice and unmoved countenance.

I was astonished at him; Mrs. Thrale not much pleased; Mr. Thrale silent and attentive; and Mr. Seward was slily laughing. Dr. johnson himself listened profoundly and laughed openly. Indeed, I believe he wishes his abusers no other Thiing than a good dinner, like Pope. [57]

Just as we had got our biscuits and toast-and-water, which make the Streatham supper, and which, indeed, is all there is any chance of eating after our late and great dinners, Mr. Lort suddenly said,

"Pray, ma'am, have you heard anything of a novel that runs about a good deal, called 'Evelina'?"

What a ferment did this question, before such a set, Put me in! I did not know whether he spoke to me, or Mrs. Thrale, and Mrs. Thrale was in the same doubt, and as she owned, felt herself in a little palpitation for me, not knowing what might come next, Between us both, therefore, he had no answer. "It has been recommended to me," continued he; "but I have no great desire to see it, because it has such a foolish name. Yet I have heard a great deal of it, too."

He then repeated "Evelina"—in a very languishing and ridiculous tone.

My heart beat so quick against my stays that I almost panted with extreme agitation, from the dread either of hearing some horrible criticism, or of being betrayed: and I munched my biscuit as if I had not eaten for a fortnight.

I believe the whole party were in some little consternation Dr. Johnson began see-sawing; Mr. Thrale awoke; Mr. E—' who I fear has picked up some notion of the affair from being so much in the house, grinned amazingly; and Mr. Seward, biting his nails and flinging himself back in his chair, I am sure had wickedness enough to enjoy the whole scene.

Mrs. Thrale was really a little fluttered, but without looking at me, said, "And pray what, Mr. Lort, what have you heard of it?"

"Why they say," answered he, "that it's an account of a young lady's first entrance into company, and of the scrapes she gets into; and they say there's a great deal of character in it, but I have not cared to look in it, because the name is so foolish- -'Evelina'!"

"Why foolish, sir?" cried Dr. Johnson. "Where's the folly of it?"

"Why, I won't say much for the name myself," said Mrs. Thrale, "to those who don't know the reason of it, which I found out, but which nobody else seems to know." She then explained the name from Evelyn, according to my own meaning.

"Well," said Dr. Johnson, " if that was the reason, it is a very good one."

"Why, have you had the book here?" cried Mr. Lort, staring.

"Ay, indeed, have we," said Mrs. Thrale; "I read it When I was last confined, and I laughed over it, and I cried over it!"

"O ho!" said Mr. Lort, "this is another thing! If you have had it here, I will certainly read it."

"Had it? ay," returned she; "and Dr. Johnson, who would not look at it at first, was so caught by it when I put it in the coach with him, that he has sung its praises ever since,—and he says Richardson would have been proud to have written it."

"O ho! this is a good hearing," cried Mr. Lort; "if Dr. Johnson can read it, I shall get it with all speed."

"You need not go far for it," said Mrs. Thrale, "for it's now upon yonder table."

I could sit still no longer; there was something so awkward, so uncommon, so strange in my then situation, that I wished myself a hundred miles off, and indeed, I had almost choked myself with the biscuit, for I could not for my life swallow it: and so I got up, and, as Mr. Lort wen to the table to look for "Evelina," I left the room, and was forced to call for water to wash down the biscuit, which literally stuck in my throat.

I heartily wished Mr. Lort at jerusalem. I did not much like going back, but the moment I recovered breath, I resolved not to make bad worse by staying longer away: but at the door of the room, I met Mrs. Thrale, who, asking me if I would have some water, took me into a back room, and burst into a hearty fit of laughter.

"This is very good sport," cried she; "the man is as innocent about the matter as a child, and we shall hear what he says about it to-morrow morning at breakfast. I made a sign to Dr. Jonnson and Seward not to tell him."

she found I was not in a humour to think it such good sport as she did, she grew more serious,. and taking my hand kindly said, "May you never, Miss Burney, know any other pain than that of hearing yourself praised! and I am sure that you must often feel."

When I told her how much I dreaded being discovered, and beggt her not to betray me any further, she again began laughing, and openly declared she should not consult me about the matter. But she told me that, as soon as I had left the room, when Mr. Lort took up "Evelina," he exclaimed contemptuously "Why, it's printed for Lowndes!" and that Dr. Johnson then told him there were things and characters in it more than worthy of Fielding. "Oh ho!" cried Mr. Lort; "what, is it better than Fielding?" "Harry Fielding," answered Dr. Johnson, "knew nothing but the shell of life."

"So you, ma'am," added the flattering Mrs. Thrale, "have found the kernel."

Are they all mad? or do they only want to make me so

CURIOSITY REGARDING THE AUTHOR OF "EVELINA."

Streatham, Sept.— Our Monday's intended great party was very small, for people are so dispersed at present in Various quarters: we had, therefore, only Sir Joshua Reynolds, two Miss Palmers, Dr. Calvert, Mr. Rose Fuller, and Lady Ladd. [58]Dr. Johnson did not return.

Sir Joshua I am much pleased with: I like his ccountenance, and I like his manners; the former I think expressive, and sensible; the latter gentle, unassuming, and engaging.

The dinner, in quantity as well as quality, would have sufficed for forty people. Sir Joshua said, when the dessert appeared, "Now if all the company should take a fancy to the same dish, there would be sufficient for all the company from any one."

After dinner, as usual, we strolled out: I ran first into the hall for my cloak-, and Mrs. Thrale, running after me, said in a low voice,

"If you are taxed with 'Evelina,' don't own it; I intend to say it is mine, for sport's sake."

You may think how much I was surprised, and how readily I agreed not to own it; but I could ask no questions, for the two Miss Palmers followed close, saying,

"Now pray, ma'am, tell us who it is?"

"No, no," cried Mrs. Thrale, "who it is, you must find out. I have told you that you dined with the author; but the rest you must make out as you can."

Miss Thrale began tittering violently, but I entreated her not to betray me; and, as soon as I could, I got Mrs. Thrale to tell me what all this meant. She then acquainted me, that, when she first came into the parlour, she found them all busy in talking of "Evelina," and heard that Sir Joshua had declared he would give fifty pounds to know the author!

"Well," said Mrs. Thrale, "thus much, then, I Will tell you; the author will dine with you to-day."

They were then all distracted to know the party.

"Why," said she, "we shall have Dr. Calvert, Lady Ladd, Rose Fuller, and Miss Burney."

"Miss Burney?" quoth they, "which Miss Burney?"

"Why, the eldest, Miss Fanny Burney; and so out of this list you must make out the author."

I shook my head at her, but begged her, at least, to go no further.

"No, no," cried she, laughing, "leave me alone; the fun will be to make them think it me."

Howeverp as I learnt at night, when they were gone, Sir Joshua was so very importunate with Mr. Thrale, and attacked him with such eagerness, that he made him confess who it was, as soon as the ladies retired.

Well, to return to our walk. The Miss Palmers grew more and more urgent.

"Did we indeed," said the eldest, "dine with the author of 'Evelina?'"

"Yes, in good truth did you."

"Why then, ma'am, it was yourself."

"I shan't tell you whethir it was or not; but were there not other people at dinner besides me? What think you of Dr. Calvert?"

"Dr. Calvert? no! no; I am sure it was not he: besides, they say it was certainly written by a woman."

"By a woman? nay, then, is not here Lady Ladd, and Miss Burney, and Hester?" [59]

"Lady Ladd I am sure it was not, nor could it be Miss Thrale's. O maam! I begin to think it was really yours! Now, was it not, Mrs. Thrale?"

Mrs. Thrale only laughed.

"A lady of our acquaintance," said Miss Palmer, "Mrs. Cholmondeley, went herself to the printer, but he would not tell."

"Would he not?" cried Mrs. Thrale, "why, then, he's an honest man."

"Oh, is he so?—nay, then, it is certainly Mrs. Thrale's."

"well, well, I told you before I should not deny it."

"Miss Burney," said she, "pray do you deny it?" in a voice that seemed to say,—I must ask round, though rather from civility than suspicion.

"Me?" cried I, "well no: if nobody else will deny it, why should I? It does not seem the fashion to deny it."

"No, in truth," cried she; "I believe nobody would think of denying it that could claim it, for it is the sweetest book in the world. My uncle could not go to bed till he had finished it, and he says he is sure he shall make love to the author, if ever he meets with her, and it should really be a woman!"

"Dear madam," cried Miss Offy, "I am sure it was you but why will you not own it at once?"

"I shall neither own nor deny anything about it."

"A gentleman whom we know very well," said Miss Palmer, "when he could learn nothing at the printer's, took the trouble to go all about Snow Hill, to see if he could find any silversmith's." "Well, he was a cunning creature!" said Mrs. Thrale; "but Dr. Johnson's favourite is Mr. Smith."

"So he is of everybody," answered she: "he and all that family; everybody says Such a family never was drawn before. But Mrs. Cholmondeley's favourite is Madame Duval; she acts her from morning to night, and ma-foi's everybody she sees. But though we all want so much to know the author, both Mrs. Cholmondeley and my uncle himself say they should be frightened to death to be in her company, because she must be such a very nice observer, that there would be no escaping her with safety."

What strange ideas are taken from mere book-reading! But what follows gave me the highest delight I can feel.

"Mr. Burke," [60]she continued, "doats on it: he began it one morning at seven o'clock, and could not leave it a moment; he sat up all night reading it. He says he has not seen such a book he can't tell when."

Mrs. Thrale gave me involuntarily a look of congratulation, and could not forbear exclaiming, "How glad she was Mr. Burke approved it!" This served to confirm the Palmers in their mistake, and they now, without further questioning, quietly and unaffectedly concluded the book to be really Mrs. Thrale's and Miss Palmer said,—"Indeed, ma'am, you Ought to write a novel every year: nobody can write like you!"

I was both delighted and diverted at this mistake, and they grew so easy and so satisfied under it, that the conversation dropped, and offy went to the harpsichord.

Not long after, the party broke up, and they took leave. I had no conversation with Sir Joshua all day; but I found myself more an object of attention to him than I wished; and he several times spoke to me, though he did not make love!

When they rose to take leave, Miss Palmer, with the air of asking the greatest of favours, hoped to see me when I returned to town; and Sir Joshua, approaching me with the most profound respect, inquired how long I should remain at Streatham? A week, I believed: and then he hoped, when I left it, they should have the honour of seeing me in Leicester Square. [61]

In short, the joke is, the people speak as if they were afraid of me, instead of my being afraid of them. It seems, when they got to the door, Miss Palmer said to Mrs. Thrale,

"Ma'am, so it's Miss Burney after all!"

"Ay, sure," answered she, "who should it be?"

"Ah! why did not you tell us sooner?" said Offy, "that we might have had a little talk about it?"

Here, therefore, end all my hopes of secrecy!

THE MEMBERS OF DR. JOHNSON'S HOUSEHOLD.

At tea-time the subject turned upon the domestic economy "" of Dr. Johnson's household. Mrs. Thrale has often acquainted me that his house is quite filled and overrun with all sorts of strange creatures, whom he admits for mere charity, and because nobody else will admit them,—for his charity is unbounded; or, rather, bounded only by his circumstances.

The account he gave of the adventures and absurdities of the set, was highly diverting, but too diffused for writing—though one or two speeches I must give. I think I shall occasionally theatricalise my dialogues.

Mrs. Thrale-Pray, Sir, how does Mrs. Williams like all this tribe?

Johnson-Madam, she does not like them at all: but their fondness for her is not greater. She and De Mullin[62]quarrel incessantly; but as they can both be occasionally of service to each other, and as neither of them have a place to go to, their animMOSity does not force them to separate.

Mrs. T.-And pray, sir, what is Mr. Macbean? [63]

Dr. J.-Madam, he is a Scotchman: he is a man of great learning, and for his learning I respect him, and I wish to serve him. He knows many languages, and knows them well; but he knows nothing of life. I advised him to write a geographical dictionary; but I have lost all hopes of his doing anything properly, since I found he gave as much labour to Capua as to Rome.

Mr. T.-And pray who is clerk of your kitchen, sir?

Dr. J.-Why, sir, I am afraid there is none; a general anarchy prevails in my kitchen, as I am told by Mr. Levat, [64]who says it is not now what it used to be!

Mrs. T.-Mr. Levat, I suppose, sir, has the office of keeping the hospital in health? for he Is an apothecary.

Dr. J.-Levat, madam, is a brutal fellow, but I have a good regard for him; for his brutality is in his manners, not his mind.

Mr. T.-But how do you get your dinners drest ?

Dr. J.-Why De Mullin has the chief management of the kitchen; but our roasting is not magnificent, for we hav no jack.

Mr. T.-No jack? Why, how do they manage without?

Dr. J.-Small joints, I believe, they manage with a string, larger are done at the tavern. I have some thoughts with profound gravityof buying a jack, because I think a jack is some credit to a house.

Mr. T.-Well, but you'll have a spit, too?

Dr. J.-No, sir, no; that would be superfluous; for we shall never use it; and if a jack is seen, a spit will be presumed!

Mrs. T.-But pray, sir, who is the Poll you talk of? She 97 that you used to abet in her quarrels with Mrs. Williams, and call out, "At her again, Poll! Never flinch, Poll>"[65]

Dr. J.-Why, I took to Poll very well at first, but she won't do upon a nearer examination.

Mrs. T.-How came she among you, sir?

Dr. J.-Why I don't rightly remember, but we could spare her very well from us. Poll is a stupid slut; I had some hopes of her at first; but when I talked to her tightly and closely, I could make nothing of her; she was wiggle waggle, and I could never persuade her to be categorical, I wish Miss Burney would come among us; if she would Only give US a week, we should furnish her with ample materials for a new scene in her next work.

ANTICIPATED VISIT FROM MRS. MONTAGU.

("The great Mrs. Montagu" deserves a somewhat longer notice than can be conveniently compressed within the limits of a footnote. She was as indisputably, in public estimation, the leading literary lady of the time, as Johnson was the leading man of letters. Her maiden name was Elizabeth Robinson. She was born at York in the year 1720, and married, in 1742, Edward Montagu, grandson of the first Earl of Sandwich. Her husband's death, in 1775, left her in the possession of a handsome fortune. Mrs. Montagu's literary celebrity was by no means dearly bought, for it rested, almost exclusively, on her

"Essay on the Writings and Genius of Shakespear," published by Dodsley in 1769. Indeed, the only other writings which she committed to the press were three "Dialogues of the Dead," appended to the Well-known "Dialogues" of her friend, Lord Lyttelton. The "Essay" is an elegantly written little work, superficial when regarded in the light of modern criticism, but marked by good sense and discrimination. One of the chief objects of the authoress was to defend Shakespeare against the strictures of Voltaire, and in this not very difficult task she has undoubtedly succeeded. Johnson's opinion of the "Essay" was unfavourable. To Sir Joshua Reynolds's remark, that it did honour to its authoress, he replied: "Yes Sir: it does her honour, but it would do nobody else honour;" and he goes on to observe that "there is not one sentence of true criticism in the book." But if the general applause which the book had excited was out of all proportion to its merits, Johnson's unqualified condemnation was more than equally disproportionate to its defects.

Of Mrs. Montagu's conversational abilities Johnson entertained a higher opinion. " Sir," he would say, "that lady exerts more mind in conversation than any person I ever met with" (Miss Reynolds's Recollections). It was probably, indeed, to the fame of her conversation, and of the has biem parties which assembled at her house, that she owed the greater part of her reputation. She was the acknowledged " Queen of the Blue Stockings,, although the epithet originated with a rival giver of literary parties, Mrs. Vesey, who, replying to the apology of a gentleman who declined an invitation to one of her meetings on the plea of want of dress, exclaimed, "Pho, pho! don't mind dress! Come in your blue stockings!" The term "Blue Stocking" (bas bleu) was thenceforward applied to the set which met at Mrs. Vesey's, and was gradually extended to other coteries of similar character.

The charitable and beneficient disposition of Mrs. Montagu was as notorious as her intellectual superiority. It may be interesting here to observe that after her husband's death, in 1775, she doubled the income of poor Anna Williams, the blind poetess who resided with Dr. Johnson, by settling upon her an annuity of ten pounds. The publication of Johnson's "Lives of the Poets," in 1781, occasioned a coolness between the doctor and Mrs. Montagu, on account of the severity with which, in that work, he had handled the character of Lord Lyttelton. In September, 1783, however, Dr. Johnson wrote to the lady to announce the death of her pensioner, Miss Williams; and shortly afterwards he informs Mrs. Thrale that he has received a reply "not only civil but tender; so I hope peace is proclaimed." Mrs. Montagu died at her house in Portman Square, in the year 1800.-ED.]

I was looking over the " Life of Cowley," which Dr. Johnson had himself given me to read, at the same time that he gave to Mrs. Thrale that of Waller.' But he bade me put it away.

"Do," cried he, "put away that now, and prattle with us; I can't make this little Burney prattle, and I am sure she prattles well; but I shall teach her another lesson than to sit thus silent before I have done with her."

"To talk," cried I, "is the only lesson I shall be backward to learn from you, sir."

"You shall give me," cried he, "a discourse upon the passions: come, begin! Tell us the necessity of regulating them

Watching over and curbing them! Did you ever read Norris's "Theory of Love?" [67]

"No, sir," said I, laughing, yet staring a little.

Dr. J.-It is well worth your reading. He will make you see that inordinate love is the root of all evil" inordinate love of wealth brings on avarice; of wine, brings on intemperance; of power, brings on cruelty; and so on. He deduces from inordinate love all human frailty."

Mrs. T.-To-morrow, sir, Mrs. Montagu dines here, and then you will have talk enough.

Dr. Johnson began to see-saw, with a countenance strongly expressive of inward fun, and after enjoying it Some time in silence, he suddenly, and with great animation, turned to me and cried,

"Down with her, Burney!—down with her!—spare her not!—attack her, fight her, and down with her at once! You are a rising wit, and she is at the top; and when I was beginning the world, and was nothing and nobody, the joy of my life was to fire at all the established wits! and then everybody loved to halloo me on. But there is no game now; every body would be glad to see me conquered: but then, when I was new, to vanquish the great ones was all the delight of my poor little dear soul! So at her, Burney—at her, and down with her!"

Oh, how we were all amused! By the way I must tell you that Mrs. Montagu is in very great estimation here, even with Dr. Johnson himself, when others do not praise her improperly. Mrs. Thrale ranks her as the first of women in the literary way. I should have told you that Miss Gregory, daughter of the Gregory who wrote the "Letters," or, "Legacy of Advice," lives with Mrs. Montagu, and was invited to accompany her. [68]

"Mark now," said Dr. Johnson, "if I contradict her tomorrow. I am determined, let her say what she will, that I will not contradict her."

Mrs. T.-Why, to be sure, sir, you did put her a little out Of countenance the last time she came. Yet you were neither rough, nor cruel, nor ill-natured, but still, when a lady changes colour, we imagine her feelings are not quite composed.

Dr. j.-Why, madam, I won't answer that I shan't Contradict her again, if she provokes me as she did then ; but a less provocation I will withstand. I believe I am not high in her good graces already ; and I begin (added he, laughing heartily), to tremble for my admission into her new house. I doubt I shall never see the inside of it.

(Mrs. Montagu is building a most superb house.) [69]

Mrs. T.-Oh, I warrant you, she fears you, indeed; but that, you know, is nothing uncommon: and dearly I love to hear your disquisitions; for certainly she is the first woman for literary knowledge in England, and if in England, I hope I may say in the world.

Dr. J.-I believe you may, madam. She diffuses more knowledge in her conversation than any woman I know, or, indeed, almost any man. Mrs. T.-I declare I know no man equal to her, take away yourself and Burke, for that art. And you who love magnificence, won't quarrel with her, as everybody else does, for her love of finery.

Dr. J.-No, I shall not quarrel with her upon that topic.

FANNY BURNEY'S INTRODUCTION TO A CELEBRATED "BLUE-STOCKING."

Wednesday.-We could not prevail with Dr. Johnson to stay till Mrs. Montagu arrived, though, by appointment, she came very early. She and Miss Gregory came by one o'clock.

There was no party to meet her. She is middle-sized, very thin, and looks infirm ; she has a sensible and penetrating countenance, and the air and manner of a woman accustomed to being distinguished, and of great parts. Dr. Johnson, who agrees in this, told us that a Mrs. Hervey, of his acquaintance, says she can remember Mrs. Montagu trying for this same air and manner. Mr. Crisp has said the same: however, nobody can now impartially see her, and not confess that she has extremely well succeeded.

My expectations, which were compounded of the praise of Mrs. Thrale, and the abuse of Mr. Crisp, were most exactly, answered, for I thought her in a medium way.

Miss Gregory is a fine young woman, and seems gentle and well-bred. A bustle with the dog Presto—Mrs. Thrale's favourite—at the entrance of these ladies into the library, prevented any formal reception; but as soon as Mrs. Montagu heard my name, she inquired very civilly after my father, and made many speeches concerning a volume of "Linguet," [70] which she has lost; but she hopes soon to be able to replace it. I am sure he is very high in her favour, because she did me the honour of addressing herself to me three or four times.

But my ease and tranquillity were soon disturbed: for she had not been in the room more than ten minutes, ere, turning to Mrs. Thrale, she said,

"Oh, ma'am—but your 'Evelina'—I have not yet got it. I sent for it, but the bookseller had it not. However, I will certainly have it."

"Ay, I hope so," answered Mrs. Thrale, "and I hope you Will like it too; for 'tis a book to be liked."

I began now a vehement nose-blowing, for the benefit of handkerchiefing my face. "

I hope though," said Mrs. Montagu, drily, "it is not in verse? I can read anything in prose, but I have a great dread of a long story in verse."

"No, ma'am, no; 'tis all in prose, I assure you. 'Tis a novel; and an exceeding—but it does nothing good to be praised too much, so I will say nothing more about it: only this, that Mr. Burke sat up all night to read it."

" Indeed? Well, I propose myself great pleasure from it and I am gratified by hearing it is written by a woman."

"And Sir Joshua Reynolds," continued Mrs. Thrale, "has been offering fifty pounds to know the author."

"Well, I will have it to read on my journey; I am going to Berkshire, and it shall be my travelling book."

" No, ma'am if you please you shall have it now. Queeny, do look it for Mrs. Montagu, and let it be put in her carriage, and go to town with her."

Miss Thrale rose to look for it, and involuntarily I rose too, intending to walk off, for my situation was inexpressibly awkward; but then I recollected that if I went away, it might seem like giving Mrs. Thrale leave and opportunity to tell my tale, and therefore I stopped at a distant window, where I busied myself in contemplating the poultry.

"And Dr. Johnson, ma'am," added my kind puffer, "says

Fielding never wrote so well—never wrote equal to this book; he says it is a better picture of life and manners than is to be found anywhere in Fielding."

"Indeed?" cried Mrs. Montagu, surprised; "that I did not expect, for I have been informed it is the work of a young lady and therefore, though I expected a very pretty book, I supposed it to be a work of mere imagination, and the name I thought attractive; but life and manners I never dreamt of finding."

"Well, ma'am, what I tell you is literally true; and for my part, I am never better pleased than when good girls write clever books—and that this is clever— But all this time we are killing Miss Burney, who wrote the book herself."

What a clap of thunder was this !-the last thing in the world I should have expected before my face? I know not what bewitched Mrs. Thrale, but this was carrying the jest further than ever. All retenu being now at an end, I fairly and abruptly took to my heels, and ran out of the room with the utmost trepidation, amidst astonished exclamations from Mrs, Montagu and Miss Gregory.

I was horribly disconcerted, but I am now so irrecoverably in for it, that I begin to leave off reproaches and expostulations; indeed, they have very little availed me while they might have been of service, but now they would pass for mere parade and affectation; and therefore since they can do no good, I gulp them down. I find them, indeed, somewhat hard of digestion, but they must make their own way as well as they can.

I determined not to make my appearance again till dinner was upon table; yet I could neither read nor write, nor indeed do any thing but consider the new situation in life into which I am thus hurried—I had almost said forced—and if I had, methinks it would be no untruth.

Miss Thrale came laughing up after me, and tried to persuade me to return. She was mightily diverted all the morning, and came to me with repeated messages of summons to attend the company, but I could not brave it again into the roon', and therefore entreated her to say I was finishing a letter. Yet I was sorry to lose so much of Mrs. Montagu.

When dinner was upon table, I followed the procession, in a tragedy step, as Mr. Thrale will have it, into the dining parlour. Dr. Johnson was returned.

The conversation was not brilliant, nor do I remember much of it; but Mrs. Montagu behaved to me just as I could have wished, since she spoke to me very little, but spoke that little with the utmost politeness. But Miss Gregory, though herself a modest girl, quite stared me out of countenance, and never took her eyes off my face.

When Mrs. Montagu's new house was talked of, Dr. Johnson, in a jocose manner, desired to know if he should be invited to see it.

"Ay, sure," cried Mrs. Montagu, looking well pleased; "or I shan't like it: but I invite you all to a house warming; I shall hope for the honour of seeing all this company at my new house next Easter day: I fix the day now that it may be remembered.'

Everybody bowed and accepted the invite but me, and I thought fitting not to hear it; for I have no notion of snapping at invites from the eminent. But Dr. Johnson, who sat next to me, Was determined I should be of the party, for he suddenly clapped his hand on my shoulder, and called out aloud,

"Little Burney, you and I will go together?"

"Yes, surely," cried Mrs. Montagu, "I shall hope for the pleasure of seeing 'Evelina.'"

"'Evelina>'" repeated he; "has Mrs. Montagu then found out 'Evelina?'"

"Yes," cried she, "and I am proud of it: I am proud that a work so commended should be a woman's."

hhow my face burnt!

"Has Mrs. Montagu," asked Dr. Johnson, "read 'Evelina?'"

"No, sir, not yet; but I shall immediately, for I feel the greatest eagerness to read it."

"I am very sorry, madam," replied he, "that you have not already, read it, because you cannot speak of it with a full conviction of its merit: which, I believe, when you have read it, you will have great pleasure in acknowledging."

Some other things were said, but I remember them not, for I could hardly keep my place: but my sweet, naughty Mrs. Thrale looked delighted for me......

When they were gone, how did Dr. Johnson astonish me by asking if I had observed what an ugly cap Miss Gregory had on? Then taking both my hands, and looking at me with an expression of much kindness, he said,

"Well, Miss Burney, Mrs. Montagu now will read 'Evelina'"...... 104 Mrs. Thrale then told me such civil things. Mrs. Montagu, it seems, during my retreat, inquired very particularly what kind of book it was?

"And I told her," continued Mrs. Thrale, "that it was a picture of life, manners, and characters. 'But won't she go on,' says she; 'surely she won't stop here?'

"'Why,' said I, 'I want her to go on in a new path—I want her to write a comedy.'

"'But,' said Mrs. Montagu, 'one thing must be considered; Fielding, who was so admirable in novel writing, never succeeded when he wrote for the stage.'"

"Very well said," cried Dr. Johnson "that was an answer which showed she considered her subject."

Mrs. Thrale continued :

"'Well, but `a propos,' said Mrs. Montagu, 'if Miss Burney does write a play, I beg I may know of it; or, if she thinks proper, see it; and all my influence is at her service. We shall all be glad to assist in spreading the fame of Miss Burney.'"

I tremble for what all this will end in. I verily think I had best stop where I am, and never again attempt writing: for after so much honour, so much success—how shall I bear a downfall?

DR. JOHNSON'S COMPLIMENTS AND GROSS SPEECHES.

Monday, Sept. 21.-I have had a thousand delightful conversations with Dr. Johnson, who, whether he loves me or not, I am sure seems to have some opinion of my discretion, for he speaks of all this house to me with unbounded confidence, neither diminishing faults, nor exaggerating praise.

Whenever he is below stairs he keeps me a prisoner, for he does not like I should quit the room a moment; if I rise he constantly calls out, "Don't you go, little Burney!"

Last night, when we were talking of compliments and of gross speeches, Mrs. Thrale most justly said, that nobody could make either like Dr. Johnson. "Your compliments, sir, are made seldom, but when they are made they have an elegance unequalled; but then when you are angry! who dares make speeches so bitter and so cruel?"

Dr. J.-Madam, I am always sorry when I make bitter speeches, and I never do it, but when I am insufferably vexed.

Mrs. T-Yes, Sir; but you suffer things to vex you, that 105 nobody else would vex at. I am sure I have had my share of scoldings from YOU!

Dr. J-It is true, you have ; but you have borne it like an angel, and you have been the better for it.

Mrs. T.-That I believe, sir: for I have received more instruction from You than from any man, or any book: and the vanity that you should think me worth instructing, always overcame the vanity[71]of being found fault with. And so you had the scolding, and I the improvement.

F.B.-And I am sure both make for the honour of both!

Dr J.-I think so too. But Mrs. Thrale is a sweet creature, and never angry; she has a temper the most delightful of any woman I ever knew.

Mrs. T-This I can tell you, sir, and without any flattery— I not only bear your reproofs when present, but in almost everything I do in your absence, I ask myself whether you would like it, and what you would say to it. Yet I believe there is nobody you dispute with oftener than me.

F.B.-But you two are so well established with one another, that you can bear a rebuff that would kill a stranger.

Dr. J.-Yes; but we disputed the same before we were so well established with one another.

Mrs. T.-Oh, sometimes I think I shall die no other death than hearing the bitter things he says to others. What he says to myself I can bear, because I know how sincerely he is my friend, and that he means to mend me; but to others it is cruel.

Dr. j.-Why, madam, you often provoke me to say severe things, by unreasonable commendation. If you would not call for my praise, I would not give you my censure; but it constantly moves my indignation to be applied to, to speak well of a thing which I think contemptible.

F.B.-Well, this I know, whoever I may hear complain of Dr. Johnson's severity, I shall always vouch for his kindness, as far as regards myself, and his indulgence.

Mrs. T.-Ay, but I hope he will trim you yet, too!

Dr. J.-I hope not: I should be very sorry to say anything that should vex my dear little Burney.

F.B.-If you did, sir, it would vex me more than you can imagine. I should sink in a minute.

Mrs-. T.-I remember, sir, when we were travelling in Wales, how you called me to account for my civility to the people. 'Madam,' you said, 'let me have no more of this idle commendation of nothing. Why is it, that whatever You see, and whoever you see, you are to be so indiscriminately lavish of praise?' 'Why! I'll tell you, sir,' said I, 'when I am with you and Mr. Thrale, and Queeny, I am obliged to be civil for four!'"

There was a cutter for you! But this I must say, for the honour of both— Mrs. Thrale speaks to Dr. Johnson with as much sincerity, (though with greater softness,) as he does to her.

SUGGESTED HUSBANDS FOR FANNY BURNEY.

Sept. 26-The present chief sport with Mrs. Thrale is disposing of me in the holy state of matrimony, and she offers me whoever comes to the house. This was begun by Mrs. Montagu, who, it seems, proposed a match for me in my absence, with Sir Joshua Reynolds!-no less a man, I assure you!

When I was dressing for dinner, Mrs. Thrale told me that Mr. Crutchley was expected.

"Who's he?" quoth I.

" A young man of very large fortune, who was a ward of Mr. Thrale. Queeny, what do you say of him for Miss Burney?"

"Him?" cried she; "no, indeed; what has Miss Burney done to have him?"

" Nay, believe me, a man of his fortune may offer himself anywhere. However, I won't recommend him."

" Why then, ma'am," cried I, with dignity, "I reject him!"

This Mr. Crutchley stayed till after breakfast the next morning. I can't tell you anything, of him, because I neither like nor dislike him. Mr. Crutchley was scarce gone, ere Mr. Smith arrived. Mr. Smith is a second cousin to Mr. Thrale, and a modest pretty sort of young man. He stayed till Friday morning. When he was gone,

"What say you to him, Miss Burney?" cried Mrs. Thrale; "I'm sure I offer you variety."

"Why I like him better than Mr. Crutchley, but I don't think I shall pine for either of them."

, Dr. Johnson," said Mrs. Thrale, "don't you think Jerry Crutchley very much improved?"

Dr. J.-Yes, madam, I think he is.

Mrs. T.-Shall he have Miss Burney?

Dr. J.-Why, I think not; at least I must know more about him; I Must inquire into his connections, his recreations, his employments, and his character, from his intimates, before I trust Miss Burney with him. And he must come down very handsomely with a settlement. I will not have him left to his generosity; for as he will marry her for her wit, and she him for his fortune, he ought to bid well, and let him come down with what he will, his price will never be equal to her worth.

Mrs. T.-She says she likes Mr. Smith better.

Dr. J.-Yes, but I won't have her like Mr. Smith without money, better than Mr. Crutchley with it. Besides, if she has Crutchley, he will use her well, to vindicate his choice. the world, madam, has a reasonable claim upon all mankind to account for their conduct; therefore, if with his great wealth, he marries a woman who has but little, he will be more attentive to display her merit, than if she was equally rich,—in order to show that the woman he has chosen deserves from the world all the respect and admiration it can bestow, or that else she would not have been his choice.

Mrs. T.-I believe young Smith is the better man.

F.B.-Well, I won't be rash in thinking of either; I will take some time for consideration before I fix.

Dr. J.-Why, I don't hold it to be delicate to offer marriage to ladies, even in jest, nor do I approve such sort of jocularity; yet for once I must break through the rules of decorum, and Propose a match myself for Miss Burney. I therefore nominnate Sir J- L-.[72]

Mrs. T.-I'll give you my word, sir, you are not the first to say that, for my master the other morning, when we were alone, said 'What would I give that Sir J— L— was married to Miss Burney; it might restore him to our family.' So spoke his Uncle and guardian.

F.B.-He, he! Ha, ha! He, he! Ha, ha!

Dr. J.-That was elegantly said of my master, and nobly said, and not in the vulgar way we have been saying it. And madam, where will you find another man in trade who will make such a speech- -who will be capable of making such a speech? Well, I am glad my master takes so to Miss Burney; I would have everybody take to Miss Burney, so as they allow 108 me to take to her most! Yet I don't know whether Sir J__ L— should have her, neither; I should be afraid for her; I don't think I would hand her to him.

F.B.-Why, now, what a fine match is here broken off!

Some time after, when we were in the library, he asked me very gravely if I loved reading?

"Yes," quoth I.

"Why do you doubt it, sir ?" cried MrsThrale.

"Because," answered he, "I never see her with a book in her hand. I have taken notice that she never has been reading whenever I have come into the room."

"Sir," quoth I, courageously, "I'm always afraid of being caught reading, lest I should pass for being studious or affected, and therefore instead of making a display of books, I always try to hide them, as is the case at this very time, for I have now your 'Life of Waller' under my gloves behind me. However, since I am piqued to it, I'll boldly produce my voucher."

And so saying, I put the book on the table, and opened it with a flourishing air. And then the laugh was on my side, for he could not help making a droll face; and if he had known Kitty Cooke,' I would have called out, "There I had you, my lad!"

A STREATH A m DINNER PARTY.

Monday was the day for our great party; and the Doctor came home, at MrsThrale's request, to meet them. The party consisted of Mr. C—, who was formerly a timber-merchant, but having amassed a fortune of one million of pounds, he has left off business. He is a good-natured busy sort of man. ;

Mrs. C—, his lady, a sort of Mrs. Nobody.

Mr. N—, another rich business leaver-off.

Mrs. N—, his lady; a pretty sort of woman, who was formerly a pupil of Dr. Hawkesworth. I had a great deal of talk with her about him, and about my favourite miss Kinnaird, whom she knew very well.

Mr. George and Mr. Thomas N—, her sons-in-law.

Mr. R—, of whom I know nothing but that he married into MrThrale's family.

Lady Ladd; I ought to have begun with her. I beg her ladyship a thousand pardons—though if she knew My offence,

I am sure I should not obtain one. She is own sister to Mr. Thrale. She is a tall and stout woman, has an air of mingled dignity and haughtiness, both of which wear off in conversation. She dresses very youthful and gaily, and attends to her person with no little complacency. She appears to me uncultivated in knowledge, though an adept in the manners of the world, And all that. She chooses to be much more lively than her brother; but liveliness sits as awkwardly upon her as her pink ribbons. in talking her over with MrsThrale who has a very proper regard for her, but who, I am sure, cannot be blind to her faults, she gave me another proof to those I have already of the uncontrolled freedom of speech which Dr. Johnson exercised to everybody, and which everybody receives quietly from him. Lady Ladd has been very handsome, but is now, I think, quite ugly—at least she has the sort of face I like not. she was a little while ago dressed in so showy a manner as to attract the doctor's notice, and when he had looked at her some time, he broke out aloud into this quotation:

"With patches, paint, and jewels on, Sure Phillis is not twenty-one But if at night you Phillis see, The dame at least is forty-three!"

I don't recollect the verses exactly, but such was their purport.

"However," said Mrs. Thrale, "Lady Ladd took it very good- naturedly, and only said, 'I know enough of that forty-three—I don't desire to hear any more of it."''

Miss Moss, a pretty girl, who played and sung, to the great fatigue of Mrs. Thrale; Mr. Rose Fuller, Mr. Embry, Mr. Seward, Dr. Johnson, the three Thrales, and myself, close the party.

In the evening the company divided pretty much into parties, and almost everybody walked upon the gravel-walk before the windows. I was going to have joined some of them, when Dr. Johnson stopped me, and asked how I did.

"I was afraid, sir," cried I "you did not intend to know me again, for you have not spoken to me before since your return from town."

"MY dear," cried he, taking both my hands, "I was not of You, I am so near sighted, and I apprehended making some Mistake." Then drawing me very unexpectedly towards him, he actually kissed me!

To be sure, I was a little surprised, having no idea of such facetiousness from him, However, I was glad nobody was in the room but MrsThrale, who stood close to us, and Mr. Embry, who was lounging on a sofa at the furthest end of the room. Mrs. Thrale laughed heartily, and said she hoped I was contented with his amends for not knowing me sooner.

A little after she said she would go and walk with the rest, if she did not fear for my reputation in being left with the doctor"

"However, as Mr. Embry is yonder, I think he'll take some care of you," she added.

"Ay, madam," said the doctor, "we shall do very well; but I assure you I sha'n't part with Miss Burney!"

And he held me by both hands; and when MrsThrale went, he drew me a chair himself facing the window, close to his own; and thus t`ete-`a-t`ete we continued almost all the evening. I say t`ete- `a-t`ete, because Mr, Embry kept at an humble distance, and offered us no interruption And though Mr, Seward soon after came in, he also seated himself at a distant corner, not presuming, he said, to break in upon us! Everybody, he added, gave way to the doctor.

Our conversation chiefly was upon the Hebrides, for he always talks to me of Scotland, out of sport; and he wished I had been of that tour—quite gravely, I assure you!

The P— family came in to tea. When they were gone Mrs. Thrale complained that she was quite worn out with that tiresome silly woman Mrs. P—, who had talked of her family and affairs till she was sick to death of hearing her.

"Madam," said Dr. Johnson, "why do you blame the woman for the only sensible thing she could do—talking of her family and her affairs? For how should a woman who is as empty as a drum, talk upon any other subject? If you speak to her of the sun, she does not know it rises in the east;—if you speak to her of the moon, she does not know it changes at the full ;—if you speak to her of the queen, she does not know she is the king's wife.—how, then, can you blame her for talking of her family and affairs?"

31   Fanny Burney's step-mother.-ED.

32   Dr. Burney's daughter by his second wife.

33   "Evelina; or a Young Lady's Entrance into the World.-This novel has given us so much pleasure in the perusal, that we do not hesitate to pronounce it one of the most sprightly, entertaining, and agreeable productions of this kind that has of late fallen under our notice. A great variety of natural incidents, some of the comic stamp, render the narrative extremely interesting. The characters, which are agreeably diversified, are conceived and drawn with propriety, and supported with spirit. The whole is written with great ease and command of language. From this commendation we must, however, except the character of a son of Neptune, whose manners are rather those of a rough, uneducated country squire than those of a genuine sea-captain." Monthly Review, April, 1778.

34   " Evelina.-The history of a young lady exposed to very critical situations. There is much more merit, as well respecting style as character and incident, than is usually to be met with in modern novels." London Review, Feb., 1778.

35   Fanny was no mistress of numbers; but the sincerity and warm affection expressed in every line of the Ode prefixed to "Evelina," would excuse far weaker verses. We quote it in full.-ED.

"Oh, Author of my being !-far more dear

To me than light, than nourishment, or rest, Hygeia's blessings, Rapture's burning tear, Or the life-blood that mantles in-my breast! If in my heart the love of Virtue glows, 'Twas planted there by an unerring rule From thy example the pure flame arose, Thy life, my precept,—thy good works, my school. Could my weak pow'rs thy num'rous virtues trace, By filial love each fear should be repress'd; The blush of Incapacity I'd chace, And stand, Recorder of thy worth, confess'd But since my niggard stars that gift refuse, Concealment is the only boon I claim Obscure be still the unsuccessful Muse, Who cannot raise, but would not sink, thy fame, Oh! of my life at once the source and joy! If e'er thy eyes these feeble lines survey, Let not their folly their intent destroy; Accept the tribute-but forget the lay."

36   Lady Hales was the mother of Miss Coussmaker, having been twice married, the second time to Sir Thomas Pym Hales, Bart., who died in 1773. They were intimate friends of the Burneys.-ED.

37   Dr. Burney had brought the work under the notice of Mrs. Thrale. Mrs. Cholmondeley was a sister of the famous actress, Peg Woffington. Her husband, the Hon. and Rev. Robert Cholmondeley, was the second son of the Earl of Cholmondeley, and nephew of Horace Walpole.-ED.

38   The sum originally paid for "Evelina" was twenty pounds, to which ten Pounds more were added after the third edition. "Evelina " passed through four editions within a year.-ED.

39   Mrs. Greville, the wife of Dr, Burney's friend and early patron, Fulke

Greville, was Fanny's godmother, and the author of a much admired "Ode to Indifference."-ED

40 Her cousin, Charles Rousseau Burney-Hetty's husband.-ED.

41 A French authoress, who wrote about the middle of the eighteenth century. Her novels, according to Dunlop ""A History of Fiction," chap. xiii. "are distinguished by their delicacy and spirit." Her best works ar: "Miss jenny Salisbury," "Le Marquis de Cressy," "Letters of Lady Catesby," etc.-ED.

42 Mrs. Williams, the blind poetess, who resided in Dr. Johnson's house. She had written to Dr. Burney, requesting the loan of a copy of "Evelina."-ED.

43 william Seward "a great favourite at Streatham," was the son of an eminent brewer, Mr. Seward, of the firm of Calvert and Seward, and was born in 1747. He was not yet a "literary lion," but he published some volumes—"Anecdotes of Distinguished Persons "—at a later date. He died in 1799.-ED.

44 Miss Frances Reynolds—Dr. Johnson's "Renny"—was the sister of the great Sir Joshua, and a miniature painter of some talent.-ED.

45 Her brother.-ED.

46 Bennet Lanpton, of Langton in Lincolnshire, was an old and much loved friend of Dr. johnson, and is frequently mentioned in Boswell's "Life." He was born about 1737, was educated at Oxford, was a good Greek scholar, and, says Boswell, "a gentleman eminent not only for worth, and learning but for an inexhaustible fund of entertaining conversation." ." He succeeded Johnson, on the death of the latter, as Professor of Ancient History to the Royal Academy, and died in 1801. Boswell has printed a charming letter, written by johnson, a few months before his death, to Langton's little daughter jane, then in her seventh year.-ED.

47 "My master" was a Common appellation for Mr, Thrale,—and One which he seems, in earnest, to have deserved. "I know no man," said johnson, "who is more master of his wife and family than Thrale, he but holds up a finger, he is obeyed." (Boswell.)- ED.

48 Suspirius the Screech Owl. See "Rambler" for Oct. 9, 1750. (This is unjust to Goldsmith. The general idea of the character of Croaker, no doubt, closely resembles that of Suspirius, and was probably borrowed from johnson; but the details which make the part so diverting are entirely of Goldsmith's invention, as anyone may see by comparing "The Good-natured Man" with "The Rambler."-ED.]

49 Mrs. Thrale tells a good story of Johnson's irrational antipathy to the Scotch. A Scotch gentleman inLondon, "at his return from the Hebrides, asked him, with a firm tone of voice, 'what he thought of his country?' 'That it is a very vile country, to be sure, sir,' returned for answer Dr. Johnson. 'Well sir!' replies the other, somewhat mortified, 'God made it!' 'Certainly he did,' answers Mr. Johnson, again, 'but we

must always remember that He made it for Scotchmen; and—comparisons are odious, Mr. S.—but God made hell!'—(Anecdotes of Dr. Johnson ED.

50   Fanny's step-mother.-ED.

51   Boswell prints these lines as follows:

"When first I drew my vital breath, A little minikin I came upon earth And then I came from a dark abode, into this gay and gaudy world,"-ED,

52   Malone gives some further particulars about Bet Flint in a note to Boswell's "Life of Johnson." She was tried, and acquitted, at the Old Bailey in September, 1758, the prosecutrix, Mary Walthow, being unable to prove "that the goods charged to have been stolen (a counterpane, a silver spoon, two napkins, etc.) were her property. Bet does not appear to have lived at that time in a very genteel style; for she paid for her ready- furnished room in Meard's-court, Dean-street, Soho, from which these articles were alleged to be stolen, only five shillings a week."-ED.

53   Margaret Caroline Rudd was in great notoriety about the year 1776, from the fame of her powers of fascination, which, it was said, had brought a man to the gallows. This man, her lover, was hanged in January, 1776, for forgery, and the fascinating Margaret appeared as evidence against him. Boswell visited her in that year, and to a lady who expressed her disapprobation of such proceedings, Johnson said: "Nay, madam, Boswell is right: I should have visited her myself, were it not that they have got a trick of putting every thing into the newspapers."-ED.

54   Kitty Fisher—more correctly, Fischer, her father being a German—an even more famous courtesan, who enjoyed the distinction of having been twice painted by Sir Joshua Reynolds -ED.

55   The blind poetess, and inmate of Dr. Johnson's house.-ED.

56   Michael Lort, D.D., Fellow of Trinity College, Cambridge, and subsequently Greek Professor. He was born in 1725, and died in 1799.-ED.

57   "I wished the man a dinner and sat still."-Pope.

58   The Miss Palmers were the nieces of Sir Joshua Reynolds. Mary, the elder, married, in 1792, the Earl of Inchiquin, afterwards created Marquis of Thomond; the younger, Theophila ("Offy"), married Robert Lovell Gwatkin, Esq. One of Sir Joshua's most charming pictures ("Simplicity") was painted, in 1788, from Offy's little daughter. Lady Ladd was the sister of Mr. Thrale.-ED.

59   Miss Thrale.-ED.

60   Edmund Burke, our "greatest man since Milton," as Macaulay called him.-ED.

61   At Sir Joshua's town house, in Leicester Square. The house is now occupied by Messrs. Puttick and Simpson, the auctioneers.-ED.

62   "de Mullin" is Mrs. Desmoulins, the daughter of Johnson's godfather,

Dr. Swinfen, a physician in Lichfield. Left in extreme indigence by the deaths of her father and husband, she found for many years an asylum in the house of Dr. Johnson, whom she survived.-ED.

63   Macbean was sometime Johnson's amanuensis. His "Dictionary of Ancient Geography" was published in 1773, with a Freface by Johnson.-ED

64   Robert Levett—not Levat, as Fanny writes it—was a Lichfield man, "an obscure practiser in pbysick amongst the lower people," and an old acquaintance of Dr. Johnson's, in whose house he was supported for many years, until his death, at a very advanced age, in 1782, "So ended the long life of a very useful and very blameless man," Johnson wrote, in communicating the intelligence to Dr, Lawrence.-ED.

65   Boswell tells us nothing of Poll, except that she was a Miss Carmichael. Domestic dissensions seem to have been the rule with this happy family, but Johnson's long-suffering was inexhaustible, On one occasion he writes Mrs. Thrale, "Williams hates everybody; Levett hates Desmoulins, who does not love Williams; Desmoulins hates them both; Poll loves none of them."-ED.

66   The lives of Cowley and Waller, from Johnson's "Lives of the Poets." They were not published till 1781, but were already in print.-ED.

67   "The Theory and Regulation of Love: A Moral Essay." By the Rev. John Norris, Oxford, 1688.-ED.

68   Miss Gregory was the daughter of a Scotch physician. She married the Rev. Archibald Alison, and was the mother of Sir Archibald Alison, the historian.-ED.

69   The house in which she died, in Portman Square.-ED.

70   No doubt Simon Nicolas Henri Linguet, a French author, who published numerous works, historical and political, both before and after this date.-ED.

71   IN the original edition: perhaps "vexation" was the word intended.-ED.

72   Sir John Ladd, Mr, Thrale's sister's son, a young profligate who subsequently married, not Miss Burney, but a woman of the town! Dr. Johnson's satirical verses on his coming of age are printed near the end of Boswell's "Life."-ED.

SECTION 2 (1779)

THE AUTHOR OF "EVELINA" IN SOCIETY: SHE VISITS BRIGHTON AND TUNBRIDGE WELLS.

(FANNY'S circle of acquaintance was largely extended in 1779, in which year she was introduced to Mrs. Horneck and her daughter Mary (Goldsmith's "Jessamy Bride"), to Mr. and Mrs. cholmondeley, to Arthur Murphy, the dramatist, and best of all, Richard Brinsley Sheridan and his beautiful wife. The Hornecks and the Cholmondeleys she met at one of those delightful parties at Sir Joshua Reynolds's house in Leicester Square,—parties composed of the wisest and wittiest in English society of the day, though nowhere among the guests could there be found a man of more genuine worth or more brilliant genius than the mild-mannered host. Mrs. Horneck had been a noted beauty in her younger days, and she, as well as her two lovely daughters, had been painted by Sir Joshua. The elder daughter, Catherine (Goldsmith's "Little Comedy"), was now 1779 Mrs. Bunbury, wife of Henry Bunbury the caricaturist. Mary, the younger, was at this time about twenty-six years of age, and was subsequently married to Colonel Gwynn, whom we shall meet with in Fanny's Diary of her Life at Court. Goldsmith, it is said, had loved Mary Horneck, though the ugly little man never ventured to tell his love; but when he died, five years before her meeting with fanny, the jessamy Bride caused his coffin to be reopened, and a lock of hair to be cut from the dead poet's head. This lock she treasured until her own death, nearly seventy years afterwards.

Mrs. Sheridan's maiden name was Eliza Anne Linley. There is an interesting notice of her in Fanny's "Early Diary" for the month of April, 1773. "Can I speak of music, and not mention Miss Linley? The town has rung of no other name this month. Miss Linley is daughter to a musician of Bath, a very sour, ill-bred, severe, and selfish man. She is believed to be very romantic; she has long been very celebrated for her singing, though never, till within this month, has she been in London. .

She has long been attached to a Mr. Sheridan, a young man of great talents, and very well spoken of, whom it is expected she will speedily marry. She has performed this Lent at the Oratorio of Drury-lane, under Mr. Stanley's direction. The applause and admiration she has met with, can only be compared to what is given Mr. Garrick. The whole town seems distracted about her. Every other diversion is forsaken. Miss Linley alone engrosses all eyes, ears, hearts."

The "young man of great talents" was, when Fanny first met him, already renowned as the author of "The Rivals" and "The School for Scandal." His wife's extraordinary beauty has been perpetuated in one of Reynolds's masterpieces, in which she is represented as St. Cecilia, sitting at an organ. Her father seems to have fully deserved the character which Fanny gives him. In 1772 Eliza, then only nineteen, ran away to France with young Sheridan, who was just of age, and, it is reported, was privately married to him at the time. They were pursued, however, by old Linley, and Eliza was brought back, to become the rage of the town as a singer. Her lover married her openly in April, 1773, and thenceforward she sang no more in public.

Fanny's account of her visits to Tunbridge Wells and Brighton will recall, to readers of her novels, the delightfully humorous descriptions of the society at those fashionable resorts, in "Camilla" and "The Wanderer." Mount Ephraim, at Tunbridge Wells, where Sophy Streatfield resided, will be recognized as the scene of the accident in which Camilla's life is saved by Sir Sedley Clarendel.-ED.]

A QUEER ADVENTURE.

ST. Martin's Street, January.

On Thursday, I had another adventure, and one that has made me grin ever since. A gentleman inquiring for my father, was asked into the parlour. The then inhabitants were only my mother and me. In entered a square old gentleman, well-wigged, formal, grave and important. He seated himself. My mother asked if he had any message for my father? "No, none." Then he regarded me with a certain dry kind of attention for some time; after which, turning suddenly to my mother, he demanded,

"Pray, ma'am, is this your daughter?"

"Yes, sir."

"O! this is Evelina, is it?"

"No, sir," cried I, staring at him, and glad none of you were in the way to say "Yes."

"No?" repeated he, incredulous; "is not your name Evelina, ma'am?"

"Dear, no, sir," again quoth I, staring harder.

"Ma'am," cried he, drily; "I beg your pardon! I had understood your name was Evelina."

Soon: after, he went away.

And when he put down his card, who should it prove but Dr. Franklin. [73]Was it not queer?

AN EVENING AT SIR JOSHUA REYNOLDS'S: A DEMONSTRATIVE "EVELINA" ENTHUSIAST.

NOW to this grand visit, which was become more tremendous than ever because of the pamphlet [74]business, and I felt almost ashamed to see Sir JOShua, and could not but conclude he would think of it too.

My mother, who changed her mind, came with me. My father promised to come before the Opera was half over.

We found the Miss Palmers alone. We were, for near an hour, quite easy, chatty, and comfortable; no pointed speech was made, and no starer entered. But when I asked the elder Miss Palmer if she would allow me to look at some of her drawings, she said,

"Not unless you will let me see something of yours."

"Of mine?" quoth I. "Oh,! I have nothing to show."

"I am sure you have; you must have."

"No, indeed; I don't draw at all."

"Draw? No, but I mean some of your writing."

"Oh, I never write—except letters."

"Letters? those are the very things I want to see."

"Oh, not such as you mean."

" Oh now, don't say so; I am sure you are about something and if you would but show me—"

"No, no, I am about nothing—I am quite out of conceit with writing." I had my thoughts full of the vile Warley.

"You out of conceit?" exclaimed she; "nay, then, if you are, who should be otherwise!"

just then, Mrs. and Miss Horneck were announced. you may suppose I thought directly of the one hundred and sixty miles[75]and may take it for granted I looked them very boldly in the face! Mrs. Horneck seated herself by my mother. Miss Palmer introduced me to her and her daughter, who seated herself next me; but not one word passed between us!

Mrs. Horneck, as I found in the course of the evening, is an exceedingly sensible, well-bred woman. Her daughter is very beautiful ; but was low-spirited and silent during the whole visit. She was, indeed, very unhappy, as Miss Palmer informed me, upon account of some ill news she had lately heard of the affairs of a gentleman to whom she is shortly to be married.

Not long after came a whole troop, consisting of Mr. Cholmondeley!—perilous name!—Miss Cholmondeley, and Miss Fanny Cholmondeley, his daughters, and Miss Forrest. Mrs. Cholmondeley, I found, was engaged elsewhere, but soon expected. [76]Now here was a trick of Sir Joshua, to make me meet all these people.

Mr. Cholmondeley is a clergyman; nothing shining either in person or manners, but rather somewhat grim in the first, and glum in the last. Yet he appears to have humour himself, and to enjoy it much in others.

Miss Cholmondeley I saw too little of to mention.

Miss Fanny Cholmondeley is a rather pretty, pale girl; very young and inartificial, and though tall and grown up, treated by her family as a child, and seemingly well content to really think herself such. She followed me whichever way I turned, and though she was too modest to stare, never ceased watching me the whole evening.

Miss Forrest is an immensely tall and not handsome young woman. Further I know not.

Next came my father, all gaiety and spirits. Then Mr. William Burke. [77]

Soon after, Sir Joshua returned home. He paid his compliments to everybody, and then brought a chair next mine, and said,

"So you were afraid to come among us?"

I don't know if I wrote to you a speech to that purpose, which I made to the Miss Palmers? and which, I Suppose, they had repeated to him. He went on, saying I might as ,Well fear hobgoblins, and that I had only to hold up my head to be above them all.

After this address, his behaviour was exactly what my wishes would have dictated to him, for my own ease and quietness; for he never once even alluded to my book, but conversed rationally, gaily, and serenely: and so I became more comfortable than I had been ever since the first entrance of company. Our confab was interrupted by the entrance of Mr. King; a gentleman who is, it seems, for ever with the Burkes; -and presently Lord Palmerston[78]was announced.

Well, while this was going forward, a violent rapping bespoke, I was sure, Mrs. Cholmondeley, and I ran from the standers, and turning my back against the door, looked over Miss Palmer's cards; for you may well imagine, I was really in a tremor at a meeting which so long has been in agitation, and with the person who, of all persons, has been most warm and enthusiastic for my book.

She had not, however, been in the room half an instant, ere „my father came up to me, and tapping me on the shoulder, said, "Fanny, here's a lady who wishes to speak to you."

I curtsied in silence, she too curtsied, and fixed her eyes full on my face: and then tapping me with her fan, she cried,

"Come, come, you must not look grave upon me."

Upon this, I te-he'd; she now looked at me yet more earnestly, and, after an odd silence, said, abruptly—

"But is it true?"

"What, ma'am?"

"It can't be!—tell me, though, is it true?"

I could only simper.

"Why don't you tell me?—but it can't be—I don't believe it!— no, you are an impostor!"

Sir Joshua and Lord Palmerston were both at her side—oh, how notably silly must I look! She again repeated her question of "Is it true?" and I again affected not to understand her: and then Sir Joshua, taking hold on her arm, attempted to pull her away, saying

"Come, come, Mrs. Cholmondeley, I won't have her overpowered here!"

I love Sir Joshua much for this, But Mrs. Cholmondeley, turning to him, said, with quickness and vehemence:—

"Why, I a'n't going to kill her! don't be afraid, I sha'n't compliment her!-I can't, indeed!"

Then, taking my hand, she led me through them all, to another part of the room, where again she examined my phiz, and viewed and reviewed my whole person.

"Now," said she, "do tell me; is it true?"

"What, ma'am?—I don't-I don't know what—"

"Pho! what,-why you know what: in short, can you read? and can you write?"

"No, ma'am!"

"I thought so," cried she I have suspected it was a trick, some time, and now I am sure of it. You are too young by half!-it can't be!"

I laughed, and would have got away, but she would not let me.

"No," cried she, "one thing you must, at least, tell me;—are you very conceited? Come, answer me," continued she. "You won't? Mrs. Burney, Dr. Burney,—come here,—tell me if she is not very conceited?—if she is not eat up with conceit by this time?"

They were both pleased to answer "Not half enough."

"Well," exclaimed she, "that is the most wonderful part of all! Why, that is yet more extraordinary than writing the book."

I then got away from her, and again looked over Miss Palmer's cards : but she was after me in a minute,

"Pray, Miss Burney," cried she, aloud, "do you know any thing of this game?"

"No, ma'am."

"No?" repeated she, "ma foi, that's pity!" [79]

This raised such a laugh, I was forced to move on; yet everybody seemed to be afraid to laugh, too, and studying to be delicate, as if they had been cautioned; which, I have since found, was really the case, and by Sir Joshua himself.

Again, however, she was at my side.

"What game do you like, Miss Burney?" cried she.

"I play at none, ma'am."

"No? Pardie, I wonder at that! Did you ever know such a toad?"

Again I moved on, and got behind Mr. W. Burke, who, turning round to me, said,—

"This is not very politic in us, Miss Burney, to play at cards, and have you listen to our follies."

There's for you! I am to pass for a censoress now.

Mrs. Cholmondeley hunted me quite round the card-table, from chair to chair, repeating various speeches of Madame Duval; and when, at last, I got behind a sofa, out of her reach, she called out aloud, " Polly, Polly ! only think! miss has danced with a lord

Some time after, contriving to again get near me, she began flirting her fan, and exclaiming, "Well, miss, I have had a beau, I assure you! ay, and a very pretty beau too, though I don't know if his lodgings were so prettily furnished, and everything, as Mr. Smith's." [80]

Then, applying to Mr. Cholmondeley, she said, "Pray, sir, what is become of my lottery ticket?"

"I don't know," answered he.

" Pardie " cried she, "you don't know nothing

I had now again made off, and, after much rambling, I at last seated myself near the card-table : but Mrs. Cholmondeley was after me in a minute, and drew a chair next mine. I now found it impossible to escape, and therefore forced myself to sit still. Lord Palmerston and Sir Joshua, in a few moments, seated themselves by us.

I must now write dialogue-fashion, to avoid the enormous length of Mrs. C.'s name.

Mrs. C.-I have been very ill; monstrous ill indeed or else I should have been at your house long ago. Sir Joshua, pray how do you do? you know, I suppose, that I don't come, to see you?

Sir Joshua could only laugh, though this was her first address to him.

Mrs. C.-Pray, miss, what's your name?

F.B.-Frances, ma'am.

Mrs. C.-Fanny ? Well, all the Fanny's are excellent and yet, my name is Mary! Pray, Miss Palmers, how are you?—though I hardly know if I shall speak to you to-night, I thought I should have never got here! I have been so out of humour with the people for keeping me. If you but knew, cried I, to whom I am going to-night, and who I shall see to-night, you would not dare keep me muzzing here!

During all these pointed speeches, her penetrating eyes were fixed upon me; and what could I do?—what, indeed, could anybody do, but colour and simper?—all the company watching us, though all, very delicately, avoided joining the confab.

Mrs. C-My Lord Palmerston, I was told to-night that nobody could see your lordship for me, for that you supped at my house every night. Dear, bless me, no ! cried I, not every night! and I looked as confused as I was able; but I am afraid I did not blush, though I+ tried hard for it.

Then, again, turning to me,

That Mr. What-d'ye-call-him, in Fleet-street, is a mighty silly fellow;—perhaps you don't know who I mean?—one T. Lowndes,—but maybe you don't know such a person?

FB.-No, indeed, I do not!—that I can safely say.

Mrs. C.-I could get nothing from him: but I told him I hoped he gave a good price ; and he answered me that he always did things genteel. What trouble and tagging we had! Mr. [I cannot recollect the name she mentioned] laid a wager the writer was a man:—I said I was sure it was a woman: but now we are both out; for it's a girl!

In this comical, queer, flighty, whimsical manner she ran on, till we were summoned to supper ; for we were not allowed to break up before: and then, when Sir Joshua and almost everybody was gone down stairs, she changed her tone, and, with a face and voice both grave, said:

"Well, Miss Burney, you must give me leave to say One thing to you; yet, perhaps you won't, neither, will you?"

"What is it, ma'am?"

"Why it is, that I admire you more than any human being and that I can't help!"

Then suddenly rising, she hurried down stairs.

While we were upon the stairs, I heard Miss Palmer say to Miss Fanny Cholmondeley, "Well, you don't find Miss Burney quite so tremendous as you expected?"

Sir Joshua made me sit next him at supper; Mr. William Burke was at my other side; though, afterwards, I lost the knight of plimton, [81]who, as he eats no suppers, made way for Mr. Gwatkin, [82]and, as the table was crowded, himself stood at the fire. He was extremely polite and flattering in his manners to me, and entirely avoided all mention or hint at "Evelina" the whole evening: indeed, I think I have met more scrupulous delicacy from Sir Joshua than from anybody, although I have heard more of his approbation than of almost any other person's.

Mr. W. Burke was immensely attentive at table; but, lest he should be thought a Mr. Smith for his pains, he took care, whoever he helped, to add, "You know I am all for the ladies!"

I was glad I was not next Mrs. Cholmondeley; but she frequently, and very provokingly, addressed herself to me; once she called out aloud, "Pray, Miss Burney, is there anything new coming out?" And another time, "Well, I wish people who can entertainme would entertain me!"

These sort of pointed speeches are almost worse than direct attacks, for there is no knowing how to look, or what to say, especially where the eyes of a whole company mark the object for Whom they are meant. To the last of these speeches I made no sort of answer but Sir Joshua very good-naturedly turned it from me, by saying,

"Well, let everyone do what they can in their different ways; do you begin yourself."

"Oh, I can't!" cried she; "I have tried, but I can't."

"Oh, so you think, then," answered he, "that all the world is made only to entertain you?"

A very lively dialogue ensued. But I grow tired of writing. One thing, however, I must mention, which, at the time, frightened me wofully.

"Pray, Sir Joshua," asked Lord Palmerston, what is this 'Warley' that is just come out?"

Was not this a cruel question? I felt in such a twitter!

"Why, I don't know," answered he; "but the reviewers, my lord, speak very well of it."

Mrs. C.-Who wrote it?

Sir Joshua.-Mr. Huddisford.

Mrs. C.-O! I don't like it at all, then! Huddisford What a name! Miss Burney, pray can you conceive anything of such a name as Huddisford?

I could not speak a word, and I dare say I looked no-how. But was it not an unlucky reference to me? Sir Joshua attempted a kind of vindication Of him; but Lord Palmerston said, drily,

"I think, Sir Joshua, it is dedicated to you?"

"Yes, my lord," answered he.

"Oh, your servant! Is it so?" cried Mrs. Cholmondeley; "then you need say no more!"

Sir Joshua laughed, and the subject, to my great relief, was dropped.

When we broke up to depart, which was not till near two in the morning, Mrs. Cholmondeley went up to my mother, and begged her permission to visit in St. Martin's-street. Then, as she left the room, she said to me, with a droll sort of threatening look,

"You have not got rid of me yet, I have been forcing myself into your house."

I must own I was not at all displeased at this, as I had very much and very reasonably feared that she would have been by then as sick of me from disappointment, as she was before eager for me from curiosity.

When we came away, Offy Palmer, laughing, said to me,

"I think this will be a breaking-in to you!"

"Ah," cried I, "if I had known of your party!"

" You would have been sick in bed, I suppose?"

I would not answer "No," yet I was glad it was over. And so concludeth this memorable evening.

FANNY BURNEY'S INTRODUCTION TO SHERIDAN.

ON Monday last, my father sent a note to Mrs. Cholmondeley, to propose our waiting on her the Wednesday following; she accepted the proposal, and accordingly on Wednesday evening, my father, mother, and self went to Hertford-street. I should have told you that Mrs. Cholmondeley, when My father some time ago called on her, sent me a message, that if

I would go to see her, I should not again be stared at or worried; and she acknowledged that my visit at Sir Joshua's had been a formidable one, and that I was watched the whole evening; but that upon the whole, the company behaved extremely well, for they only ogled!

Well, we were received by Mrs. Cholmondeley with great politeness, and in a manner that showed she intended to throw aside Madame Duval, and to conduct herself towards me in a new style.

Mr. and Misses Cholmondeley and Miss Forrest were with her; but who else think you?—why Mrs. Sheridan! I was absolutely charmed at the sight of her. I think her quite as beautiful as ever, and even more captivating; for she has now a look of ease and happiness that animates her whole face.

Miss Linley was with her; she is very handsome, but nothing near her sister: the elegance of Mrs. Sheridan's beauty is unequalled by any I ever saw, except Mrs. Crewe. [83]I was pleased with her in all respects. She is much more lively and agreeable than I had any idea of finding her; she was very gay, and very unaffected, and totally free from airs of any kind. Miss Linley was very much out of spirits; she did not speak three words the whole evening, and looked wholly unmoved at all that passed. Indeed, she appeared to be heavy and inanimate.

Mrs. Cholmondeley sat next me. She is determined, I believe, to make me like her: and she will, I believe, have full success; for she is very clever, very entertaining, and very much unlike anybody else.

The first subject started was the Opera, and all joined in the praise of Pacchierotti. [84]Mrs. Sheridan declared she could not hear him without tears, and that he was the first Italian singer who ever affected her to such a degree.

Then they talked of the intended marriage of the Duke of Dorset, to Miss Cumberland, and many ridiculous anecdotes were related. The conversation naturally fell upon Mr. Cumberland[85]and he was finely cut up!

"What a man is that! ' said Mrs. Cholmondeley: "I Cannot bear him—so querulous, so dissatisfied, so determined to like nobody, and nothing but himself!"

After this, Miss More[86]was mentioned and I was asked what I thought of her?

"Don't be formal with me if you are, I sha'n't like you!"

"I have no hope that you will any way!"

"Oh, fie! fie! but as to Miss More—I don't like her at all: that is, I detest her! She does nothing but flatter and fawn; and then she thinks ill of nobody. Oh, there's no supporting the company of professed flatterers. She gives me such doses of it, that I cannot endure her; but I always sit still and make no answer, but receive it as if I thought it my due: that is the only way to quiet her. [87]She is really detestable. I hope, Miss Burney, you don't think I admire all geniuses? The only person I flatter," continued she, "is Garrick; and he likes it so much, that it pays one by the spirits it gives him. Other people that I like, I dare not flatter."

A rat-tat-tat-tat ensued, and the Earl of Harcourt was announced. When he had paid his compliments to Mrs. Cholmondeley, speaking of the lady from whose house he was just come, he said,

"Mrs. Vesey[88] 'Is vastly agreeable, but her fear of ceremony is really troublesome ; for her eagerness to break a circle is such, that she insists upon everybody's sitting with their backs one to another ; that is, the chairs are drawn into little parties of three together, in a confused manner, all over the room."

"Why, then," said my father, "they may have the pleasure of caballing and cutting up one another, even in the same room."

"Oh, I like the notion of all things," cried Mrs. Cholmondeley, "I shall certainly adopt it then she drew her chair into the middle of our circle. Lord Harcourt turned his round, and his back to most of us, and my father did the same. You can't imagin.e a more absurd sight.

Just then the door opened, and Mr. Sheridan entered.

Was I not in luck? Not that I believe the meeting was accidental; but I had more wished to meet him and his wife than any people I know not.

I could not endure my ridiculous situation, but replaced myself in an orderly manner immediately. Mr. Sheridan stared at the mall, and Mrs. Cholmondeley said she intended it as a hint for a comedy.

Mr. Sheridan has a very fine figure, and a good though I don't think a handsome face. He is tall, and very upright, and his appearance and address are at once manly and fashionable, without the smallest tincture of foppery or modish graces. In short, I like him vastly, and think him every way worthy his utiful companion.

And let me tell you what I know will give you as much pleasure as it gave me,—that, by all I Could observe in the course of the evening, and we stayed very late, they are extreely happy in each other: he evidently adores her, and she as evidently idolises him. The world has by no means done him justice.

When he had paid his compliments to all his acquaince, he went behind the sofa on which Mrs. Sheridan and Miss OFFy Cholmondeley were seated, and entered into earnest conversation with them.

Upon Lord Harcourt's again paying Mrs. Cholmondeley some compliment. she said,

"Well, my lord, after this I shall be quite sublime for some days! I shan't descend into common life till—till Saturday. And then I shall drop into the vulgar style—I shall be in the ma foi Way."

I do really believe she could not resist this, for she had seemed determined to be quiet.

When next there was a rat-tat, Mrs. Cholmondeley and Lord Harcourt, and my father again, at the command of the former, moved into the middle of the room, and then Sir Joshua Reynolds and Dr. Warton entered.

No further company came. You may imagine there was a [89]Joseph Warton, author of the "Essay on the Genius and Writings of Pope."-ED. general roar at the breaking of the circle, and when they got into order, Mr. Sheridan seated himself in the place Mrs. Cholmondeley had left, between my father and myself.

And now I must tell you a little conversation which I did not hear myself till I came home; it was between Mr. Sheridan and my father.

"Dr. Burney," cried the former, "have you no older daughters? Can this possibly be the authoress of 'Evelina'?"

And then he said abundance of fine things, and begged my father to introduce him to me.

"Why, it will be a very formidable thing to her," answered he, "to be introduced to you."

"Well then, by and by," returned he.

Some time after this, my eyes happening to meet his, he waived the ceremony of introduction, and in a low voice said,

"I have been telling Dr. Burney that I have long expected to see in Miss Burney a lady of the gravest appearance, with the quickest parts."

I was never much more astonished than at this unexpected address, as among all my numerous puffers the name of Sheridan has never reached me, and I did really imagine he had never deigned to look at my trash.

Of course I could make no verbal answer, and he proceeded then to speak of "Evelina" in terms of the highest praise but I was in such a ferment from surprise (not to say pleasure that I have no recollection of his expressions. I only remember telling him that I was much amazed he had spared time to read it, and that he repeatedly called it a most surprising book; and sometime after he added, "But I hope, Miss Burney, you don't intend to throw away your pen?"

"You should take care, sir," said I, "what you say: for you know not what weight it may have."

He wished it might have any, he said, and soon after turned again to my father.

I protest, since the approbation of the Streathamites, I hav met with none so flattering to me as this of Mr. Sheridan, in so very unexpected.

About this time Mrs. Cholmondeley was making much spO by wishing for an acrostic on her name. She said she had several times begged for one in vain, and began to entertain thoughts of writing one herself.

"For," said she, "I am very famous for my rhymes, though I never made a line of poetry in my life."

"An acrostic on your name," said Mr. Sheridan, "would be a very formidable task; it must be so long that I think it should be divided into cantos." "Miss Burney," cried Sir Joshua, who was now reseated, "Are not you a writer of verses?"

F.B.-No, sir.

Mrs C.-O don't believe her. I have made a resolution ,Aot to believe anything she says.

Mr. S.-I think a lady should not write verses till she is past receiving them.

Mrs. C. (rising and stalking majestically towards him).-Mr. Sheridan, pray, sir, what may you mean by this insinuation; did I not say I writ verses?)

Mr. S.- Oh, but you—

Mrs. C.-Say no more, sir! You have made your meaning but too plain already. There now, I think that's a speech for a tragedy

Some time after, Sir Joshua, returning to his standing-place, entered into confab with Miss Linley and your slave upon various matters, during which Mr. Sheridan, joining us, said,

"Sir Joshua, I have been telling Miss Burney that she must not suffer her pen to lie idle—ought she?"

Sir J.-No, indeed, ought she not.

Mr. S.-Do you then, Sir Joshua, persuade her. But perhaps you have begun something? May we ask? Will you answer a question candidly?

F.B.-I don't know, but as candidly as Mrs. Candour I think I certainly shall.

Mr. S.-What then are you about now?

F.B.-Why, twirling my fan, I think!

Mr. S.-No, no; but what are you about at home? However, it is not a fair question, so I won't press it.

Yet he looked very inquisitive ; but I was glad to get off without any downright answer.

Sir J-Anything in the dialogue way, I think, she must succeed in; and I am sure invention will not be wanting,

Mr. S.-No, indeed ; I think, and say, she should write a comedy.

SIr J.-I am sure I think so; and hope she will.

I could only answer by incredulous exclamations.

"Consider" continued Sir Joshua, " you have already had all the applause and fame you can have given you in the closet; but the acclamation of a theatre will be new to you."

And then he put down his trumpet, and began a violen clapping of his hands.

I actually shook from head to foot ! I felt myself already in Drury Lane, amidst the hubbub of a first night.

"Oh, no!" cried I, "there may be a noise, but it will b, just the reverse." And

I returned his salute with a hissing.

Mr. Sheridan joined Sir Joshua Very warmly.

"O sir," cried I, "you should not run on so, you don't know what mischief you may do!"

Mr. S.-I wish I may-I shall be very glad to be accessory,

Sir j.-She has, certainly, something of a knack at characters; where she got it I don't know, and how she got it, I can'l imagine; but she certainly has it. And to throw it away is——

Mr. S.-Oh, she won't, she will write a comedy, she has promised me she will!

F.B.-Oh! if you both run on in this manner, I shall—"

I was going to say get under the chair, but Mr. Sheridan, interrupting me with a laugh, said,

"Set about one ? very well, that's right."

"Ay," cried Sir Joshua, "that's very right. And You (to Mr. Sheridan) would take anything of hers, would you not? unsight, unseen?" [90]What a point blank question! who but Sir Joshua would have ventured it!

" Yes," answered Mr. Sheridan, with quickness, "and make her a bow and my best thanks into the bargain."

Now my dear Susy, tell me, did you ever hear the fellow to such a speech as this! it was all I could do to sit it.

"Mr. Sheridan," I exclaimed, "are you not mocking me?"

"No, upon my honour! this is what I have meditated to say to you the first time I should have the pleasure of seeing you."

To be sure, as Mrs. Thrale says, if folks are to be spoilt, there is nothing in the world so pleasant as spoiling ! But I was never so much astonished, and seldom have been so much delighted, as by this attack of Mr. Sheridan. Afterwards he took my father aside, and formally repeated his opinion that I should write for the stage, and his desire to see my play, with encomiums the most flattering of "Evelina."

And now, my dear Susy, if I should attempt the stage, I think I may be fairly acquitted of presumption, and however I may fall, that I was strongly pressed to try by Mrs. Thrale, and by Mr. Sheridan, the most successful and powerful of all dramatic living authors, will abundantly excuse my temerity.

AN ARISTOCRATIC RADICAL OF THE LAST CENTURY.

Streatham, February.-I have been here so long, MY dearest Susan, Without writing a word, that now I hardly know where or how to begin, But I will try to draw up a concise account of what has passed for this last fortnight, and then endeavour to be more minute.

Mrs. Thrale and Dr. Johnson vied with each other in the kindness of their reception of me. Mr. Thrale was, as usual at first, cold and quiet, but soon, as usual also, warmed into sociality,

The next day Sir Philip Jennings Clerke came. He is not at all a man of letters, but extremely well-bred, nay, elegant, in his manners, and sensible and agreeable in his conversation, He is a professed minority man, and very active and zealous in the opposition. He had, when I came, a bill in agitation concerning contractors—too long a matter to explain upon paper—but which was levelled against bribery and corruption in the ministry, and which he was to make a motion upon in __the House of Commons the next week. [91]

Men of such different principles as Dr. Johnson and Sir Philip YOU W, may imagine, can not have much sympathy or cordiality in their political debates; however, the very superior abilities of the former, and the remarkable good breeding of the latterp have kept both upon good terms; though they have had several arguments, in which each has exerted his utmost force for conquest.

The heads of one of their debates I must try to remember, because I should be sorry to forget. Sir Philip explained his bill; Dr. Johnson at first scoffed at it; Mr. Thrale betted a guinea the motion would not pass, and Sir Philip, that he should divide a hundred and fifty upon it.[92]

Sir Philip, addressing himmself to Mrs. Thrale, hoped she would not suffer the Tories to warp her judgment, and told me he hoped my father had not tainted my principles; and then he further explained his bill, and indeed made it appear so equitable, that Mrs. Thrale gave in to it, and wished her husband to vote for it. He still bung back ; but, to our general surprise, Dr. Johnson having made more particular inquiries into its merits, first softened towards it, and then declared it a very rational and fair bill, and joined with Mrs, Thrale in soliciting Mr. Thrale's vote.

Sir Philip was, and with very good reason, quite delighted. He opened upon politics more amply, and freely declared his opinions, which were so strongly against the government, and so much bordering upon the republican principles, that Dr. Johnson suddenly took fire; he called back his recantation begged Mr. Thrale not to vote for Sir Philip's bill, and grew' very animated against his antagonist.

"The bill," said he, "ought to be opposed by all honest men ! in itself, and considered simply it is equitable, and I would forward it; but when we find what a faction it is to support and encourage, it ought not to be listened to. All men should oppose it who do not wish well to sedition!"

These, and several other expressions yet more strong, he made use of; and had Sir Philip had less unalterable politeness, I believe they would have had a vehement quarrel. He maintained his ground, however, with calmness and steadiness, though he had neither argument nor wit at all equal to such an opponent.

Dr. Johnson pursued him with unabating vigour and dexterity, and at length, though he could not convince, he so entirely baffled him, that Sir Philip was self-compelled to be quiet-which, with a very good grace, he confessed.

Dr. Johnson then, recollecting himself, and thinking, as he owned afterwards, that the dispute grew too serious, with a skill all his own, suddenly and unexpectedly turned it to burlesque; and taking Sir Philip by the hand at the moment we arose after supper, and were separating for the night,

"Sir Philip," said he, "you are too liberal a man for the party to which you belong; I shall have much pride in the honour of converting you; for I really believe, if you were not spoiled by bad company, the spirit of faction would not bav possessed you. Go, then, sir, to the House, but make not your motion! Give up your bill, and surprise the world by turning to the side of truth and reason. Rise, sir, when they least expect you, and address your fellow-patriots to this Purpose:—Gentlemen, I have, for many a weary day, been deceived and seduced by you. I have now opened my eyes; I see that you are all scoundrels—the subversion of all government is your aim. Gentlemen, I will no longer herd among rascals in whose infamy my name and character must be included. I therefore renounce you all, gentlemen, as you deserve to be renounced.' "

Then, shaking his hand heartily, he added,

"Go, sir, go to bed; meditate upon this recantation, and rise in the morning a more honest man than you laid down.

MR. MURPHY, THE DRAMATIST.

On Thursday, while my dear father was here, who should be announced but Mr. Murphy; [93]the man of all other strangers to me whom I most longed to see.

He is tall and well made, has a very gentlemanlike appearance, and a quietness of manner upon his first address that, to me, is very pleasing. His face looks sensible, and his deportment is perfectly easy and polite.

When he had been welcomed by Mrs. Thrale, and had gone through the reception-salutations of Dr. Johnson and my father, Mrs. Thrale, advancing to me, said,

But here is a lady I must introduce to you, Mr. Murphy here is another F. B."

"Indeed!" cried he, taking my hand; "is this a sister of Miss Brown's?"

"No, no; this is Miss Burney."

"What!" cried he, staring; "is this—is this—this is not the lady that—that—"

"Yes, but it is," answered she, laughing.

"'No, you don't say so? You don't mean the lady that—"

"Yes yes I do; no less a lady, I assure you."

He then said he was very glad of the honour of seeing me. I sneaked away. When we came upstairs, Mrs. Thrale charged me to make myself agreeable to Mr. Murphy.

"He may be of use to you, in what I am most eager for, your writing a play: he knows stage business so well; and if you but take a fancy to one another, he may be more able to serve you than all of us put together. My ambition is, that Johnson should write your prologue, and Murphy your epilogue, then I shall be quite happy."

At tea-time, when I went into the library, I found Johnson reading, and Mrs. Thrale in close conference with Mr. Murphy.

"If I," said Mr. Murphy, looking very archly, "had writte a certain book—a book I won't name, but a book I have lately read—I would next write a comedy."

"Good," cried Mrs. Thrale, colouring with pleasure; "you think so too?"

"Yes, indeed; I thought so while I was reading it; it struc me repeatedly."

" Don't look at me, Miss Burney," cried Mrs. Thrale, "for this is no doing of mine. Well, I wonder what Miss Burney will do twenty years hence, when she can blush no more; for now she can never hear the name of her book."

Mr. M.-Nay, I name no book; at least no author: how can I, for I don't know the author; there is no name given to it: I only say, whoever wrote that book ought to write a comedy. Dr. Johnson might write it for aught I know.

F. B.-Oh, yes!

Mr. M.-Nay, I have often told him he does not know his own strength, or he would write a comedy, and so I think.

Dr. j. (laughingSuppose Burney and I begin together?

Mr. M.-Ah, I wish you would! I wish you would Beaumont and Fletcher us!

F.B.-My father asked me, this morning, how my head stood. If he should have asked me this evening, I don't know what answer I must have made.

Mr. M.-I have no wish to turn anybody's head: I speak what I really think;—comedy is the forte of that book. I laughed over it most violently: and if the author—I won't say who [all the time looking away from me]—will write a comedy I will most readily, and with great pleasure, give any advice or assistance in my power.

"Well, now you are a sweet man!" cried Mrs. Thrale, who looked ready to kiss him. "Did not I tell you, Miss Burney, that Mr. Murphy was the man?"

Mr. M.-All I can do, I shall be very happy to do; and at least I will undertake to say I can tell what the sovereigns of the upper gallery will bear: for they are the most formidable part of an audience. I have had so much experience in this sort of work, that I believe I can always tell what will be hissed at least. And if Miss Burney will write, and will show me—

.Dr. J.- Come, come, have done with this now; why should you overpower her? Let's have no more of it. I don't mean to dissent from what you say; I think well of it, and approve of it; but you have said enough of it.

Mr. Murphy, who equally loves and reverences Dr. Johnson, instantly changed the subject.

Yesterday, at night, I asked Dr. Johnson if he would permit me to take a great liberty with him? He assented with the most encouraging smile. And then I said,

"I believe, sir, you heard part of what passed between Mr. Murphy and me the other evening, concerning-a a comedy. Now, if I should make such an attempt, would you be so good as to allow me, any time before Michaelmas, to put it in the coach, for you to look over as you go to town?"

"To be sure, my dear!—What, have you begun a comedy then?

I told him how the affair stood. He then gave me advice which just accorded with my wishes, viz., not to make known that I had any such intention; to keep my own counsel; not to whisper even the name of it; to raise no expectations, which were always prejudicial, and finally, to have it performed while the town knew nothing of whose it was. I readily assured him of my hearty concurrence in his opinion; but he somewhat distressed me when I told him that Mr. Murphy must be in my confidence, as he had offered his services, by desiring he might be the last to see it.

What I shall do, I know not, for he has, himself, begged to be the first. Mrs. Thrale, however, shall guide me between them. He spoke highly of Mr. Murphy, too, for he really loves him. He said he would not have it in the coach, but I should read it to him; however, I could sooner drown or hang!

When I would have offered some apology for the attempt, he stopt me, and desired I would never make any.

"For," said he, "if it succeeds, it makes its own apology, if not——"

"ifnot," quoth I, "I cannot do worse than Dr. Goldsmith, when his play[94]failed,—go home and cry"

He laughed, but told me, repeatedly (I mean twice, which, for him, is very remarkable), that I might depend upon all the service in his power; and, he added, it would be well to make Murphy the last judge, " for he knows the stage," he said, and I am quite ignorant of it."

Afterwards, grasping my hand with the most affectionate warmth, he said,

"I wish you success! I wish you well ! my dear little Burney !"

When, at length, I told him I could stay no longer, and bid him good night, he said, "There is none like you, my dear little Burney ! there is none like you !— good night, my darling!"

A BEAUTY WEEPING AT WILL,

I FIND MIss Streatfield' a very amiable girl, and extremely handsome; not so wise as I expected, but very well; however, had she not chanced to have had so uncommon an education, with respect to literature or learning, I believe she would not have made her way among the wits by the force of her natural parts.

Mr. Seward, you know, told me that she had tears at command, and I begin to think so too, for when Mrs. Thrale, who had previously told me I should see her cry, began coaxing her to stay, and saying, "If you go, I shall know you don't love me so well as Lady Gresham,"—she did cry, not loud indeed, nor much, but the tears came into her eyes, and rolled down her fine cheeks.

"Come hither, Miss Burney," cried Mrs. Thrale, "come and see Miss Streatfield cry! "

I thought it a mere badinage. I went to them, but when I saw real tears, I was shocked, and saying "No, I won't look NE at her," ran away frightened, lest she should think I laughed at her, which Mrs. Thrale did so openly, that, as I told her, had she served me so, I should have been affronted with her ever after.

miss Streatfield, however, whether from a sweetness not to be ruffled, or from not perceiving there was any room for taking offence, gently wiped her eyes, and was perfectly composed!

MR. MURPHY'S CONCERN REGARDING FANNY BURNEY'S COEDY.

Streatham, May, Friday. Once more, my dearest Susy, I will attempt journalising, and endeavour, according to my promise, to keep up something of the kind during our absence, however brief and curtailed.

To-day, while Mrs. Thrale was chatting with me in my room, we saw Mr. Murphy drive into the courtyard. Down stairs flew Mrs. Thrale, but, in a few minutes, up she flew again, 'crying,

"Mr. Murphy is crazy for your play—he won't let me rest for it— do pray let me run away with the first act."

Little as I like to have it seen in this unfinished state, she was too urgent to be resisted, so off she made with it.

I did not shew my phiz till I was summoned to dinner. Mr. Murphy, probably out of flummery, made us wait some minutes, and, when he did come, said,

I had much ado not to keep you all longer, for I could hardly get away from some new acquaintances I was just making."

As he could not stay to sleep here, he had only time, after dinner, to finish the first act. He was pleased to commend it very liberally; he has pointed out two places where he thinks I might enlarge, but has not criticised one word; on the contrary, the dialogue he has honoured with high praise.

Brighthelmstone, May 26. The road from Streatham hither is beautiful: Mr., Mrs., Miss Thrale, and Miss Susan Thrale, and I, travelled in a coach, with four horses, and two of the servants in a chaise, besides two men on horseback; so we were obliged to stop for some time at three places on the road.

We got home by about nine o'clock. Mr. Thrale's house is in West Street, which is the court end of the town here, as well as in London. 'Tis a neat, small house, and I have a snug comfortable room to myself. The sea is not many yards from our windows. Our journey was delightfully pleasant, the day being heavenly, the roads in fine order, the prospects charming, and everybody good-humoured and cheerful.

Thursday. just before we went to dinner, a chaise drove up to the door, and from it issued Mr. Murphy. He met with, a very joyful reception; and Mr. Thrale, for the first time in his life, said he was "a good fellow": [95]for he makes it a sort Of TUle to salute him with the title of "scoundrel," or "rascal." They are very old friends; and I question if Mr. Thrale loves any man so well.

He made me many very flattering speeches, of his eagerness to go on with my play, to know what became of the several characters, and to what place I should next conduct them; assuring me that the first act had run in his head ever since he had read it.

In the evening we all, adjourned to Major H-'s, where, besides his own family, we found Lord Mordaunt, son to the Earl of Peterborough,—a pretty, languid, tonnish young man; Mr. Fisher, who is said to be a scholar, but is nothing enchanting as a gentleman; young Fitzgerald, as much the thing as ever; and Mr. Lucius Corcannon.

Mr. Murphy was the life of the party: he was in good spirits,, and extremely entertaining; he told a million of stories, admirably well; but stories won't do upon paper, therefore I shall not attempt to present you with them.

This morning, as soon as breakfast was over, Mr. Murphy said,

"I must now go to the seat by the seaside, with my new set of acquaintance, from whom I expect no little entertainment."

"Ay," said Mrs. Thrale, "and there you'll find us all! I believe this rogue means me for Lady Smatter; but Mrs. Voluble[96]must speak the epilogue, Mr. Murphy."

"That must depend upon who performs the part," answered he.

"Don't talk of it now," cried I, "for Mr. Thrale knows nothing of it."

"I think," cried Mr. Murphy, "you might touch upon his character in 'Censor.'"

"Ay," cried Mr. Thrale, "I expect a knock some time or other; but, when it comes, I'll carry all my myrmidons to cat- call!"

Mr. Murphy then made me fetch him the second act, and walked off with it.

A SCENE ON THE BRIGHTON PARADE.

We afterwards went on the parade, where the soldiers were mustering, and found Captain Fuller's men all half intoxicated, and laughing so violently as we passed by them, that they could hardly stand upright. The captain stormed at them most angrily; but, turning to us, said,

" These poor fellows have just been paid their arrears, and it is so unusual to them to have a sixpence in their pockets, that they know not how to keep it there."

The wind being extremely high, our caps and gowns were blown about most abominably; and this increased the risibility of the merry light infantry. Captain 'Fuller's desire to keep order made me laugh as much as the men's incapacity to obey him; for, finding our flying drapery provoked their mirth, he went up to the biggest grinner, and, shaking him violently by the shoulders, said, "What do you laugh for, sirrah? do you laugh at the ladies?" and, as soon as he had given the reprimand, it struck him. to be so ridiculous, that he was obliged to turn quick round, and commit the very fault he was attacking most furiously.

MR. MURPHY CONSIDERS THE DIALOGUE IS CHARMING: A CESORIOUS LADY.

After tea, the bishop, his lady, Lord Mordaunt, and Mrs. H— seated themselves to play at whist, and Mr. Murphy, coming Up to me, said,

"I have had no opportunity, Miss Burney, to tell you how much I have been entertained this morning, but I have a great deal to say to you about it; I am extremely pleased with it, indeed. The dialogue is charming; and the—"

"What's that?" cried Mrs. Thrale, "Mr. Murphy always flirting with Miss Burney? And here, too, where everybody's watched!"

And she cast her eyes towards Mrs. H—, who is as censorious a country lady as ever locked up all her ideas in a country town. She has told us sneering anecdotes of every woman and every officer in Brighthelm stone. Mr. Murphy, checked by Mrs. Thrale's exclamation, stopt the conversation, and said he must run away, but would return in half-an-hour.

"Don't expect, however, Miss Burney," he said, "I shall bring with me what you are thinking of; no, I can't part with it yet! "

What! at it again cried Mrs. Thrale. " This flirting is incessant ; but it's all to Mr. Murphy's credit."

Mrs. Thrale told me afterwards, that she made these speeches to divert the attention of the company from our subject; for that she found they were all upon the watch the moment Mr. Murphy addressed me, and that the bishop and his lady almost threw down their cards, from eagerness to discover what he meant.

The supper was very gay: Mrs. Thrale was in high spirits, and her wit flashed with incessant brilliancy; Mr. Murphy told several stories with admirable humour; and the Bishop of Peterborough was a worthy third in contributing towards general entertainment. He turns out most gaily sociable. Mrs. H— was discussed, and, poor lady, not very mercifully.

Mrs. Thrale says she lived upon the Steyn, for the pleasure of viewing, all day long, who walked with who, how often the same persons were seen together, and what visits were made by gentlemen to ladies, or ladies to gentlemen. "She often tells me," said the captain,," of my men. 'Oh,' she says, 'Captain Fuller, your men are always after the ladies!'"

"Nay," cried Mrs. Thrale, "I should have thought the officers might have contented her; but if she takes in the soldiers too, she must have business enough."

"Oh, she gets no satisfaction by her complaints; for I only say, 'Why, ma'am, we are all young!—all young and gay!—and how can we do better than follow the ladies?'"

A MILITIA CAPTAIN OFFICIATES As BARBER.

Saturday, May 29. After breakfast, Mrs. and Miss Thrale took me to Widget's, the milliner and library-woman on the Steyn. After a little dawdling conversation, Captain Fuller came in to have a little chat. He said he had just gone through a great operation—"I have been," he said, "cutting off the hair of all my men."

"And why ?

"Why, the Duke of Richmond ordered that it should be done, and the fellows swore that they would not submit to it; so I was forced to be the operator myself. I told them they would look as smart again when they had got on their caps; but it went much against them, they vowed, at first, they would not bear such usage; some said they would sooner be run through the body, and others, that the duke should as soon have their heads. I told them I would soon try that, and fell to work myself with them."

"And how did they bear it ?

"Oh, poor fellows, with great good-nature, when they found his honour was their barber: but I thought proper to submit to bearing all their oaths, and all their jokes; for they had no other comfort but to hope I should have enough of it, and such sort of wit. Three or four of them, however, escaped, but I Shall find them out. I told them I had a good mind to cut my own hair off too, and then they would have a Captain Crop. I shall soothe them to-morrow with a present of new feathers for all their caps."

"HEARTS HAVE AT YE ALL."

Streatham, Sunday, June 13. After church we all strolled the grounds, and the topic of our discourse was Miss Streatfield. Mrs. Thrale asserted that she had a power of captivation that was irresistible ; that her beauty, joined to her softness, her caressing manners, her tearful eyes, and alluring looks, would insinuate her into the heart of any man she thought worth attacking.

Sir Philip[97]declared himself of a totally different opinion, ?,:'and quoted Dr. Johnson against her, who had told him that, taking away her Greek, she was as ignorant as a butterfly.

Mr. Seward declared her Greek was all against her, with him, for that, instead of reading Pope, Swift, or "The Spectator"— books from which she might derive useful knowledge and improvement—it had led her to devote all her reading time to the first eight books of Homer.

"But," said Mrs. Thrale, "her Greek, you must own, has made all her celebrity:—you would have heard no more of her than of any other pretty girl, but for that."

"What I object to," said Sir Philip, "is her avowed Preference for this parson. Surely it is very indelicate in any lady to let all the world know with whom she is in love ! "

"The parson," said the severe Mr. Seward, "I suppose, spoke first,—or she would as soon have been in love with you, or with me!"

You will easily believe I gave him no pleasant look. He wanted me to slacken my pace, and tell him, in confidence, my private opinion of her : but I told him, very truly, that as I knew her chiefly by account, not by acquaintance, I had not absolutely formed my opinion.

"Were I to live with her four days," said this odd man, "I believe the fifth I should want to take her to church."

"You'd be devilish tired of her, though," said Sir Philip, "in half a year. A crying wife will never do!"

"Oh, yes," cried he, "the pleasure of soothing her would make amends."

"Ah," cried Mrs. Thrale, "I would insure her power of crying herself into any of your hearts she pleased. I made her cry to Miss Burney, to show how beautiful she looked in tears." "

"If I had been her," said Mr. Seward, "I would never have visited you again."

"Oh, but she liked it," answered Mrs. T., "for she knows how well she does it. Miss Burney would have run away, but she came forward on purpose to show herself. I would have done so by nobody else - but Sophy Streatfield is never happier than when the tears trickle from her fine eyes in company."

"Suppose, Miss Burney," said Mr. Seward, "we make her the heroine of our comedy? and call it "Hearts have at ye all?""

"Excellent," cried I, "it can't be better."

GIDDY MISS BROWN.

At dinner we had three persons added to our company,—my dear father, Miss Streatfield, and Miss Brown.

Miss Brown, as I foresaw, proved the queen of the day. Miss Streatfield requires longer time to make conquests. She is, indeed, much more really beautiful than Fanny Brown; but Fanny Brown is much more showy, and her open, goodhumoured, gay, laughing face inspires an almost immediate wish of conversing and merry-making with her. Indeed, the two days she spent here have raised her greatly in my regard. She is a charming girl, and so natural, and easy, and sweet-tempered, that there is no being half an hour in her company without ardently wishing her well.

Next day at breakfast, our party was Sir Philip, Mr. Fuller, Miss Streatfield, Miss Brown, the Thrales, and I.

The first office performed was dressing Miss Brown. She had put on bright, jonquil ribbons. Mrs. Thrale exclaimed against them immediately; Mr. Fuller half joined her, and away she went, and brought green ribbons of her own, which she made Miss Brown run up stairs with to put on. This she did with the utmost good humour; but dress is the last thing in which she excels; for she has lived so much abroad, and so much with foreigners at home, that she never appears habited as an Englishwoman, nor as a high-bred foreigner, but rather as an Italian Opera-dancer; and her wild, careless, giddy manner, her loud hearty laugh, and general negligence of appearance, contribute to give her that air and look. I like her so much, that I am quite sorry she is not better advised, either by her own or some friend's judgment.

Miss Brown, however, was queen of the breakfast: for though her giddiness made everybody take liberties with her, her goodhumour made everybody love her, and her gaiety made everybody desirous to associate with her. Sir Philip played with her as with a young and sportive kitten; Mr. Fuller laughed and chatted with her; and Mr. Seward, when here, teases and torments her. The truth is, he cannot bear her, and she, in return, equally fears and dislikes him, but still she cannot help attracting his notice.

SOPHY STREATFIELD AGAIN WEEPS TO ORDER.

Wednesday, June 16.—We had.at breakfast a scene, of its sort, the most curious I ever saw.

The persons were Sir Philip, Mr. Seward, Dr. Delap, [98]Miss Streatfield, Mrs. and Miss Thrale, and I. The discourse turning I know not how, upon Miss Streatfield, Mrs. Thrale said,

"Ay I made her cry once for Miss Burney as pretty as could be, but nobody does cry so pretty as the S. S. I'm sure, when she cried for Seward, I never saw her look half so lovely."

"For Seward?" cried Sir Philip; "did she cry for Seward? What a happy dog! I hope she'll never cry for me, for if she does, I won't answer for the consequences!"

"Seward," said Mrs. Thrale, "had affronted Johnson, and then Johnson affronted Seward, and then the S. S. cried."

"OH," cried Sir Philip, "that I had but been here!"

"Nay," answered Mrs. Thrale, "you'd only have seen how like three fools three sensible persons behaved: for my part, I was quite sick of it, and of them too."

Sir P.- But what did Seward do? was he not melted?

Mrs. T.-Not he; he was thinking only of his own affront, and taking fire at that.

Mr. S.-Why, yes, I did take fire, for I went and planted my back to it.

S.S.-And Mrs. Thrale kept stuffing me with toast-and-water.

Sir P.-But what did Seward do with himself? Was not he in extacy? What did he do or say?

Mr. S.-Oh, I said pho, pho, don't let's have any more of this,— it's making it of too much consequence: no more piping, pray.

Sir P.-Well, I have heard so much of these tears, that I would give the universe to have a sight of them.

Mrs. T.-Well, she shall cry again if you like it.

S.S.-No, pray, Mrs. Thrale.

Sir P.- Oh, pray, do ! pray let me see a little of it.

Mrs. T.-Yes, do cry a little, Sopby [in a wheedling voice], pray do! Consider, now, you are going to-day, and it's very hard if you won't cry a little: indeed, S. S., you ought to cry.

Now for the wonder of wonders. When Mrs, Thrale, in a coaxing voice, suited to a nurse soothing a baby, had run on for some time,—while all the rest of us, in laughter, joined in the request,—two crystal tears came into the soft eyes of the S. S., and rolled gently down her cheeks! Such a sight I never saw before, nor could I have believed. She offered not to conceal ordissipate them: on the contrary, she really contrived to have them seen by everybody. She looked, indeed, uncommonly handsome; for her pretty face was not, like Chloe's, blubbered; it was smooth and elegant, and neither her features nor complexion were at all ruffled; nay, indeed, she was smiling all the time.

"Look, look!" cried Mrs. Thrale; "see if the tears are not come already."

Loud and rude bursts of laughter broke from us all at once. How, indeed, could they be restrained? Yet we all stared, and looked and re-looked again and again, twenty times, ere we could believe our eyes. Sir Philip, I thought, would have died in convulsions; for his laughter and his politeness, struggling furiously with one another, made him almost black in the face. Mr. Seward looked half vexed that her crying for him was now so much lowered in its flattery, yet grinned incessantly; Miss Thrale laughed as much as contempt would allow her: but Dr. Delap seemed petrified with astonishment.

When our mirth abated, Sir Philip, colouring violently with his efforts to speak, said,

"I thank you, ma'am, I'm much obliged to you."

But I really believe he spoke without knowing what he was saying.

"What a wonderful command," said Dr. Delap, very gravely, "that lady must have over herself!"

She now took out a handkerchief, and wiped her eyes.

"Sir Philip," cried Mr. Seward, "how can you suffer her to dry her own eyes?—you, who sit next her?"

"I dare not dry them for her," answered he, "because I am not the right man."

"But if I sat next her," returned he, "she would not dry them herself."

"I wish," cried Dr. Delap, "I had a bottle to put them in; 'tis a thousand'pities they should be wasted."

"There, now," said Mrs. Thrale, "she looks for all the world as if nothing had happened; for, you know, nothing has happened!"

"Would you cry, Miss Burney," said Sir Philip, "if we asked you?"

"She can cry, I doubt not," said Mr. Seward, "on any Proper occasion."

"But I must know," said I, "what for." I did not say this loud enough for the S. S. to hear me, but if I had, she would not have taken it for the reflection it meant. She seemed, the whole time, totally insensible to the numerous strange and, indeed, impertinent speeches which were made and to be very well satisfied that she was only manifesting a tenderness of disposition, that increased her beauty of countenance. At least, I can put no other construction upon her conduct which was, without exception, the strangest I ever saw. Without any pretence of affliction,-to weep merely because she was bid, though bid in a manner to forbid any one else,—to be in good spirits all the time,—to see the whole company expiring of laughter at her tears, without being at all offended, and, at last, to dry them up, and go on with the same sort of conversation she held before they started!

" EVERYTHING A BORE."

Sunday, June 20,-While I was sitting with Mr. Thrale, in the library, Mr. Seward entered. As soon as the first inquiries were over, he spoke about what he calls our comedy, and he pressed and teazed me to set about it. But he grew, in the evening, so queer, so ennuy`e, that, in a fit of absurdity, I called him "Mr. Dry;" and the name took so with Mrs. Thrale, that I know not when he will lose it. Indeed, there is something in this young man's alternate drollery and lassitude, entertaining qualities and wearying complaints, that provoke me to more pertness than I practise to almost anybody.

The play, he said, should have the double title of "The Indifferent Man, or Everything a Bore;" and I protested Mr. Dry should be the hero. And then we ran on, jointly planning a succession of ridiculous scenes;—he lashing himself pretty freely though not half so freely, or so much to the purpose, as I lashed him; for I attacked him, through the channel of Mr, Dry, upon his ennui, his causeless melancholy, his complaining languors, his yawning inattention, and his restless discontent. You may easily imagine I was in pretty high spirits to go so far: in truth, nothing else could either have prompted or excused my facetiousness : and his own manners are so cavalier, that they always, with me, stimulate a sympathising return.

He repeatedly begged me to go to work, and commit the projected scenes to paper: but I thought that might be carrying the jest too far; for as I was in no humour to spare him, writtten raillery might, perhaps, have been less to his taste than verbal.

He challenged me to meet him the next morning, before breakfast, in the library, that we might work together at some scenes, but I thought it as well to let the matter drop, and did not make my entry till they were all assembled.

He, however, ran upon nothing else ; and, as soon as we happened to be left together, he again attacked me.

"Come," said he, "have you nothing ready yet? I dare say you have half an act in your pocket."

"No," quoth I, "I have quite forgot the whole business; I was only in the humour for it last night."

"How shall it begin?" cried he; "with Mr. Dry in his study?— his slippers just on, his hair about his ears,—exclaiming, 'O what a bore is life!—What is to be done next?"

"Next?" cried I, "what, before he has done anything at all?"

"Oh, he has dressed himself, you know.—Well, then he takes up a book—"

"For example, this," cried I, giving him Clarendon's History.

He took it up in character, and flinging it away, cried

"No—this will never do,—a history by a party writer is vodious."

I then gave him Robertson's "America."

"This," cried he, "is of all reading the most melancholy;—an account of possessions we have lost by our own folly."

I then gave him Baretti's "Spanish Travels."

"Who," cried he, flinging it aside, "can read travels by a fellow who never speaks a word of truth."

Then I gave him a volume of "Clarissa."

"Pho," cried he, "a novel writ by a bookseller!—there is but one novel now one can bear to read,—and that's written by a young lady."

I hastened to stop him with Dalrymple's Memoirs, and then proceeded to give him various others, upon all which he made severe, splenetic, yet comical comments;—and we continued thus employed till he was summoned to accompany Mr. Thrale to town.

The next morning, Wednesday, I had some very serious talk with Mr. Seward,—and such as gave me no inclination for railery, though it was concerning his ennui; on the contrary, I resolved, athe the moment, never to rally him upon that subject again, for his account of himself filled me with compassion.

He told me that he had never been well for tbree hours in a day in his life, and that when he was thought only tired he was really so ill that he believed scarce another man would stay in company. I was quite shocked at this account, and told him, honestly, that I had done him so little justice as to attribute all his languors to affectation.

PROPOSED MATCH BETWEEN MR. SEWARD AND THE WEPER-

AT-WILL.

When Mrs. Thrale joined us, Mr. Seward told us he had just seen Dr. Jebb.—Sir Richard, I mean,—and that he had advised him to marry.

"No," cried Mrs. Thrale, "that will do nothing for you; but if you should marry, I have a wife for you."

"Who?" cried he, "the S. S.?"

"The S. S.?—no!—she's the last person for you,—her extreme softness, and tenderness, and weeping, would add languor to languor, and irritate all your disorders; 'twould be drink to a dropsical man."

"No, no,-it would soothe me."

"Not a whit ! it would only fatigue you. The wife for you is Lady Anne Lindsay. She has birth, wit, and beauty, she has no fortune, and she'd readily accept you; and she is such a spirit that she'd animate you, I warrant you! O, she would trim you well! you'd be all alive presently. She'd take all the care of the money affairs,—and allow you out of them eighteen pence a week! That's the wife for you!"

Mr. Seward was by no means " agreeable " to the proposal; he turned the conversation upon the S. S., and gave us an account of two visits he had made her, and spoke in favour of her manner of living, temper, and character. When he had run on in this strain for some time, Mrs. Thrale cried,

"Well, so you are grown very fond of her?"

"Oh dear, no!" answered he, drily, "not at all!"

" Why, I began to think," said Mrs. Thrale, "you intended to supplant the parson."

"No, I don't: I don't know what sort of an old woman she'd make; the tears won't do then. Besides, I don't think her so sensible as I used to do."

"But she's very pleasing," cried I, "and very amiable."

"Yes, she's pleasing,—that's certain; but I don't think she reads much; the Greek has spoilt her."

"Well, but you can read for yourself."

"That's true ; but does she work well?"

"I believe she does, and that's a better thing."

"Ay; so it is," said he, saucily, "for ladies; ladies should rather write than read."

"But authors," cried I, "before they write should read."

Returning again to the S. S., and being again rallied about her by Mrs. Thrale, who said she believed at last he would end there,-he said,

"Why, if I must marry—if I was bid to choose between that and racking on the wheel, I believe I should go to her."

We all laughed at this exquisite compliment; but, as he said, it was a compliment, for though it proved no passion for her, it proved a preference.

"However," he continued, "it won't do."

"Upon my word," exclaimed I, "you settle it all your own way!- -the lady would be ready at any rate!"

"Oh yes ! any man might marry Sophy Streatfield."

I quite stopt to exclaim against him.

"I mean," said he, "if he'd pay his court to her."

THE FATE OF "THE WITLINGS."

(FANNY BUrney to Mr. Crisp.)

Friday, July 30This seems a strange, unseasonable period for my undertaking, but yet, my dear daddy, when you have read my conVersation with Mr. Sheridan, I believe you will agree that I must have been wholly insensible, nay, almost ungrateful, to resist encouragement such as he gave me—nay, more than encouragement, entreaties, all of which he warmly repeated to my father.

Now, as to the play itself, I own I had wished to have been the bearer of it when I visit Chesington; but you seem so urgent, and my father himself is so desirous to carry it you, that I have given that plan up.

O my dear daddy, if your next letter were to contain your real opinion of it, how should I dread to open it! Be, however, as honest as your good nature and delicacy will allow you to be, and assure yourself I shall be very certain that all your criticisms will proceed from your earnest wishes to obviate those of others, and that you would have much more pleasure in being my panegyrist.

As to Mrs. Gast, I should be glad to know what I would refuse to a sister of yours. Make her, therefore, of your coterie, if she is with you while the piece is in your possession.

And now let me tell you what I wish in regard to this affair. I should like that your first reading should have nothing to do with me-that you should go quick through it, or let my father read it to you-forgetting all the time, as much as you can, that Fannikin is the writer, or even that it is a play in manuscript, and capable of alterations ;-and then, when you have done, I should like to have three lines, telling me, as nearly as you can trust my candour, its general effect. After that take it to your own desk, and lash it at your leisure.

(Fanny Burney to Dr. Burney.)

The fatal knell, then, is knolled, and down among the dead men sink the poor " Witlings "-for ever, and for ever, and for ever!

I give a sigh, whether I will or not, to their memory! for, however worthless, they were mes enfans. You, my dear sir, who enjoyed, I really think, even more than myself, the astonishing success of my first attempt, would, I believe, even more than myself, be hurt at the failure of my second; and I am sure I speak from the bottom of a very honest heart, when I most solemnly declare, that upon your account any disgrace would mortify and afflict me more than upon my own ; for whatever appears with your knowledge, will be naturally supposed to have met with your approbation, and, perhaps, your assistance; therefore, though all particular censure would fall where it ought—upon me—yet any general censure of the whole, and the plan, would cruelly, but certainly involve you in its severity.

You bid me open my heart to you,—and so, my dearest sir, I will, for it is the greatest happiness of my life that I dare be sincere to you. I expected many objections to be raised—a thousand errors to be pointed out-and a million of alterations to be proposed; but the suppression of the piece were words I did not expect; indeed, after the warm approbation of Mrs. Thrale, and the repeated commendations and flattery of Mr. Murphy, how could I?

I do not, therefore, pretend to wish you should think a decision, for which I was so little prepared, has given me no disturbance ; for I must be a far more egregious witling than any of those I tried to draw, to imagine you could ever credit that I wrote without some remote hope of success now—though I literally did when I composed "Evelina"!

But ny mortification is not at throwing away the characters, or the contrivance;—it is all at throwing away the time,—which I with difficulty stole, and which I have buried in the mere trouble of writing.

(Fanny Burney to Mr. Crisp.)

Well! there are plays that are to be saved, and plays that are not to be saved! so good night, Mr. Dabbler!—good night, Lady Smatter,—Mrs. Sapient,—Mrs. Voluble,—Mrs. Wheedle,—Censor,— Cecilia,—Beaufort,—and you, you great oaf, Bobby!—good night! good night!

And good morning, Miss Fanny Burney!—I hope you have opened your eyes for some time, and will not close them in so drowsy a fit again—at least till the full of the moon.

I won't tell you, I have been absolutely ravie with delight at the fall of the curtain; but I intend to take the affair in the tant miemx manner, and to console myself for your censure by this greatest proof I have ever received of the sincerity, candour, and, let me add, esteem, of my dear daddy. And as I happen to love myself rather more than my play, this consolation is not a very trifling one.

As to all you say of my reputation and so forth, I perceive the kindness of your endeavours to put me in humour with myself, and prevent my taking huff, which, if I did, I should deserve to receive, upon any future trial, hollow praise from you,—and the rest from the public.[99]

The only bad thing in this affair is, that I cannot take the comfort of my poor friend Dabbler, by calling you a crabbed fellow, because you write with almost more kindness than ever neither can I (though I try hard) persuade myself that you have not a grain of taste in your whole composition. This, however, seriously I do believe, that when my two daddies put their heads together to concert for me that hissing, groaning, catcalling epistle they sent me, they felt as sorry for poor little Miss Bayes as she could possibly do for herself.
[100]

"QUITE WHAT WE CALL," AND "GIVE ME LEAVE To TELL YO."

We HAd Lady Ladd at Streatham; Mr. Stephen Fuller, the sensible, but deaf old gentleman I have formerly mentioned, dined here also; as did Mr. R— ,[101]whose trite, settled, tonish emptiness of discourse is a never-failing source of laughter and diversion.

"Well, I say, what, Miss Burney, so you had a very good party last Tuesday?—what we call the family party—in that Sort of way? Pray who had you?"

"Mr. Chamier." [102]

"Mr. Chamier, ay? Give me leave to tell you, Miss Burney, that Mr. Chamier is what we call a very sensible man!"

"Certainly. And Mr. Pepys." [103]

"Mr. Pepys? Ay, very good—very good in that sort of way. I am quite sorry I could not be here; but I was so much indisposed— quite what we call the nursing party."

"I'm very sorry; but I hope little Sharp[104]is well?

"Ma'am, your most humble! you're a very good lady, indeed!—quite what we call a good lady! Little Sharp is perfectly well: that sort of attention, and things of that sort,—the bow-wow system is very well. But pray, Miss Burney, give me leave to ask, in that sort of way, had you anybody else?"

Yes, Lady Ladd and Mr. Seward."

"So, so!—quite the family system! Give me leave to tell you, Miss Burney, this commands attention!—what we call a respectable invitation! I am sorry I could not come, indeed; for we young men, Miss Burney, we make it what we call a sort of rule to take notice of this sort of attention. But I was extremely indisposed, indeed—what we call the walnut system had quite—— Pray what's the news, Miss Burney?—in that sort of way, is there any news?"

"None, that I have heard. Have you heard any?"

"Why, very bad! very bad, indeed!—quite what we call poor old England! I was told, in town,—fact—fact, I assure you—that these Dons intend us an invasion this very month, they and the Monsieurs intend us the respectable salute this very month;—the powder system, in that sort of way! Give me leave to tell you, Miss Burney, this is what we call a disagreeable visit, in that sort of way."

I think, if possible, his language looks more absurd upon paper even than it sounds in conversation, from the perpetual recurrence of the same words and expressions—-

THE CRYING BEAUTY AND HER MOTHER.

BrighthelMSTONE, October 12-On Tuesday Mr., Mrs., Miss Thrale, and "yours, ma'am, yours," set out on their expedition. The day was very pleasant, and the journey delightful.

We dined very comfortably at Sevenoaks, and thence made but one stage to Tunbridge. It was so dark when we went through the town that I could see it very indistinctly. The Wells, however, are about seven miles yet further, so that we saw that night nothing ; but I assure you, I felt that I was entering into a new country pretty roughly, for the roads were so sidelum and jumblum, as Miss L— called those of Teignmouth, that I expected an overturn every minute. Safely, however, we reached the Sussex Hotel, at Tunbridge Wells.

Having looked at our rooms, and arranged our affairs, we proceeded to Mount Ephraim, where Miss Streatfield resides. We found her with only her mother, and spent the evening there.

Mrs. Streatfield is very—very little, but perfectly well made, thin, genteel, and delicate. She has been quite beautiful, and has still so much of beauty left, that to call it only the remains of a fine face seems hardly doing her justice. She is very lively, and an excellent mimic, and is, I think, as much superior to her daughter in natural gifts as her daughter is to her in acquired ones: and how infinitely preferable are parts without education to education without parts!

The fair S. S. is really in higher beauty than I have ever yet seen her; and she was so caressing, so soft, so amiable, that I felt myself insensibly inclining to her with an affectionate regard. "If it was not for that little, gush," as Dr. Delap Said, I should certainly have taken a very great fancy to her ; but tears so ready-oh, they blot out my fair opinion of her! Yet whenever I am with her, I like, nay, almost love her, for her manners are exceedingly captivating ; but when I quit her, I do not find that she improves by being thought over-no, nor talked over; for Mrs. Thrale, who is always disposed to half adore her in her presence, can never converse about her without exciting her own contempt by recapitulating what has passed. This, however, must always be certain, whatever may be doubtful, that she is a girl in no respect like any other.

But I have not yet done with the mother: I have told you of her vivacity and her mimicry, but her character is yet not half told. She has a kind of whimsical conceit and odd affectation, that, joined to a very singular sort of humour, makes her always seem to be rehearsing some scene in a comedy. She takes off, if she mentions them, all her own children, and, though she quite adores them, renders them ridiculous with all her power. She laughs at herself for her smallness and for her vagaries, just with the same ease and ridicule as if she were speaking Of some other person ; and, while perpetually hinting at being old and broken, she is continually frisking, flaunting, and playing tricks, like a young coquet.

When I was introduced to her by Mrs. Thrale, who said, "Give me leave, ma'am, to present to you a friend of your daughter's—Miss Burney," she advanced to me with a tripping pace, and, taking one of my fingers, said, "Allow me, ma'am, will you, to create a little -acquaintance with you."

And, indeed, I readily entered into an alliance with her, for I found nothing at Tunbridge half so entertaining, except, indeed, Miss Birch, of whom hereafter.

A BEWITCHING PRODIGY.

Tunbridge Wells is a place that to me appeared very Singular; the country is all rock, and every part of it is either up or down hill, scarce ten yards square being level ground in the whole place: the houses, too, are scattered about in a strange wild manner, and look as if they had been dropt where they stand by accident, for they form neither streets nor squares, but seem strewed promiscuously, except, indeed, where the shopkeepers live, who have got two or three dirty little lanes, much like dirty little lanes in other places,

In the evening we all went to the rooms. The rooms, as they are called, consisted for this evening, of only one apartment, as there was not company enough to make more necessary, and a very plain, unadorned, and ordinary apartment that was.

The next morning we had the company of two young ladies at breakfast-the S. S. and a Miss Birch, a little girl but ten years old, whom the S. S. invited, well foreseeing how much we should all be obliged to her. This Miss Birch is a niece of the charming Mrs. Pleydell, [105]and so like her, that I should have taken her for her daughter. yet she is not, now, quite so handsome; but as she will soon know how to display her beauty to the utmost advantage, I fancy, in a few years, she will yet more resemble her lovely and most bewitching aunt. Everybody, she said, tells her how like she is to her aunt Pleydell.

As you, therefore, have seen that sweet woman, only imagine her ten years old, and you will see her sweet niece. Nor does the resemblance rest with the person; she sings like her, laughs like her, talks like her, caresses like her, and alternately softens and animates just like her. Her conversation is not merely like that of a woman already, but like that of a most uncommonly informed, cultivated, and sagacious woman; and at the same time that her understanding is thus wonderfully premature, she can, at pleasure, throw off all this rationality, and make herself a mere playful, giddy, romping child. One moment, with mingled gravity and sarcasm, she discusses characters, and the next, with schoolgirl spirits, she jumps round the room; then, suddenly, she asks, "Do you know such or such a song?" and instantly, with mixed grace and buffoonery, singles out an object, and sings it; and then, before there has been time to applaud her, she runs into the middle of the room, to try some new step in a dance; and after all this, without waiting till her vagaries grow tiresome, she flings herself, with an affectionate air upon somebody's lap, and there, composed and thoughtful, she continues quiet till she again enters into rational conversation.

Her voice is really charming—infinitely the most powerful, as well as sweet, I ever heard at her age. Were she well and constantly taught, she might, I should think, do anything,—

for two or three Italian songs, which she learnt out of only five months' teaching by Parsons, she sung like a little angel, with respect to taste, feeling, and expression; but she now learns of nobody, and is so fond of French songs, for the sake, she says, of the sentiment, that I fear she will have her wonderful abilities all thrown away. Oh, how I wish my father had the charge of her!

She has spent four years out of her little life in France, which has made her distractedly fond of the French operas, "Rose et Colas," "Annette et Lubin," etc., and she told us the story quite through of several I never heard of, always singing the sujet when she came to the airs, and comically changing parts in the duets. She speaks French with the same fluency as English, and every now and then, addressing herself to the S. S.—"Que je vous adore!"—"Ah, permettez que je me mette `a vos pieds!" etc., with a dying languor that was equally laughable and lovely.

When I found, by her taught songs, what a delightful singer she was capable of becoming, I really had not patience to hear her little French airs, and entreated her to give them up, but the little rogue instantly began pestering me with them, singing one after another with a comical sort of malice, and following me round the room, when I said I would not listen to her, to say, "But is not this pretty?—and this?—and this?" singing away with all her might and main.

She sung without any accompaniment, as we had no instrument ; but the S. S. says she plays too, very well. Indeed, I fancy she can do well whatever she pleases.

We hardly knew how to get away from her when the carriage was ready to take us from Tunbridge, and Mrs. Thrale was so much enchanted with her that she went on the Pantiles and bought her a very beautiful inkstand.

"I don't mean, Miss Birch," she said, when she gave it her, "to present you this toy as to a child, but merely to beg you will do me the favour to accept something that may make you now and then remember us."

She was much delighted with this present, and told me, in a whisper, that she should put a drawing of it in her journal.

So you see, Susy, other children have had this whim. But something being said of novels, the S. S. said—

"Selina, do you ever read them?"—And, with a sigh, the little girl answered—

"But too often!—I wish I did not: The only thing i did not like in this seducing little creature was our leave-taking. The S. S. had, as we expected, her fine eyes suffused with tears, and nothing would serve the little Selina, who admires the S. S. passionately, but that she, also, must weep-and weep, therefore, she did, and that in a manner as pretty to look at, as soft, as melting, and as little to her discomposure, as the weeping of her fair exemplar. The child's success in this pathetic art made the tears of both appear to the whole party to be lodged, as the English merchant says, "very near the eyes!"

Doubtful as it is whether we shall ever see this sweet syren again, nothing, as Mrs. Thrale said to her, can be more certain than that we shall hear of her again, let her go whither she will.

Charmed as we all were with her, we all agreed that to have the care of her would be distraction! "She seems the girl in the world," Mrs. Thrale wisely said, "to attain the highest reach of human perfection as a man's mistress!—as such she would be a second Cleopatra, and have the world at her command."

Poor thing! I hope to heaven she willescape such sovereignty and such honours!

AT BRIGHTON: A "CURE." THE JEALOUS CUMBERLANDS.

We left Tunbridge Wells, and got, by dinner time, to our first stage, Uckfield. Our next stage brought us to Brighthelmstone, where I fancy we shall stay till the Parliament calls away Mr. Thrale. [106]

The morning after our arrival, our first visit was from Mr Kipping, the apothecary, a character so curious that Foote[107]designed him for his next piece, before he knew he had already written his last. He is a prating, good-humoured old gossip, who runs on in as incoherent and unconnected a style of discourse as Rose Fuller, though not so tonish.

The rest of the morning we spent, as usual at this place, upon the Steyn, and in booksellers' shops. Mrs. Thrale entered all our names at Thomas's, the fashionable bookseller; but we find he has now a rival, situated also upon the Steyn, who seems to carry away all the custom and all the company. This is a Mr. Bowen, who is just come from London, and who seems just the man to carry the world before him as a shop, keeper. Extremely civil, attentive to watch opportunities Of obliging, and assiduous to make use of them—skilful in discovering the taste or turn of mind of his Customers, and adroit in Putting in their way just such temptations as they are least able to withstand. Mrs. Thrale, at the same time that she sees his management and contrivance, so much admires his sagacity and dexterity, that, though open-eyed, she is as easily wrought upon to part with her money, as any of the many dupes in this place, whom he persuades to require indispensably whatever he shows them. He did not, however, then at all suspect who I was, for he showed me nothing but schemes for raffles, and books, pocket-cases, etc., which weie put up for those purposes. It is plain I c I can have no authoress air, since so discerning a bookseller thought me a fine lady spendthrift, who only wanted occasions to get rid of money.

Sunday morning, as we came out of church, we saw Mrs. Cumberland, one of her sons, and both her daughters. Mrs. Thrale spoke to them, but I believe they did not recollect me. They are reckoned the flashers of the place, yet everybody laughs at them for their airs, affectations, and tonish graces and impertinences.

In the evening, Mrs. Dickens, a lady of Mrs. Thrale's acquaintance, invited us to drink tea at the rooms with her, which we did, and found them much more full and lively than the preceding night. The folks of most consequence with respect to rank, were Lady Pembroke and Lady Di Beauclerk, [108]both of whom have still very pleasing remains of the beauty for which they have been so much admired. But the present beauty, whose remains our children i.e. nieces) may talk of, is a Mrs. Musters, an exceedingly pretty woman, who is the reigning toast of the season.

While Mrs. Thrale, Mrs. Dickens, and I were walking about after tea, we were joined by a Mr. Cure, a gentleman of the former's acquaintance. After a little while he said-

"Miss Thrale is very much grown since she was here last year ; and besides, I think she's vastly altered."

"Do you, sir," cried she, "I can't say I think so."

"Oh vastly!—but young ladies at that age are always altering. To tell you the truth, I did not know her at all."

This, for a little while, passed quietly; but soon after, he exclaimed,

"Ma'am, do you know I have not yet read 'Evelina?"

"Have not you so, sir?" cried she, laughing.

"No, and I think I never shall, for there's no getting it. the booksellers say they never can keep it a moment, and the folks that hire it keep lending it from one to another in such a manner that it is never returned to the library. It's very provoking."

"But," said Mrs. Thrale, "what makes you exclaim about it so to me?"

"Why, because, if you recollect, the last thing you said to me when we parted last year, was—be sure you read 'Evelina.' So as soon as I saw you I recollected it all again. But I wish Miss Thrale would turn more this way."

"Why, what do you mean, Mr. Cure? do you know Miss Thrale now?"

"Yes, to be sure," answered he, looking full at me, "though I protest I should not have guessed at her had I seen her with anybody but you."

"Oh ho!" cried Mrs. Thrale, laughing, "so you mean Miss Burney all this time."

Mr. Cure looked aghast. As soon, I suppose, as he was able, he repeated, in a low voice, "Miss Burney! so then that lady is the authoress of 'Evelina' all this time."

And, rather abruptly, he left us and joined another party.

I suppose he told his story to as many as he talked to, for, in a short time, I found myself so violently stared at that I could hardly look any way without being put quite out of countenance,-particularly by young Mr. Cumberland, a handsome, soft-looking youth, who fixed his eyes upon me incessantly, though but the evening before, when I saw him at Hicks's, he looked as if it would have been a diminution of his dignity to have regarded me twice. One thing proved quite disagreeable to me, and that was the whole behaviour of the whole tribe of the Cumberlands, which I must explain,

Mr. Cumberland, [109]when he saw Mrs. Thrale, flew With eagerness to her and made her take his seat, and he talked to her, with great friendliness and intimacy, as he has been always accustomed to do,-and inquired very particularly concerning her daughter, expressing an earnest desire to see her. But when, some time after, Mrs. Thrale said, "Oh, there is my daughter, with Miss Burney," he changed the discourse abruptly,—never came near Miss Thrale, and neither then nor since, when he has met Mrs. Thrale, has again mentioned her name: and the whole evening lie seemed determined to avoid us both.

Mrs. Cumberland contented herself with only looking at me as at a person she had no reason or business to know.

The two daughters, but especially the eldest, as well as the son, were by no means so quiet; they stared at me every time I came near them as if I had been a thing for a show; surveyed me from head to foot, and then again, and again returned to my face, with so determined and so unabating a curiosity, that it really made me uncomfortable.

All the folks here impute the whole of this conduct to its having transpired that I am to bring out a play this season; for Mr. Cumberland, though in all other respects an agreeable and a good man, is so notorious for hating and envying and spiting all authors in the dramatic line, that he is hardly decent in his behaviour towards them.

He has little reason, at present at least, to bear me any ill-will; but if he is capable of such weakness and malignity as to have taken an aversion to me merely because I can make use of pen and ink, he deserves not to hear of my having suppressed my play, or of anything else that can gratify so illiberal a disposition.

Dr. Johnson, Mr. Cholmondeley, and Mr. and Mrs. Thrale have all repeatedly said to me, "Cumberland no doubt hates you heartily by this time;" but it always appeared to me a speech of mingled fun and flattery, and I never dreamed of its being possible to be true.

A few days since, after tea at Mrs. Dickens's, we all went to the rooms. There was a great deal of company, and among them the Cumberlands. The eldest of the girls, who was walking with Mrs. Musters, quite turned round her whole person every time we passed each other, to keep me in sight, and stare at me as long as possible; so did her brother, I never saw anything so ill-bred and impertinent; I protest I was ready to quit the rooms to avoid them - till at last Miss Thrale, catching Miss Cumberland's eye, gave her so full, determined, and downing a stare, that whether cured by shame or by resentment, she forbore from that time to look at either of us. Miss Thrale, with a sort of good-natured dryness, said, "Whenever you are disturbed with any of these starers, apply to me,—I'll warrant I'll cure them. I dare say the girl hates me for it ; but what shall I be the worse for that? I would have served master Dickey[110]so too, only I could not catch his eye."

Oct. 20-We have had a visit from Dr. Delap. He told me that he had another tragedy, and that I should have it to read.

He was very curious to see Mr. Cumberland, who, it seems, has given evident marks of displeasure at his name whenever Mrs. Thrale has mentioned it. That poor man is so wonderfully narrow-minded in his authorship capacity, though otherwise good, humane and generous, that he changes countenance at either seeing or hearing of any writer whatsoever. Mrs. Thrale, with whom, this foible excepted, he is a great favourite, is so enraged with him for his littleness of soul in this respect, that merely to plague him, she vowed at the rooms she would walk all the evening between Dr. Delap and me. I wished so little to increase his unpleasant feelings, that I determined to keep with Miss Thrale and Miss Dickens entirely. One time, though, Mrs. Thrale, when she was sitting by Dr. Delap, called me suddenly to her, and when I was seated, said, "Now let's see if Mr. Cumberland will come and speak to me !" But he always turns resolutely another way when he sees her with either of us; though at all other times he is particularly fond of her company.

"It would actually serve him right," says she, "to make Dr. Delap and you strut at each side of me, one with a dagger, and the other with a mask, as tragedy and comedy."

"I think, Miss Burney," said the doctor, "you and I seem to stand in the same predicament. What shall we do for the Poor man? suppose we burn a play apiece?"

"Depend upon it," said Mrs. Thrale, "he has heard, in town, that you are both to bring one out this season, and perhaps one of his own may be deferred on that account."

On the announcement of the carriage, we went into the next room for our cloaks, where Mrs. Thrale and Mr. Cumberland were in deep conversation.

"Oh, here's Miss Burney! " said Mrs. Thrale aloud. Mr Cumberland turned round, but withdrew his eyes instantly; and I, determined not to interrupt them, made Miss Thrale walk away with me. In about ten minutes she left him and we all came home.

As soon as we were in the carriage,

"It has been," said Mrs. Thrale, warmly, "all I could do not to affront Mr. Cumberland to-night!"

"Oh, I hope not cried I, "I would not have you for the world!"

" Why, I have refrained ; but with great difficulty."

And then she told me the conversation she had just had with him. As soon as I made off, he said, with a spiteful tone of voice,

"Oh, that young lady is an author, I hear!"

"Yes," answered Mrs. Thrale, "author of 'Evelina.'"

"Humph,—I am told it has some humour!"

"Ay, indeed! Johnson says nothing like it has appeared for years!"

"So," cried he, biting his lips, and waving uneasily in his chair, "so, so!"

" Yes," continued she, " and Sir Joshua Reynolds told Mr. Thrale he would give fifty pounds to know the author!"

"So, so—oh, vastly well!" cried he, putting his hand on his forehead.

"Nay," added she, "Burke himself sat up all night to finish it!"

This seemed quite too much for him; he put both his hands to his face, and waving backwards and forwards, said,

"Oh, vastly well!—this will do for anything!" with a tone as much as to say, Pray, no more!

Then Mrs. Thrale bid him good night, longing, she said, to call Miss Thrale first, and say, "So you won't speak to my daughter?— why, she is no author."

AN AMUSING CHARACTER: His VIEWS ON MANY SUBJECTS.

October 20.-I must now have the honour to present to you a new acquaintance, who this day dined here.

Mr. B-y, [111]an Irish gentleman, late a commissary in Germany. He is between sixty and seventy, but means to pass for about thirty; gallant, complaisant, obsequious, and humble to the fair sex, for whom he has an awful reverence; but when not immediately addressing them, swaggering, blustering, puffing, and domineering. These are his two apparent characters; but the real man is worthy, moral, religious, though conceited and parading.

He is as fond of quotations as my poor Lady Smatter, [112]and, like her, knows little beyond a song, and always blunders about the author of that. His whole conversation consists in little French phrases, picked up during his residence abroad, and in anecdotes and story-telling, which are sure to be retold daily and daily in the same words.

Speaking of the ball in the evening, to which we were all going, "Ah, madam!" said he to Mrs. Thrale, "there was a time when— fol-de-rol, fol-de-rol [rising, and dancing and Singing], fol-de-rol!—I could dance with the best of them; but now a man, forty and upwards, as my Lord Ligonier used to say—but--fol-de-rol!—there was a time!"

"Ay, so there was, Mr. B——y," said Mrs. Thrale, "and I think you and I together made a very venerable appearance!"

"Ah! madam, I remember once, at Bath, I was called out to dance with one of the finest young ladies I ever saw. I was just preparing to do my best, when a gentleman of my acquaintance was so cruel as to whisper me— 'B——y! the eyes of all Europe are upon you!' for that was the phrase of the times. 'B——y!' says he, 'the eyes of all Europe are upon you!'— I vow, ma'am, enough to make a man tremble!-fol-de-rol, fol-de-rol! [dancing]—the eyes of all Europe are upon you!—I declare, ma'am, enough to put a man out of countenance."

I am absolutely almost ill with laughing. This Mr. B——y half convulses me ; yet I cannot make you laugh by writing his speeches, because it is the manner which accompanies them, that, more than the matter, renders them so peculiarly ridiculous. His extreme pomposity, the solemn stiffness of his person, the conceited twinkling of his little old eyes, and the quaint importance of his delivery, are so much more like some pragmatical old coxcomb represented on the stage, than like anything in real and common life, that I think, were I a man, I should sometimes be betrayed into clapping him for acting so Well. As it is, I am sure no character in any comedy I ever saw has made me laugh more extravagantly.

He dines and spends the evening here constantly, to my great satisfaction.

At dinner, when Mrs. Thrale offers him a seat next her, he regularly says,

"But where are les charmantes?" meaning Miss T. and me. "I can do nothing till they are accommodated!"

And, whenever he drinks a glass of Wine, he never fails to touch either Mrs. Thrale's, or my glass, with "est-il permis?"

But at the same time that he is so courteous, he is proud to a most sublime excess, and thinks every person to whom he speaks honoured beyond measure by his notice, nay, he does not even look at anybody without evidently displaying that such notice is more the effect of his benign condescension, than of any pretension on their part to deserve such a mark of his perceiving their existence. But you will think me mad about this man.

Nov. 3-Last Monday we went again to the ball. Mr. B——y, who was there, and seated himself next to Lady Pembroke, at the top of the room, looked most sublimely happy! He continues still to afford me the highest diversion.

As he is notorious for his contempt of all artists, whom he looks upon with little more respect than upon day-labourers, the other day, when painting was discussed, he spoke of Sir Joshua Reynolds as if he had been upon a level with a carpenter or farrier.

"Did you ever," said Mrs. Thrale, "see his Nativity?"

"No, madam,—but I know his pictures very well; I knew him many years ago, in Minorca; he drew my picture there; and then he knew how to take a moderate price; but now, I vow, ma'am, 'tis scandalous—scandalous indeed! to pay a fellow here seventy guineas for scratching out a head!"

"Sir," cried Dr. Delap, "you must not run down Sir Joshua Reynolds, because he is Miss Burney's friend."

"Sir," answered he, "I don't want to run the man down; I like him well enough in his proper place; he is as decent as any man of that sort I ever knew; but for all that, sir, his prices are shameful. Why, he would not (looking at the poor doctor with an enraged contempt] he would not do your head under seventy guineas!"

"Well," said Mrs. Thrale, "he had one portrait at the last exhibition, that I think hardly could be paid enough for; it was of a Mr. Stuart; I had never done admiring it."

"What stuff is this, ma'am!" cried Mr. B-y, "how can two or three dabs of paint ever be worth such a sum as that?"

"Sir," said Mr. Selwyn[113] (always willing to draw him out "you know not how much he is improved since you knew him in Minorca; he is now the finest painter, perhaps, in the world."

"Pho, pho, sir," cried he, "how can you talk so? you, Mr. Selwin, who have seen so many capital pictures abroad?

"Come, come, sir," said the ever odd Dr. Delap, "you must not go on so undervaluing him, for, I tell you, he is a friend of Miss Burney's."

"Sir," said Mr. B—y, "I tell you again I have no objection to the man; I have dined in his company two or three times; a very decent man he is, fit to keep company with gentlemen; but, ma'am, what are all your modern dabblers put together to one ancient? nothing!—a set of—not a Rubens among them! I vow, ma'am, not a Rubens among them!" .....

To go on with the subject I left off with last—my favourite subject you will think it—Mr. B-y. I must inform you that his commendation was more astonishing to me than anybody's could be, as I had really taken it for granted he had hardly noticed my existence. But he has also spoken very well of Dr. Delap-that is to say, in a very condescending manner. " That Mr. Delap," said he, " seems a good sort of .man ; I wish all the cloth were like him; but, lackaday! 'tis no such thing; the clergy in general are but odd dogs."

Whenever plays are mentioned, we have also a regular speech about them. "I never," he says, "go to a tragedy,—it's too affecting; tragedy enough in real life: tragedies are only fit for fair females; for my part, I cannot bear to see Othello tearing about in that violent manner—and fair little Desdemona, ma'am, 'tis too affecting! to see your kings and your princes tearing their pretty locks,—oh, there's no standing it! 'A straw-crown'd monarch,'—what is that, Mrs. Thrale?

'A straw-crown'd monarch in mock majesty.'

I can't recollect now where that is; but for my part, I really Cannot bear to see such sights. And then out come the white handkerchiefs, and all their pretty eyes are wiping, and then come poison and daggers, and all that kind of thing,— O ma'am, 'tis too much; but yet the fair tender hearts, the pretty little females, all like it!"

This speech, word for word, I have already heard from him literally four times.

When Mr. Garrick was mentioned, he honoured him with much the same style of compliment as he had done Sir Joshua Reynolds.

"Ay, ay," said he, "that Garrick was another of those fellows that people run mad about. Ma'am, 'tis a shaine to think of such things! an actor living like a person of quality scandalous! I vow, scandalous!"

"Well,—commend me to Mr. B—y!" cried Mrs. Thrale "for he is your only man to put down all the people that everybody else sets up."

"Why, ma'am," answered he, "I like all these people very well in their proper places ; but to see such a set of poor beings living like persons of quality,—'tis preposterous! common sense, madam, common sense is against that kind of thing. As to Garrick, he was a very good mimic, an entertaining fellow enough, and all that kind of thing - but for an actor to live like a person of quality—oh, scandalous!"

Some time after the musical tribe was mentioned. He was at cards at the time with Mr. Selwyn, Dr. Delap, and Mr. Thrale, while we "fair females," as he always calls us, were speaking of Agujari. [114]He constrained himself from flying out as long as he was able ; but upon our mentioning her having fifty pounds a song, he suddenly, in a great rage, called out, "Catgut and rosin !ma'am, 'tis scandalous!" . . .

The other day, at dinner, the subject was married life, and among various husbands and wives Lord L— being mentioned, Mr. B—y pronounced his panegyric, and called him his friend. Mr. Selwyn, though with much gentleness, differed from him in opinion, and declared he could not think well of him, as he knew his lady, who was an amiable woman, was used very ill by him.

"How, sir? " cried Mr. B—y.

"I have known him," answered Mr. Selwyn, "frequently pinch her till she has been ready to cry with pain, though she has endeavoured to prevent its being observed."

"And I," said Mrs. Thrale, "know that he pulled her nose, in his frantic brutality, till he broke-some of the vessels of it, and when she was dying she still found the torture he had given her by it so great, that it was one of her last complaints."

The general, who is all for love and gallantry, far from attempting to vindicate his friend, quite swelled with indignation It this account, and, after a pause, big with anger, exclaimed,

"Wretched doings, sir, wretched doings!"

"Nay, I have known him," added Mr. Selwyn, "insist upon handing her to her carriage, and then, with an affected kindness, pretend to kiss her hand, instead of which he has almost bit a piece out of it."

"Pitiful!—pitiful! sir," cried the General, "I know nothing more shabby!"

"He was equally inhuman to his daughter," said Mrs. Thrale, "for, in one of his rages, he almost throttled her."

"Wretched doings!" again exclaimed Mr. B—y, "what! cruel to a fair female! Oh fie! fie! fie!—a fellow who can be cruel to females and children, or animals, must be a pitiful fellow indeed. I wish we had had him here in the sea. I should like to have had him stripped, and that kind of thing, and been well banged by ten of our clippers here with a cat-o'-nine-tails. Cruel to a fair female? Oh fie! fie! fie!"

I know not how this may read, but I assure you its sound was ludicrous enough.

However, I have never yet told you his most favourite story, though we have regularly heard it three or four times a day —And this is about his health.

"Some years ago," he says,—" let's see, how many? in the year '71,—ay, '71, '72—thereabouts—I was taken very ill, and, by ill-luck, I was persuaded to ask advice of one of these Dr. Gallipots:—oh, how I hate them all! Sir, they are the vilest pick-pockets—know nothing, sir! nothing in the world! poor ignorant mortals! and then they pretend—In short, sir, I hate them all!- I have suffered so much by them, sir—lost four years of the happiness of my life—let's see, '71, '72, '73, '74—ay, four years, sir!—mistook my case, sir !—and all that kind of thing. Why, sir, my feet swelled as big as two horses' heads! I vow I will never consult one of these Dr. Gallipot fellows again! lost me, sir, four years of the happiness of my life!—why, I grew quite an object!—you would hardly have known me!—lost all the calves of my legs!—had not an ounce of flesh left!—and as to the rouge— why, my face was the colour of that candle!—those deuced Gallipot fellows!— why, they robbed me of four years—let me see, ay, '71, '72—"

And then it was all given again!

We had a large party of gentlemen to dinner. Among them was Mr. Hamilton, commonly called Single-speech Hamilton, from having made one remarkable speech in the House of Commons against government, and receiving some douceur to be silent ever after. This Mr. Hamilton is extremely tall and handsome; has an air of haughty and fashionable superiority; is intelligent, dry, sarcastic, and clever. I should have received much pleasure from his conversational powers, had I not previously been prejudiced against him, by hearing that he is infinitely artful, double, and crafty.

The dinner conversation was too general to be well remembered; neither, indeed, shall I attempt more than partial scraps relating to matters of what passed when we adjourned to tea.

Mr. Hamilton, Mr. Selwyn, Mr. Tidy, and Mr. Thrale seated themselves to whist ; the rest looked on : but the General, as he always does, took up the newspaper, and, with various comments, made aloud, as he went on reading to himself, diverted the whole company. Now he would cry, "Strange! strange that!"—presently, "What stuff! I don't believe a word of it!"—a little after, "Mr. Bate, [115]I wish your ears were cropped!"—then, "Ha! ha! ha! funnibus! funnibus! indeed!"—and, at last, in a great rage, he exclaimed, "What a fellow is this, to presume to arraign the conduct of persons of quality!"

Having diverted himself and us in this manner, till he had read every column methodically through, he began all over again, and presently called out, "Ha! ha! here's a pretty thing!" and then, in a plaintive voice, languished out some wretched verses.

73 This was not the famous philosopher and statesman, but the Rev. Thomas Franklin, D.D., who was born in 1721, and died in 1784. He published various translations from the classics, as well as plays and miscellaneous works; but is best known for his translation of Sophocles, published in 1759.-ED.

74 "Warley: a Satire," then just published, by a Mr. Huddisford. "Dear little Burney's" name was coupled in it with that of Sir Joshua Reynolds, in a manner which seemed to imply that Sir Joshua had special reasons for desiring her approbation. It will be remembered that, before he knew that Miss Burney was the author of "Evelina," Sir Joshua had jestingly remarked that If the author proved to be a woman, he should be sure to make love to her. See ante, p. 94.-ED.

75 Mrs. Horneck and Mrs. Bunbury (her eldest daughter) had declared that they would walk a hundred and sixty miles, to see the author of "Evelina."-ED.

76 See note 37 ante, p. 68.-ED,

77 A kinsman of the great Edmund Burke, and, like him, a politician and member of Parliament. Goldsmith has drawn his character in "Retaliation."

 "Here lies honest William, whose heart was a mint, While the owner ne'er knew half the good that was in 't; The pupil of impulse, it forced him along, His conduct still right, with his argument wrong Still aiming at honour, yet fearing to roam, The coachman was tipsy, the chariot drove home; Would-you ask for his merits ? alas! he had none; What was good was spontaneous, his faults were his own."-ED.

78 Henry Temple, second Viscount Palmerston, and father of the celebrated Lord Palmerston.-ED.

79 Mrs. Cholmondeley imitates the language of Madame Duval, the Prench woman in "Evelina."-ED.

80 A character in "Evelina."-ED.

81 Sir Joshua Reynolds, who was born at Plympton, in Devonshire, in 1723-ED.

82 Mr. Qwatkin afterwards married Miss Offy Palmer.-ED.

83 Afterwards Lady Crewe; the daughter of Mr, and Mrs. Greville, and a famous Political beauty. At a supper after the Westminster election on the Prince of Wales toasting, "True blue and Mrs. Crewe," the lady responded, "True blue and all of you."-ED.

84 A celebrated Italian singer and intimate friend of the Burneys.-ED.

85 See note 15 ante, p. xxvi. The intended marriage above referred to above came to nothing, Miss Cumberland, the eldest daughter of the dramatist subsequently marrying Lord Edward Bentinck, son of the Duke of Portland.-ED.

86 Miss Hannah More, the authoress.-ED.

87 Hannah More gave Dr. Johnson, when she was first introduced to him, such a surfeit of flattery, that at last, losing patience, he turned to her

and said, "Madam, before you flatter a man so grossly to his face, you should consider whether or not your flattery is worth his having."-ED.

88   Mrs. Vesey was the lady at whose house were held the assemblies from which the term "blue-stocking" first came into use. (.See ante, p. 98.) Fanny writes of her in 1779, "She is an exceeding well-bred woman, and of agreeable manners; but all her name in the world must, I think, have been acquired by her dexterity and skill in selecting parties, and by her address in rendering them easy with one another—an art, hoever, that seems to imply no mean understanding."-ED.

90   Sheridan was at this time manager of Drury-lane Theatre-ED.

91   Sir P. J. Clerke's bill was moved on the 12th of February. It passed the first and second readings, but was afterwards lost on the motion for going into committee. It was entitled a "Bill for restraining any person, being a member of the House of Commons, from being concerned himself, or any person in trust for him, in any contract made by the commissioners of his Majesty's Treasury, the commissioners of the Navy, the board of Ordnance, or by any other person or persons for the public service, Unless the said contract shall be made at a public bidding."-ED.

93   Arthur Murphy, the well-known dramatic author, a very intimate friend of the Thrales. He was born in Ireland in 1727, and died at Knightsbridge in 1805. Among his most successful plays were "The Orphan of China " and "The Way to Keep Hirn."-ED.

94   "The', Good-natured Man."-ED

95   Sophy Streatfield, a young lady who understood Greek, and was consequently looked upon as a prodigy of learning. Mrs. Thrale appears to have been slightly jealous of her about this time, though without serious cause. In January, 1779, she writes (in "Thraliana"): "Mr. Thrale has fallen in love, really and seriously, with Sophy Streatfield; but there is no wonder in that; she is very pretty, very gentle, soft and insinuating; hangs about him, dances round him, cries when she parts from him, squeezes his hand slily, and with her sweet eyes full of tears looks fondly in his face—and all for love of me, as she pretends, that I can hardly sometimes help laughing in her face. A man must not be a man, but an it, to resist such artillery."-ED.

96   Characters in the comedy which Fanny was then engaged upon.-ED.

97   Sir Philip Jennings Clerke-ED,

98   The Rev. John Delap, D.D., born 1725, died 1812. He was a man "of deep learning, but totally ignorant of life and manners," and wrote several tragedies, two or three of which were acted, but generally without success,-ED.

99   Mrs. Piozzi (then Mrs. Thrale) relates this story in her "Anecdotes of Dr. Johnson." "I came into the room one evening where he [Johnson] and a gentleman [Seward], whose abilities we all respect exceedingly, were sitting. A lady [Miss Streatfield], who walked in two minutes

before me, had blown 'em both into a flame by whispering something to Mr. S-d, which he endeavoured to explain away so as not to affront the doctor, whose suspicions were all alive. 'And have a care, sir,' said he, just as I came in, 'the Old Lion will not bear to be tickled.' The other was pale with rage, the lady wept at the confusion she had caused, and I could only say with Lady Macbeth— 'Soh! you've displaced the mirth, broke the good meeting With most admired disorder.'-ED.

100   The following note is in the hand-writing of Miss Burney, at a subsequent period. The objection of Mr. Crisp to the MS play of 'The Witlings,' was its resemblance to Moliere's 'Femmes Savantes,' and consequent immense inferiority. It is, however, a curious fact, and to the author a consolatory one, that she had literally never read the 'Femmes Savantes' when she composed 'The Witlings.'"

101   Mr. Rose Fuller.-ED.

102   Anthony Chamier, M.P. for Tamworth, and an intimate friend of Dr. Burney's. He was Under Secretary of State from 1775 till his death in 1780. We find him at one of Dr. Burney's famous music-parties in 1775. Fanny writes of him then as "an extremely agreeable man, and the very pink of gallantry." ("Early Diary," vol, ii. p. 106.)-ED.

103   Afterwards Sir William Weller Pepys, Master in Chancery, and brother of the physician, Sir Lucas Pepys. He was an ardent lover of literature, and gave "blue-stocking" parties, which Dr. Burney frequently attended. Fanny extols his urbanity and benevolence. See "Memoirs of Dr. Burney," vol. ii. p. 285.-ED.

104   His dog.-ED.

105   Mrs. Pleydell was a friend of Dr. Burney's, and greatly admired for ber beauty and the sweetness of her disposition. She was the daughter of Governor Holwell, one of the survivors from the Dlac Hole of Calcutta.-ED.

106   Mr. Thrale was Member of Parliament for Southwark.-ED.

107   Samuel Foote, the famous actor and writer of farces,-ED.

108   Lady Diana Spencer, eldest daughter of Charles, second Duke of Marlborough. She was born in 1734, married in 177 to Vicount Bolingbroke, divorced from him in 17b8, and married soon after to Dr. Johnson's friend, Topbam Beauclerk. Lady Di was an amateur artist, and the productions of her pencil were much admired by Horace Walpole and other persons of fashion. Elizabeth, Countess of Pembroke, was the sister of Lady Di Beauclerk, being the second daughter of the Duke of Marlborough.-ED.

109   See note 15 ante, p. xxvi.-Ep.

110   Young Cumberland, son of the author.-ED.

111   General Blakeney.-ED.

112   A character in Fanny's suppressed comedy, "The Witlings."-ED.

113   Not the celebrated George Selwyn, but a wealthy banker of that name.-ED.

114   Lucrezia Agujari was one of the most admired Italian singers of the day. She died at Parma in 1783.-ED.

115   The Rev. Henry Bate, afterwards Sir Henry Bate Dudley, editor of the "Morning Post" from its establishment in 1772 till 1780, in which year his connection with that paper came to an end in consequence of a quarrel with his coadjutors. On the 1st of November, 1780, he brought out the "Morning Herald" in opposition to his old paper, the "Post." He assumed the name of Dudley in 1784, was created a baronet in 1813, and died in 1824. Gainsborough has painted the portrait of this ornament of the Church, who was notorious, in his younger days, for his physical strength, and not less so for the very unclerical use which he made of it. He was popularly known as the "Fighting Parson."-ED.

SECTION 3 17801781

A SEASON AT BATH: MR.THRALE'S DEATH.

[THERE is a long hiatus here in the published " Diary," and upon its resumption we find Fanny at Bath with the Thrales, in April, 1780; but from her letters to Mr. Crisp we learn that she returned, at Christmas, 1779, to her father's house in St. Martin's -street, and spent there the intervening period, frequently visiting, and being visited by, the Thrales. Bath was at this time the most fashionable summer resort in the kingdom. Fanny had been there before, in 1776 or 1777, but of that visit no account remains to us. She has recorded, however, in " "Evelina," her general impression of the place. "The charming city of Bath answered all my expectations. The Crescent, the prospect from it, and the elegant symmetry of the Circus, delighted me. The Parades, I own, rather disappointed me; one of them is scarce preferable to some of the best paved streets in London; and the other, though it affords a beautiful prospect, a charming view of Prior-park and of the Avon, yet wanted something in itself of more striking elegance than a mere broad pavement, to satisfy the ideas I had formed of it.

"At the pump-room, I was amazed at the public exhibition of the ladies in the bath; it is true, their heads are covered with bonnets; but the very idea of being seen, in such a situation, by whoever pleases to look, is indelicate."

We may be sure Fanny never exhibited herself in such a situation. Of her drinking the waters, even, there is no mention in her Bath journal Of 1780. But the journal records a continual succession of visits and diversions, and keeps us entertained with the most life-like and amusing descriptions of Bath society. The house occupied by Mr. Thrale and his party was at the corner of the South-parade, and Fanny's room commanded that beautiful prospect of Prior-park and the Avon which had charmed Evelina.

Amid all these gaieties there are glimpses of more serious scenes. The Gordon riots took place in June, 1780, and the alarm they occasioned spread far and wide over the country. The present section, too, closes with a melancholy incident—the death of Mr. Thrale. He had been long ailing, and had had a paralytic stroke in 1779. He died on the 4th of April, 1781. Probably no one felt the loss more keenly than Thrale's old friend, 'Dr. Johnson, in whose "Prayers and Meditations" occurs the following touching entry:—

"Good Friday, 13th April, 1781. On Wednesday, 11th, was buried my dear friend Thrale, who died on Wednesday, 4th ; and with him were buried many of my hopes and pleasures. About five, I think, on Wednesday morning he expired. I felt almost the last flutter of his pulse, and looked for the last time upon the face that for fifteen years had never been turned upon me but with respect or benignity."-ED.]

A YOUTHFUL PRODIGY.

Bath, April 7-The journey was very comfortable ; Mr. Thrale was charmingly well and in very good spirits, and Mrs. Thrale must be charming, well or ill. We only went to Maidenhead Bridge the first night, where I found the caution given me by Mr. Smelt, [116]of not attempting to travel near Windsor on a hunting-day, was a very necessary one, as we were with difficulty accommodated even the day after the hunt; several stragglers remaining at all the inns, and we heard of nothing but the king and royal huntsmen and huntswomen. The second day we slept at SDeen Hill, and the third day we reached Devizes.

And here Mrs. Thrale and I were much pleased with our hostess, Mrs. Laurence, who seemed something above her station in her inn. While we were at cards before supper, we were much surprised by the sounds of a pianoforte. I jumped up, and ran to listen whence it proceeded. I found it came from the next room, where the overture to the "Buona Figliuola" was performing. The playing was very decent, but as the music was not quite new to me, my curiosity was not whole ages in satisfying, and therefore I returned to finish the rubber.

Don't I begin to talk in an old-cattish manner of cards?

Well, another deal was hardly played, ere we heard the sound of a voice, and out I ran again. The singing, however, detained me not long, and so back I whisked; but the performance, however indifferent in itself yet' surprised us at the Bear however indifferent in itself, yet surprised us at Devizes, and therefore Mrs. Thrale determined to know from whom it came. Accordingly, she tapped at the door. A very handsome girl, about thirteen years old, with fine dark hair upon a finely-formed forehead, opened it. Mrs. Thrale made an apology for her intrusion, but the poor girl blushed and retreated into a corner of the room: another girl, however, advanced, and obligingly and gracefully invited us in and gave us all chairs. She was just sixteen extremely pretty, and with a countenance better than her features, though those were also very good. Mrs. Thrale made her many compliments, which she received with a mingled modesty and pleasure, both becoming and interesting. She was, indeed, a sweetly pleasing girl.

We found they were both daughters of our hostess, and born and bred at Devizes. We were extremely pleased with them, and made them a long visit, which I wished to have been longer. But though those pretty girls struck us so much, the wonder of the family was yet to be produced. This was their brother, a most lovely boy of ten years of age who seems to be not merely the wonder of their family, but of the times, for his astonishing skill in drawing. [117]They protest he has never had any instruction, yet showed us some of his productions that were really beautiful. Those that were copies were delightful, those of his own composition amazing, though far inferior. I was equally struck with the boy and his works.

We found that he had been taken to town, and that all the painters had been very kind to him, and Sir Joshua Reynolds had pronounced him, the mother said, the most promising genius he had ever met with. Mr. Hoare has been so charmed with this sweet boy's drawings that he intends sending him to Italy with his own son.

This house was full of books, as well as paintings, drawings, and music and all the family seem not only ingenious and industrious, but amiable; added to which, they are strikingly handsome.

LORD MULGRAVE ON THE "SERVICES."

Bath.-I shall now skip to our arrival at this beautiful city which I really admire more than I did, if possible, when I first saw it. The houses are so elegant, the streets are so beautiful, the prospects so enchanting, I could fill whole pages upon the general beauty of the place and country, but that I have neither time for myself, nor incitement for you, as I know nothing tires so much as description.

Monday.-Lord Mulgrave, Augustus Phipps, Miss Cooper, Dr. Harrington, and Dr. Woodward dined with us.

I like Lord Mulgrave[118]very much. He has more wit, and a greater readiness of repartee, than any man I have met with this age. During dinner he was all brilliancy, but I drew myself into a little scrape with him, from which I much wanted some of his wit to extricate myself. Mrs. Thrale was speaking of the House of Commons, and lamenting that she had never heard any debates there.

"And now," said she, "1 cannot, for this General Johnson has turned us all out most barbarously."

"General Johnson?" repeated Lord Mulgrave.

"Ay, or colonel—I don't know what the man was, but I know he was no man of gallantry."

"Whatever he was," said his lordship, "I hope he was a land officer."

"I hope so too, my lord," said she.

"No, no, no," cried Mr. Thrale, "it was Commodore Johnson."

"That's bad, indeed said Lord Mulgrave, laughing. "I thought, by his manners, he had belonged to the army."

"True," said I "they were hardly polished enough for the sea."

This I said `a demi-voix, and meant only for Mrs. Thrale, but Lord Mulgrave heard and drew up upon them, and pointing his finger at me with a threatening air, exclaimed,

"Don't you speak, Miss Burney? What's this, indeed?"

They all stared, and to be sure I rouged pretty high.

"Miss Burney," said Mrs. Thrale, "should be more respectful to be sure, for she has a brother at sea herself."

" I know it," said he, "and for all her, we shall see him come back from Kamschatka as polished a beau as any he will find."

Poor Jem! God send him safe back, polished or rough.

LordMulgrave's brother Edmund is just entered into the army.

"He told me t'other day," said his lordship, "that he did not like the thoughts of being a parson.

"'Very well,' said I, 'you are old enough to choose for yourself; what will you be then?'

"'Why, a soldier,' says he.

"'A soldier? will you so? Why, then, the best thing you can do is to embark with your brother Henry immediately, for you won't know what to do in a regiment by yourself.' Well, no sooner said than done! Henry was just going to the West Indies in Lord Harrington's regiment, and Edmund ordered a chaise and drove to Portsmouth after him. The whole was settled in half an hour."

SARAH, DUCHESS OF MARLBOROUGH.

My sister Gast, in her younger days, was a great favourite with an old lady who was a particular crony and intimate of old Sarah Marlborough, who, though much of the jade, had undoubtedly very strong parts, and was indeed remarkably clever. When Mrs. Hinde (the old lady) would sometimes talk to her about books, she'd cry out, "Prithee, don't talk to me about books; I never read any books but men and cards!" But let anybody read her book, and then tell me if she did not draw characters with as masterly a hand as Sir Joshua Reynolds.— Mr. Crisp to Fanny Burney (April 27.)

THE BYRONS.

Sunday-We had Mrs. Byron and Augusta, [119]and Mrs. Lee, to spend the afternoon. Augusta opened her whole heart to me, as we sat together, and told me all the affairs of her family. Her brother, Captain George Byron, is lately returned from the West Indies, and has brought a wife with him from Earbadoes, though he was there only three weeks, and knew not this girl he has married till ten days before he left it!—a pleasant circumstance for this proud family!

Poor Mrs. Byron seems destined for mortification and humiliation; yet such is her native fire, and so wonderful are her spirits, that she bears up against all calamity, and though half mad one day with sorrow and vexation, is fit the next to entertain an assembly of company;-and so to entertain them as to make the happiest person in the company, by comparison with herself, seem sad.

Augusta is a very amiably ingenuous girl, and I love her the more for her love of her sisters: she talked to me of them all, but chiefly of Sophia, the youngest next to herself, but who, having an independent fortune, has quarrelled with her mother, and lives with one of her sisters, Mrs. Byron, who married a first cousin, And son of Lord Byron. '

"Ah, Miss Burney," she says continually, "if you knew Sophy, you would never bear me! she is so much better than I am, and so handsome, and so good, and so clever,-and I used to talk to her of you by the hour together. She longs so to know you! 'Come,' she says, 'now tell me something more about your darling, Miss Burney.' But I ought to hope you may never see her, for if you did I should be so jealous."

MR. HENRY WILL BE SO MORTIFIED."

Friday was a busy and comical day. We had an engagement of long standing, to drink tea with Miss L-, whither we all went, and a most queer evening did we spend.

When we entered, she and all her company were looking out of the window; however, she found us out in a few minutes, and made us welcome in a strain of delight and humbleness at receiving us, that put her into a flutter of spirits, from which she never recovered all the evening.

Her fat, jolly mother took her seat at the top of the room; next to her sat a lady in a riding habit, whom I soon found to be Mrs. Dobson; [120]below her sat a gentlewoman, prim, upright, neat, and mean; and, next to her, sat another, thin, haggard, wrinkled, fine, and tawdry, with a thousand frippery ornaments and old-fashioned furbelows; she was excellently nick-named, by Mrs. Thrale, the Duchess of Monmouth. On the opposite side was placed Mrs. Thrale, and, next to her, Queeny. For my own part, little liking the appearance of the set, and half dreading Mrs. Dobson, from whose notice I wished to escape, I had made up myself to one of the now deserted windows, and Mr. Thrale had followed me. As to Miss L-, she came to stand by me, and her panic, I fancy, returned, for she seemed quite panting with a desire to say something, and an incapacity to utter it.

It proved happy for me that I had taken this place, for in a few minutes the mean, neat woman, whose name was Aubrey, asked if Miss Thrale was Miss Thrale?

"Yes, ma'am."

"And pray, ma'am, who is that other young lady?" "

A daughter of Dr. Burney's, ma'am."

"What!" cried Mrs. Dobson, "is that the lady that has favoured us with that excellent novel?"

"Yes, ma'am."

.Then burst forth a whole volley from all at once. "Very extraordinary, indeed!" said one;—"Dear heart, who'd have thought it?" said another,—"I never saw the like in my life!" said a third. And Mrs. Dobson, entering more into detail, began praising it through, but chiefly Evelina herself, which she said was the most natural character she had ever met in any book.

Mr. and Mrs. Whalley now arrived, and I was obliged to go to a chair-when such staring followed; they could not have opened their eyes wider when they first looked at the Guildhall giants! I looked with all the gravity and demureness possible, in order to keep them from coming plump to the subject again, and, indeed this, for a while, kept them off.

Soon after, Dr. Harrington[121]arrived, which closed our party. Miss L— went whispering to him, and then came up to me, with a look of dismay, and said,

"O, ma'am, I'm so prodigiously concerned; Mr. Henry won't come!"

"Who, ma'am?"

"Mr. Henry, ma'am, the doctor's son. But, to be sure, he does not know you are here, or else—but I'm quite concerned, indeed, for here now we shall have no young gentlemen!"

"O, all the better," cried I, "I hope we shall be able to do very well without."

"O yes, ma'am, to be sure. I don't mean for any common young gentlemen; but Mr. Henry, ma'am, it's quite another thing;— however, I think he might have come but I did not bappen to mention in my card that you was to be here, and so—but I think it serves him right for not coming to see me."

Soon after the mamma hobbled to me, and began a furious Panegyric upon my book, saying at the same time, "I wonder, Miss, how you could get at them low characters. As to the lords and ladies, that's no wonder at all ; but, as to t'others, why, I have not stirred night nor morning while I've been reading it; if I don't wonder how you could be so clever!"

And much, much more. And, scarcely had she unburthened herself, ere Miss L— trotted back to me, crying, in a tone of mingled triumph and vexation,

"Well, ma'am, Mr. Henry will be very much mortified when he knows who has been here; that he will, indeed; however, I'm sure he deserves it!"

I made some common sort of reply, that I hoped he was better engaged, which she vehemently declared was impossible.

We had now some music. Miss L- sung various old elegies of Jackson, Dr. Harrington, and Linley, and O how I dismalled in hearing them! Mr. Whalley, too, sung "Robin Gray," and divers other melancholic ballads, and Miss Thrale Sang "Ti seguiro fedele." But the first time there was a cessation of harmony, Miss L- again respectfully approaching me, cried,

"O Well, all my comfort is that Mr. Henry will be prodigiously mortified! But there's a ball to-night, so I suppose he's gone to that. However, I'm sure if he had known of meeting you young ladies here—but it's all good enough for him, for not coming."

"Nay," cried I, "if meeting young ladies is a motive with him, he can have nothing to regret while at a ball, where he will see many more than he could here."

"O, ma'am, as to that—but I say no more, because it mayn't be proper; but, to be sure, if Mr. Henry had known—however, he'll be well mortified!" . . .

I was not two minutes relieved, ere Miss I- returned, to again assure me how glad she was that Mr. Henry would be mortified. The poor lady was quite heart-broken that we did not meet.

ALL THE BEST FAMILIES IN THE NAVY.

Tuesday.-Lord Mulgrave called this morning. He is returned to Bath for only a few days. He was not in his usual spirits; yet he failed not to give me a rub for my old offence, which he seems determined not to forget ; for upon something being said, to which, however, I had not attended, about seamen, he cast an arch glance at me, and cried out,

"Miss Burney, I know, will take our parts-if I remember right, she is one of the greatest of our enemies!"

"All the sea captains," said Mrs. Thrale, "fall upon Miss Burney: Captain Cotton, my cousin, was for ever plaguing her about her spite to the navy."

This, however, was for the character of Captain Mirvan, [122]which, in a comical and good-humoured way, Captain Cotton pretended highly to resent, and so, he told me, did all the captains in the navy.

Augusta Byron, too, tells me that the admiral, her father, very often talks of Captain Mirvan, and though the book is very high in his favour, is not half pleased with the captain's being such a brute.

However, I have this to comfort me-that the more I see of sea captains, the less reason I have to be ashamed of Captain Mirvan; for they have all so irresistible a propensity to wanton mischief—to roasting beaus, and detesting old women, that I quite rejoice I showed the book to no one ere printed, lest I should have been prevailed upon to soften his character. Some time after, while Lord Mulgrave was talking of Captain G. Byron's marrying a girl at Barbadoes, whom he had not known a week, he turned suddenly to me, and called out,

"See, Miss Burney, what you have to expect—your brother will bring a bride from Kamschatka, without doubt!"

"That," said I, "may perhaps be as well as a Hottentot, for when he was last out, he threatened us with a sister from the Cape of Good Hope."

Thursday,-Lord Mulgrave and Dr. Harrington dined here. Lord Mulgrave was delightful;—his wit is of so gay, so forcible, so splendid a kind that when he is disposed to exert it, he not only engrosses attention from all the rest of the company, but demands the full use of all one's faculties to keep pace in understanding the speeches, allusions, and sarcasms which he sports. But he will never, I believe, be tired of attacking me about the sea; "he will make me 'eat it that leak,' I assure YOU.

During dinner he was speaking very highly of a sea officer whose name, I think, was Reynolds.

"And who is he?" asked Mrs. Thrale, to which his lordship answered, "Brother to Lord—something, but I forget what;" and then, laughing and looking at me, he added, "We have all the great families in the navy—ay, and all the best families, too,—have we not, Miss Burney? The sea is so favourable an element to genius, that there all high-souled younger brothers with empty pockets are sure of thriving: nay, I can say even more for it, for it not only fosters the talents of the spirited younger brothers, it also lightens the dullness even of that Poor animal—an elder brother; so that it is always the most desirable place both for best and worst."

"Well, your lordship is always ready to praise it," said Mrs. Thrale, "and I only wish we had a few more like you in the service,—and long may you live, both to defend and to ornament it!"

"Defence," answered he with quickness, "it does not want, and, for ornament, it is above all!"

THE LADY OF BATH EASTON.

Saturday.-In the afternoon we all went to the Whalleys, where we found a large and a highly dressed company, at the head of which sat Lady Miller. [123]

As soon as my discourse was over with Mr. Whalley, Lady Miller arose, and went to Mrs. Thrale, and whispered something to her. Mrs. Thrale then rose, too, and said,

"If your ladyship will give me leave, I will first introduce my daughter to you" making Miss Thrale, who was next her mother, make her reverences. "

"And now," she continued, "Miss Burney, Lady Miller desires to be introduced to you."

Up I jumped and walked forward ; Lady Miller, very civilly, more than met me half way, and said very polite things, of her wish to know me, and regret that she had not sooner met me, and then we both returned to our seats.

Do you know now that notwithstanding Bath Easton is so much laughed at in London, nothing here is more tonish than to visit Lady Miller, who is extremely curious in her company, admitting few people who are not of rank or of fame, and excluding of those all who are not people of character very unblemished.

Some time after, Lady Miller took a seat next mine on the sofa, to play at cards, and was excessively civil indeed-scolded Mrs. Thrale for not sooner making us acquainted, and had the politeness to offer to take me to the balls herself, as she heard Mr. and Mrs. Thrale did not choose to go.

After all this, it is hardly fair to tell you what I think of her. However, the truth is, I always, to the best of my intentions, speak honestly what I think of the folks I see, without being biassed either by their civilities or neglect ; and that you will ,allow is being a very faithful historian.

well then, Lady Miller is a round, plump, coarse looking dame of about forty, and while all her aim is to appear an elegant woman of fashion, all her success is to seem an ordinary woman in very common life, with fine clothes on. Her manners are bustling, her air is mock-important, and her manners very inelegant.

So much for the lady of Bath Easton; who, however, seems extremely good-natured, and who is, I am sure, extremely civil.

A FASHIONABLE CONCERT.

June 4.-To go on with Saturday evening. We left the Whalleys at nine, and then proceeded to Sir J. C—, who had invited us to a concert at his house.

We found such a crowd of chairs and carriages we could hardly make our way. I had never seen any of the family, consisting of Sir J. and three daughters, but had been particularly invited. The two rooms for the company were quite full when we arrived, and a large party was standing upon the first floor landing-place. just as I got up stairs, I was much surprised to hear my name called by a man's voice, who stood in the crowd upon the landing-place, and who said,

"Miss Burney, better go up another flight (pointing up stairs)- -if you'll take my advice, you'll go up another flight, for there's no room anywhere else."

I then recollected the voice, for I could not see the face, of Lord Mulgrave, and I began at first to suppose I must really do as he said, for there seemed not room for a sparrow, and I have heard the Sharp family do actually send their company all over their house when they give concerts. However, by degrees we squeezed ourselves into the outer room, and then Mrs. Lambart made way up to me, to introduce me to Miss C—, who is extremely handsome, genteel, and pleasing, though tonish, and who did the honours, in spite of the crowd, in a manner to satisfy everybody. After that, she herself introduced me to her next sister, Arabella, who is very fat, but not ugly. As to Sir J., He was seated behind a door in the music-room, where, being lame, he was obliged to keep still, and I never once saw his face, though I was upon the point of falling over him; for, at one time, as I had squeezed just into the musicroom, and was leaning against the door, which was open, and which Lord Althorp, the Duchess of Devonshire's brother, was also lolling against, the pressure pushed Sir James's chair, and the door beginning to move, I thought we should have fallen backwards. Lord Althorp moved off instantly, and I started forwards without making any disturbance, and then Mr. Travell came to assure me all was safe behind the door, and so the matter rested quietly, though not without giving me a ridiculous fright.

Mr. Travell, ma'am, if I have not yet introduced him to you, I must tell you - 'is known throughout Bath by the name of Beau Travell; he is a most approved connoisseur in beauty, gives the ton to all the world, sets up young ladies in the beau monde, and is the sovereign arbitrator of fashions, and decider of fashionable people. I had never the honour of being addressed by him before, though I have met him at the dean's and at Mrs. Lainbart's. So you may believe I was properly struck.

Though the rooms were so crowded, I saw but two faces I knew— -Lord Huntingdon, whom I have drank tea with at Mrs. Cholmley's. [124]and Miss Philips ; but the rest were all showy tonish people, who are only to be seen by going to the rooms, which we never do.

Some time after, Lord Mulgrave crowded in among us, and cried out to me, "So you would not take my advice!"

I told him he had really alarmed me, for I had taken him Seriously.

He laughed at the notion of sending me up to the garrets, and then poked himself into the concert-room.

oh, but I forgot to mention Dr. Harrington, with whom I 'had much conversation, and who was dry, comical, and very agreeable. I also saw Mr. Henry, but as Miss L- was not present, nothing ensued. [125]

Miss C- herself brought me a cup of ice, the room being crowded that the man could not get near me. How ridiculous to invite so many more people than could be accommodated! Lord Mulgrave was soon sick of the heat, and finding me distressed what to do with my cup, he very good -naturedly took it from me, but carried not only that, but himself also, away, which I did not equally rejoice at.

You may laugh, perhaps, that I have all this time said never A word of the music, but the truth is I heard scarce a note. There were quartettos and overtures by gentlemen performers whose names and faces I know not, and such was the never ceasing rattling and noise in the card-room, where I was kept almost all the evening, that a general humming of musical sounds, and now and then a twang, was all I could hear.

Nothing can well be more ridiculous than a concert of this sort; and Dr. Harrington told me that the confusion amongst the musicians was equal to that amongst the company ; for that, when called upon to open the concert, they found no music. The Miss C—'s had prepared nothing, nor yet solicited their dilettante's to prepare for them. Miss Harrington, his daughter, who played upon the harpsichord, and by the very little I could sometimes hear, I believe very well, complained that she had never touched so vile an instrument, and that she was quite disturbed at being obliged to play upon it.

About the time that I got against the door, as I have mentioned, of the music room, the young ladies were preparing to perform, and with the assistance of Mr. Henry, they sang catches. Oh, such singing! worse squalling, more out of tune, and more execrable in every respect, never did I hear. We did not get away till late.

A BATH ALDERMAN's RAREE SHOW.

Sunday.-We had an excellent sermon from the Bishop of Peterborough, who preached merely at the request of Mrs. Thrale.

At dinner we had the bishop and Dr. Harrington; and the bishop, who was in very high spirits, proposed a frolic, which was, that we should all go to Spring Gardens, where he should give us tea, and thence proceed to Mr. Ferry's, to see a very curious house and garden. Mrs. Thrale pleaded that she had invited company to tea at home, but the bishop said we would go early, and should return in time, and was so gaily authoritative that he gained his point. He had been so long accustomed to command, as master of Westminster school, that he cannot prevail with himself, I believe, ever to be overcome.

Dr. Harrington was engaged to a patient, and could not be of our party. But the three Thrales, the bishop and I, pursued our scheme, crossed the Avon, had a sweet walk through the meadows, and drank tea at Spring Gardens, where the bishop did the honours with a spirit, a gaiety, and an activity that jovialised us all, and really we were prodigiously lively. We then walked on to Mr. Ferry's habitation.

Mr. Ferry is a Bath alderman; his house and garden exhibit the house and garden of Mr. Tattersall, enlarged. just the same taste prevails, the same paltry ornaments, the same crowd of buildings, the same unmeaning decorations, and the same unsuccessful attempts at making something of nothing.

They kept us half an hour in the garden, while they were preparing for our reception in the house, where after parading through four or five little vulgarly showy closets, not rooms, we were conducted into a very gaudy little apartment, where the master of the house sat reclining on his arm, as if in contemplation, though everything conspired to show that the house and its inhabitants were carefully arranged for our reception. The bishop had sent in his name by way of gaining admission.

The bishop, with a gravity of demeanour difficult to himself to sustain, apologised for our intrusion, and returned thanks for seeing the house and garden. Mr. Ferry started from his pensive attitude, and begged us to be seated, and then a curtain was drawn, and we perceived through a glass a perspective view of ships, boats, and water. This raree-show over, the maid who officiated as show-woman had a hint given her and presently a trap-door opened, and up jumped a covered table, ornamented with various devices. When we had expressed our delight at this long enough to satisfy Mr. Ferry, another hint was given, and presently down dropped an eagle from the ceiling whose talons were put into a certain hook in the top of the covering of the table, and when the admiration at this was over, up again flew the eagle, conveying in his talons the cover, and leaving under it a repast of cakes, sweetmeats, oranges, and jellies.

When our raptures upon this feat subsided, the maid received another signal, and then seated herself in an armchair, which presently sank down underground, and up in its room came a barber's block, with a vast quantity of black wool on it, and a high head-dress.

This, you may be sure, was more applauded than all the rest; we were en extase, and having properly expressed our gratitude, were soon after suffered to decamp.

FLIGHTY CAPTAIN BOUCHIER.

Tuesday.-This morning, by appointment, we met a party at the pump-room, thence to proceed to Spring Gardens, to a public breakfast. The folks, however, were not to their time, and we sallied forth only with the addition of Miss Weston and Miss Byron.

As soon as we entered the gardens Augusta, who had hold of my arm, called out, "Ah! there's the man I danced with at the ball! and he plagued me to death, asking me if I liked this and that, and the other, and, when I said 'No,' he asked me what I did like? So, I suppose he thought me a fool, and so indeed, I am! only you are so good to me that I wrote my sister Sophy word that you had almost made me quite vain; and she wrote to me t'other day a private letter, and told me how glad she was you were come back, for, indeed, I had written her word I should be quite sick of my life here, if it was not for sometimes seeing you."

The gentleman to whom she pointed presently made up to us, And I found he was Captain Bouchier, the saine who had rattled away at Mr. Whalley's. He instantly joined Miss Weston and consequently our party, and was in the same style of flighty raillery as before. He seems to have a very good understanding, and very quick parts, but he is rather too conscious of both however, he was really very entertaining, and as he abided wholly by Miss Weston, whose delicacy gave way to gaiety and flash, whether she would or not, I was very glad that he made one among us.

The rest of the company soon came, and were Mr. and Mrs. Whalley, Mrs. Lambart, Mrs. Aubrey, Colonel Campbell, an old officer and old acquaintance of Mr. Thrale, and some others, both male and female, whose names I know not.

We all sat in one box, but we had three tea-makers. Miss Weston presided at that to which I belonged, and Augusta, Captain Bouchier, and herself were of our set. And gay enough we were, for the careless rattle of Captain Bouchier, which paid no regard to the daintiness of Miss Weston, made her obliged in her own defence, to abate her finery, and laugh, and rally, and rail, in her turn. But, at 'last, I really began to fear that this flighty officer would bring on a serious quarrel, for, among other subjects he was sporting, he unfortunately started that of the Bath Easton vase, which he ridiculed without mercy, and yet, according to all I have heard of it, without any injustice; but Mrs. Whalley, who overheard him, was quite irritated with him. Sir John an Lady Miller are her friends, and she thought it incumbent upon her to vindicate even this vain folly, which she did weakly and warmly, while Captain Bouchier only laughed and ridiculed them the more. Mrs. Whalley then coloured, and grew quite enraged, reasoning upon the wickedness of laughing at her good friends, and talking of generosity and sentiment. Meanwhile, he scampered from side to side to avoid her; laughed, shouted, and tried every way of braving it out; but was compelled at last to be serious, and enter into a solemn defence of his intentions, which were, he said, to ridicule the vase, not the Millers.

A YOUNG AND AGREEABLE INFIDEL.

Wednesday.-The party was Mr. and Mrs. Vanbrugh—the former a good sort of man-the latter, Captain Bouchier says, reckons herself a woman of humour, but she kept it prodigious snug; Lord Huntingdon, a very deaf old lord Sir Robert Pigot, a very thin old baronet ; Mr. Tyson, a very civil master of the ceremonies ; Mr. and Mrs. White, a very insignificant couple; Sir James C——, a bawling old man; two Misses C——, a pair of tonish misses; Mrs. and Miss Byron; Miss W——, and certain others I knew nothing of. Augusta Byron, according to custom, had entered into conversation with me, and we were talking about her sisters, and her affairs, when Mr. E- -(whose name I forgot to mention) came to inform me that Mrs. Lambart begged to speak to me. She was upon a sofa with Miss W——, who, it seemed, desired much to be introduced to me, and so I took a chair facing them.

Miss W—— is young and pleasing in her appearance,not pretty, but agreeable in her face, and soft, gentle, and well bred in her manners. Our conversation, for some time, was upon the common Bath topics; but when Mrs. Lambart left us—called to receive more company—we went insensibly into graver matters.

As I soon found, by the looks and expressions of this young lady that she was of a peculiar cast, I left all choice of subjects to herself, determined quietly to follow as she led ; and very soon, and I am sure I know not how, we had for topics the follies and vices of mankind, and, indeed, she spared not for lashing them. The women she rather excused than defended, laying to the door of the men their faults and imperfections; but the men, she said, were all bad—all, in one word, and without exception, sensualists.

I stared much at a severity of speech for which her softness of manner had so ill prepared me ; and she, perceiving my surprise, said,

"I am sure I ought to apologise for speaking my opinion to you- -you, who have so just and so uncommon a knowledge of human nature. I have long wished ardently to have the honour of conversing with you ; but your party has, altogether, been regarded as so formidable, that I have not had courage to approach it."

I made—as what could I do else?—disqualifying speeches, and she then led to discoursing of happiness and misery: the latter she held to be the invariable lot of us all; and "one word," she added, "we have in our language, and in all others, for which there is never any essential necessity, and that is pleasure!"

And her eyes filled with tears as she spoke.

"How you amaze me!" cried I; "I have met with misanthropes before, but never with so complete a one; and I can hardly think I hear right when I see how young you are!" \ She then, in rather indirect terms, gave me to understand that she was miserable at home, and in very direct terms, that she was wretched abroad; and openly said, that to affliction she was born, and in affliction she must die, for that the world was so vilely formed as to render happiness impossible for its inhabitants.

There was something in this freedom of repining that I could by no means approve, and, as I found by all her manner that she had a disposition to even respect whatever I said, I now grew very serious, and frankly told her that I could not think it consistent with either truth or religion to cherish such notions.

"One thing," answered she, "there is, which I believe might make me happy, but for that I have no inclination: it is an amorous disposition; but that I do not possess. I can make myself no happiness by intrigue."

"I hope not, indeed!" cried I, almost confounded by her extraordinary notions and speeches; "but, surely, there are worthier objects of happiness attainable!"

"No, I believe there are not, and the reason the men are happier than us, is because they are more sensual!"

"I would not think such thoughts," cried I, clasping my hands with an involuntary vehemence, "for worlds!"

The Misses C— then interrupted us, and seated themselves next to us; but Miss W— paid them little attention at first, and soon after none at all; but, in a low voice, continued her discourse with me, recurring to the same subject of happiness and misery, upon which, after again asserting the folly of ever hoping for the former, she made this speech,

"There may be, indeed, one moment of happiness, which must be the finding one worthy of exciting a passion which one should dare own to himself. That would, indeed, be a moment worth living for! but that can never happen— I am sure not to me—the men are so low, so vicious, so worthless! No, there is not one such to be found!"

What a strange girl! I could do little more than listen to her, from surprise at all she said.

"If, however," she continued, "I had your talents I could, bad as this world is, be happy in it. There is nothing, there is nobody I envy like you. With such resources as yours there can never be ennui; the mind may always be employed, and always be gay! Oh, if I could write as you write!"

"Try," cried I, "that is all that is wanting! try, and you will soon do much better things!"

"O no! I have tried, but I cannot succeed."

"Perhaps you are too diffident. But is it possible you can be serious in so dreadful an assertion as that you are never happy? Are you sure that some real misfortune would not show you that your present misery is imaginary?"

"I don't know," answered she, looking down, "perhaps it is So,— but in that case 'tis a misery so much the harder to be cured."

"You surprise me more and more," cried I; "is it possible you can so rationally see the disease of a disordered imagination, and yet allow it such power over your mind?"

"Yes, for it is the only source from which I draw any shadow of felicity. Sometimes when in the country, I give way to my imagination for whole days, and then I forget the world and its cares, and feel some enjoyment of existence."

"Tell me what is then your notion of felicity? Whither does your castle-building carry you?"

"O, quite out of the world—I know not where, but I am surrounded with sylphs, and I forget everything besides."

"Well, you are a most extraordinary character, indeed; I must confess I have seen nothing like you!"

"I hope, however, I shall find something like myself, and, like the magnet rolling in the dust, attract some metal as I go."

"That you may attract what you please, is of all things the most likely; but if you wait to be happy for a friend resembling yourself, I shall no longer wonder at your despondency."

"Oh!" cried she, raising her eyes in ecstasy, "could I find such a one!—male or female—for sex would be indifferent to me. With such a one I would go to live directly."

I half laughed, but was perplexed in my own mind whether to be- sad or merry at such a speech.

"But then," she continued, "after making, should I lose such a friend, I would not survive."

"Not survive?" repeated I, "what can you mean?"

She looked down, but said nothing.

"Surely you cannot mean," said I, very gravely indeed, "to Put a violent end to your life."

"I should not," said she, again looking up, "hesitate a moment."

I was quite thunderstruck, and for some time could not say A word; but when I did speak, it was in a style of exhortation so serious and earnest, I am ashamed to write it to you, lest 'You should think it too much.

She gave me an attention that was even respectful, but when I urged her to tell me by what right she thought herself entitled to rush unlicensed on eternity, she said, "By the right of believing I shall be extinct." I really felt horror-struck.

"Where, for heaven's sake," I cried, "where have you picked up such dreadful reasoning?"

"In Hume," said she; " I have read his Essays repeatedly."

"I am sorry to find they have power to do so much mischief; you should not have read them, at least till a man equal to Hume in abilities had answered him. Have you read any more infidel writers?"

"Yes, Bolingbroke, the divinest of all writers."

"And do you read nothing upon the right side?"

"Yes, the bible, till I was sick to death of it, every Sunday evening to my mother."

Have you read Beattie on the Immutability of Truth?" [126]

"No."

"Give me leave then to recommend it to you. After Hume's Essays you ought to read it. And even for lighter reading, if you were to look at Mason's 'Elegy on Lady Coventry,' it might be of no disservice to you."

This was the chief of our conversation, which indeed made an impression upon me I shall not easily get rid of. A young and agreeable infidel is even a shocking sight, and with her romantic, flighty, and unguarded turn of mind, what could happen to her that could give surprise?

BALL-ROOM FLIRTATIONS.

Friday.-In the evening was the last ball expected to be at Bath this season, and therefore knowing we could go to no other, it was settled we should go to this. Of our party were Mrs. Byron and Augusta, Miss Philips, and Charlotte Lewis.

Mrs. Byron was placed at the upper end of the room by Mr. Tyson, because she is honourable, and her daughter next to her; I, of course, the lowest of our party; but the moment Mr. Tyson had arranged us, Augusta arose, and nothing would satisfy her but taking a seat not only next to but below me; nor could I for my life get the better of the affectionate humility with which she quite supplicated me to be content. She was soon after followed by Captain Brisbane, a young officer who had met her in Spring Gardens, and seemed much struck with her, and was now presented to her by Mr. Tyson for her partner.

Captain Brisbane is a very pretty sort of young man, but did not much enliven us. Soon after I perceived Captain Bouchier, who, after talking some time with Mrs. Thrale, and various parties, made up to us, and upon Augusta's being called upon to dance a minuet, took her place, and began a very lively sort of chit-chat.

I had, however, no small difficulty to keep him from abusing my friend Augusta. He had once danced with her, and their commerce had not been much to her advantage. I defended her upon the score of her amiable simplicity and unaffected ingenuousness, but I could not have the courage to contradict him when he said he had no notion she was very brilliant by the conversation he had had with her. Augusta, indeed, is nothing less than brilliant: but she is natural, artless, and very affectionate. just before she went to dance her minuet, upon my admiring her bouquet, which was the most beautiful in the room, she tore from it the only two moss roses in it, and so spoilt it all before her exhibition, merely that I might have the best of it.

Country dances were now preparing, and after a little further chat, Captain Bouchier asked me for the honour of my hand, but I had previously resolved not to dance, and therefore declined his offer. But he took, of the sudden, a fancy to prate with me, and therefore budged not after the refusal.

He told me this was the worst ball for company there had been the whole season ; and, with a wicked laugh that was too Significant to be misunderstood, said, "And, as you have been to no other, perhaps you will give this for a specimen of a Bath ball!"

He told me he had very lately met with Hannah More, and then mentioned Mrs. Montagu and Mrs. Carter, whence he took occasion to say most high and fine things of the ladies of the present age,—their writings, and talents; and I soon found he had no small reverence for us blue-stockings.

About this time Charlotte, [127]who had confessedly dressed herself for dancing, but whose pretty face had by some means been overlooked, drawled towards us, and asked me why I would not dance?

"I never intended it," said I, "but I hoped to have seen you."

"No," said she, yawning, "no more shall I,—I don't choose."

"Don't you ?" said Captain Bouchier, dryly, "why not?

"Why, because I don't like it."

"O fie!" cried he; "consider how cruel that is."

"I must consider myself," said she, pertly; "for I don't choose to heat myself this hot weather."

just then a young man came forward, and requested her hand. She coloured, looked excessively silly, and walked off with him to join the dancers. When, between the dances, she came our way, he plagued her, `a la Sir Clement. [128]

"Well," cried he, "so you have been dancing this hot night! I thought you would have considered yourself better?"

"Oh," said she, "I could not help it—I had much rather not;—it was quite disagreeable to me."

" No, no,—pardon me there!" said he, maliciously; "I saw pleasure dance first in your eyes; I never saw you look more delighted: you were quite the queen of smiles!"

She looked as if she could have killed him; and yet, from giddiness and good-humour, was compelled to join in the laugh.

After this we went to tea. When that was over, and we all returned to the ball-room, Captain Bouchier followed me, and again took a seat next mine, which he kept, without once moving, the whole night.

He again applied to me to dance, but I was more steady than Charlotte; and he was called upon, and reproached by Captain Brisbane and others for sitting still when there were so few dancers; but he told them he could not endure being pressed into the service, or serving at all under the master of the ceremonies.

Well, I have no more time for particulars, though we had much more converse ; for so it happened that we talked all the evening almost together, as Mrs. Thrale and Mrs. Byron were engaged with each other: Miss Thrale, who did not dance, was fairly jockeyed out of her place next me by Captain Bouchier, and the other young ladies were with their partners. Before we broke up, this captain asked me if I should be at the play next night?—"Yes," I could not but say, as we had had places taken some time; but I did not half like it, for his manner of asking plainly implied, "If you go, why I will!"

When we made our exit, he saw me safe out of the rooms, with as much attention as if we had actually been partners. As we were near home we did not get into chairs; and Mr. Travell joined us in our walk.

"Why, what a flirtation"cried Mrs. Thrale; "why, Burney, this is a man of taste!—Pray, Mr. Travell, will it do? What has he."

"Twenty thousand pounds, ma'am," answered the beau.

"O ho! has he so?—Well, well, we'll think of It."

Finding her so facetious, I determined not to acquaint her with the query concerning the play, knowing that, if I did, and he appeared there, she would be outrageous in merriment. She is a most dear creature, but never restrains her tongue in anything, nor, indeed, any of her feelings:—she laughs, cries, scolds, sports, reasons, makes fun,—does everything she has an inclination to do, without any study of prudence, or thought of blame; and pure and artless as is this character, it often draws both herself and others into scrapes, which a little discretion would avoid.

FURTHER FLIRTATIONS.

Saturday morning I spent in visiting. At dinner we had Mrs. Lambart and Colonel Campbell. All the discourse was upon Augusta Byron's having made a conquest of Captain Brisbane, and the match was soon concluded upon,—at least, they all allowed it would be decided this night, when she was to go with us to the play; and if Captain Brisbane was there, why then he was in for it, and the thing was done.

Well—Augusta came at the usual time; Colonel Campbell took leave, but Mrs. Lambart accompanied us to the play: and, in the lobby, the first object we saw was Captain Brisbane. He immediately advanced to us, and, joining our party, followed us into our box.

Nothing could equal the wickedness of Mrs. Thrale and Mrs. Lambart; they smiled at each other with such significance! Fortunately, however, Augusta did not observe them.

Well, we took our seats, and Captain Brisbane, by getting into the next box, on a line with ours, placed himself next to Augusta: [129]but hardly had Mrs. T. and L. composed their faces, ere I heard the box-door open. Every one looked round but me, and I had reasons for avoiding such curiosity,—reasons well enough founded, for instantly grins, broader than before, widened the mouths of the two married ladies, while even Miss Thrale began a titter that half choaked her, and Augusta, nodding to me with an arch smirk, said, "Miss Burney, I wish you joy!"

To be sure I could have no doubt who entered, but, very innocently, I demanded of them all the cause of their mirth. They scrupled not explaining themselves; and I found my caution, in not mentioning the query that had been put to me, availed me nothing, for the captain was already a marked man in my service!

He placed himself exactly behind me, but very quietly and silently, and did not, for some minutes, speak to me; afterwards, however, he did a little,-except when my favourite, Mr. Lee, who acted Old Norval, in "Douglas," was on the stage, and then he was strictly silent. I am in no cue to write our discourse ; but it was pleasant and entertaining enough at the time, and his observations upon the play and the players were lively and comical. But I was prodigiously worried by my own party, who took every opportunity to inquire how I was entertained and so forth,—and to snigger.

Two young ladies, who seemed about eighteen, and sat above us Were somuch shocked by the death of Douglas, that both burst into a loud fit of roaring, like little children,—and sobbed on, afterwards, for almost half the farce! I was quite astonished; and Miss Weston complained that they really disturbed her sorrows ; but Captain Bouchier was highly diverted, and went to give them comfort, as if they had been babies, telling them it was all over, and that they need not cry any more.

Monday.-At breakfast, Mrs. Thrale said,

"Ah, you never tell me your love-secrets, but I could tell you one if I chose it!"

This produced entreaties - and entreaties thus much further-

"Why, I know very well who is in love with Fanny Burney!"

I told her that was more than I did, but owned it was not difficult to guess who she meant, though I could not tell what.

"Captain Bouchier," said she. "But you did not tell me so, nor he either; I had it from Mr. Tyson, our master of the ceremonies, who told me you made a conquest of him at the ball; and he knows these matters pretty well; 'tis his trade to know them."

"Well-a-day!" quoth I—"'tis unlucky we did not meet a little sooner, for this very day he is ordered away with his troop into Norfolk."

BATH EASTON AND SCEPTICAL MISS W

Thursday, June 8.-We went to Bath Easton. Mrs.Lambart went with us.

The house is charmingly situated, well fitted up, convenient, and pleasant, and not large, but commodious and elegant. Thursday is still their public day for company, though the business of the vase is over for this season.

The room into which we were conducted was so much crowded we could hardly make our way. Lady Miller came to the door, and, as she had first done to the rest of us, took my hand, and led me up to a most prodigious fat old lady, and introduced me to her. This was Mrs. Riggs, her ladyship's mother, who seems to have Bath Easton and its owners under her feet.

I was smiled upon with a graciousness designedly marked, and seemed most uncommonly welcome. Mrs. Riggs looked as if she could have shouted for joy at sight of me! She is mighty merry and facetious, Sir John was very quiet, but very civil.

I saw the place appropriated for the vase, but at this time it was removed. As it was hot, Sir John Miller offered us to walk round the house, and see his greenhouse, etc. So away we set off, Harriet Bowdler accompanying me, and some others following.

We had not strolled far ere we were overtaken by another party, and among them I perceived Miss W— my new sceptical friend. She joined me immediately, and I found she was by no means in so sad a humour as when I saw her last. on the contrary, she seemed flightily gay.

"Were you never here before?" she asked me.

"No."

"No? why what an acquisition you are then! I suppose you will contribute to the vase?"

"No, indeed!"

"No more you ought; you are quite too good for it."

"No, not that; but I have no great passion for making the trial. You, I suppose, have contributed?"

"No, never—I can't. I have tried, but I could never write verses in my life—never get beyond Cupid and stupid."

"Did Cupid, then, always come in your way? what a mischievous urchin!"

"No, he has not been very mischievous to me this year."

"Not this year? Oh, very well! He has spared you, then, for a whole twelvemonth!"

She laughed, and we were interrupted by more company. . .

Some time after, while I was talking with Miss W— and Harriet Bowdler, Mrs. Riggs came up to us, and with an expression of comical admiration, fixed her eyes upon me, and for some time amused herself with apparently watching me. Mrs. Lambart, who was at cards, turned round and begged me to give her her cloak, for she felt rheumatic; I could not readily find it, and, after looking some time, I was obliged to give her my own; but while I was hunting, Mrs. Riggs followed me, laughing, nodding, and looking much delighted, and every now and then saying,

"That's right, Evelina—Ah! look for it, Evelina!-Evelina always did so—she always looked for people's cloaks, and was obliging and well-bred!"

I grinned a little, to be sure, but tried to escape her, by again getting between Miss W— and Harriet Bowdler; but Mrs.Riggs still kept opposite to me, expressing from time to time, by uplifted hands and eyes, comical applause, Harriet Bowdler modestly mumbled some praise, but addressed it to Miss Thrale. I begged a truce, and retired to a chair in a corner, at the request of Miss W— to have a t`ete-`a-t`ete, for which, however, her strange levity gave me no great desire. She begged to know if I had written anything else. I assured her never.

"The 'Sylph,'" said she, "I am told, was yours."

"I had nothing at all to do with that or anything else that ever was published but 'Evelina;' you, I suppose, read the 'Sylph' for its name's sake?"

"No; I never read novels—I hate them; I never read 'Evelina' till I was quite persecuted by hearing it talked of. 'Sir Charles Grandison' I tried once, but could not bear it; Sir Charles for a lover! no lover for me! for a guardian or the trustee of an estate, he might do very well—but for a lover!"

"What—when he bows upon your hand! would not that do?"

She kept me by her side for a full hour, and we again talked over our former conversation; and I enquired what first led her to seeking infidel books?

"Pope," she said; he was himself a deist, she believed, and his praise of Bolingbroke made her mad to read his books, and then the rest followed easily. She also gave me an account of her private and domestic life; of her misery at home, her search of dissipation, and her incapability of happiness.

CURIOSITY ABOUT THE " EVELINA " SET.

Our conversation would have lasted till leave-taking, but for our being interrupted by Miss Miller, a most beautiful little ,girl of ten years old. Miss W- begged her to sing us a French song. She coquetted, but Mrs. Riggs came to us, and said if I wished it I did her grand-daughter great honour, and she insisted upon her obedience. The little girl laughed and complied, and we went into another room to hear her, followed by the Misses Caldwell. She sung in a pretty childish manner enough.

When we became more intimate, she said,

"Ma'am, I have a great favour to request of you, if you please!"

I begged to know what it was, and assured her I would grant it ; and to be out of the way of these misses, I led her to the window.

"Ma'am," said the little girl, will you then be so good as to tell me where Evelina is now?"

I was a little surprised at the question, and told her I had not heard lately.

"Oh, ma'am, but I am sure you know! " cried she, "for you know you wrote it; and mamma was so good as to let me hear her read it; and pray, ma'am, do tell me where she is? and whether Miss Branghton and Miss Polly went to see her when she was married to Lord Orville?"

I promised her I would inquire, and let her know.

"And pray, ma'am, is Madame Duval with her now?" And several other questions she asked me, with a childish simplicity that was very diverting. She took the whole for a true story, and was quite eager to know what was become of all the people. And when I said I would inquire, and tell her when we next met, "Oh, but, ma'am," she said, "had not you better write it down, because then there would be more of it, you know?"

ALARM AT THE No POPERY RIOTS.

[THE DISGraceful "No Popery" riots, which filled London with terror, and the whole country with alarm, in June, 1780, were occasioned by the recent relaxation of the severe penal laws against the Catholics. The rioters were headed by Lord George Gordon, a crazy enthusiast. Dr. Johnson has given a lively account of the disturbance in his "Letters to Mrs. Thrale," some excerpts from which will, perhaps, be not unacceptable to the reader.

"9th June, 1780. on Friday (June 2 the good protestants met in Saint George's Fields, at the summons of Lord George Gordon; and marching to Westminster, insulted the lords and commons, who all bore it with great tameness. At night the outrages began by the demolition of the mass-house by Lincoln's Inn.

"An exact journal of a week's defiance of government I cannot give you. On Monday Mr. Strahan, who had been insulted, spoke to Lord Mansfield, who had, I think, been insulted too, of the licentiousness of the populace; and his lordship treated it as a very slight irregularity. On Tuesday night they pulled down Fielding's[130]house, and burnt his goods in the street. They had gutted on Monday Sir George Savile's house, but the building was saved. On Tuesday evening, leaving Fielding's ruins, they went to Newgate to demand their companions, who had been seized demolishing the chapel. The keeper could not release them but by the mayor's permission, which he went to ask; at his return he found all the prisoners released, and Newgate in a blaze. They then went to Bloomsbury, and fastened upon Lord Mansfield's house, which they pulled down; and as for his goods, they totally burnt them. They have since gone to Caen-wood, but a guard was there before them. They plundered some papists, I think, and burnt a mass-house in Moorfields the same night.

"On Wednesday I walked with Dr. Scot to look at Newgate and found it in ruins, with the fire yet glowing. As I went by, the Protestants were plundering the sessions-house at the Old Bailey. There were not, I believe, a hundred; but they did their work at leisure, in full security, without sentinels without trepidation, as men lawfully employed in full day. Such is the cowardice of a commercial place. On Wednesday they broke open the Fleet, and the King's Bench, and the Marshalsea, and Woodstreet Compter, and Clerkenwell Bridewell, and released all the prisoners. At night they set fire to the Fleet, and to the King's Bench, and I know not how many other places; and one might see the glare of conflagration fill the sky from many parts. The sight was dreadful.

The King said in council, 'That the magistrates had not done their duty, but that he would do his own;' and a proclamation was published, directing us to keep our servants within doors, as the peace was now to be preserved by force. The soldiers were sent out to different parts, and the town is now at quiet.

What has happened at your house[131]you will know: the harm is only a few butts of beer; and, I think, you may be sure that the danger is over."

10th June, 1780. The soldiers are stationed so as to be everywhere within call. There is no longer any body of rioters, and the individuals are hunted to their holes, and led to prison. Lord George was last night sent to the Tower. . . .

Government now acts again with its proper force - and we are all under the protection of the King and the law."-ED.

When we came home our newspaper accounts of the tumults In town with Lord George Gordon and his mob, alarmed us very much ; but we had still no notion of the real danger you were all in.

Next day we drank tea with the Dowdlers. At our return home we were informed a mob was surrounding a new Roman Catholic chapel. At first we disbelieved it, but presently one of the servants came and told us they were knocking it to pieces; and in half an hour, looking out of our windows, we saw it in flames: and listening, we heard loud and violent shouts!

I shall write no particulars - the horrible subject you have had more than your share of. Mrs. Thrale and I sat up till four o'clock, and walked about the parades, and at two we went with a large party to the spot, and saw the beautiful new building consuming; the mob then were all quiet—all still and silent, and everybody seemed but as spectators.

Saturday morning, to my inexpressible concern, brought me no letters from town, and my uneasiness to hear from you made me quite wretched. Mrs. Thrale had letters from Sir Philip Clerke and Mr. Perkins, to acquaint her that her town-house had been three times attacked, but was at last saved by guards; her children, plate, money, and valuables all removed. Streatham also threatened, and emptied of all its furniture.

The same morning also we saw a Bath and Bristol paper, in which Mr. Thrale was asserted to be a papist. This villanous falsehood terrified us even for his personal safety, and Mrs. Thrale and I agreed it was best to leave Bath directly, and travel about the country.

She left to me the task of acquainting Mr. Thrale with these particulars, being herself too much disturbed to be capable of such a task. I did it as well as I could, and succeeded so far that, by being lightly told of it, he treated it lightly, and bore it with much steadiness and composure. We then soon settled to decamp.

We had no time nor spirits pour prendre cong`e stuff, but determined to call upon the Bowdlers and Miss Cooper. They were all sorry to part, and Miss Cooper, to my equal surprise and pleasure, fairly made a declaration of her passion for me, assuring me she had never before taken so great a fancy to a new acquaintance, and beginning warmly the request I meant to make myself, of continuing our intimacy in town.

(Fanny Burney to Dr. Burney.

Bath, June 9, 1780,

My dearest sir, How are you? where are you? and what is to come next? The accounts from town are so frightful, that I am uneasy, not only for the city at large, but for every individual I know in it. Does this martial law confine you quite to the house? Folks here say that it must, and that no business of any kind can be transacted. Oh, what dreadful times ! Yet I rejoice extremely that the opposition members have fared little better than the ministerial. Had such a mob been confirm(d friends of either or of any party, I think the nation must have been at their disposal ; for, if headed by popular or skilful leaders, who and what could have resisted them?—I mean, if they are as formidable as we are here told.

Dr. Johnson has written to Mrs. Thrale, without even mentioning the existence of this mob; perhaps at this very moment he thinks it "a humbug upon the nation," as George Bodens called the parliament,

A private letter to Bull, the bookseller, brought word this morning that much slaughter has been made by the military among the mob. Never, I am sure, can any set of wretches less deserve quarter or pity ; yet it is impossible not to shudder at hearing of their destruction. Nothing less, however, would do; they were too outrageous and powerful for civil power.

But what is it they want? who is going to turn papist? who, indeed, is thinking in an alarming way of religion?—this pious mob, and George Gordon excepted?

All the stage-coaches that come into Bath from London are Chalked over with "No Popery," and Dr. Harrington called here just now, and says the same was chalked this morning upon his door, and is scrawled in several places about the town. Wagers have been laid that the popish chapel here will be pulled or burnt down in a few days; but I believe not a word of the matter, nor do I find that anybody is at all alarmed. Bath, indeed, ought to be held sacred as a sanctuary for invalids; and I doubt not but the news of the firing in town will prevent all tumults out of it.

Now, if, after all the intolerable provocation given by the mob, after all the leniency and forbearance of the ministry, and after the shrinking Of the minority, we shall by and by hear that this firing was a massacre—will it not be villanous and horrible? And yet as soon as safety is secured—though by this means alone all now agree it can be secured—nothing would less surprise me than to hear the seekers of popularity make this assertion.

Friday night.-The above I writ this morning, before I recollected this was not post-day, and all is altered here since. The threats I despised were but too well grounded, for, to our utter amazement and consternation, the new Roman Catholic chapel in this town was set on fire at about nine o'clock. It is now burning with a fury that is dreadful, and the house of the priest belonging to it is in flames also. The poor persecuted man himself has I believe escaped with life, though pelted, followed, and very ill used. Mrs. Thrale and I have been walking about with the footmen several times. The whole town is still and orderly. The rioters do their work with great composure, and though there are knots of people in every corner, all execrating the authors of such outrages, nobody dares oppose them. An attempt indeed was made, but it was ill-conducted, faintly followed, and soon put an end to by a secret fear of exciting vengeance.

Alas! to what have we all lived!—the poor invalids here will probably lose all chance of life, from terror. Mr. Hay, our apothecary, has been attending the removal of two, who were confined to their beds in the street where the chapel is burning. The Catholics throughout the place are all threatened with destruction, and we met several porters, between ten and eleven at night, privately removing goods, walking on tiptoe, and scarcely breathing.

I firmly believe, by the deliberate villany with which this riot is conducted, that it wil! go on in the same desperate way as in town, and only be stopped by the same desperate means. Our plan for going to Bristol is at an end. We are told it would be madness, as there are seven Romish chapels in it; but we are determined upon removing somewhere to-morrow; for why should we, who can go, stay to witness such horrid scenes?

Satarday Afternoon, June 10-I was most cruelly disappointed in not having one word to-day. I am half crazy with doubt and disturbance in not hearing. Everybody here is terrified to death. We have intelligence that Mr. Thrale's house in town is filled with soldiers, and threatened by the mob with destruction. Perhaps he may himself be a marked man for their fury. We are going directly from Bath, and intend to stop only at villages. To-night we shall stop at Warminster, not daring to go to Devizes. This place is now well guarded, but still we dare not await the event of to-night; all the catholics in the town have privately escaped.

I know not now when I shall hear from you. I am in agony for news. Our head-quarters will be Brighthelmstone, where I do most humbly and fervently entreat you to write—do, dearest sir, write, if but one word—if but only you name yourself! Nothing but your own hand can now tranquillize me. The reports about London here quite distract me. If it were possible to send ine a line by the diligence to Brighton, how grateful I should be for such an indulgence!

HASTY DEPARTURE FROM BATH.
(FANNY BUrney to Dr. Burney. Salisbury, June 11, 1780
Here we are, dearest sir, and here we mean to pass this night.

We did not leave Bath till eight o'clock yesterday evening, at which time it was filled with dragoons, militia, and armed constables, not armed with muskets, but bludgeons: these latter were all chairmen, who were sworn by the mayor in the morning for petty constables. A popish private chapel, and the houses of all the catholics, were guarded between seven and eight, and the inhabitants ordered to keep house.

We set out in the coach-and-four, with two men on horseback, and got to Warminster, a small town in Somersetshire, a little before twelve.

This morning two more servants came after us from Bath, and brought us word that the precautions taken by the magistrates last night had good success, for no attempt of any sort had been renewed towards a riot. But the happiest tidings to me were contained in a letter which they brought, which had arrived after our departure, by the diligence, from Mr. Perkins,[132]with an account that all was quiet in London, and that Lord G. Gordon was sent to the Tower. I am now again tolerably easy, but I shall not be really comfortable, or free from some fears, till I hear from St. Martin's-street.

The Borough house has been quite preserved. I know not how long we may be on the road, but nowhere long",enough for receiving a letter till we come to Brighthelmstone.

We stopped in our way at Wilton, and spent half the day at that beautiful place. just before we arrived there, Lord Arundel had sent to the officers in the place, to entreat a party of guards immediately, for the safety of his house, as he had intelligence that a mob was on the road from London to attack it:—he is a catholic. His request was immediately complied with.

We intended to have gone to a private town, but find all quiet here, and therefore prefer it as much more commodious. There is no Romish chapel in the town; mass has always been performed for the catholics of the place at a Mrs. Arundel's in the Close—a relation of his lordship's, whose house is fifteen miles off. I have inquired about the Harris's; [133]I find they are here and all well.

THE GORDON RIOTS.

(CHARLOTTE Burney[134] to Fanny Burney.)

I am very sorry, my dear Fanny, to hear how much you have suffered from your apprehension about us. Susan will tell you why none of us wrote before Friday; and she says, she has told you what dreadful havoc and devastation- the mob have made here in all parts of the town. However, We are pretty quiet and tranquil again now. Papa goes on with his business pretty much as usual, and so far from the military keeping people within doors (as you say in your letter to my father, you suppose to be the case), the streets were never more crowded— everybody is wandering about in order to see the ruins of the places that the mob have destroyed.

There are two camps, one in St. James's, and the other in Hyde Park, which together with the military law, makes almost every one here think he is safe again. I expect we shall all have "a passion for a scarlet coat" now.

I hardly know what to tell you that won't be stale news. They say that duplicates of the handbill that I have enclosed were distributed all over the town on Wednesday and Thursday last; however, thank heaven, everybody says now that Mr. Thrale's house and brewery are as safe as we can wish them. There was a brewer in Turnstile that had his house gutted and burnt, because, the mob said, "he was a papish, and sold popish beer." Did you ever hear of such diabolical ruffians?

To add to the pleasantness of our situation, there have been gangs of women going about to rob and plunder. Miss Kirwans went on Friday afternoon to walk in the Museum gardens, and were stopped by a set of women, and robbed of all the money they had. The mob had proscribed the mews, for they said, "the king should not have a horse to ride upon!" They besieged the new Somerset House, with intention to destroy it, but were repulsed by some soldiers placed there for that purpose.

Mr. Sleepe has been here a day or two, and says the folks at Watford, where he comes from, "approve very Much Of having the Catholic chapels destroyed, for they say it's a shame the pope should come here!" There is a house hereabouts that they had chalked upon last week, "Empty, and No Popery!"

I am heartily rejoiced, my dearest Fanny, that you have got away from Bath, and hope and trust that at Brighthelmstone you will be as safe as we are here.

It sounds almost incredible, but they say, that on Wednesday night last, when the mob were more powerful, more numerous, and outrageous than ever, there was, nevertheless, a number of exceeding genteel people at Ranelagh, though they knew not but their houses might be on fire at the time!

A SUGGESTED VISIT To GRUB-STREET.

(FANNY BUrney to Mrs. Thrale.)

Since I wrote last I have drunk tea with Dr. Johnson. My father took me to Bolt-court, and we found him, most fortunately, with only one brass-headed cane gentleman. Since that I have had the pleasure to meet him again at Mrs. Reynolds's, when he offered to take me with him to Grub-street, to see the ruins of the house demolished there in the late riots, by a mob that, as he observed, could be no friend to the Muses! He inquired if I had ever yet visited Grub-street ? but was obliged to restrain his anger when I answered "No," because he acknowledged he had never paid his respects to it

Himself. "However," says he, "you and I, Burney, will go together; we have a very good right to go, so we'll visit the mansions of our progenitors, and take up our own freedon, together." There's for you, madam! What can be grander?

FANNY BURNEY'S BROTHER IS PROMOTED.
(Fanny Burney to Mrs. Thrale.) Chesington, Nov. 4.
I had no other adventure in London, but a most delightful incident has happened since I came hither. We had just done tea on Friday, and Mrs. Hamilton, Kitty, Jem, and Mr. Crisp, were sitting down to cards, when we were surprised by an express from London, and it brought a "Whereas we think fit" from the Admiralty, to appoint Captain Burney to the command of the "Latona," during the absence of the Honourable Captain Conway. This is one of the best frigates in the navy, of thirty-eight guns, and immediately, I believe, ready for service. Jem was almost frantic with ecstacy of joy: he sang, laughed, drank to his own success, and danced about the room with Miss Kitty till He put her quite out of breath. His hope is to get out immediately, and have a brush with some of the Dons, Monsieurs, or Mynheers, while he is in possession of a ship of sufficient force to attack any frigate he may meet.

Mrs. Thrale wrote to Fanny from Streatham, Dec. 22:—) I have picked up something to please you; Dr. Johnson pronounced an actual eulogium upon Captain Burney, to his yesterday's listeners—how amiable he was, and how gentle in his manner, etc., tho' he had lived so many years with sailors and savages.

THE DEATH OF MR. THRALE.
(Fanny Burney to Mrs. Thrale[135])
m Wednesday Evening, April 4, 1781
You bid me write to you, and so I will; you bid me pray for you, and so, indeed, I do, for the restoration of your sweet peace of mind. I pray for your resignation to this hard blow, for the continued union and exertion of your virtues with your talents, and for the happiest reward their exertion can meet with, in the gratitude and prosperity of your children. These are my prayers for my beloved Mrs. Thrale; but these are not my only ones; no, the unfailing warmth of her kindness for myself I have rarely, for a long time past, slept without first petitioning.

I ran away without seeing you again when I found you repented that sweet compliance with my request which I had won from you. For the world would I not have pursued you, had I first seen your prohibition, nor could I endure to owe that consent to teasing which I only solicited from tenderness. Still, however, I think you had better have suffered me to follow you; I might have been of some use; I hardly could have been in your way. But I grieve now to have forced you to an interview which I would have spared myself as well as you, had I foreseen how little it would have answered my purpose.

Yet though I cannot help feeling disappointed, I am not surprised; for in any case at all similar, I am sure I should have the same eagerness for solitude.

I tell you nothing of how sincerely I sympathise in your affliction; yet I believe that Mr. Crutchley and Dr. Johnson alone do so more earnestly; and I have some melancholy comfort in flattering myself that, allowing for the difference of our characters, that true regard which I felt was as truly returned. Nothing but kindness did I ever meet with; he ever loved to have me, not merely with his family, but with himself; and gratefully shall I ever remember a thousand kind expressions of esteem and good opinion, which are now crowding upon my memory.

---

116   Mr. Smelt was a friend of Dr. Burney's, and highly esteemed by Fanny both for his character and talents. He had been tutor to the Prince of Wales (afterwards George IV.). We shall meet with him later.-ED,

117   This boy was afterwards the celebrated painter, Sir Thomas Lawrence, President of the Royal Academy.

118   Constantine John Phipps, second Baron Mulgrave in the Irish peerage. He was born in 1744; served with distinction in the navy, and made a voyage of discovery towards the North Pole in 1773. His account of this voyage was published in the following year. He became Baron Mulgrave on the death of his father, the first Baron, in 1775; was raised to the English peerage under the title of Lord Mulgrave in 1790, and died in 1792.-ED.

119   Mrs. Byron was the wife of Admiral the Hon. John Byron ("Foul-weather Jack"), and grandmother of the poet. Her daughter Augusta subsequently married Vice-Admiral Parker, and died in 1824.-ED.

120   Mrs. Dobson was authoress of an abridged translation of "Petrarch's Life," and of the "History of the Troubadours."-ED.

121   Dr. Harrington was a physician, and a friend of Dr. Burney. His son, "Mr. Henry"—the Rev. Henry Harrington—was the editor of "Nugaae Antiquae.""-ED.

122   The rough-mannered, brutal sea-captain in "Evelina."-ED.

123   Lady Miller, of Bath Easton—the lady of the Vase. Horace Walpole gives an amusing description of the flummery which was indulged in every week at Bath Easton under her presidency. "You must know, that near Bath is erected a new Parnassus, composed of three laurels, a myrtle-tree, a weeping-willow, and a view of the Avon, which has now been christened Helicon. Ten years ago there lived a Madam (Briggs], an old rough humourist, who passed for a wit; her daughter, who passed for nothing, married to a captain [Miller], full of good-natured officiousness. These good folks were friends of Miss Rich, who carried me to dine with them at Bath Easton, now Pindus. They caught a little of what was then called taste, built, and planted, and begot children, till

the whole caravan were forced to go abroad to retrieve. Alas! Mrs. Miller is returned a beauty, a genius, a Sappho, a tenth muse, as romantic as Mademoiselle Scuderi, and as sophisticated as Mrs. Vesey. The captain's fingers are loaded with cameos, his tongue runs over with virt'u; and that both may contribute to the improvement of their own country, they have introduced bouts-rim`es as a new discovery. They hold a Parnassus-fair every Thursday, give out rhymes and themes, and all the flux of quality at Bath contend for the prizes. A Roman vase, dressed with pink ribands and myrtles, receives the poetry, which is drawn out every festival: six judges of these Olympic games retire and select the brightest compositions, which the respective successful acknowledge, kneel to Mrs. Calliope (Miller), kiss her fair hand, and are crowned by it with myrtle." Works, vol. v. P. 183-ED.

124   Not our old acquaintance, Mrs. Cholmondeley, but a lady whom Fanny met for the first time during this season at Bath.-ED.

125   See ante, note 121, p. 170.-ED.

126   Beattie's "Essay on Truth," published in 1770, and containing a feeble attack on Hume. Commonplace as the book is, it was received with rapture by the Orthodox, and Reynolds painted a fine picture of Beattie, standing with the "Essay" under his arm, while the angel of Truth beside him, drives away three demonic figures, in whose faces we trace a resemblance to the portraits of Hume, Voltaire, and Gibbon. For this piece of flattery the painter was justly rebuked by Goldsmith, whose sympathies were certainly not on the side of infidelity. "It very ill becomeF a mann Of your eminence and character," said the poet, "to debase so high a genius as Voltaire before so mean a writer as Beattie. Beattie and his book will be forgotten in ten years, while Voltaire's fame will last for ever. Take care it does not perpetuate this picture, to the shame of such a man as you."-ED.

127   Charlotte Lewis.-ED.

128   Sir Clement Willoughby, a rakish baronet in "Evelina."-ED.

129   This flirtation came to nothing, as Captain Brisbane proved himself a jilt. The following month Miss Burney wrote to Mrs. Thrale as follows:— "Your account of Miss M-'s being taken in, and taken in by Captain Brisbane, astonishes me! surely not half we have heard either of her adorers, or her talents, can have been true. Mrs. Byron has lost too little to have anything to lament, except, indeed, the time she sacrificed to foolish conversation, and the civilities she threw away upon so worthless a subject. Augusta has nothing to reproach herself with, and riches and wisdom must be rare indeed, if she fares not as well with respect to both, as she would have done with an adventurer whose pocket, it seems, was as empty as his head."-ED.

130   Sir John Fielding, the magistrate; brother of the novelist.-ED.

131   Mr Thrale's brewery in Southwark. His town house in Grosvenor Square was threatened by the mob, but escaped destruction.-ED.

132   The manager of Mr. Thrale's brewery.-ED.

133   James Harris, of Salisbury, and his family. Mr. Harris was the author of "Hermes, an Enquiry concerning Universal Grammar," and was characterised by Dr. Johnson as a "sound, solid scholar." He was an enthusiast on the subject of music, and had made Dr. Burney's acquaintance at the opera in 1773.-ED.

134   Fanny's younger sister, some of whose lively and amusing letters and fragments of journal are printed in the "Early Diary." Unlike Fanny, she was a bit of a flirt, and she seems to have been altogether a very charming young woman, who fully sustained the Burney reputation for sprightliness and good humour.-ED.

135   This letter was written in reply to a few words from Mrs. Thrale, in which, alluding to her husband's sudden death, she begs Miss Burney to "write to me—pray for me!" The hurried note from Mrs. Thrale is thus endorsed by Miss Burney:—"Written a few hours after the death of Mr. Thrale, which happened by a sudden stroke of apoplexy, on the morning of a day on which half the fashion of London had been invited to an intended assembly at his house in Grosvenor Square." [Mr. Thrale, who had long suffered from ill health, had been contemplating a journey to Spa, and thence to Italy. His physicians, however, were strongly opposed to the scheme, and Fanny writes, just before his death, that it was settled that a great meeting of hi friends should take place, and that they should endeavour to prevail with him to give it up; in which she has little doubt of their succeeding.-ED.]

SECTION 4 ^{17812.)}

MISS BURNEY EXTENDS THE CIRCLE OF HER ACQUAINTANCE.

[DURING the years 1781 and 1782 Fanny was engaged upon her second novel, "Cecilia," which was published in July, 1782. It is not necessary here to discuss the merits of a work with which everyone ought to be acquainted. We may safely leave the task of criticising "Cecilia" to an unimpeachable authority, Edmund Burke, whose magnificent, but just eulogy of the book will be found on Of the present volume. In the following section of " The Diary" Fanny records one of the most memorable events of her life,—her introduction to Burke, in June, 1782, at Sir Joshua Reynolds's house on Richmond Hill. Rer letter to Mr. Crisp, printed in the " Memoirs of Dr. Burney," gives a more detailed account than that in the " Diary," of the conversation which passed on this occasion. Other men of genius were present, among them Gibbon the historian, whom she then met for the first time; but Fanny had eyes and ears for none but Burke. Nor was she singular in yielding thus completely to the fascination of the great Irishman's manner and conversation. Wherever he appeared, in what society soever he mingled, Burke was still the man of distinction. As Johnson said, you could not stand under a shed with Burke for a few minutes, during a shower of rain, without feeling that you were in the company of an extraordinary man.

Mr. Thrale's death produced no immediate change in the situation of affairs at Streatham. Dr. Johnson's visits were as frequent and as protracted as before; Fanny continued to be numbered among the dearest friends of the widow. Not yet had arisen that infatuation which eventually alienated from Mrs. Thrale the sympathy of her former friends, and subjected her, justly or unjustly, to such severe and general condemnation. But to this topic we shall revert at a later period.

The great brewer had left his wife and family in affluent circumstances. The executors to his Will were Dr. Johnson, Mr. Henry Smith, Mr. Cator and Mr. Crutchley, together with Mrs. Thrale. Of the last-named gentleman we shall hear a good deal in the following pages. He and Mr. Cator were both chosen members of parliament In the same year—1784: Mr. Cator for Ipswich, Mr. Crutchley for Horsham. Early in the summer following Thrale's decease the brewery was sold for the handsome sum of 135,000 pounds, to David Barclay, the Quaker, who took Thrale's old manager, Perkins into Partnership. Thus was Vfounded the famous house Of Barclay and Perkins.-ED-]

YOUNG MR. CRUTCHLEY RUFFLES MISS BURNEY.
Streatham, May.
Miss Owen and I arrived here without incident, which, in a journey of six or seven miles, was really marvellous. Mrs. Thrale came from the Borough with two of the executors, Dr. Johnson and Mr Crutchley soon after us. She had been sadly worried, and in the evening frightened us all by again fainting away. Dear

creature! she is all agitation of mind and of body: but she is now wonnderfully recovered though in continual fevers about her affairs, which are mighty difficult and complicate indeed. Yet the behaviour of all the executors is exactly to her wish. Mr. Crutchley, In particular, was he a darling son or only brother could not possibly be more truly devoted to her. Indeed., I am very happy in the revolution in my own mind in favour of this young man, whom formerly I so little liked; for I now see so much of him, business and inclination uniting to bring him hither continually, that if he were disagreeable to me, I should spend my time in a most comfortless manner. On the contrary, I both respect and esteem him very highly; for his whole conduct manifests so much goodness of heart and excellence of principle, that he is Un homme comme ill y en a peu; and that first appearance of coldness, pride, reserve, and sneering, all wears off upon further acquaintance, and leaves behind nothing but good-humour and good-will. And this you must allow to be very candid, when I tell you that, but yesterday, he affronted me so much by a Piece Of impertinence that I had a very serious quarrel with im.

Sunday morning nobody went to church but Mr. Crutchley, Miss Thrale, and myself; and some time after, when I was sauntering upon the lawn before the house, Mr. Crutchley joined ine. We were returning together into the house, when, Mrs. Thrale, popping her head out of her dressing-room window, called out,

"How nicely these men domesticate among us, Miss Burney! Why, they take to us as natural as life!"

"Well, well," cried Mr. Crutchley, "I have sent for my horse, and I shall release you early to-morrow morning, I think yonder comes Sir Philip." [136]

"Oh! you'll have enough to do with him," cried she, laughing; "he is well prepared to plague you, I assure you."

"Is he?—and what about?"

"Why, about Miss Burney. He asked me the other day what was my present establishment. 'Mr. Crutchley and Miss Burney,' I answered. 'How well those two names go together,' cried he; 'I think they can't do better than make a match of it: I will consent, I am sure,' he added; and to-day, I dare say, you will hear enough of it."

I leave you to judge if I was pleased at this stuff thus communicated; but Mrs. Thrale, with all her excellence, can give up no occasion of making sport, however unseasonable, or even painful.

" I am very much obliged to him, indeed cried I, dryly; and Mr. Crutchley called out, "Thank him !-thank him! " in a voice of pride and of pique that spoke him mortally angry.

I instantly came into the house, leaving him to talk it out with Mrs. Thrale, to whom I heard him add, "So this is Sir Philip's kindness!" and her answer, "I wish you no worse luck!"

Now, what think you of this? was it not highly insolent?—and from a man who has behaved to me hitherto with the utmost deference, good-nature, and civility, and given me a thousand reasons, by every possible opportunity, to think myself very high indeed in his good opinion and good graces? But these rich men think themselves the constant prey of all portionless girls, and are always upon their guard, and suspicious of some design to take them in. This sort of disposition I had very early observed in Mr. Crutchley, and therefore I had been more distant and cold with him than with anybody I ever met with ; but latterly his character had risen so much in my mind, and his behaviour was so much improved, that I had let things take their own course, and no more shunned than I sought him; for I evidently saw his doubts concerning me and my plots were all at an end, and his civility and attentions were daily increasing, so that I had become very comfortable with him, and well pleased with his society.

I need not, I think, add that I determined to see as little of this most fearful and haughty gentleman in future as was in my power, since no good qualities can compensate for such arrogance of suspicion; and, therefore, as I had reason enough to suppose he would, in haste, resume his own reserve, I resolved, without much effort, to be beforehand with him in resuming mine.

Miss BURNEY SULKS ON.

At dinner we had a large and most disagreeable party of Irish ladies, whom Mrs. Thrale was necessitated to invite from motives of business and various connections.

I was obliged to be seated between Miss O'Riley and Mr. Crutchley, to whom you may believe I was not very courteous, especially as I had some apprehension of Sir Philip. Mr. Crutchley, however, to my great surprise, was quite as civil as ever, and endeavoured to be as chatty; but there I begged to be excused, only answering upon the reply, and that very dryly, for I was indeed horribly provoked with him.

I was much diverted during dinner by this Miss O'Riley, who took it in her humour to attack Mr. Crutchley repeatedly, though so discouraging a beau never did I see! Her forwardness, and his excessive and inordinate coldness, made a contrast that, added to her brogue, which was broad, kept me in a grin irrepressible.

In the afternoon we had also Mr. Wallace, the attorney general, a most squat and squab looking man. In the evening, when the Irish ladies, the Perkinses, Lambarts, and Sir Philip, had gone, Mrs. Thrale walked out with Mr. Wallace, whom she had some business to talk over with; and then, when only Miss Owen, Miss T., and I remained, Mr. Crutchley, after repeatedly addressing me, and gaining pretty dry answers, called out suddenly,

"Why, Miss Burney! why, what's the matter?"

"Nothing."

"Why, are you stricken, or smitten, or ill?"

"None of the three."

"Oh, then, you are setting down all these Irish folks."

"No, indeed; I don't think them worth the trouble."

"Oh, but I am sure you are; only I interrupted you."

I went on no further with the argument, and Miss Thrale proposed our walking out to meet her mother. We all agreed and Mr. Crutchley would not be satisfied without walking near me, though I really had no patience to talk with him, and wished him at Jericho.

"What's the matter?" said he; "have you had a quarrel?"

"NO."

"Are you affronted?"

Not a word. Then again he called to Miss Thrale-

" Why, Queeny—why, she's quite in a rage! What have you done to her?"

I still sulked on, vexed to be teased ; but, though with a gaiety that showed he had no suspicion of the cause, he grew more and more urgent, trying every means to make me tell him what was the matter, till at last, much provoked, I said-

" I must be strangely in want of a confidant, indeed, to take you for one!"

"Why, what an insolent speech!" cried he, half serious and half laughing, but casting up his eyes and hands with astonishment. He then let me be quiet some time,- but in a few minutes renewed his inquiries, with added eagerness, begging me to tell him if nobody else.

A likely matter! thought I; nor did I scruple to tell him, when forced to answer, that no one had such little chance of success in such a request.

"Why so?" cried he; "for I am the best person in the world to trust with a secret, as I always forget it."

He continued working at me till we joined Mrs. Thrale and the attorney-general. And then Miss Thrale, stimulated by him, came to inquire if I had really taken anything amiss of her. "No," I assured her.

"Is it of me, then?" cried Mr. Crutchley, as if sure I should say no; but I made no other answer than to desire him to desist questioning me. . . .

He then grew quite violent, and at last went on with his questions till, by being quite silent, he could no longer doubt who it was. He seemed then wholly amazed, and entreated to know what he had done; but I tried only to avoid him.

Soon after the attorney-general took his leave, during which ceremony Mr. Crutchley, coming behind me, exclaimed,-

"Who'd think of this creature's having any venom in her"

"Oh, yes," answered I, "when she's provoked."

" But have I provoked you?"

Again I got off. Taking Miss Thrale by the arm, we hurried away, leaving him with Mrs. Thrale and Miss Owen. He was presently, however, with us again ; and when he came to my side and found me really trying to talk of other matters with Miss Thrale, and avoid him, he called out,-

"Upon my life, this is too bad! Do tell me, Miss Burney, what is the matter? If you won't, I protest I'll call Mrs. Thrale, and make her work at you herself."

"I assure you," answered I, "that it will be to no purpose for I must offend myself by telling it, and therefore I shall mention it to nobody."

"But what in the world have I done?"

"Nothing; you have done nothing."

"What have I said, then? Only let me beg your pardon, only let me know what it is, that I may beg your pardon."

I then took up the teasing myself, and quite insisted upon his leaving us, and joining Mrs. Thrale. He begged me to tell Miss Thrale, and let her mediate, and entreated her to be his agent; which, in order to get rid of him, she promised; and he then slackened his pace, though very reluctantly, while we quickened ours. He was, however, which I very little expected, too uneasy to stay long away; and when we had walked on quite out of hearing of Mrs. Thrale and Miss Owen, he suddenly galloped after us.

"How odd it is of you," said Miss Thrale, "to come and intrude yourself in this manner upon anybody that tries so to avoid you!"

"Have you done anything for me?" cried he. I don't believe you have said a word."

"Not I, truly!" answered she; "if I can keep my own self, out of scrapes, it's all I can pretend to."

"Well, but do tell me, Miss Burney,—pray tell me! indeed, this is quite too bad; I sha'n't have a wink of sleep all night! If I have offended you, I am very sorry indeed; but I am sure I did not mean—"

"No, sir!" interrupted I, "I don't suppose you did mean to offend me, nor do I know why you should. I expect from you neither good nor ill,—civility I think myself entitled to, and that is all I have any desire for."

"Good heaven!" exclaimed he. "Tell me, however, but what it is, and if I have said any thing unguardedly, I am extremely sorry, and I most sincerely beg your pardon. If You would tell me, I am sure I could explain it off, because I am sure it has been done undesignedly."

"No, it does not admit of any explanation ; so pray don't mention it any more."

"Only tell me what part of the day it was."

Whether this unconsciousness was real, or only to draw me in so that he might come to the point, and make his apology with greater ease, I know not; but I assured him it was in vain he asked, and again desired him to puzzle himself with no further recollections.

"Oh," cried he, "but I shall think of every thing I have ever said to you for this half year. I am sure, whatever it was, it must have been unmeant and unguarded."

"That, Sir, I never doubted; and probably you thought me hard enough to hear any thing without minding it."

"Good heaven, Miss Burney! why, there is nobody I would not sooner offend,—nobody in the world! Queeny knows it. If Queeny would speak, she could tell you so. Is it not true, Miss Thrale?"

"I shall say nothing about it; if I can keep my own neck out of the collar, it's enough for me."

"But won't it plead something for me that you are sure, and must be sure, it was by blunder, and not design? . . . I beg you will think no more of it. I—I believe I know what it is; and, indeed, I was far from meaning to give you the smallest offence, and I most earnestly beg your pardon. There is nothing I would not do to assure you how sorry I am. But I hope it will be all over by the time the candles come. I shall look to see, and I hope—I beg—you will have the same countenance again."

I now felt really appeased, and so I told him. We then talked of other matters till we reached home, though it was not without difficulty I could even yet keep him quiet. I see that Mr. Crutchley, though of a cold and proud disposition, is generous, amiable, and delicate, and, when not touched upon the tender string of gallantry, concerning which he piques himself upon invariable hardness and immoveability, his sentiments are not merely just, but refined.

Too MUCH OF MANY THINGS.

Sunday.-We had Mr. and Mrs. Davenant here. They are very lively and agreeable, and I like them more' and more. Mrs. Davenant is one of the saucy women of the ton, indeed; but she has good parts, and is gay and entertaining; and her sposo, who passionately adores her, though five years her junior, is one of the best-tempered and most pleasant-charactered young men imaginable . . .

"Mrs. Davenant is very agreeable," said I to Mr. Crutchley, "I like her much. Don't you?"

"Yes, very much," said he; "she is lively and entertaining;" and then a moment after, "'Tis wonderful," he exclaimed, "that such a thing as that can captivate a man!"

"Nay," cried I, "nobody more, for her husband quite adores her." "So I find," said he; "and Mrs. Thrale says men in general like her."

"They certainly do," cried I, "and all the oddity is in you who do not, not in them who do."

"May be so," answered he, "but it don't do for me, indeed."

We then came to two gates, and there I stopped short, to wait till they joined us ; and Mr. Crutchley, turning about and looking at Mrs. Davenant, as she came forward, said, rather in a muttering voice, and to himself than to me, "What a thing for an attachment! No, no, it would not do for me!—too much glare! too much flippancy! too much hoop! too much gauze! too much slipper! too much neck! Oh, hide it! hide it! muffle it up! muffle it up! If it is but in a fur cloak, I am for muffling it all up!"

A "POOR WRETCH OF A PAINTER."

I HAD NEW specimens to-day of the oddities of Mr. Crutchley, whom I do not yet quite understand, though I have seen so much of him. In the course of our walks to-day we chanced, at one time, to be somewhat before the rest of the company, band soon got into a very serious conversation; though we began it by his relating a most ludicrous incident which had happened to him last winter.

There is a certain poor wretch of a villainous painter, one Mr. Lowe, [137]who is in some measure under Dr. Johnson's protection, and whom, therefore, he recommends to all the people he thinks can afford to sit for their pictures. Among these he made Mr. Seward very readily, and then applied to Mr. Crutchley.

"But now," said Mr. Crutchley, as he told me the circumstance, "I have not a notion of sitting for my picture,—for who wants it? I may as well give the man the money without; but no, they all said that would not do so well, and Dr. Johnson asked me to give him my picture. 'And I assure you, sir,' says he, 'I shall put it in very good company, for I have portraits of some very respectable people in my dining-room.' 'Ay, sir,' says I, 'that's sufficient reason why you should not have mine, for I am sure it has no business in such society.' So then Mrs. Thrale asked me to give it to her. 'Ay sure, ma'am,' says I, 'you do me great honour; but pray, first, will you do me the favour to tell me what door you intend to put it behind?' However, after all I could say in opposition, I was obliged to go to the painter's. And I found him in such a condition! a room all dirt and filth, brats squalling and wrangling, up two pair of stairs, and a closet, of which the door was open, that Seward well said was quite Pandora's box—it was the repository of all the nastiness, and stench, and filth, and food, and drink, and - oh, it was too bad to be borne! and 'Oh!' says I, 'Mr. Lowe, I beg your pardon for running away, but I have just recollected another engagement;' so I poked the three guineas in his hand, and told him I would come again another time, and then ran out of the house with all my might."

DR. JOHNSON IN A RAGE.

June.—Wednesday—We had a terrible noisy day. Mr. and Mrs. Cator came to dinner, and brought with them Miss Collison, a niece. Mrs. Nesbitt was also here, and Mr. Pepys. [138]

The long war which has been proclaimed among the wits concerning Lord Lyttelton's "Life," by Dr. Johnson, and which a whole tribe of "blues," with Mrs. Montagu at their head, have vowed to execrate and revenge, now broke out with all the fury of the first actual hostilities, stimulated by long concerted schemes and much spiteful information. Mr. Pepys, Dr. Johnson well knew, was one of Mrs. Montagu's steadiest abettors; and, therefore, as he had some time determined to defend himself with the first of them he met, this day he fell the sacrifice to his wrath.

In a long tête-à-tête which I accidentally had with Mr. Pepys before the company was assembled, he told me his apprehensions of an attack, and entreated me earnestly to endeavour to prevent it; modestly avowing he was no antagonist for Dr. Johnson; and yet declaring his personal friendship for Lord Lyttelton made him so much hurt by the "Life," that he feared he could not discuss the matter without a quarrel, which, especially in the house of Mrs. Thrale, he wished to avoid.

It was, however, utterly impossible for me to serve him. I could have stopped Mrs. Thrale with ease, and Mr. Seward with a hint, had either of them begun the subject; but, unfortunately, in the middle of dinner, it was begun by Dr. Johnson himself, to oppose whom, especially as he spoke with great anger, would have been madness and folly.

Never before have I seen Dr. Johnson speak with so much passion.

"Mr. Pepys," he cried, in a voice the most enraged, "I understand you are offended by my 'Life of Lord Lyttelton.' What is it you have to say against it?

Come forth, man Here am I, ready to answer any charge you can bring!"

"No, sir," cried Mr. Pepys, "not at present; I must beg leave to decline the subject. I told Miss Burney before dinner that I hoped it would not be started."

I was quite frightened to hear my own name mentioned ina .debate which began so seriously; but Dr. Johnson made not -to this any answer, he repeated his attack and his challenge, and a violent disputation ensued, in which this great but mortal man did, to own the truth, appear unreasonably furious and grossly severe. I never saw him so before, and I heartily hope I never shall again. He has been long provoked, and justly enough, at the sneaking complaints and murmurs of the Lytteltonians; and, therefore, his long-excited wrath, which hitherto had met no object, now burst forth with a vehemence and bitterness almost incredible.

Mr. Pepys meantime never appeared to so much advantage; he preserved his temper, uttered all that belonged merely to himself with modesty, and all that more immediately related to Lord Lyttelton with spirit. Indeed, Dr. Johnson, in the very midst of the dispute, had the candour and liberality to make him a personal compliment, by saying

"Sir, all that you say, while you are vindicating one who cannot thank you, makes me only think better of you than I ever did before. Yet still I think you do me wrong," etc., etc.

Some time after, in the heat of the argument, he called out,—

" The more my Lord Lyttelton is inquired after, the worse he will appear; Mr. Seward has just heard two stories of him, which corroborate all I have related."

He then desired Mr. Seward to repeat them. Poor Mr. Seward looked almost as frightened as myself at the very mention of his name; but he quietly and immediately told the stories, which consisted of fresh instances, from good authorities, of Lord Lyttelton's illiberal behaviour to Shenstone; and then he flung himself back in his chair, and spoke no more during the whole debate, which I am sure he was ready to vote a bore.

One happy circumstance, however, attended the quarrel, which was the presence of Mr. Cator, who would by no means be prevented talking himself, either by reverence for Dr. Johnson, or ignorance of the subject in question; on the contrary, he gave his opinion, quite uncalled upon every thing that was said by either party, and that with an importance and pomposity, yet with an emptiness and verbosity, that rendered the whole dispute, when in his hands, nothing more than ridiculous, and compelled even the disputants themselves, all inflamed as they were, to laugh. To give a specimen—one speech will do for a thousand.

"As to this here question of Lord Lyttelton, I can't speak to it to the purpose, as I have not read his 'Life,' for I have only read the 'Life of Pope;' I have got the books though, for I sent for them last week, and they came to me on Wednesday, and then I began them; but I have not yet read 'Lord Lyttelton.' 'Pope' I have begun, and that is what I am now reading. But what I have to say about Lord Lyttelton is this here: Mr. Seward says that Lord Lyttelton's steward dunned Mr. Shenstone for his rent, by which I understand he was a tenant of Lord Lyttelton's. Well, if he was a tenant of Lord Lyttelton's, why should not he pay his rent?"

Who could contradict this?

When dinner was quite over, and we left the men to their wine, we hoped they would finish the affair; but Dr. Johnson was determined to talk it through, and make a battle of it, though Mr. Pepys tried to be off continually. When they were all summoned to tea, they entered still warm and violent. Mr. Cator had the book in his hand, and was reading the "Life of Lyttelton," that he might better, he said, understand the cause, though not a creature cared if he had never heard of it.

Mr. Pepys came up to me and said-

"Just what I had so much wished to avoid! I have been crushed in the very onset."

I could make him no answer, for Dr. Johnson immediately called him off, and harangued and attacked him with a vehemence and continuity that quite concerned both Mrs. Thrale and myself, and that made Mr. Pepys, at last, resolutely silent, however called upon. This now grew more unpleasant than ever; till Mr. Cator, having some time studied his book, exclaimed—

"What I am now going to say, as I have not yet read the 'Life of Lord Lyttelton' quite through, must be considered as being only said aside, because what I am going to say—"

"I wish, sir," cried Mrs. Thrale, "it had been all said aside; here is too much about it, indeed, and I should be very glad to hear no more of it."

This speech, which she made with great spirit and dignity, had an admirable effect. Everybody was silenced. Mr. Cator, thus interrupted in the midst of his proposition, looked quite amazed; Mr. Pepys was much gratified by the interference; and Dr. Johnson, after a pause, said-

"Well, madam, you shall hear no more of it; yet I will defend myself in every part and in every atom!"

And from this time the subject was wholly dropped. This dear violent doctor was conscious he had been wrong, and therefore he most candidly bore the reproof. . . .

When the leave-taking time arrived, Dr. Johnson called to Mr. Pepys to shake hands, an invitation which was most coldly and forcibly accepted. [139]

THE MISERABLE HOST AND MELANCHOLY GUEST.

Monday, june 17.-There passed, some time ago, an 'agreement' between Mr. Crutchley and Mr. Seward, that the latter is to make a visit to the former, at his country house in Berkshire; and to-day the time was settled; but a more ridiculous scene never was exhibited. The host elect and the guest elect tried which should show least expectation of pleasure from the meeting, and neither of them thought it at all worth while to disguise his terror of being weary of the other. Mr. Seward seemed quite melancholy and depressed in the prospect of making, and Mr. Crutchley absolutely miserable in that of receiving, the visit. Yet nothing so ludicrous as the distress of both, since nothing less necessary than that either should have such a punishment inflicted. I cannot remember half the absurd things that passed - but a few, by way of specimen, I will give.

"How long do you intend to stay with me, Seward?" cried Mr. Crutchley; "how long do you think you can bear it?"

"O, I don't know; I sha'n't fix," answered the other: just as I find it."

"Well, but—when shall you come? Friday or Saturday? I think you'd better not come till Saturday."

"Why, yes, I believe on Friday."

" On Friday! Oh, you'll have too much of it! what shall I do with you?"

"Why, on Sunday we'll dine at the Lyells'. Mrs. Lyell is a charming woman; one of the most elegant creatures I ever saw."

"Wonderfully so," cried Mr. Crutchley; "I like her extremely—an insipid idiot! She never opens her mouth but in a whisper; I never heard her speak a word in my life. But what must I do with you on Monday? will you come away?"

"Oh, no; I'll stay and see it out."

" Why, how long shall you stay? Why, I must come away myself on Tuesday."

"O, I sha'n't settle yet," cried Mr. Seward, very dryly. "I shall put up six shirts, and then do as I find it."

" Six shirts!" exclaimed Mr. Crutchley '; and then, with equal dryness, added—"Oh, I suppose you wear two a-day."

And so on. . . .

June 26.-Mr. Crutchley said he had just brought Mr. Seward to town in his phaeton, alive. He gave a diverting account of the visit, which I fancy proved much better than either party pretended to expect, as I find Mr. Seward not only went a day sooner, but stayed two days later, than was proposed; and Mr. Crutchley, on his part, said he had invited him to repeat his visit at any time when he knew not in what other manner "to knock down a day or two. When he was at my place," continued Mr. Crutchley, "he did himself up pretty handsomely; he ate cherries till he complained most bitterly of indigestion, and he poured down madeira and port most plentifully, but without relief. Then he desired to have some peppermint-water, and he drank three glasses; still that would not do, and he said he njust have a large quantity of ginger. We had no such thing in the house. However, he had brought some, it seems, with him, and then he took that, but still to no purpose. At last, he desired some brandy, and tossed off a glass of that; and, after all, he asked for a dose of rhubarb. Then we had to send and inquire all over the house for this rhubarb, but our folks had hardly ever heard of such a thing. I advised him to take a good bumper of gin and gunpowder, for that seemed almost all he had left untried."

Two CELEBRATED DUCHESSEs DISCUSSED.

Wednesday, June 26.-Dr. Johnson, who had been in town .some days, returned, and Mr. Crutchley came also, as well as my father. I did not see the two latter till summoned to dinner; and then Dr. Johnson seizing my hand, while with one of his own he gave me a no very gentle tap on the shoulder, half drolly and half reproachfully called out—

"Ah, you little baggage, you! and have you known how long I have been here, and never to come to me?"

And the truth is, in whatever sportive mood he expresses it, he really likes not I should be absent from him half a minute whenever he is here, and not in his own apartment.

Dr. Johnson, as usual, kept me in chat with him 'in the library after all the rest had dispersed ; but when Mr. Crutchley returned again, he went upstairs, and, as I was finishing some work I had in hand, Mr. Crutchley, either from civility or a sudden turn to loquacity, forbore his books, to talk.

Among other folks, we discussed the two rival duchesses, Rutland and Devonshire. [140] "The former," he said, "must, he fancied, be very weak and silly, as he knew that she endured being admired to her face, and complimented perpetually, both upon her beauty and her dress;" and when I asked whether he was one who joined in trying her—

"Me!" cried he, "no, indeed! I never complimented any body; that is, I never said to any body a thing I did not think, unless I was openly laughing at them, and making sport for other people."

" Oh," cried I, "if everybody went by this rule, what a world of conversation would be curtailed! The Duchess of Devonshire, I fancy, has better parts."

Oh yes; and a fine, pleasant, open countenance. She came to my sister's once, in Lincolnshire, when I was there, in order to see hare-hunting, which was then quite new to her."

" She is very amiable, I believe," said I, "for all her friends love and speak highly of her."

"Oh, yes, very much so - perfectly good-humoured and unaffected. And her horse was led, and she was frightened; and we told her that was the hare, and that was the dog; and the dog pointed to the hare, and the hare ran away from the dog and then she took courage, and then she was timid;—and, upon my word, she did it all very prettily! For my part, I liked it so well, that in half an hour I took to my own horse, and rode away."

MR. CRUTCHLEY IS BANTERED ABOUT HIS PRIDE.

While we were at church on Sunday morning, we heard a sermon, upon which, by means of a speech I chanced to make, we have been talking ever since. The subject was treating of humility, and declaiming against pride; in the midst of which Mrs. Thrale whispered-

"This sermon is all against us; that is, four of us: Queeny, Burney, Susan, and I, are all as proud as possible—Mr. Crutchley and Sophy[141]are humble enough."

"Good heavens!" cried I, "Mr. Crutchley!—why he is the proudest among us!"

This speech she instantly repeated, and just at that moment the preacher said—"Those -who are the weakest are ever the soonest puffed up."

He instantly made me a bow, with an expressive laugh, that thanked me for the compliment. To be sure it happened most untimely.

As soon as we came out of church, he called out-

"Well, Miss Burney, this is what I never can forgive! Am I so proud?"

"I am sure if you are," cried Mrs. Thrale, "you have imposed upon me, for I always thought you the humblest man I knew. Look how Burney casts up her eyes! Why, are you so proud, after all, Mr. Crutchley?"

"I hope not," cried he, rather gravely "but I little thought of ever going to Streatham church to hear I was the proudest man in it."

"Well, but," said I, "does it follow you certainly are so because I say so?"

"Why yes, I suppose I am if you see it, for you are one that see all things and people right."

"Well, it's very odd," said Mrs. Thrale, "I wonder how she found you out."

"I wonder," cried I, laughing, "how you missed finding him out."

"Oh! worse and worse!" cried he. "Why there's no bearing this!"

"I protest, then," said Mrs. Thrale, "he has always taken me in; he seemed to me the humblest creature I knew; always speaking so ill of himself—always depreciating all that belongs to him."

"Why, I did not say," quoth I, "that he had more vanity than other men; on the contrary, I think he has none."

"Well distinguished," cried she; "a man may be proud enough, and yet have no vanity."

"Well, but what is this pride?" cried Mr. Crutchley; "what is it shown in?— what are its symptoms and marks?"

"A general contempt," answered I, undaunted, "of every body and of every thing."

"Well said, Miss Burney!" exclaimed Mrs. Thrale. "Why that's true enough, and so he has."

"A total indifference," continued I, "of what is thought of him by others, and a disdain alike of happiness or misery."

"Bravo, Burney!" cried Mrs. Thrale, "that's true enough!"

"Indeed," cried Mr. Crutchley, "you are quite mistaken. Indeed, nobody in the world is half so anxious about the opinions of others; I am wretched—I am miserable if I think myself thought ill of; not, indeed, by everybody, but by those whose good opinion I have tried—there if I fall, no man Can be more unhappy."

"Oh, perhaps," returned I, "there may be two or three people in the world you may wish should think well of you, but that is nothing to the general character."

"Oh, no ! many more. I am now four-and-thirty, and perhaps, indeed, in all my life I have not tried to gain the esteem of more than four-and-thirty people, but——"

"Oh, leave out the thirty!" cried I, "and then you may be nearer the truth."

"No, indeed: ten, at least, I daresay I have tried for, but, perhaps, I have not succeeded with two. However, I am thus even with the world; for if it likes me not, I can do without it—I can live alone; and that, indeed, I prefer to any thing I can meet with; for those with whom I like to live are so much above me, that I sink into nothing in their society; so I think it best to run away from them."

"That is to say," cried I, "you are angry you cannot yourself excel—and this is not pride"

"Why, no, indeed; but it is melancholy to be always behind—to hear conversation in which one is unable to join—"

"Unwilling," quoth I, "you mean."

"No, indeed, but really unable; and therefore what can I do so well as to run home? As to an inferior, I hope I think that of nobody; and as to my equals, and such as I am on a par with, heaven knows I can ill bear them!—I would rather live alone to all eternity!"

This conversation lasted till we got home, when Mrs. Thrale said-

"Well, Mr. Crutchley, has she convinced you ?"

"I don't know," cried I, "but he has convinced me."

"Why, how you smote him," cried Mrs. Thrale, "but I think you make your part good as you go on."

"The great difference," said I, "which I think there is between Mr. Seward and Mr. Crutchley, who in some things are very much alike, is this—Mr. Seward has a great deal of vanity and no pride, Mr. Crutchley a great deal of pride and no vanity."

"just, and true, and wise!" said dear Mrs. Thrale, "for Seward is always talking of himself, and always with approbation; Mr. Crutchley seldom mentions himself, and when he does, it is with dislike. And which have I, most pride or most vanity?"

"Oh, most vanity, certa!" quoth I.

At Supper we had only Sir Philip and Mr. Crutchley. The conversation of the morning was then again renewed. -

"Oh!" cried Mrs. Thrale, "what a smoking did Miss Burney give Mr. Crutchley!"

"A smoking, indeed!" cried He. "Never had I such a one before! Never did I think to get such a character! I had no notion of it."

"Nay, then," said I, "why should you, now?"

"But what is all this?" cried Sir Philip, delighted enough at any mischief between Mr. Crutchley and me, or between any male and female, for he only wishes something to go forward, And thinks a quarrel or dispute next best to foridness and flirting.

"Why, Miss Burney," answered she, "gave Mr, Crutchley this morning a noble trimming. I had always thought him very humble, but she shewed me my mistake, and said I had not distinguished pride from vanity."

"Oh, never was I so mauled in my life," said he.

Enough, however, of this rattle, which lasted till we all went to bed, and which Mrs. Thrale most kindly kept up, by way of rioting me from thinking, and which Mr. Crutchley himself bore with the utmost good nature, from having noticed that I was out of spirits. . . .

July 2-The other morning Mrs. Thrale ran hastily into my room, her eyes full of tears, and cried,—

"What an extraordinary man is this Crutchley! I declare he has quite melted me! He came to me just now, and thinking I was uneasy I could do no more for Perkins, [142]though he cared not himself if the man were drowned, he offered to lend him a thousand pounds, merely by way of giving pleasure to me!"

MISS SOPHY STREATHIELD IS COMMENTED ON

Well-it was, I think, Saturday, Aug. 25, that Mrs Thrale brought me back. [143]We then took up Mr. Crutchley, who had come to his town-house upon business, and who accompanied us thither for a visit of three days.

In the evening Mr. Seward also came. He has been making the western tour, and gave us, with a seriousness that kept me continually grinning, some account of a doctor, apothecary, or 'chemist' belonging to every town at which he had stopped.

And when we all laughed at his thus following up the faculty, he undauntedly said,—

"I think it the best way to get information; I know no better method to learn what is going forward anywhere than to send for the chief physician of the place, so I commonly consult him the first day I stop at a place, and when I have fee'd him, and made acquaintance, he puts me in a way to find out what is worth looking at."

A most curious mode of picking up a cicerone!

After this, still pursuing his favourite topic, he began to inquire into the particulars of Mr. Crutchley's late illness - but that gentleman, who is as much in the opposite extreme, of disdaining even any decent care of himself, as Mr. Seward is in the other, of devoting almost all his thoughts to his health cut the matter very short, and would not talk upon it at all.

"But, if I had known sooner," said Mr. Seward, "that you were ill, I should have come to see you."

"Should you?" cried Mr. Crutchley, with a loud laugh; "very kind, indeed!— it would have been charming to see you when I am ill, when I am afraid of undertaking you even when well!"

Some time after Sophy Streatfield was talked of,-Oh, with how much impertinence as if she was at the service of any man who would make proposals to her! Yet Mr. Seward spoke of her with praise and tenderness all the time, as if, though firmly of this opinion, he was warmly her admirer. From such admirers and such admiration heaven guard me! Mr. Crutchley said but little; but that little was bitter enough.

"However," said Mr. Seward, "after all that can be said, there is nobody whose manners are more engaging, nobody more amiable than the little Sophy; and she is certainly very pretty; I must own I have always been afraid to trust myself with her."

Here Mr. Crutchley looked very sneeringly.

"Nay, squire," cried Mr. Seward, "she is very dangerous, I can tell you; and if she had you at a fair trial, she would make an impression that would soften even your hard heart."

"No need of any further trial," answered he, laughing, "for she has done that already; and so soft was the impression that it is absolutely all dissolved!—melted quite away, and not a trace of it left!"

Mr. Seward then proposed that she should marry Sir John Miller, [144]who has just lost his wife and very gravely said, he had a great mind to set out for Tunbridge, and carry her with him to Bath, and so make the match without delay!

"But surely," said Mrs. Thrale, "if you fail, you will think yourself bound in honour to marry her yourself?"

"Why, that's the thing," said he; "no, I can't take the little Sophy myself; I should have too many rivals; no, that won't do."

How abominably conceited and sure these pretty gentlemen are! However, Mr. Crutchley here made a speech that half won my heart.

"I wish," said he, "Miss Streatfield was here at this moment to cuff you, Seward!"

"Cuff me!" cried he. "What, the little Sophy!—and why?"

"For disposing of her so freely. I think a man deserves to be cuffed for saying any lady will marry him."

I seconded this speech with much approbation.

GARRULOUS MR. MUSGRAVE.

August, Monday.-We were to have Mr. Cator and other company to dinner; and all breakfast Mr. Seward kept plaguing poor Mr. Musgrave, who is an incessant talker, about the difficulty he would have in making his part good with Mr. Cator, who, he assured him, would out-talk him if he did not take care. And Mr. Crutchley recommended to him to "wait for a sneeze," in order to put in; so that he was almost rallied into a passion, though, being very good-natured, he made light of it, and it blew over.

In the middle of dinner I was seized with a violent laughing fit, by seeing Mr. Musgrave, who had sat quite silent, turn very solemnly to Mr. Seward and say in a reproachful tone,—

"Seward, you said I should be fighting to talk all the talk, and here I have not spoke once."

"Well, sir," cried Mr. Seward, nodding at him, 'why don't you put in?"

"Why, I lost an opportunity just now, when Mr. Cator -talked of climates; I had something I could have said about them very well."

After this, however, he made himself amends ; for when we left the men to their wine, he began such a violent dispute with Mr Cator, that Mr. Jenkinson and Mr. Crutchley left the field of battle, and went out to join the ladies in their walk round the grounds ; and that breaking up the party, the rest soon followed.

By the way, I happened not to walk myself, which was most ludicrously noticed by Mr. Musgrave; who, while we were at tea, suddenly crossed the circle to come up to me, and say,—

"You did not walk, Miss Burney?"

"No, sir."

"Very much in the right—very much in the right, indeed! You were studying? Oh, very right! never lose a moment! Such an understanding as yours it would be a shame to neglect; it ought to be cultivated every moment."

And then he hurried back to his seat.

In the evening, when all the company was gone but our three gentlemen, Seward, Crutchley, and Musgrave, we took a walk round the grounds by moonlight - and Mr. Musgrave started with rapture at the appearance of the moon, now full, now cloudy, now clear, now obscured, every three yards we moved.

A PARTING SHOT AT MR. CRUTCHLEY.

Friday, Sept. 11.-And now, if I am not mistaken, I come to relate the conclusion of Mr. Crutchley's most extraordinary summer career at Streatham, which place, I believe, he has now left without much intention to frequently revisit. However, this is mere conjecture; but he really had a run of ill-luck not very inviting to a man of his cold and splenetic turn to play the same game.

When we were just going to supper, we heard a disturbance among the dogs; and Mrs. and Miss Thrale went out to see what was the matter, while Dr. Johnson and I remained quiet. Soon returning,

"A friend! a friend!" she cried, and was followed by Mr. Crutchley. He would not eat with us, but was chatty and in goodhumour, and as usual, when in spirits, saucily sarcastic. For instance, it is generally half my employment in hot evenings here to rescue some or other poor buzzing idiot of an insect from the flame of a candle. This, accordingly, I was performing with a Harry Longlegs, which, after much trial to catch, eluded me, and escaped, nobody could see how. Mr. Crutchley vowed I had caught and squeezed him to death in my hand.

"No, indeed," cried I, "when I catch them, I put them out of the window."

"Ay, their bodies," said he, laughing; "but their legs, I suppose, you keep."

"Not I, indeed; I hold them very safe in the palm of my hand."

Oh!" said he, "the palm of your hand! why, it would not hold a fly! But what have you done with the poor wretch! thrown him under the table slily?:

"What good would that do?"

"Oh, help to establish your full character for mercy."

Now was not that a speech to provoke Miss Grizzle herself? However, I only made up a saucy lip.

"Come," cried he, offering to take my hand, "where is he? Which hand is he in? Let me examine?"

"No, no, I thank you; I sha'n't make you my confessor, whenever I take one."

He did not much like this; but I did not mean he should.

Afterwards he told us a most unaccountably ridiculous story of a crying wife. A gentleman, he said, of his acquaintance had married lately his own kept mistress; and last Sunday he had dined with the bride and bridegroom, but, to his utter astonishment, without any apparent reason in the world, in the middle of dinner or tea, she burst into a violent fit of crying, and went out of the room, though there was not the least quarrel, and the sposo seemed all fondness and attention.

"What, then," said I, somewhat maliciously, I grant, "had you been saying to er?"

"Oh, thank you!" said he, with a half-affronted bow, "I expected this! I declare I thought you would conclude it was me!"

MANAGER HELIOGABALUS.

Somebody told me (but not your father) that the Opera singers would not be likely to get any money out of Sheridan This year. "Why that fellow grows fat," says I, "like Heliogabalus, upon the tongues of nightingales." Did I tell you that bright thing before?—Mrs. Thrale to Fanny Burney.

SISTER AUTHORESSES.

(Fanny Burney to Mrs. Philips, late Miss Susan Burney.) February, 1782.

As I have a frank and a subject, I will leave my bothers, and write you and my dear brother Molesworth[145]a little account of a rout I have just been at, at the house of Mr. Paradise.

You will wonder, perhaps, in this time of hurry, why I went thither ; but when I tell you Pacchierotti[146]was there, you will not think it surprising.

There was a crowd of company; Charlotte and I went together; my father came afterwards. Mrs. Paradise received us very graciously, and led me immediately up to Miss Thrale, who was sitting by the Pac.

We were very late, for we had waited cruelly for the coach, and Pac. had sung a song out of "Artaxerxes," composed for a tenor, which we lost, to my infinite regret. Afterwards he sang "Dolce speme" delightfully.

Mrs. Paradise, leaning over the Kirwans and Charlotte, who hardly got a seat all night for the crowd, said she begged to speak to me. I squeezed my great person out, and she then said,-

"Miss Burney, Lady Say and Sele desires the honour of being introduced to you."

Her ladyship stood by her side. She seems pretty near fifty-at least turned forty ; her head was full of feathers, flowers, jewels, and gew-gaws, and as high as Lady Archer's her dress was trimmed with beads, silver, persian sashes, and all sorts of fine fancies; her face is thin and fiery, and her whole manner spoke a lady all alive.

"Miss Burney," cried she, with great quickness, and a look all curiosity, "I am very happy to see you; I have longed to see you a great while. I have read your performance, and I am quite delighted with it. I think it's the most elegant novel I ever read in my life. Such a style! I am quite surprised at it. I can't think where you got so much invention!"

You may believe this was a reception not to make me very loquacious. I did not know which way to turn my head.

"I must introduce You," continued her ladyship, "to my sister; she'll be quite delighted to see you. She has written a novel herself so you are sister authoresseS. A most elegant thing it is, I assure You; almost as pretty as yours, only not quite so elegant. She has written two novels, only one is not so pretty as the other. But I shall insist upon your seeing them. One is in letters, like yours, only yours is prettiest ; it's called the 'Mausoleum of Julia'!"

What unfeeling things, thought I, are my sisters! I'm sure I never heard them go about thus praising me. Mrs. Paradise then again came forward, and taking my hand, led me up to her ladyship's sister, Lady Hawke, saying aloud, and with a courteous smirk,

"Miss Burney, ma'am, authoress of 'Evelina.'"

"Yes," cried my friend, Lady Say and Sele, who followed me close, "it's the authoress of 'Evelina,' so you are sister authoresses!"

Lady Hawke arose and curtsied. She is much younger than her sister, and rather pretty; extremely languishing, delicate, and pathetic; apparently accustomed to be reckoned the genius of her family, and well contented to be looked upon as a creature dropped from the clouds. I was then seated between their ladyships, and Lady S. and S., drawing as near to me as possible, said,-

"Well, and so you wrote this pretty book ! -and pray did your papa know of it?"

"No, ma'am; not till some months after the publication."

"So I've heard - it's surprising! I can't think how you invented it!—there's a vast deal of invention in it! And you've got so much humour, too! Now my sister has no humour; hers is all sentiment. You can't think how I was entertained with that old grandmother and her son!"

I suppose she meant Tom Branghton for the son.

"How much pleasure you must have had in writing it; had not you?"

"Yes, ma'am."

"So has my sister; she's never without a pen in her band; she can't help writing for her life. When Lord Hawke is travelling about with her, she keeps writing all the way."

"Yes," said Lady Hawke; "I really can't help writing. One has great pleasure in writing the things; has one not, Miss Burney?

"Yes, ma'am."

"But your novel," cried Lady Say and Sele, "is in such a style!- -so elegant! I am vastly glad you made it end happily. I hate a novel that don't end happy."

"Yes," said Lady Hawke, with a languid smile, "I was vastly glad when she married Lord Orville. I was sadly afraid it would not have been."

"My sister intends," said Lady Say and Sele, "to print her 'Mausoleum,' just for her own friends and acquaintances."

"Yes," said Lady Hawke; "I have never printed yet."

"I saw Lady Hawke's name," quoth I to my first friend, "ascribed to the play of 'Variety.'"[147]

"Did you indeed?" cried Lady Say, in an ecstasy. "Sister! do you know Miss

Burney saw your name in the newspapers, about the play!"

"Did she?" said Lady Hawke, smiling complacently. "But I really did not write it; I never wrote a play in my life."

"Well," cried Lady Say, "but do repeat that sweet part that I am so fond of—you know what I mean; Miss Burney must hear it,—out of your novel, you know!"

Lady H.-No, I can't ; I have forgot it.

Lady S.-Oh, no! I am sure you have not; I insist upon it.

Lady H.-But I know you can repeat it yourself; you have so fine a memory; I am sure you can repeat it;

Lady S.-Oh, but I should not do it justice! that's all,—I should not do it justice!

Lady Hawke then bent forward, and repeated—"'If, when he made the declaration of his love, the sensibility that beamed in his eyes was felt in his heart, what pleasing sensations and soft alarms might not that tender avowal awaken!'"

"And from what, ma'am," cried I, astonished, and imagining I had mistaken them, "is this taken?"

"From my sister's novel!" answered the delighted Lady Say and Sele, expecting my raptures to be equal to her own; "it's in the 'Mausoleum,'—did not you know that? Well, I can't think how you can write these sweet novels! And it's all just like that part. Lord Hawke himself says it's all poetry. For my part, I'm sure I never could write so. I suppose, Miss Burney, you are producing another,—a'n't you?"

"No, ma'am."

"oh, I dare say you are. I dare say you are writing one this Very minute!"

Mrs. Paradise now came up to me again, followed by a square man, middle-aged, and hum-drum, who, I found was Lord Say and Sele, afterwards from the Kirwans, for though they introduced him to me, I was so confounded by their vehemence and their manners, that I did not hear his name.

"Miss Burney," said Mrs. P.,, presenting me to him, "authoress of 'Evelina.'"

"Yes," cried Lady Say and Sele, starting up, "'tis the authoress of 'Evelina!'"

"Of what ? " cried he.

"Of 'Evelina.' You'd never think it,—she looks so young, to have so much invention, and such an elegant style! Well, I could write a play, I think, but I'm sure I could never write a novel."

"Oh, yes, you could, if you would try," said Lady Hawke.

"Oh, no, I could not," answered she; "I could not get a style— that's the thing—I could not tell how to get a style! and a novel's nothing without a style, you know!"

"Why no," said Lady Hawke; "that's true. But then you write such charming letters, you know!"

"Letters!" repeated Lady S. and S. simpering; "do you tbink so? Do you know I wrote a long letter to Mrs. Ray just before I came here, this very afternoon,—quite a long letter! I did, I assure you!"

Here Mrs. Paradise came forward with another gentleman, younger, slimmer, and smarter, and saying to me, "Sir Gregory Page Turner," said to him, "Miss Burney, authoress of 'Evelina.'"

At which Lady Say and Sele, In fresh transport, again rose, and rapturously again repeated—

"Yes, she's authoress of 'Evelina'! Have you read it?"

"No; is it to be had?"

"Oh dear, yes! it's been printed these two years! You'd never think it! But it's the most elegant novel I ever read in my life. Writ in such a style!"

"Certainly," said he very civilly; "I have every inducement to get it. Pray where is it to be had? everywhere, I suppose?"

"Oh, nowhere, I hope," cried I, wishing at that moment it had been never in human ken.

My square friend, Lord Say and Sele, then putting his head forward, said, very solemnly, "I'll purchase it!"

His lady then mentioned to me a hundred novels that I had never heard of, asking my opinion of them, and whether I knew the authors? Lady Hawke only occasionally and languidly joining in the discourse: and then Lady S. and S., sudclertl rising, begged me not to move, for she should be back again in a minute, and flew to the next room.

I took, however, the first opportunity of Lady Hawke's casting down her eyes, and reclining her delicate head, to make away from this terrible set; and, just as I was got by the pianoforte, where I hoped Pacchierotti would soon present himself, Mrs. Paradise again came to me, and said,-

"Miss Burney, Lady Say and Sele wishes vastly to cultivate your acquaintance, and begs to know if she may have the honour of your company to an assembly at her house next Friday?—and I will do myself the pleasure to call for you if you will give me leave."

"Her ladyship does me much honour, but I am unfortunately engaged," was my answer, with as much promptness as I could command.

A DINNER AT SIR JOSHUA'S, WITH BURKE AND GiBBON.

June.-Among the many I have been obliged to shirk this year, for the sake of living almost solely with "Cecilia," none have had less patience with my retirement than Miss Palmer, who, bitterly believing I intended never to visit her again, has forborne sending me any invitations: but, about three weeks ago, my father had a note from Sir Joshua Reynolds, to ask him to dine at Richmond, and meet the Bishop of St. Asaph, [148]and, therefore, to make my peace, I scribbled a note to Miss Palmer to this purpose,—

"After the many kind invitations I have been obliged to refuse, will you, my dear Miss Palmer, should I offer to accompany my father to-morrow, bid me remember the old proverb,

'Those who will not when they may, When they will, they shall have nay?'— F.B."

This was graciously received; and the next morning Sir Joshua and Miss

Palmer called for my father and me, accompanied by Lord Cork. We had a mighty pleasant ride, Miss Palmer and I " made up," though she scolded most violently about my long absence, and attacked me about the book without mercy. The book, in short, to my great consternation, I find is talked of and expected all the town over. My dear father himself, I do verily believe, mentions it to everybody; he is fond of it to enthusiasm, and does not foresee the danger of raising such general expectation, which fills me with the horrors every time I am tormented with the thought.

Sir Joshua's house is delightfully situated, almost at the top of Richmond Hill. We walked till near dinner-time upon the terrace, and there met Mr. Richard Burke, the brother of the orator. Miss Palmer, stopping him, said,-

"Are you coming to dine with us?"

"No," he answered ; "I shall dine at the Star and Garter."

"How did you come—with Mrs. Burke, or alone?"

"Alone."

"What, on horseback?"

"Ay, sure!" cried he, laughing; "up and ride! Now's the time."

And he made a fine flourish with his hand, and passed us. He is just made under-secretary at the Treasury. He is a tall and handsome man, and seems to have much dry drollery; but we saw no more of him.

After our return to the house, and while Sir Joshua and I were t`ete-`a-t`ete, Lord Cork and my father being still walking, and Miss Palmer having, I suppose, some orders to give about the dinner, the " knight of Plympton " was desiring my opinion of the prospect from his window, and comparing it with Mr. Burke's, as he told me after I had spoken it,—when the Bishop of St. Asaph and his daughter, Miss Georgiana Shipley, were announced. Sir Joshua, to divert himself, in introducing me to the bishop, said, "Miss Burney, my lord; otherwise 'Evelina.'"

The bishop is a well-looking man, and seemed grave, quiet, and sensible. I have heard much more of him, but nothing more appeared. Miss Georgiana, however, was showy enough for two. She is a very tall and rather handsome girl; but the expression of her face is, to me, disagreeable. She has almost a constant smile, not of softness, nor of insipidity, but of selfsufficiency and internal satisfaction. She is very much accomplished, and her fame for painting and for scholarship, I know You are well acquainted with. I believe her to have very good parts and much quickness , but she is so full of herself, so earnest to obtain notice, and so happy in her confidence of deserving it, that I have been not less charmed with any youn lady I have seen for many a day. I have met with her before, at Mrs. Pepys', but never before was introduced to her.

Miss Palmer soon joined us ; and, in a short time, entered more company,— three gentlemen and one lady; but there was no more ceremony used of introductions. The lady, I concluded was Mrs. Burke, wife of the Mr. Burke, and was not mistaken.

One of the gentlemen I recollected to be young Burke, her son, whom I once met at Sir Joshua's in town, and another of them I knew for Mr. Gibbon:

but the third I had never seen before. I had been told that the Burke was not expected yet I could conclude this gentleman to be no other; he had just the air, the manner, the appearance, I had prepared myself to look for in him, and there was an evident, a striking superiority in his demeanour, his eye, his motions, that announced him no common man.

I could not get at Miss Palmer to satisfy my doubts, and we were soon called downstairs to dinner. Sir Joshua and the "unknown" stopped to speak with one another upon the stairs; and, when they followed us, Sir Joshua, in taking his place at the table, asked me to sit next to him; I willingly complied. "And then," he added, "Mr. Burke shall sit on the other side of you." "Oh, no, indeed!" cried Miss Georgiana, who also had placed herself next Sir Joshua; "I won't consent to that; Mr. Burke must sit next me; I won't agree to part with him. Pray, come and sit down quiet, Mr. Burke."

Mr. Burke,-for him it was,-smiled and obeyed.

"I only meant," said Sir Joshua, "to have made my peace with Mr. Burke, by giving him that place, because he has been scolding me for not introducing him to Miss Burney. However, I must do it now;—Mr. Burke!—Miss Burney!"

We both half rose, and Mr. Burke said,—

" I have been complaining to Sir Joshua that he left me wholly to my own sagacity; however, it did not here deceive me."

" Oh dear, then," said Miss Georgiana, looking a little consternated, "perhaps you won't thank me for calling you to this place!"

Nothing was said, and so we all began dinner,-youngBurke making himself my next neighbour.

Captain Phillips[149]knows Mr. Burke. Has he or has he not told you how delightful a creature he is? If he has not, pray in my name, abuse him without mercy; if he has, pray ask if he will subscribe to my account of him, which herewith shall follow.

He is tall, his figure is noble, his air commanding, his address graceful, his voice is clear, penetrating, sonorous, and powerful, his language is copious, various, and eloquent; his manners are attractive, his conversation is delightful.

What says Captain Phillips? Have I chanced to see him in his happiest hour? or is he all this in common? Since we lost Garrick I have seen nobody so enchanting.

I can give you, however, very little of what was said, for the conversation was not suivie, Mr. Burke darting from subject to subject with as much rapidity as entertainment. Neither is the charm of his discourse more in the matter than the manner: all, therefore, that is related from him loses half its effect in not being related by him. Such little sketches as I can recollect take however.

From the window of the dining-parlour, Sir Joshua directed us to look at a pretty white house which belonged to Lady Di Beauclerk.

"I am extremely glad," said Mr. Burke, "to see her at last so well housed; poor woman! the bowl has long rolled in misery; I rejoice that it has now found its balance. I never, myself, so much enjoyed the sight of happiness in another, as in that woman when I first saw her after the death of her husband. It was really enlivening to behold her placed in that sweet house, released from all her cares, a thousand pounds a-year at her own disposal, and—her husband was dead! Oh, it was pleasant, it was delightful to see her enjoyment of her situation!"

"But, without considering the circumstances," said Mr. Gibbon, "this may appear very strange, though, when they are fairly stated, it is perfectly rational and unavoidable."

"Very true," said Mr. Burke, "if the circumstances are not considered, Lady Di may seem highly reprehensible."

He then, addressing himself particularly to me, as the person least likely to be acquainted with the character of Mr. Beauclerk, drew it himself in strong and marked expressions, describing the misery he gave his wife, his singular ill-treatment of her, and the necessary relief the death of such a man must give. [150]

He then reminded Sir Joshua of a day in which they had dined at Mr. Beauclerk's, soon after his marriage with Lord Bolingbroke's divorced wife, in company with Goldsmith, and told a new story of poor Goldsmith's eternal blundering.

A LETTER FROM BURKE To FANNY BURNEY.

Whitehall, July 29, 1782.

Madam, I should feel exceedingly to blame if I could refuse to myself the natural satisfaction, and to you the just but poor return, of my best thanks for the very great instruction and entertainment I have received from the new present you have bestowed on the public. There are few—I believe I may say fairly there are none at all—that will not find themselves better informed concerning human nature, and their stock of observation enriched, by reading your "Cecilia." They certainly will, letheir experience in life and manners be what it may. The arrogance of age must submit to be taught by youth. You have crowded into a few small volumes an incredible variety of characters; most of them well planned, well supported, and well contrasted with each other. If there be any fault in this respect, It is one in which you are in no great danger of being imitated. justly as your characters are drawn, perhaps they are too numerous. But I beg pardon; I fear it is quite in vain to preach economy to those who are come young to excessive and sudden opulence.

I might trespass on your delicacy if I should fill my letter to u with what I fill my conversation to others. I should be troublesome to you alone If I should tell you all I feel and think on the natural vein of humour, the tender pathetic, the comprehensive and noble moral, and the sagacious observance, that appear quite throughout that extraordinary performance.

In an age distinguished by producing extraordinary women, I hardly dare to tell you where my opinion would place you amongst them. I respect your modesty, that will not endure the commendations which your merit forces from everybody.

I have the honour to be, with great gratitude, respect, and esteem, madam, your most obedient and most humble servant, EDM. BURKE.

My best compliments and congratulations to Dr. Burney on the great honour acquired to his family.

Miss BURNEY SITS FOR HER PORTRAIT.

ChesingtoN, Monday, Aug. 12-I Set Out for this ever dear place, accompanied by Edward, [151]who was sent for to paint Mr. Crisp for my father. I am sure you will rejoice in this. I was a little dumpish in the journey, for I seemed leaving my Susan again. However, I read a "Rambler" or two, and "composed the harmony of my temper," as well as I could, for the sake of Edward, who was not only faultless of this, but who is, I almost think, faultless of all things. I have thought him more amiable and deserving, than ever, since this last sojourn under the same roof with him; and, as it happened, I have owed to him almost all the comfort I have this time met with here.

We came in a chaise, which was well loaded with canvasses, .pencils, and painting materials ; for Mr. Crisp was to be three times painted, and Mrs. Gast once. My sweet father came down Gascoign-lane to meet us, in very pood spirits and very good health. Next came dear daddy Crisp, looking vastly well, and, as usual, high in glee and kindness at the meeting. Then the affectionate Kitty, the good Mrs. Hamilton, the gentle Miss Young, and the enthusiastic Mrs. Gast.

The instant dinner was over, to my utter surprise and consternation, I was called into the room appropriated for Edward and his pictures, and informed I was to sit to him for Mr. Crisp! Remonstrances were unavailing, and declarations of aversion to the design were only ridiculed; both daddies interfered, and, when I ran off, brought me back between them, and compelled my obedience;—and from that time to this, nothing has gone forward but picture-sitting.

GENERAL PAOLI.
(Fanny Burney to Mr. crisp. Oct. 15, 1782.

.....I am very sorry you could not come to Streatham at the time Mrs. Thrale hoped to see you, for when shall we be likely to meet there again? You would have been much pleased, I am sure, by meeting with General Paoli,' who spent the day there, and was extremely communicative and agreeable. I had seen him in large companies, but was never made known to him before; nevertheless, he conversed with me as if well acquainted not only with myself, but my connexions,—inquiring of me when I had last seen Mrs. Montagu? and calling Sir Joshua Reynolds, when he spoke of him, my friend. He is a very pleasing man, tall and genteel in his person, remarkably well bred, and very mild and soft in his manners.

I will try to give you a little specimen of his conversation, because I know you love to hear particulars of all out-of-theway persons. His English is blundering but not unpretty. Speaking of his first acquaintance with Mr. Boswell,—

"He came," he said, "to my country, and he fetched me some letter of recommending him; but I was of the belief he might be an impostor, and I supposed, in my minte, he was an espy; for I look away from him, and in a moment I look to him again, and I behold his tablets. Oh! he was to the work of writing down all I say! Indeed I was angry. But soon I discover he was no impostor and no espy; and I only find I was myself the monster he had come to discern. Oh,-is a very good man! I love him indeed; so cheerful! so gay! so pleasant! but at the first, oh! I was indeed angry."[152]

After this he told us a story of an expectation he had of being robbed, and of the protection he found from a very large dog that he is very fond of. "

I walk out," he said, "in the night; I go towards the field; I behold a man—oh, ugly one! I proceed—he follow; I go on—he address me. 'You have one dog,' he says. 'Yes,' say I to him. 'Is a fierce dog?' he says; 'is he fiery?' 'Yes,' reply I, 'he can bite.' 'I would not attack in the night,' says he, 'a house to have such dog in it.' Then I conclude he was a breaker" so I turn to him—oh, very rough! not gentle—and I say, very fierce, 'He shall destroy you, if you are ten!'"

Afterwards, speaking of the Irish giant, who is now shown in town, he said,-"He is so large I am as a baby! I look at him—oh! I find myself so little as a child! Indeed, my indignation it rises when I see him hold up his hand so high. I am as nothing; and I find myself in the power of a man who fetches from me half a crown."

This language, which is all spoke very pompously by him, sounds comical from himself, though I know not how it may read.

---

136   Sir Philip Jennings Clerke.-ED,

137   Mauritius Lowe, a natural son of Lord Southwell. He sent a large picture of the Deluge to the Royal Academy in 1783, and was so distressed at its rejection, that Johnson compassionately wrote to Sirjoshua Reynolds in his behalf, entreating that the verdict might be re-considered. His intercession was successful, and the picture was admitted. We know nothing of Mr. Lowe's work.-ED.

138   Afterwards Sir William PWeller Pepys. See note 103, ante, p. 148.-ED.

139   "The moment he was gone, 'Now,' says Dr. Johnson, 'is Pepys gone home hating me, who love him better than I did before. He spoke in defence of his dead friend; but though I hope I spoke better, who spoke against him, yet all my eloquence will gain me nothing but an honest man for my enemy!'" (Mrs. Piozzi's "Anecdotes of Johnson.")-ED.

140   The celebrated Georgiana, Duchess of Devonshire, equally famous for her personal attractions and her political enthusiasm in the Whig interest. Her canvassing, and, it is said, her kisses, largely contributed to the return of Charles james Fox for Westminster in the election of 1784. She was the daughter of John, first Earl Spencer ; was born 1757; married, 1774, to William, fifth Duke of Devonshire; and died, 1806. Her portrait was painted by both Reynolds and Gainsborough.

    Mary Isabella, Duchess of Rutland, was the youngest daughter of the Duke of Beaufort, and was married, in 1775, to Charles Mariners, fourth Duke of Rutland. She died, 1831.-ED.

141   Susan and Sophy were younger daughters of Mrs. Thrale-ED.

142   The manager of Mr. Thrale's brewery.-ED.

143   i.e. To Streatham: Fanny had been home in the interval.-ED.

144   Of Bath Easton: husband of the lady of the "Vase." See note 123, ante, P. 174.-ED.

145   Captain Molesworth Phillips, who had recently married Susan Burney.-ED.

146   Gasparo Pacchierotti, a celebrated Italian singer, and a very intimate friend of the Burney family.-ED.

147   "Variety," a comedy, was produced at Drury Lane, Feb. 25, 1782, and ran nine nights. Genest calls it a dull play, with little or no plot. The author is unknown.-ED.

148   Dr. Jonathan Shipley.-ED.

149   The husband of Fanny Burney's sister, Susan.-ED.

150   Poor Lady Di was throughout unfortunate in her marriages. Her first husband, Lord Bolingbroke, to whom she was married in 1757, brutally used her, and drove her to seek elsewhere the affection which he failed to bestow. She was divorced from him in 1768, and married, immediately afterwards, to Topham Beauclerk, who, in his turn, ill-treated her. Mr. Beauclerk died in March, 1780. He was greatly esteemed by Johnson, but his good qualities appear to have been rather of the head than of the heart.-ED.

151   Her cousin Edward Burney, the painter. A reproduction of his portrait of Fanny forms the frontispiece to the present volume.-ED.

152   Pasquale Paoli, the famous Corsican general and patriot. He maintained the independence of his country against the Genoese for nearly ten years. in 1769, upon the submission of Corsica to France, to which the Genoese had ceded it, Paoli settled in England, where he enjoyed a pension of 1200 pounds a year from the English Government. More details respecting this delightful interview between Fanny and the General are given in the "Memoirs of Dr. Burney" (vol. ii. p. 255, from which we select the following extracts:—

"He is a very pleasing man; tall and genteel in his person, remarkably attentive, obliging, and polite; and as soft and mild in his speech, as if he came from feeding sheep in Corsica, like a shepherd; rather than as if he had left the warlike field where he had led his armies to battle.

"When Mrs. Thrale named me, he started back, though smilingly, and said; 'I am very glad enough to see you in the face, Miss Evelina, which I have wished for long enough. O charming book! I give it you my word I have read it often enough. It is my favourite studioso for apprehending the English language; which is difficult often. I pray you, Miss Evelina, write some more little volumes of the quickest.'

"I disclaimed the name, and was walking away; but he followed me with an apology. 'I pray your pardon, Mademoiselle. My ideas got in a blunder often. It is Miss Borni what name I meant to accentuate, I pray your pardon, Miss Evelina."'-ED.

SECTION 5 1782

"CECILIA": A PAEAN OF PRAISE: LAMENTATIONS.

["THIS is the last visit remembered, or, at least, narrated, of Streatham." With these words Madame D'Arblay concludes the account given in the "Memoirs of Dr. Burney," of her meeting with General Paoli. In the autumn Of 1782 Mrs. Thrale went, with her daughters and Dr. Johnson, to Brighthelmstone, where Fanny joined them. On their return to London, November 20, the Thrales settled for the winter in Argyle-street, and Fanny repaired to her father's residence in St. Martin's-street. She saw much of Mrs. Thrale during the winter, but in the following April that lady quitted London for Bath, where she resided until her marriage with Signor Piozzi in the summer of 1784. She maintained an affectionate correspondence with Fanny until after the marriage, but from the date of their parting in London, they saw no more of each other, except for one brief interval in May, 1784, for several years.

We must here give an account, as concise as possible, of the transaction which was so bitterly resented by the friends of Mrs. Thrale, but in which her conduct seems to us, taking all the circumstances fairly into consideration, to have been less deserving of condemnation than their uncharitableness. She had first seen Piozzi, an Italian singer, at a party at Dr. Burney's in 1777, and her behaviour to him on that occasion had certainly afforded no premonition of her subsequent infatuation. Piozzi, who was nearly of the same age as herself, was, as Miss Seward describes him, "a handsome man, with gentle, pleasing, unaffected manners, and with very eminent skill in his profession." He was requested by Dr. Burney to sing; rather unfortunately, it would appear, for the company, which included Johnson and the Grevilles, was by no means composed of musical enthusiasts, and Mrs. Thrale, in particular, "knew not a flat from a sharp, nor a crotchet from a quaver." However, he complied; and Mrs. Thrale, after sitting awhile in silence, finding the proceedings dull, was seized with a desire to enliven them. "In a fit of utter recklessness, she suddenly, but softly, arose, and stealing on tiptoe behind Signor Piozzi, who was accompanying himself on the pianoforte to an animated aria parlante, with his back to the company and his face to the wall, she ludicrously began imitating him by squaring her elbows, elevating them with ecstatic shrugs of the shoulders, and casting up her eyes, while languishingly reclining her head; as if she were not less enthusiastically, though somewhat more suddenly, struck with the transports of harmony than himself.

"But the amusement which such an unlooked-for exhibition -caused to the party, was momentary; for Dr. Burney, shocked lest the poor signor should observe, and be hurt by this mimicry, glided gently round to Mrs. Thrale, and, with something between pleasantry and severity, whispered to her, 'Because, madam, you have no ear yourself for music, will you destroy the attention of all who, in that one point, are otherwise gifted?'"[153]

This deserved rebuke the lively lady took in perfectly good part, and the incident passed without further notice. She does not appear to have met with Piozzi again, Until, in July, 1780, she Pppicked him up " at Brighton. She now finds him " amazingly like her father," and insists that he shall teach Hester music. From this point the fever gradually increased. In August, 1781, little more than four months after her husband's death, Piozzi has become "a prodigious favourite" with her; she has even developed a taste for his music, which "fills the mind with emotions one would not be without, though inconvenient enough sometimes." In the spring Of 1783, soon after her arrival at Bath, they were formally engaged, but the urgent remonstrances of her friends and family caused the engagement to be broken off, and Piozzi went to Italy. Her infatuation, however, was too strong to be overcome. Under the struggle, long protracted, her health gave way, and at length, by the advice of her doctor, and with the sullen consent of Miss Thrale, Piozzi was summoned to Bath. He, too, had been faithful, and he lost no time in obeying the summons. They were married, according to the Roman Catholic rites, in London, and again, on the 25th of July, 1784, in a Protestant church at Bath, her three elder daughters, of whom the eldest, Hester ("Queeny"), was not yet twenty years of age, having quitted Bath before his arrival.

Mrs. Piozzi left England with her husband and her youngest daughter, Cecilia, and lived for some years in Italy, where she compiled her well known "Anecdotes of Dr. Johnson." Her wedded life with Piozzi was certainly happy, and he gave her no reason to repent the step she had taken. The indignation of her former friends, especially of Dr. Johnson, was carried to a length which, the cause being considered, appears little short of ridiculous. Mrs. Thrale's second marriage may have been ill-advised, but it was neither criminal nor disgraceful. Piozzi was incontestably a respectable man and a constant lover ; but that an Italian musician, who depended upon his talents for his livelihood, should become the husband of the celebrated Mrs. Thrale, and the stepfather of four young ladies of fashion, the daughters of a brewer, and the heiresses to his large fortune,- -there was the rub! The dislike of Dr. Johnson and his friends to the marriage was, from a worldly point of view, justifiable enough, but it argues ill for their generosity of mind that they should have attached such overwhelming importance to such petty considerations. Mrs. Piozzi has been blamed for deserting her three elder daughters; but the fact is, it was her daughters who deserted her, and refused to recognise her husband. Her only fault, if fault it can be called, was in declining to sacrifice the whole happiness of her life to the supposed requirements of their rank in society. In condemning her friends for their severity and illiberality, we must, however, make an exception in favour of Fanny. She, like the rest, had been averse to the match, but her cordiality to Mrs. Piozzi remained undiminished; and when, soon after the marriage, their correspondence was discontinued, to be renewed only after the lapse of many years, it was not Fanny, but Mrs. Piozzi, who broke it off, instigated, Fanny always believed, by her husband.

Her separation from Mrs. Thrale was not the only event which brought sorrow to Fanny during the years to which the following section of the Diary relates. Mr. Crisp, the person dearest to her of all human beings outside her own family, died at Chesington, of an attack of his old malady, the gout, on the 24th of April, 1783, aged seventy-five. Fanny and Susan were with him at the last, and Fanny's love was rewarded, her anguish soothed yet deepened, when, almost with his dying breath, her Daddy Crisp called her "the dearest thing to him on earth."

Towards the end of 1784 another heavy blow fell upon Fanny, in the loss of Dr. Johnson, who died on the 13th of December. The touching references in the Diary to his last illness form an interesting supplement to Boswell's narrative.

But the picture of Fanny's life during these years is not without bright touches. As such we may reckon the great, and deserved success of her novel, "Cecilia"; the commencement of her acquaintance with two ladies who were hereafter to be numbered among her dearest friends—the venerable Mrs. Delany, and Mrs. Locke, of Norbury Park, Surrey; and last, not least, the growing intimacy between Edmund Burke and the family of Dr. Burney.-ED.]

AT BRIGHTON AGAIN, THE "FAmous Miss BURNEY."
BrighthelMSTONE, Oct. 26.
My journey was incidentless - but the Moment I came into Brighthelmstone I was met by Mrs. Thrale, who had most eagerly been waiting for me a long while, and therefore I dismounted, and walked home with her. It would be very superfluous to tell you how she received me, for you cannot but know, from her impatient letters, what I had reason to expect of kindness and welcome.

Dr. Johnson received me, too, with his usual goodness, and with a salute so loud, that the two young beaus, Cotton and Swinerton, have never done laughing about it.

Mrs. Thrale spent two or three hours in my room, talking over all her affairs, and then we wished each other bon repos, and— retired. Grandissima conclusion!

Oh, but let me not forget that a fine note came from Mr. Pepys, who is here with his family, saying he was pressd`e de vivre, and entreating to see Mrs. and Miss T., Dr. Johnson, and Cecilia at his house the next day. I hate mightily this method of naming me from my heroines, of whose honour I think I am more jealous than of my own.

Oct. 27-The Pepyses came to visit me in form, but I was dressing; in the evening, however, Mrs. and Miss T. took me to them. Dr. Johnson would not go ; he told me it was my day, and I should be crowned, for Mr. Pepys was wild about "Cecilia." We found at Mr. Pepys' nobody but his wife, his brother, Dr. Pepys, [154]and Dr. Pepys' lady, Countess of Rothes. Mr. Pepys received me with such distinction, that it was very evident how much the book, with the most flattering opinion of it, was in his head; however, he behaved very prettily, and only mentioned it by allusions; most particularly upon the character of Meadows, which he took various opportunities of pronouncing to be the "best hit possible" upon the present race of fine gentlemen. We did not stay with them long, but called upon Miss Benson, and proceeded to the rooms. Mr. Pepys was very unwilling to part with us, and wanted to frighten me from going, by saying,—

"And has Miss Burney the courage to venture to the Rooms? I wonder she dares!"

I did not seem to understand him, though to mistake him was impossible. However, I thought of him again when I was at the rooms, for most violent was the staring and whispering as I passed and repassed ! insomuch that I shall by no means be in any haste to go again to them. Susan and Sophy Thrale, who were with their aunt, Mrs. Scott, told Queeny upon our return that they heard nothing said, whichever way they turned, but "That's she!" "That's the famous Miss Burney!" I shall certainly escape going any more, if it is in my power.

Monday, Od. 28.—Mr. Pepys had but just left me, when Mrs. Thrale sent Susan with a particular request to see me in her dressing- room, where I found her with a milliner.

"Oh, Miss Burney," she cried, "I could not help promising Mrs. Cockran that she should have a sight of you—she has begged it so hard."

You may believe I stared; and the woman, whose eyes almost looked ready to eat me, eagerly came up to me, exclaiming,-

"Oh, ma'am, you don't know what a favour this is to see you! I have longed for it so long! It is quite a comfort to me, indeed. Oh, ma'am, how clever you must be! All the ladies I deal with are quite distracted about 'Cecilia,'—and I got it myself. Oh, ma'am, how sensible you must be! It does my heart good to see you."

DR. JOHNSON DOGMATISES.

Oct. 29.-We had a large party at home in the evening. I was presently engaged by Mr. Pepys, and he was joined by Mr. Coxe, and he by Miss Benson. Mr. Pepys led the conversation, and it was all upon criticism and poetry. The little set was broken up by my retreat, and Mr. Pepys joined Dr. Johnson, with whom he entered into an argument upon some lines of Gray, and upon Pope's definition of wit, in which he was so roughly confuted, and so severely ridiculed, that he was hurt and piqued beyond all power of disguise, and, in the midst of the discourse, suddenly turned from him, and, wishing Mrs. Thrale good night, very abruptly withdrew.

Dr. Johnson was certainly right with respect to the argument and to reason ; but his opposition was so warm, and his wit so satirical and exulting, that I was really quite grieved to see how unamiable he appeared, and how greatly he made himself dreaded by all, and by many abhorred. What pity that he will not curb the vehemence of his love of victory and superiority.

The sum of the dispute was this. Wit being talked of, Mr. Pepys repeated,—

"True wit is Nature to advantage dress'd, What oft was thought, but ne'er so well express'd."

"That, sir," cried Dr. Johnson, "is a definition both false and foolish. Let wit be dressed how it will, it will equally be wit, and neither the more nor the less for any advantage dress can give it."

Mr. P.-But, sir, may not wit be so ill expressed, and so obscure, by a bad speaker, as to be lost?

Dr. J.-The fault, then, sir, must be with the hearer. If a man cannot distinguish wit from words, he little deserves to hear it.

Mr. P.-But, sir, what Pope means—

Dr. J.-Sir, what Pope means, if he means what he says, is both false and foolish. In the first place, 'what oft was thought,' is all the worse for being often thought, because to be wit, it ought to be newly thought.

Mr. P.-But, sir, 'tis the expression makes it new.

Dr. J.-How can the expression make it new? It may make it clear, or may make it elegant - but how new? You are confounding words with things.

Mr. P.-But, sir, if one man says a thing very ill, may not another man say it so much better that—

Dr. J.-That other man, sir, deserves but small praise for the amendment; he is but the tailor to the first man's thoughts.

Mr. P.-True, sir, he may be but the tailor; but then the difference is as great as between a man in a gold lace suit and a man in a blanket.

Dr. J.-just so, sir, I thank you for that; the difference is precisely such, since it consists neither in the gold lace suit nor the blanket, but in the man by whom they are worn.

This was the summary; the various contemptuous sarcasms intermixed would fill, and very unpleasantly, a quire.

A CUNNING RUNAWAY HEIRESS.

Oct. 30.-Lady Warren is immensely tall, and extremely beautiful; she is now but just nineteen, though she has been married two or three years. She is giddy, gay, chatty, goodhumoured, and a little affected; she hazards all that occurs to her, seems to think the world at her feet, and is so young and gay and handsome that she is not much mistaken. She is, in short, an inferior Lady Honoria Pemberton; [155]somewhat beneath her in parts and understanding, but strongly in that class of character. I had no conversation with her myself; but her voice is loud and deep, and all she said was for the whole room.

Marriages being talked of, "I'll tell you," cried she, "a story; that is, it sha'n't be a story, but a fact. A lady of my acquaintance, who had 650,000 fortune, ran away to Scotland with a gentleman she liked vastly; so she was a little doubtful of him, and had a mind to try him: so when they stopped to dine, and change horses, and all that, she said, 'Now, as I have a great regard for you, I dare say you have for me - so I will tell you a secret: I have got no fortune at all, in reality, but only 5,000 pounds; for all the rest is a mere pretence : but if you like me for myself, and not for my fortune, you won't mind that.' So the gentleman said, 'Oh, I don't regard it at all, and you are the same charming angel that ever you was,' and all those sort of things that people say to one, and then went out to see about the chaise. So he did not come back; but when dinner was ready, the lady said 'Pray, where is he?' 'Lor, ma'am,' said they, 'why, that gentleman has been gone ever so long!' So she came back by herself; and now she's married to somebody else, and has her 50,000 pounds fortune all safe."

DR. JOHNSON A BORE.

Saturday, November 2.-We went to Lady Shelley's. Dr. Johnson, again, excepted in the invitation. He is almost constantly omitted, either from too much respect or too much fear. I am sorry for it, as he hates being alone, and as, though he scolds the others, he is well enough satisfied himself, and having given vent to all his own occasional anger or ill-humour, he is ready to begin again, and is never aware that those who have so been "downed" by him, never can much covet So triumphant a visitor. In contests of wit, the victor is as ill off in future consequences as the vanquished in present ridicule.

Monday, November 4.-This was a grand and busy day. Mr. Swinerton has been some time arranging a meeting for all our house, with Lady De Ferrars, whom you may remember as Charlotte Ellerker, and her lord and sisters: and this morning it took place, by mutual appointment, at his lodgings, where we met to breakfast. Dr. Johnson, who already knew Lord De Ferrars, and Mrs. and Miss Thrale, and myself, arrived first and then came the Lord and Lady, and Miss Ellerker and her youngest sister, Harriet. Lord De Ferrars is very ugly, but extremely well-bred, gentle, unassuming, sensible, and pleasing. His lady is much improved since we knew her in former days, and seems good-humoured, lively, and rather agreeable. Miss Ellerker is nothing altered.

I happened to be standing by Dr. Johnson when all the ladies came in; but, as I dread him before strangers, from the staring attention he attracts both for himself and all with whom he talks, I endeavoured to change my ground. However, he kept prating a sort of comical nonsense that detained me some minutes whether I would or not; but when we were all taking places at the breakfast-table I made another effort to escape. It proved vain; he drew his chair next to mine, and went rattling on in a humorous sort of comparison he was drawing of himself to me,—not one word of which could I enjoy, or can I remember, from the hurry I was in to get out of his way. In short, I felt so awkward from being thus marked out, that I was reduced to whisper a request to Mr. Swinerton to put a chair between us, for which I presently made a space: for I have often known him stop all conversation with me, when he has ceased to have me for his next neighbour. Mr. Swinerton who is an extremely good-natured young man, and so intimate here that 1 make no scruple with him, instantly complied, and placed himself between us.

But no sooner was this done, than Dr. Johnson, half seriously, and very loudly, took him to task.

"'How now, sir! what do you mean by this? Would you separate me from Miss Burney?

Mr. Swinerton, a little startled, began some apologies, and Mrs. Thrale winked at him to give up the place; but he was willing to oblige me, though he grew more and more frightened every minute, and coloured violently as the Doctor continued Is remonstrance, which he did with rather unmerciful raillery, upon his taking advantage of being in his own house to thus supplant him, and cram; but when he had borne it for about ten minutes, his face became so hot with the fear of hearing something worse, that he ran from the field, and took a chair between Lady De Ferrars and Mrs. Thrale.

I think I shall take warning by this failure, to trust only to my own expedients for avoiding his public notice in future. However it stopped here; for Lord De Ferrars came in, and took the disputed place without knowing of the contest, and all was quiet.

Miss BURNEY WILL NOT BE PERSUADED To DANCE.

..... LATE as it was, it was settled we should go to the ball, the last for the season being this night. My own objections about going not being strong enough to combat the ado my mentioning them would have occasioned, I joined in the party, without demur.

The ball was half over, and all the company seated to tea. Mr. Wade[156]came to receive us all, as usual, and we had a table procured for us, and went to tea ourselves, for something to do. When this repast was over, the company returned to their recreation. The room was very thin, and almost half the ladies danced with one another, though there were men enough present, I believe, had they chosen such exertion; but the Meadowses at balls are in crowds. Some of the ladies were in riding habits, and they made admirable men. 'Tis tonnish to be so much undressed at the last ball.

None of our usual friends, the Shelleys, Hatsels, Dickens, or Pepys, were here, and we, therefore, made no party - but Mrs. Thrale and I stood at the top of the room to look on the dancing, and as we were thus disengaged, she was seized with a violent desire to make one among them, and I felt myself an equal inclination. She proposed, as so many women danced together, that we two should, and nothing should I have liked so well; but I begged her to give up the scheme, as that would have occasioned more fuss and observation than our dancing with all the men that ever were born.

While we were debating this matter, a gentleman suddenly said to me,-"Did you walk far this morning, Miss Burney?" And, looking at him, I saw Mr. Metcalf, [157]whose graciousness rather surprised me, for he only made to Mrs. Thrale a cold and distant bow, and it seems he declares, aloud and around, his aversion to literary ladies. That he can endure, and even seek me is, I presume, only from the general perverseness of mankind, because he sees I have always turned from him; not, however, from disliking him, for he is a shrewd, sensible, keen, and very clever man; but merely from a dryness on his own side that has excited retaliation.

"Yes," I answered, "we walked a good way."

"Dr. Johnson," said he, "told me in the morning you were no walker; but I informed him then I had had the pleasure of seeing you upon the Newmarket Hill."

"Oh, he does not know," cried I, "whether I am a walker or not- -he does not see me walk, because he never walks himself." . . .

Here he was called away by some gentleman, but presently came to me again.

"Miss Burney," he said, "shall you dance?"""

"No, sir, not to-night."

"A gentleman," he added, "has desired me to speak to you for him."

Now, Susanna, for the grand moment!—the height—the zenith of my glory in the ton meridian! I again said I did not mean to dance, and to silence all objection, he expressively said,—

"'Tis Captain Kaye[158]who sends me."

Is not this magnificent? Pray congratulate me!

I was really very much surprised, but repeated my refusal, with all customary civilities to soften it. He was leaving me with this answer, when this most flashy young officer, choosing to trust his cause to himself, came forward, and desired to be introduced to me. Mr. Metcalf performed that ceremony, and he then, with as much respect and deference as if soliciting a countess, said,—

"May I flatter myself you will do me the honour of dancing With me?"

I thanked him, and said the same thing over again. He looked much disappointed, and very unwilling to give up his plan.

"If you have not," he said, "any particular dislike to dancing, it will be doing, not only me, but the Whole room much honour, if you will make one in a set."

"You do me much honour, sir," I answered, "but I must beg you to excuse me."

"I hope not," cried he, "I hope out of charity you will dance, as it is the last ball, and the company is so thin."

"Oh, it will do Very Well without me; Mr. Wade himself says he dies to-night a very respectable death."

"And will you not have the goodness to help it on a little in its last stage ? "

"No," said I, laughing; "why should we wish it to be kept lingering?"

"Lingering!" repeated he, looking round at the dancers, "no, surely it is not quite so desperate; and if you will but join in, you will give it new existence."

I was a little thrown off my guard at this unexpected earnestness, so different to the ton of the day, and I began hardly to know What to answer, my real objection being such as I could by no means publish, though his urgency and his politeness joined would have made me give up any other.

"This is a very quiet dance," he continued. "there is nothing fatiguing in it."

"You are very good," said I, "but I cannot really dance to-night."

I was sorry to seem so obstinate, but he was just the man to make every body inquire whom he danced with; and any one Who wished for general attention could do no better than to be his partner. The ever-mischievous Mrs. Thrale, calling to Mr. Selwyn, who stood by us, said,-

"Why, here's a man in love !-quite, downright in love with Miss Burney, if ever I saw one!"

"He is quite mortified, at least," he answered; "I never saw a man look more mortified."

"Well, he did not deserve it," said she; "he knew how to beg, and he ought not to have been so served."

I begged her to be silent, for Mr. Metcalf returned to me. "

"Were you too much tired," he said, "with your walk this morning, to try at a dance?"

I excused myself as well as I could, and we presently went into the card-room to vary the scene. When we returned to the ball-room I was very glad to see my new captain had just taken out Lady Anne Lindsay, who is here with Lady Margaret Fordyce, and who dances remarkably well, and was every way a more suitable partner for him. He was to leave the town, with his regiment, the next day.

Tuesday.-Mrs. Thrale took me out to walk with her. We met Lady De Ferrars and Miss Ellerker in our ramble, and the very moment the ball was mentioned, this dear and queer creature called out,—

"Ay, there was a sad ado, ladies dancing with ladies, and all sorts of odd things; and that handsome and fine Mr. Kaye broke his heart almost to dance with Miss Burney; but she refused him, and so, in despair, he took out Lady Anne Lindsay."

DR. JOHNSON HELD IN GENERAL DREAD.

Thursday.-Mr. Metcalf called upon Dr. Johnson, and took him out for an airing. Mr. Hamilton is gone, and Mr. Metcalf is now the only person out of this house that voluntarily communicates with the doctor. He has been in a terrible severe bumour of late, and has really frightened all the people, till they almost ran from him. To me only I think he is now kind, for Mrs. Thrale fares worse than anybody. 'Tis very strange and very melancholy that he will not a little more accommodate his manners and language to those of other people. He likes Mr. Metcalf, however, and so do I, for he is very clever and entertaining when he pleases.

Poor Dr. Delap confessed to us, that the reason he now came so seldom, though he formerly almost lived with us when at this place, was his being too unwell to cope with Dr. Johnson. And the other day Mr. Selwyn having refused an invitation from Mr. Hamilton to meet the doctor, because he preferred being here upon a day when he was out, suddenly rose at the time he was expected to return, and said he must run away, "for fear the doctor should call him to account."

SHORT, FAT, HANDSOME MISS MONCKTON: DUCAL INIFFERENCE.

Sunday, November 10, brings in a new person. Th e Honourable Miss Monckton, [159]who is here with her mother, the Dowager Lady Galway, has sent various messages of her earnest desire to be acquainted with Mrs. Thrale and your humble servant to command. Dr. Johnson 'she already knew,, for she is one of those who stand foremost in collecting all extraordinary or curious people to her London conversaziones, which, like those of Mrs. Vesey, mix the rank and file literature, and exclude all beside. Well—after divers intimations Of this sort, it was at last settled that Lady De Ferrars should bring her here this morning.

In the evening came Lady De Ferrars, Miss Monckton, and Miss Ellerker. Miss Monckton is between thirty and forty very short, very fat, but handsome ; splendidly and fantastically dressed, rouged not unbecomingly, yet evidently and palpably desirous of gaining notice and admiration. She has an easy levity in her air, manner, voice, and discourse, that speak all within to be comfortable; and her rage of seeing anything curious may be satisfied, if she pleases, by looking in a mirror.

I can give you no account of the conversation, as it was broken, and not entertaining. Miss Monckton went early, having another engagement, but the other ladies stayed very late. She told us, however, one story extremely well worth recarding. The Duke of Devonshire was standing near a very fine glass lustre in a corner of a room, at an assembly, and in a house of people who, Miss Monckton said, were by no means in a style of life to hold expense as immaterial ; and, by carelessly lolling back, he threw the lustre down and it was broke. He shewed not, however, the smallest concern or confusion at the accident, but coolly said, "I wonder how I did that!" He then removed to the opposite corner, and to shew, I suppose, he had forgotten what he had done, leaned his head in the same manner, and down came the opposite lustre ! He looked at it very calmly, and, with a philosophical dryness, merely said, "This is singular enough!" and walked to another part of the room, without either distress or apology.

MISS MONCKTON's ASSEMBLY: SACQUES AND RUFFLES.

December 8.-Now for Miss Monckton's assembly.

I had begged Mrs. Thrale to call for me, [160]that I might have her countenance and assistance upon my entrance. Miss Thrale came also. Every thing was in a new style. We got out of the coach into a hall full of servants, not one of which inquired our names, or took any notice of us. We proceeded, and went upstairs, and, when we arrived at a door, stopped and looked behind us. No servant had followed or preceded us. We deliberated what was to be done. To announce ourselves was rather awkward, neither could we be sure we were going into the right apartment. I proposed going up higher, till we met with somebody; Miss Thrale thought we should go down and call some of the servants; but Mrs. Thrale, after a ridiculous consultation, determined to try her fortune by opening the door. This being done, we entered a room full of tea-things, and one maid-servant.

"Well," cried Mrs. Thrale, laughing, "what is to be done now? I suppose we are come so early that nothing is ready."

The maid stared, but said,—"There's company in the next room."

Then we considered again how to make ourselves known; and then Mrs. Thrale again resolved to take courage and enter. She therefore opened another door, and went into another apartment. I held back, but looked after, and observing that she made no curtsey, concluded she was gone into some wrong place. Miss Thrale followed, and after her went little I, wondering who was to receive, or what was to become of us.

Miss Monckton lives with her mother, the old Dowager Lady Galway, in a noble house in Charles-street, Berkeleysquare, The room was large and magnificent. There was not much company, for we were very early. Lady Galway sat at the side of the fire, and received nobody. She seems very old, and was dressed with a little round white cap, and not a single hair, no cushlori, roll, nor any thing else but the little round cap, which was flat upon her forehead. Such part of the company as already knew her made their compliments to her where she sat, and the rest were never taken up to her, but belonged wholly to Miss Monckton.

Miss Monckton's own manner of receiving her guests was scarce more laborious ; for she kept her seat when they entered, and only turned rOUnd her head to nod it, and say "How do you do?" after which they found what accommodation they could for themselves.

As soon, however, as she perceived Mrs. and Miss Thrale, which was not till they had been some minutes in the room, she arose to welcome them, contrary to her general Custom, and merely because it was their first visit. Our long train making my entrance some time after theirs, gave me the advantage of being immediately seen by her, and she advanced to me with quickness, and very politely thanked me for coming, and said,—

"I fear you think me very rude for taking the liberty of sending to you."

"No, indeed, you did me much honour," quoth I.

She then broke further into her general rules, by making way for me to a good place, and seating me herself, and then taking a chair next me, and beginning a little chat. I really felt myself much obliged to her for this seasonable attention, for I was presently separated from Mrs. Thrale, and entirely surrounded by strangers, all dressed superbly, and all looking saucily ; and as nobody's names were spoken, I had no chance to discover any acquaintances. Mr. Metcalf, indeed, came and spoke to me the instant I came in, and I should have been very happy to have had him for my neighbour; but he was engaged in attending to Dr. Johnson, who was standing near the fire, and environed with listeners.

Some new people now coming in, and placing themselves in a regular way, Miss Monckton exclaimed,—"My whole care is to prevent a circle;" and hastily rising, she pulled about the chairs, and planted the people in groups, with as dexterous a disorder as you would desire to see.

The company in general were dressed with more brilliancy than at any rout I ever was at, as most of them were going to the Duchess of Cumberland's, and attired for that purpose. just behind me sat Mrs. Hampden, still very beautiful, but insufferably affected. Another lady, in full dress, and very pretty, came in soon after, and got herself a chair just before me ; and then a conversation began between her and Mrs. Hampden, of which I will give you a specimen.

"How disagreeable these sacques are! I am so incommoded with these nasty ruffles! I am going to Cumberland House—are you?"

"To be sure," said Mrs. Hampden, "what else, do you think, would make me bear this weight of dress? I can't bear a sacque."

"Why, I thought you said you should always wear them?"

"Oh, yes, but I have changed my mind since then—as many people do."

"Well, I think it vastly disagreeable indeed," said the other, "you Can't think how I am encumbered with these ruffles!"

" Oh I am quite oppressed with them," said Mrs. Hampden, "I can hardly bear myself up."

" And I dined in this way!" cried the other; "only think—dining in a sacque!"

"Oh," answered Mrs. Hampden, "it really puts me quite out of spirits."

After this they found some subject less popular, and the lady unknown leaned over me, without any ceremony, to whisper with Mrs. Hampden. I should have offered her my place if she had made any apology, but as it was, I thought she might take her own way. In the course of the evening, however, I had the pleasure to observe a striking change in her manners; for as soon as she picked up, I know not how, my name, she ceased her whispering, looked at me with the civilest smiles, spoke to me two or three times, and calling to a fine beau, said—

"Do pray sit this way, that you may screen Miss Burney as well as me from that fire,"

I did not, however, sufficiently like her beginning, to accept her challenge of talking, and only coldly answered by yes, no, or a bow.

AT MISS MONCKTON'S: "CECILIA" EXTOLLED BY THE "OLD WIS," AND By BURKE.

Then came in Sir Joshua Reynolds, and he soon drew a chair near mine, and from that time I was never without some friend at my elbow.

Have you seen," said he, "Mrs. Montagu lately?"

"No, not very lately."

"But within these few months?"

"No, not since last year."

"Oh, you must see her, then. You ought to see and to hear her— 't will be worth your while. Have you heard of the fine long letter she has written?"

"Yes, but I have not met with it."

"I have."

"And who is it to?"

"The old Duchess of Portland. [161]She desired Mrs. Montagu's opinion of 'Cecilia,' and she has written it at full length. I was in a party at her grace's, and heard of nothing but you. She is so delighted, and so sensibly, so rationally, that I only wish you could have heard her. And old Mrs. Delany had been forced to begin it, though she had said she should never read any more; however, when we met, she was reading it already for the third time."

After this Mrs. Burke saw me, and with much civility and softness of manner, came and talked with me, while her husband without seeing me, went behind my chair to speak to Mrs Hampden.

Miss Monckton, returning to me, then said—

" Miss Burney, I had the pleasure yesterday of seeing Mrs. Greville. [162]

I suppose she concluded I was very intimate with her.

"I have not seen her," said I, "many years."

"I know, however," cried she, looking surprised, "she is your godmother."

"But she does not do her duty and answer for me, for I never see her."

"Oh, you have answered very well for yourself! But I know by that your name is Fanny."

She then tripped to somebody else, and Mr. Burke very quietly came from Mrs. Hampden, and sat down in the vacant place at my side. I could then wait no longer, for I found he was more near-sighted than myself; I, therefore, turned towards him and bowed: he seemed quite amazed, and really made me ashamed, however delighted, by the expressive civility and distinction with which he instantly rose to return my bow, and stood the whole time he was making his compliments upon seeing me, and calling himself the blindest of men for not finding me out sooner. And Mrs. Burke, who was seated near me, said, loud enough for me to hear her—

"See, see what a flirtation Mr. Burke is beginning with Miss Burney and before my face too!"

These ceremonies over, he sat down by me, and began a conversation which you, my dearest Susy, would be glad to hear, for my sake, word for word; but which I really could not listen to with sufficient ease, from shame at his warm eulogiums, to remember With any accuracy. The geneial substance, however, take as I recollect it.

After many most eloquent compliments upon the book, too delicate either to shock or sicken the nicest ear, he very empbatically congratulated me upon its most universal success, said, "he was now too late to speak of it, since he could only echo the voice of the whole nation" and added, with a laugh, "I had hoped to have made some merit of my enthusiasm; but the moment I went about to hear what others say, I found myself merely one in a multitude."

He then told me that, notwithstanding his admiration, he was the man who had dared to find some faults with so favourite and fashionable a work. I entreated him to tell me what they were, and assured him nothing would make me so happy as to correct them under his direction. He then enumerated them: and I will tell you what they are, that you may not conclude I write nothing but the fairer part of my adventures, which I really always relate very honestly, though so fair they are at this time, that it hardly seems possible they should not be dressed up.

The masquerade he thought too long, and that something might be spared from Harrel's grand assembly; he did not like Morrice's part of the pantheon; and he wished the conclusion either more happy or more miserable "for in a work of imagination," said he, "there is no medium."

I was not easy enough to answer him, or I have much, though perhaps not good for much, to say in defence of following life and nature as much in the conclusion as in the progress of a tale; and when is life and nature completely happy or miserable?

Looking very archly at me, and around him, he said,—

"Are you sitting here for characters? Nothing, by the way, struck me more in reading your book than the admirable skill with which your ingenious characters make themselves known by their own words."

He then went on to tell me that I had done the most wonderful of wonders in pleasing the old wits, particularly the Duchess of Portland and Mrs. Delany, who resisted reading the book till they were teased into it, and, since they began, could do nothing else - and he failed not to point out, with his utmost eloquence, the difficulty Of giving satisfaction to those who piqued themselves upon being past receiving it.

"But," said he, "I have one other fault to find, and a more material one than any I have mentioned."

"I am the more obliged to you. What is it?"

"The disposal of this book. I have much advice to offer to you upon that subject. Why did not you send for your own friend out of the city? he would have taken care you should not part with it so much below par."

He meant Mr. Briggs. [163]

Sir Joshua Reynolds now joined us.

" Are you telling her," said he, "of our conversation with the old wits? I am glad you hear it from Mr. Burke, Miss Burney, for he can tell it so much better than I can, and remember their very words."

" Nothing else would they talk of for three whole hours," said he, "and we were there at the third reading of the bill."

"I believe I was in good hands," said I, "if they talked of it to you?"

"Why, yes," answered Sir Joshua, laughing, "we joined in from time to time. Gibbon says he read the whole five volumes in a day."

"'Tis impossible," cried Mr. Burke, "it cost me three days and you know I never parted with it from the time I first opened it."

A WRITER OF ROMANCES.

Soon after the parties changed again and young Mr. Burke[164]came and sat by me. He is a very civil and obliging, and a sensible and agreeable young man. Old Lady Galway trotted from her corner, in the middle of the evening, and leaning her hands upon the backs of two chairs, put her little round head through two fine high dressed ladies on purpose to peep at me, and then trotted back to her place! Ha, ha!

Miss Monckton now came to us again, and I congratulated her upon her power in making Dr. Johnson sit in a group upon which she immediately said to him,—

"Sir, Miss Burney says you like best to sit in a circle."

"Does she?" said he, laughing; "Ay, never mind what she says. Don't you know she is a writer of romances?"

"Yes, that I do, indeed," said Miss Monckton, and every one joined in a laugh that put me horribly out of countenance.

"She may write romances and speak truth," said my dear Sir Joshua, who, as well as young Burke, and Mr. Metcalf, and two strangers, joined now in our little party.

"But, indeed, Dr. Johnson," said Miss Monckton, "you must see Mrs. Siddons. Won't you see her in some fine part?"

"Why, if I must, madam, I've no choice."

"She says, sir, she shall be very much afraid of you."

"Madam, that cannot be true."

"Not true," cried Miss Monckton, staring, "yes it is."

"It cannot be, madam."

"But she said so to me ; I heard her say it myself."

"Madam, it is not possible! remember, therefore, in future, that even fiction should be supported by probability."

Miss Monckton looked all amazement, but insisted upon the -truth of what she had said.

"I do not believe, madam," said he, warmly, "she knows my name."

" "Oh, that is rating her too low," said a gentleman stranger.

"By not knowing my name," continued he, "I do not mean so literally; but that, when she sees it abused in a newspaper, she may possibly recollect that she has seen it abused in a newspaper before."

"Well, sir," said Miss Monckton, "but you must see her for all this."

"Well, madam, if you desire it, I will go. See her I shall not, nor hear her; but I'll go, and that will do. The last time I was at a play, I was ordered there by Mrs. Abington, or Mrs. Somebody, I do not well remember who; but I placed myself in the middle of the first row of the front boxes, to show that when I was called I came."

The talk upon this matter went on very long, and with great spirit. At last, a large party of ladies arose at the same time', and I tripped after them; Miss Monckton, however, made me come back, for she said I must else wait in the other room till those ladies' carriages drove away.

When I returned, Sir Joshua came and desired he might convey me home; I declined the offer, and he pressed it a good deal, drolly saying,—

"Why, I am old enough, a'n't I?" And when he found me stout, he said to Dr. Johnson,—"Sir, is not this very hard? Nobody thinks me very young, yet Miss Burney won't give me the privilege of age in letting me see her home? She says I a'n't old enough." [165]

I had never said any such thing.

"Ay," sir," said the doctor, "did I not tell you she was a riter of romances?"

MRS. WALSINGHAM.

December 15.-To-day, by an invitation of ten days standing, I waited upon Mrs. Walsingham. She is a woman high in fame for her talents, [166]and a wit by birth, as the daughter of Sir Charles Hanbury Williams.

She has the character of being only civil to people of birth, fame, or wealth, and extremely insolent to all others. Of this, however, I could see nothing, since she at least took care to invite no company to her own house whom she was disposed to disdain. Her reception of me appeared rather singular. She was violently dressed,—a large hoop, flowers in her small and full dressed cap, ribands and ornaments extremely shown, and a fan in her hand. She was very polite, said much of her particular pleasure in seeing Me, and kept advancing to me near, that involuntarily I retreated from her, not knowing er design, and kept, therefore, getting further and further back as she came forward, till I was stopped from any power of moving by the wainscot. I then necessarily stood still, and she saluted me.

We then quietly sat down, and my father began a very lively conversation upon various subjects; she kept it up with attention and good breeding, often referring to me, and seemig curious to know my notions.

The rest of the company who came to dinner were Mrs. Montagu, Mr. Percy, Speaker of the Irish House of Commons, his lady and daughter, and Sir Joshua Reynolds and Miss Palmer. I was excessively glad to see the latter, who clung to me all the visit, and took off from its formality and grandeur by her chatting and intimacy.

Mrs. Walsingham lives in a splendid house in Stratford place, elegantly fitted up, chiefly by her own paintings and drawingsl which are reckoned extremely clever. I hate that word, but cannot think of another.

We did not stay late, for my father and I were both engaged to Miss Monckton's; so was Sir Joshua, who accompanied us.

MRS. SIDDONS.

I WAS EXTremely happy to have my dear father with me at Miss Monckton's. We found Mrs. Siddons, the actress, there. She is a woman of excellent character, and therefore I am very glad she is thus patronised, since Mrs. Abington, and so many frail fair ones, have been thus noticed by the great. She behaved with great propriety ; very calm, modest, quiet, and unaffected - She has a very fine countenance, and her eyes 'look both intelligent and soft. She has, however, a steadiness in her manner and deportment by no means engaging. Mrs. Thrale, who was there, said,—"Why, this is a leaden goddess we are all worshipping! however, we shall soon gild it."

A lady who sat near me then began a dialogue with Mr. Erskine, [167]who had placed himself exactly opposite to Mrs. Siddons; and they debated together upon her manner of studying her parts, disputing upon the point with great warmth, yet not only forbearing to ask Mrs. Siddons herself which was right, but quite over-powering her with their loquacity, when she attempted, unasked, to explain the matter. Most vehement praise of all she did followed, and the lady turned to me, and said,-

"What invitation, Miss Burney, is here, for genius to display itself!— Everybody, I hear, is at work for Mrs. Siddons; but if you would work for her, what an inducement to excel you would both of you have!—Dr. Burney—."

"Oh, pray, ma'am," cried I, "don't say to him—"

"Oh, but I will!—if my influence can do you any mischief, you may depend upon having it."

She then repeated what she had said to my father, and he instantly said,—

"Your ladyship may be sure of my interest."

I whispered afterwards to know who she was, and heard she Was Lady Lucan.

DR. JOHNSON'S INMATES'AT BOLT-COURT.

On Tuesday, Dec. 24, I went in the evening to call on Mrs. Thrale, and tore myself away from her to go to Bolt-court to see Dr. Johnson, who is very unwell. He received me with great kindness, and bade me come oftener, which I will try to contrive. He told me he heard of nothing but me, call upon him who would ; and, though he pretended to grow], he was evidently delighted for me. His usual set, Mrs. Williams and Mrs. De Mullins, were with him; and some queer man of a parson who, after grinning at me some time, said,—

"Pray, Mrs. De Mullins, is the fifth volume of 'Cecilia' at home yet? Dr. Johnson made me read it, ma'am."

"Sir, he did it much honour."

"Made you, sir?" said the doctor, "you give an ill account of your own taste or understanding, if you wanted any making to read such a book as 'Cecilia.'"

"Oh, sir, I don't mean that; for I am sure I left every thing in the world to go on with it."

A shilling was now wanted for some purpose or other, and none of them happened to have one ; I begged that I might lend one.

"Ay, do," said the doctor, "I will borrow of you ; authors are like privateers, always fair game for one another."

"True, sir," said the parson, "one author is always robbing another."

"I don't know that, sir," cried the doctor; "there sits an author who, to my knowledge, has robbed nobody. I have never once caught her at a theft. The rogue keeps her resources to herself!"

THE TWO MR. CAMBRIDGES IMPROVE UPON **ACUAINTANCE.**

THURSDAY.-In the morning Mr. Cambridge[168]came, and made a long visit. He is entertaining, Original, and well-bred; somewhat formal, but extremely civil and obliging, and, I believe, remarkably honourable and strict in his principles and actions. I wished I could have been easy and chatty with him as I hear he is so much my friend, and as I like him very much; but, in truth, he listens to every syllable I utter with so grave a deference, that it intimidates and silences me. When he was about taking leave, he said,—

"Shall you go to Mrs. Ord's[169]tomorrow?"

"Yes, sir."

"I thought so," said he, smiling, "and hoped it. Where shall you go to-night?"

"No where,—I shall be at home."

"At home? Are you sure?"

"Yes."

"Why, then, Miss Burney, my son[170] and I dine to-day in your neighbourhood, at the Archbishop of York's, and, if you please, we will come here in the evening."

This was agreed to. And our evening was really a charming one. The two Mr. Cambridges came at about eight o'clock, and the good Mr. Hoole[171]was here. My father came downstairs to them in high spirits and good humour, and he and the elder Mr. Cambridge not only talked enough for us all, but so well and so pleasantly that no person present had even a wish to speak for himself. Mr. Cambridge has the best stock of good stories I almost ever heard; and, though a little too precise in his manner, he is always well-bred, and almost always entertaining. Our sweet father kept up the ball with him admirably, whether in anecdotes, serious disquisitions, philosophy, or fun; for all which Mr. Cambridge has both talents and inclination.

The son rises extremely in my opinion and liking. He is sensible, rational, and highly cultivated ; very modest in all he asserts, and attentive and pleasing in his behaviour ; and he is wholly free from the coxcombical airs, either of impertinence, or negligence and nonchalance, that almost all the young men I meet, except also young Burke, are tainted with. What chiefly, however, pleased me in him was observing that he quite adores his father. He attended to all his stories with a face that never told he had heard them before; and, though he spoke but little himself, he seemed as well entertained as if he had been the leading person in the company,—a post which, nevertheless, I believe he could extremely well sustain; and, no doubt, much the better for being in no haste to aspire to it. I have seldom, altogether, had an evening with which I hav, been better pleased.

THE SHILLING, THE CHAIRMAN, AND THE GREEN-SHOP **GIRL.**

Saturday, Dec. 28.-My father and I dined and spent the day at Sir Joshua Reynolds's, after many preceding disappointments. I had a whispering conversation with Mrs. Reynolds, [172]which made me laugh, from her excessive oddness and absurdity.

"I had the most unfortunate thing in the world happen to me," she said, "about Mrs. Montagu, and I always am in some distress or misfortune with that lady. She did me the honour to invite me to dine with her last week,—and I am sure there is nobody in the world can be more obliged to Mrs. Montagu taking such notice of any body;—but just when the day came I was so unlucky as to be ill, and that, you know, made it quite improper to go to dine with Mrs. Montagu, for fear of disagreeable consequences. So this vexed me very much, for I had nobody to send to her that was proper to appear before Mrs. Montagu; for to own the truth, you must know I have no servant but a maid, and I could not think of sending such a person to Mrs. Montagu. So I thought it best to send a chairman, and to tell him only to ring at the bell, and to wait for no answer; because then the porter might tell Mrs. Montagu my servant brought the note, for the porter could not tell but he might be my servant.

But my maid was so stupid, she took the shilling I gave her for the chairman, and went to a green-shop, and bid the woman send somebody with the note, and she left the shilling with her; so the green-woman, I suppose, thought she might keep the shilling, and instead of sending a chairman she sent her own errand-girl; and she was all dirt and rags. But this is not all; for,when the girl got to the house, nothing would serve her but she would give the note to Mrs. Montagu, and wait for an answer; so then, you know, Mrs. Montagu saw this ragged green-shop girl. I was never so shocked in my life, for when she brought me back the note I knew at once how it all was. Only think what a mortification, to have Mrs. Montagu see such a person as that! She must think it very odd of me indeed to send a green-shop girl to such a house as hers!"

MR. SOAME JENYNS'S EULOGY ON "CECILIA."

Friday, [Jan. 17, 1783. Now for this grand interview with Soame Jenyns. [173] I went with my dear father who was quite enchanted at the affair. Dear soul, how he feeds upon all that brings fame to "Cecilia!" his eagerness upon this subject, and his pleasure in it, are truly enthusiastic, and, I think, rather increase by fulness than grow satiated.

We were late; there was a good deal of company, not in groups, nor yet in a circle, but seated square round the room, in order following,—Miss Ellerker, Mrs. Soame Jenyns, Mrs. Thrale, her daughter, Mrs. Buller, Mr. Cambridge, senior, Mr. Soame Jenyns, Mr. Selwin, Mr. Cambridge, junior, Miss Burgoyne, a lady or two I knew not, and three or four men.

Mrs. Ord almost ran to the door to receive us, and every creature of this company, contrary to all present custom in large meetings, stood up.

"Why have you been so late?" cried Mrs. Ord, "we have been waiting for you this hour. I was afraid there was some mistake."

"My father could not come sooner."

"But why would not you let me send my coach for you? Mr. Soame Jenyns has been dying with impatience; some of us thought you would not come; others thought it only coquetry; but come, let us repair the time as we can, and introduce you to one another without further delay."

You may believe how happy I felt at this "some thought," and "others," which instantly betrayed that everybody was apprised they were to see this famous rencounter; and lest I should mark it less, every body still stood up. Mr. Jenyns now, with all the speed in his power, hastened up to me, and began a long harangue of which I know hardly a word, upon the pleasure and favour, and honour, and what not, of meeting me, and upon the delight, and information, and amusement of reading "Cecilia."

I made all possible reverences, and tried to get to a seat, but Mrs. Ord, when I turned from him, took my hand, and leading me to the top of the room, presented me to Mrs. Jenyns. Reverences were repeated here, in silence, however, so they did very well. I then hoped to escape to Mrs. Thrale, who held out her hand to me, pointing to a chair by her own, and saying,-

"Must I, too, make interest to be introduced to Miss Burney?"

This, however, was not allowed; Mrs. Ord again took my hand, and parading me to the sofa, said,—

"Come, Miss Burney, and let me place you by Mrs. Buller."

I was glad, by this time, to be placed any where, for not till then did the company seat themselves.

Mr. Cambridge, sen., then came up to speak to me, but had hardly asked how I did before Mrs. Ord brought Mr. jenyns to me again, and made him my right-hand neighbour, saying,-

"There! now I have put you fairly together, I have done with you."

Mr. Soame jenyns then, thus called upon—could he do less?—began an eulogy unrivalled, I think, for extravagance of praise. All creation was open to me; no human being ever began that book and had power to put it down; pathos, humour, interest, moral—O heavens! I heard, however, but the leading words; though every body else, the whole roon, being silent, doubtless heard how they hung together. Had I been carried to a theatre to hear an oration upon my own performances, I could hardly have felt more confounded.

I bowed my head during the first two or three sentences, by way of marking that I thought them over; but over they were not the more. I then turned away, but I only met Mrs. Buller, who took up the panegyric where Mr. jenyns stopped for breath.

In short, the things that were said, with the attention of the whole company, would have drawn blushes into the cheeks of Agujari or Garrick. I was almost upon the point of running away. I changed so often from hot to cold that I really felt myself in a fever and an ague. I never even attempted to speak to them, and I looked with all the frigidity I possibly could, in hopes they would tire of bestowing such honours on a subject so ungrateful.

One moment I had hopes that Mr. G. Cambridge, in Christian charity, was coming to offer some interruption ; for, when these speeches were in their height, he came and sat down on a chair immediately opposite Miss Thrale, and equally near, in profile, to me; but he merely said, "I hope Dr. Burney has not wanted his pamphlet?" Even Mrs. Thrale would not come near me, and told me afterwards it had been such a settled thing before my arrival, that I was to belong to Mr. Soame Jenyns, that she did not dare.

The moment they were gone, "Well, Miss Burney," said Mrs. Ord, "have you and Mr. Jenyns had a great deal of conversation together?"

"O yes, a great deal on my part!"

"Why you don't look quite recovered from it yet—did not you like it?"

"O yes, it was perfectly agreeable to me!"

"Did he oppress you?" cried Mr. Cambridge, and then he began a very warm praise of him for his talents, wit, and understanding, his knowledge, writings, and humour.

I should have been very ready to have joined with him, had I not feared he meant an implied reproach to me, for not being more grateful for the praise of a man such as he described. I am sorry he was present if that is the case; but the truth is, the evening was not merely disagreeable but painful to me.

AN ITALIAN SINGER'S VIEWS OF ENGLAND.

Saturday.-While Mr. George Cambridge was here Pacchierotti called-very grave, but very sweet. Mr. G. C. asked if he spoke English.

"O, very well," cried I, "pray try him; he is very amiable, and I fancy you will like him."

Pacchierotti began with complaining of the variable weather. "

I cannot," he said, "be well such an inconsistent day."

We laughed at the word "inconsistent," and Mr. Cambridge said,-

"It is curious to see what new modes all languages may take in the hands of foreigners. The natives dare not try such experiments; and, therefore, we all talk pretty much alike ; but a foreigner is obliged to hazard new expressions, and very often he shews us a force and power in our words, by an unusual adaptation of them, that we were not ourselves aware tlley would admit."

And then, to draw Pacchierotti out, he began a dispute, of the different merits of Italy and England; defending his own country merely to make him abuse it; while Pacchierotti most eagerly took up the gauntlet on the part of Italy.

"This is a climate," said Pacchierotti, "never in the same case for half an hour at a time; it shall be fair, and wet, and dry, and humid, forty times in a morning in the least. I am tired to be so played with, sir, by your climate."

"We have one thing, however, Mr. Pacchierotti," he answered, "which I hope you allow makes some amends, and that is our verdure; in Italy you cannot boast that."

"But it seem to me, sir, to be of no utility so much evergreen is rather too much for my humble opinion."

"And then your insects, Mr. Pacchierotti! those alone are a most dreadful drawback upon the comfort of your fine climate."

"I must own," said Pacchierotti, "Italy is rather disagreeable for the insects; but is it not better, sir, than an atmosphere so bad as they cannot live in it?"

"Why, as i can't defend our atmosphere, I must shift my ground, and talk to you of our fires, which draw together society."

"O indeed, good sir, your societies are not very invigorating! Twenty people of your gentlemen and ladies to sit about a fire, and not to pronounce one word, is very dull!"

We laughed heartily at this retort courteous.

RAPTURES OF THE "OLD WITS" OVER "CECILIA."

[MARY DELany was the daughter of Bernard Granville, younger brother of George Granville, Baron Lansdowne, the poet and friend of Wycherley and Pope. She was born on the 14th Of May, 1700. Her uncle, Lord Lansdowne, was a better friend to the Muses than to his young niece, for he forced poor Mary Granville, at the age of seventeen, to marry one Alexander Pendarves, a coarse, hard drinking Cornish squire, of more than three times her age. Pendarves died some six years later, and his widow married, in 1743, Dr. Patrick

Delany, the friend of Swift. With Delany she lived happily for fifteen years, and after his death in 1768, Mrs. Delany devoted most of her time to her bosom friend, the dowager Duchess of Portland (see note 161, ante, p. 251, at whose seat at Bulstrode she usually spent the summer, while during the winter she resided at her own house in St. James's-place, where she was constantly visited by the Duchess. On the death of the Duchess in July, 1785, King George bestowed upon Mrs. Delany, whose means were not such as to make an addition to them a matter of indifference, a furnished house at Windsor and a pension Of 300 pounds a year. These she enjoyed for less than three years, dying on the 15th of April, 1788.

The strong attachment which grew up between her and Fanny renders Mrs. Delany a very interesting figure in the "Diary." Nor wasFanny's enthusiasm for her aged friend misdirected. Speakin of Mrs' Delany, Edmund Burke said: "She was a perfect pattern of a perfect fine lady: a real fine lady of other days. Her manners were faultless; her deportment was of marked elegance; her speech was all sweetness; and her air and address were all dignity. I have always looked up to Mrs. Delany, as the model of an accomplished gentlewoman of former times." [174] ED.]

Sunday, January ig-And now for Mrs. Delany. I spent one hour with Mrs. Thrale, and then called for Mrs. Chapone, [175]and we proceeded together to St. James's-place.

Mrs. Delany was alone in her drawing-room, which is entirely hung round with pictures of her own painting, and Ornaments of her own designing. She came to the door to receive us. She is still tall, though some of her height may be lost: not much, however, for she is remarkably upright. She has no remains of beauty in feature, but in countenance I never but once saw more, and that was in my sweet maternal grandmother. Benevolence, softness, piety, and gentleness are all resident in her face ; and the resemblance with which she struck me to my dear grandmother, in her first appearance, grew so much stronger from all that came from her mind, which seems to contain nothing but purity and native humility, that I almost longed to embrace her; and I am sure if I had the recollection of that saint-like woman would have been so strong that I should never have refrained from crying over her.

Mrs. Chapone presented me to her, and taking my hand* she said,— "You must pardon me if I give you an old-fashioned reception, for I know nothing new." And she saluted me. I did not, as with Mrs. Walsingham, retreat from her.

"Can you forgive, Miss Burney," she continued, "this great liberty I have taken with you, of asking for your company to dinner? I wished so impatiently to see one from whom I have received such extraordinary pleasure, that, as I could not be alone this morning, I could not bear to put it off to another day; and, if you had been so good to come in the evening, I might, perhaps, have had company; and I hear so ill that I cannot, as I wish to do, attend to more than one at a time; for age makes me stupid even more than I am by nature; and how grieved and mortified I must have been to know I had Miss Burney in the room, and not to hear her!"

She then mentioned her regret that we could not stay and spend the evening with her, which had been told her in our card of accepting her invitation, as we were both engaged, which, for my part, I heartily regretted.

"I am particularly sorry," she added, "on account of the Duchess dowager of Portland, who is so good as to come to me in an evening, as she knows I am too infirm to wait upon her grace myself: and she wished so much to see Miss Burney. But she said she would come as early as possible."

Soon after we went to dinner, which was plain, neat, well cooked, and elegantly served. When it was over, I began to speak; and now, my Chesington auditors, look to yourselves!

"Will you give me leave, ma'am, to ask if you remember any body of the name of Crisp?"

"Crisp?" cried she, "What! Mrs. Ann Crisp?"

"Yes, ma'am."

"O surely! extremely well! a charming, an excellent woman she was; we were very good friends once; I visited her at Burford, and her sister Mrs. Gast."

Then came my turn, and I talked of the brother - but I won't write what I said. Mrs. Delany said she knew him but very little; and by no means so much as she should have liked. I reminded her of a letter he wrote her from abroad, which she immediately recollected.

This Chesingtonian talk lasted till we went upstairs, and then she shewed me the new art which she had invented. It is staining paper of all possible colours, and then cutting it out, so finely, and delicately, that when it is pasted on paper or vellum, it has all the appearance of being pencilled, except that, by being raised, it has still a richer and more natural look. The effect is extremely beautiful. She invented it at tseventy-five! She told me she did four flowers the first year; sixteen the second; and the third, one hundred and sixty; and after that many more. They are all from nature, and consist of the most curious flowers, plants, and weeds, that are to (be found. She has been supplied with patterns from all the great gardens, and all the great florists in the kingdom. Her plan was to finish one thousand; but, alas! her eyes now fail her though she has only twenty undone of her task,

about seven o'clock, the Duchess dowager of Portland came. She is not near so old as Mrs. Delany; nor, to me, is her face by any means so pleasing; but yet there is sweetness, and dignity, and intelligence in it. Mrs. Delany received her with the same respectful ceremony as if it was her first visit, though she regularly goes to her every evening. But what she at first took as an honour and condescension, she has so much of true humility of mind, that no use can make her see in any other light. She immediately presented me to her. Her grace courtesied and smiled with the most flattering air of pleasure, and said she was particularly happy in meeting with me. We then took our places, and Mrs. Delany said,—

"Miss Burney, ma'am, is acquainted with Mr. Crisp, whom your grace knew so well ; and she tells me he and his sister have been so good as to remember me, and to mention me to her."

The duchess instantly asked me a thousand questions about him—where he lived, how he had his health, and whether his fondness for the polite arts still continued. She said he was one of the most ingenious and agreeable men she had ever known, and regretted his having sequestered himself so much from the society of his former friends.

IN the course of this conversation I found the duchess very charming, high-bred, courteous, sensible, and spirited ; not merely free from pride, but free from affability-its most mortifying deputy.

After this she asked me if I had seen Mrs. SiddOns, and what I thought of her. I answered that I admired her very much.

"If Miss Burney approves her," said the duchess, "no approbation, I am sure, can do her so much credit ; for no One can so perfectly judge of characters or of human nature."

"Ah, ma'am," cried Mrs. Delany, archly, "and does your grace remember protesting you would never read 'Cecilia?'"

"Yes," said she, laughing, "I declared that five volumes could never be attacked; but since I began I have read it three times."

"O terrible!" cried I, "to make them out fifteen."

"The reason," continued she, "I held out so long against reading them, was remembering the cry there was in favour of 'Clarissa' and 'Sir Charles Grandison,' when they came out, and those I never could read. I was teased into trying both of them; but I was disgusted with their tediousness, and could not read eleven letters, with all the effort I could make: so much about my sisters and my brothers, and all my uncles and my aunts!"

"But if your grace had gone on with 'Clarissa,'" said Mrs. Chapone, "the latter part must certainly have affected you, and charmed you." [176]

"O, I hate any thing so dismal! Every body that did read it had melancholy faces for a week. 'Cecilia' is as pathetic as I can bear, and more sometimes; yet, in the midst of the sorrow, there is a spirit in the writing, a fire in the whole composition, that keep off that heavy depression given by Richardson. Cry, to be sure, we did. Mrs. Delany, shall you ever forget how we cried? But then we had so much laughter to make us amends, we were never left to sink under our concern."

I am really ashamed to write on.

"For my part," said Mrs. Chapone, "when I first read it, I did not cry at all; I was in an agitation that half killed me, that shook all nerves, and made me unable to sleep at nights, from the suspense I was in! but I could not cry, for excess of eagerness."

"I only wish," said the duchess, "Miss Burney could have been in some corner, amusing herself with listening to us,

when Lord Weymouth, and the Bishop of Exeter, and Mr. Lightfoot, and Mrs. Delany, and I, were all discussing the point -of the name. So earnest we were, she must have been diverted with us. Nothing, the nearest our own hearts and interests, could have been debated more warmly. The bishop was quite as eager as any of us; but what cooled us a little, at last, was Mr. Lightfoot's thinking we were seriously going to quarrel; and while Mrs. Delany and I were disputing about Mrs. Delvile, he very gravely said, 'Why, ladies, this is only a matter of imagination; it is not a fact: don't be so earnest.'"

"Ah, ma'am," said Mrs. Delany, "how hard your grace was upon Mrs. Delvile: so elegant, so sensible, so judicious, so charming a woman."

"O, I hate her," cried the duchess, "resisting that sweet Cecilia; coaxing her, too, all the time, with such hypocritical flattery."

"I shall never forget," said Mrs. Delany, "your grace's earnestness when we came to that part where Mrs. Delvile bursts a blood vessel. Down dropped the book, and just with the same energy as if your grace had heard some real and important news, You called out, 'I'm glad of it with all my heart!'"

"What disputes, too," said Mrs. Chapone, "there are about Briggs. I was in a room some time ago where somebody said there could be no such character; and a poor little mean city man, who was there, started up and said, 'But there is though, for I'se one myself!'"

"The Harrels!—O, then the Harrels!" cried Mrs. Delany.

"If you speak of the Harrels, and of the morality of the book," cried the duchess, with a solemn sort of voice, "we shall, indeed, never give Miss Burney her due: so striking, so pure, so genuine, SO instructive."

"Yes," cried Mrs. Chapone, "let us complain how we will of the torture she has given our nerves, we must all join in saying she has bettered us by every line."

"No book," said Mrs. Delany, "ever was so useful as this, because none other that is so good was ever so much read."

I think I need now write no more. I could, indeed, hear no more; for this last so serious praise, from characters so respectable, so moral, and so aged, quite affected me; and though I had wished a thousand times during the discourse to run out of the room, when they gave me finally this solemn sanction to the meaning and intention of my writing, I found it not without difficulty that I could keep the tears out of my eyes; and when I told what had passed to our sweet father, his cup quite ran over.

The duchess had the good sense and judgment to feel she had drawn up her panegyric to a climax, and therefore here she stopped; so, however, did not we, for our coach was ready.

ILLNESS AND DEATH OF MR. CRISP.
(FANNY BUrney to Mr. Crisp.) April 12, 1783.
My dearest—dearest daddy,

I am more grieved at the long and most disappointing continuation of your illness than I know how to tell YOU ; and though my last account, I thank heaven, is better, I find you still suffer so much, that my congratulations in my letter to Susan, upon what I thought your recovery, must have appeared quite crazy, if you did not know me as well as you do, and were not sure what affliction the discovery of my mistake would bring to myself. I think I never yet so much wished to be at Chesington, as at this time, that I might see how YOU go On, and not be kept in such painful suspense from post to post.

Why did you tell me of the DelaDYS, Portlands, Cambridges, etc., as if any of them came into competition with yourself? When you are better, I shall send you a most fierce and sharp remonstrance upon this subject. At present I must be content with saying, I will undoubtedly accept your most kind invitation as soon as I possibly can. Meantime, if my letters will give you any amusement, I will write oftener than ever, and supply you with all the prog I get myself.

Susan, who is my reader, must be your writer, and let me know if such tittle-tattle as I can collect serves to divert some of those many moments of languor and weariness that creep between pain and ease, and that call more for mental food than for bodily medicine. Your love to your Fannikin, I well know, makes all trash interesting to you that seems to concern her ; and I have no greater pleasure, when absent, than in letting you and my dear Susan be acquainted with my proceedings. I don't mean by this to exclude the rest of the dear Chesington set—far from it— -but a sister and a daddy must come first.

God bless and restore you, my most dear daddy! You know not how kindly I take your thinking of me, and inquiring about me, in an illness that might so well make you forget us all; but Susan assures me your heart is as affectionate as ever to your ever and ever faithful and loving child, F. B.

[Mr. Crisp's illness became so alarming, that Miss Burney hastened to Chesington, where she had been only a few days when her valued friend breathed his last. In reply to a letter, in which she had given Dr. Burney an account of Mr. Crisp's increasing sufferings, the doctor wrote:

"Ah! my dear Fanny, your last letter has broke all our hearts! your former accounts kept off despair; but this brings it back in all its horrors. I wish, if it were possible, that you would let him know how much I loved him, and how heavily I shall feel his loss when all this hurry subsides, and lets me have time to brood over my sorrows. I have always thought that, in many particulars, his equal was not to be found. His wit, learning, taste, penetration, and, when well, his conviviality, pleasantry, and kindness of heart to me and mine, will ever be thought of with the most profound and desponding regret."

After the last mournful duties had been performed at Chesington, [177]Miss Burney returned to her father's house in St. Martin's-street; but some time elapsed ere she recovered composure sufficient to resume her journal.]

DR. JOHNSON ATTACKED BY PARALYSIS.

Thursday, june 19.-We heard to-day that Dr. Johnson had been taken ill, in a way that gave a dreadful shock to himself, and a most anxious alarm to his friends. Mr. Seward brought the news here, and my father and I instantly went to his house. He had earnestly desired me, when we lived so much together at Streatham, to see him frequently if he should be ill. He saw my father, but he had medical people with him, and could not admit me upstairs, but he sent me down a most kind message, that he thanked me for calling, and when he was better should hope to see me often. I had the satisfaction to hear from Mrs. Williams that the physicians had pronounced him to be in no danger, and expected a speedy recovery.

The stroke was confined to his tongue. Mrs. Williams told me a most striking and touching circumstance that attended the attack. It was at about four o'clock in the morning: he found himself with a paralytic affection; he rose, and composed in his own mind a Latin prayer to the Almighty, "that whatever were the sufferings for which he must prepare himself, it would please Him, through the grace and mediation of our blessed Saviour, to spare his intellects, and let them all fall upon his body." When he had composed this, internally, he endeavoured to speak it aloud, but found his voice was gone.

June 20.-I Went in the morning to Dr. Johnson, and heard a good account of him. Dr. Rose, Dr. Dunbar, and Sam Rose, the Doctor's son, dined with us. We expected the rest of our party early though the absence of Dr. Johnson, whom they were all invited to meet, took off the spirit of the evening.

July 1.-I had the satisfaction to hear from Sir Joshua that Dr. Johnson had dined with him at the Club. I look upon him, therefore, now, as quite recovered. I called the next morning to congratulate him, and found him very gay and very good-humoured.

A PLEASANT DAY WITH THE CAMBRIDGES.

July 15.-To-day my father, my mother, and I, went by appointment to dine and spend the day at Twickenham with the Cambridges. Soon after our arrival Mr. C. asked if we should like to walk, to which we most readily agreed.

We had not strolled far before we were followed by

Mr. George. No sooner did his father perceive him, than, hastily coming up to my side, he began a separate conversation with me; and leaving his son the charge of all the rest, he made me walk off with him from them all. It was really a droll manoeuvre, but he seemed to enjoy it highly, and though he said not a word of his design, I am sure it reminded me of his own old trick to his son, when listening to a dull story, in saying to the relator,— "Tell the rest of that to George." And if George was in as good-humour with his party as his father was with his why, all were well pleased. As soon as we had fairly got away from them, Mr. Cambridge, with the kindest smiles of satisfaction, said,—"I give you my word I never was more pleased at any thing in my life than I am now at having you here to-day."

I told him that I had felt so glad at seeing him again, after so long an absence, that I had really half a mind to have made up to him myself, and shook hands.

"You cannot imagine," said he, "how you flatter me !-and there is nothing, I do assure you, of which I am prouder, than seeing you have got the better of your fear of me, and feeling that I am not afraid of you."

"Of me, sir?—but how should you be?"

"Nay, I give you my word, if I was not conscious of the greatest purity of mind, I should more fear you than any body in the world. You know everything, everybody," he continued, "so wonderfully well!"

We then, I know not how, fell into discussing the characters of forward and flippant women; and I told him it was my fortune to be, in general, a very great favourite with them, though I felt so little gratitude for that honour, that the smallest discernment would show them it was all thrown away.

"Why, it is very difficult," said he, "for a woman to get rid of those forward characters without making them her enemies. But with a man it is different. Now I have a very peculiar happiness, which I will tell you. I never took very much to a very amiable woman but I found she took also to me, and I have the good fortune to be in the perfect confidence of some of the first women in this kingdom; but then there are a great many women that I dislike, and think very impertinent and foolish, and, do you know, they all dislike me too!—they absolutely cannot bear me! Now, I don't know, of those two things, which is the greatest happiness."

How characteristic this!—do you not hear him saying it?

We.now renewed our conversation upon various of our acquaintances, particularly Mr. Pepys, Mr. Langton, and Mrs. Montagu. We stayed in this field, sitting and sauntering, near an hour. We then went to a stile, just by the riverside, where the prospect is very beautiful, and there we seated ourselves. Nothing could be more pleasant, though the wind was so high I was almost blown into the water.

He now traced to me great part of his life and conduct in former times, and told me a thousand excellent anecdotes of himself and his associates. He summed them all up in a way that gave me equal esteem and regard for him, in saying he found society the only thing for lasting happiness ; that, if he had not met a woman he could permanently love, he must with every other advantage have been miserable- but that such was his good fortune, that "to and at this moment," he said, "there is no sight so pleasing to me as seeing Mrs. Cambridge enter a room ; and that after having been married to her for forty years. And the next most pleasing sight to me is an amiable woman."

He then assured me that almost all the felicity of his life both had consisted, and did still consist, in female society. It was, indeed, he said, very rare but there was nothing like it.

"And if agreeable women," cried I, "are rare, much more so, I think, are agreeable men; at least, among my acquaintance they are very few, indeed, that are highly agreeable."

"Yes, and when they are so," said he, "it is difficult for you to have their society with any intimacy or comfort; there'are always so many reasons why you cannot know them."

We continued chatting until we came to the end of the meadow, and there we stopped, and again were joined by the company.

Mr. Cambridge now proposed the water, to which I eagerly agreed.

We had an exceeding pleasant excursion. We went up the river beyond the Duke of Montagu's, and the water was smooth and delightful. Methinks I should like much to sail from the very source to the mouth of the Thames. . . .

After dinner we again repaired to the lawn, in a general body ; but -we- had scarce moved ten paces, before Mr. Cambridge again walked off with me, to a seat that had a very "fine view of Petersham wood, and there we renewed our confabulation.

He now shewed me a note from Mr. Gibbon, sent to engage himself to Twickenham on the unfortunate day he got his ducking. [178]It is the most affected little piece of writing I ever saw. He shall attend him, he says, at Twickenham, and upon the water, as soon as the weather is propitious, and the Thames, that amiable creature, is ready, to receive him.

Nothing, to be sure, could be so apt as such a reception as that "amiable creature" happened to give him! Mr. Cambridge said it was "God's revenge against conceit."

DR. JOHNSON's HEROic FORBEARANCE.

Tuesday, December 9-This evening at Mrs. Vesey's, Mr. George Cambridge came, and took the chair half beside me. I told him of some new members for Dr. Johnson's club! [179]

"I think," said he, " it sounds more like some club that one reads of in the 'Spectator,' than like a real club in these times; for the forfeits of a whole year will not amount to those of a single night in other clubs. Does Pepys belong to it?"

"Oh no! he is quite of another party! He is head man on the side of the defenders of Lord Lyttelton. Besides, he has had enough of Dr. Johnson; for they had a grand battle upon the 'Life of Lyttelton,' at Streatham."

"And had they really a serious quarrel? I never imagined it had amounted to that."

"yes, serious enough, I assure you. I never saw Dr. Johnson really in a passion but then: and dreadful, indeed, it was to see. I wished myself away a thousand times. It was a frightful scene. He so red, poor Mr. Pepys so pale!"

"But how did it begin? What did he say?"

" Oh, Dr. Johnson came to the point without much ceremony. He called out aloud, before a large company, at dinner, 'What have you to say, sir, to me or of me? Come forth, man! I hear you object to my "Life of Lord Lyttelton." What are your objections? If you have anything to say, let's hear it. Come forth, man, when I call you!'"

"What a call, indeed! Why, then, he fairly bullied him into a quarrel!"

"Yes. And I was the more sorry, because Mr. Pepys had begged of me, before they met, not to let Lord Lyttelton be mentioned. Now I had no more power to prevent it than this macaroon cake in my hand."

"It was behaving ill to Mrs. Thrale, certainly, to quarrel in her house."

" Yes; but he never repeated it; though he wished of all things to have gone through just such another scene with Mrs, Montagu, and to refrain was an act of heroic forbearance."

"Why, I rather wonder he did not ; for she was the head of the set of Lytteltonians."

"Oh, he knows that; he calls Mr. Pepys only her prime minister."

"And what does he call her ?

"Queen,' to be sure! 'Queen of the blues.' She came to Streatham one morning, and I saw he was dying to attack her. But he had made a promise to Mrs. Thrale to have no more quarrels in her house, and so he forced himself to forbear. Indeed he was very much concerned, when it was over, for what had passed; and very candid and generous in acknowledging it. He is too noble to adhere to wrong."

"And how did Mrs. Montagu herself behave?"

"Very stately, indeed, at first. She turned from him very stiffly, and with a most distant air, and without even courteseying to him, and with a firm intention to keep to what she had publicly declared—that she would never speak to him more! However, he went up to her himself, longing to begin! and very roughly said,—'Well, madam, what's become of your fine new house? I hear no more of it.'

" But how did she bear this?"

" Why she was obliged to answer him; and she soon grew so frightened—as everybody else does—that she was as civil as ever."

he laughed heartily at this account. But I told him Dr. Johnson was now much softened. He had acquainted me, when I saw him last, that he had written to her upon the death of Mrs. Williams, because she had allowed her something yearly, which now ceased. 'And I had a very kind answer from her,' said he.

"'Well then, sir,' cried I, 'I hope peace now will be again proclaimed.'"

"'Why, I am now,' said he, 'come to that time when I wish all bitterness and animosity to be at an end. I have never done her any serious harm—nor would I; though I could give her a bite!— but she must provoke me much first. In volatile talk, indeed, I may have spoken of her not much to her mind; for in the tumult of conversation malice is apt to grow sprightly! and there, I hope, I am not yet decrepid!'"

He quite laughed aloud at this characteristic speech.

I most readily assured the doctor that I had never yet seen him limp."

"SWEET BEWITCHING MRS. LOCKE."

Friday, April 23, 1784.-The sweet and most bewitching Mrs. Locke called upon me in the evening, with her son George. I let her in and did so rejoice I had not gone to Mrs. Vesey's. But I rejoiced for only a short time; she came but to take leave, for she was going to Norbury the very next morning. I was quite heavy all the evening. She does truly interest both head and heart. I love her already. And she was so kind, so caressing, so soft ; pressed me so much to fix a time for going to Norbury ; said such sweet things of Mrs. Phillips; and kissed me so affectionately in quitting me, that I was quite melted by her.

What a charm has London lost for me by her departure sweet crea ture that she is ; born and bred to dispense pleasure and delight to all who see or know her! She, Mrs. Thrale and Mrs. Delany, in their several ways all excellent, possess the joint powers of winning the affections, while they delight the intellects, to the highest summit I can even conceive of human attraction. The heart-fascination of Mrs. Thrale, indeed, few know - but those few must confess and must feel her sweetness, to them, is as captivating as her wit is brilliant to all.

MRS. THRALE'S SECOND MARRIAGE.

(MRS. THRale to Fanny Burney.) Mortimer-st., Cavendish-sq. Tuesday night, May [11], 1784.

I am come, dearest Burney. It is neither dream nor fiction, though I love you dearly, or I would not have come. Absence and distance do nothing towards wearing out real affection so you shall always find it in your true and tender H. L. T.

I am somewhat shaken bodily, but 'tis the mental shocks that have made me unable to bear the corporeal ones. 'Tis past ten o'clock, however, and I must lay myself down with the sweet expectation of seeing my charming friend in the morning to breakfast. I love Dr. Burney too well to fear him, and he loves me too well to say a word which should make me love him less.

May 17.-Let me now, my Susy, acquaint you a little more connectedly than I have done of late how I have gone on. The rest of that week I devoted almost wholly to sweet Mrs. Thrale, whose society was truly the most delightful of cordials to me, however, at times, mixed with bitters the least palatable. Were I not sensible of her goodness, and full of incurable affection for her, should I not be a monster? . . .

I parted most reluctantly with my dear Mrs. Thrale, whom, when or how I shall see again heaven only knows ! but in sorrow we parted—on my side in real affliction.

[Towards the end of July in this year, Mrs. Thrale's second marriage took place with Mr. Piozzi, and Miss Burney Went about the same time to Norbury Park, where she passed some weeks with Mr and Mrs. Locke. The following "sketch" of a letter, and memorandum of what had recently passed between Mrs. Piozzi and herself, is from the journal of that period.]

(Fanny Burney to Mrs. Piozzi.)

Norbury Park, Aug. 10, 1784.

When my wondering eyes first looked over the letter I received last night, my mind instantly dictated a high-spirited vindication of the consistency, integrity, and faithfulness of the friendship thus abruptly reproached and cast away. But a sleepless night gave me leisure to recollect that you were ever as generous as precipitate, and that your own heart would do justice to mine, in the cooler judgment of future reflection. Committing myself, therefore, to that period, I determined Simply to assure you, that if my last letter hurt either you or Mr. Piozzi, I am no less sorry than surprised; and that if it offended you, I sincerely beg your pardon.

Not to that time, however, can I wait to acknowledge the pain an accusation so unexpected has caused me, nor the heartfelt satisfaction with which I shall receive, when you are able to write it, a softer renewal of regard.

May heaven direct and bless you! F. B.

N.B.—This is the sketch of the answer which F. B. most painfully wrote to the unmerited reproach of not sending "cordial congratulations" upon a marriage which she had uniformly, openly, and with deep and avowed affliction, thought wrong.

(Mrs. Piozzi to Fanny Burney) Wellbeck-st., NO, 33, Cavendish-sq., Friday, Aug. 13, 1784.

Give yourself no serious concern, sweetest Burney. All is well, and I am too happy myself to make a friend otherwise; quiet your kind heart immediately, and love my husband if you love his and your H. L. Piozzi.

N.B.-To this kind note, F. B. wrote the warmest and most affectionate and heartfelt reply; but never received another word! And here and thus stopped a correspondence of six years of almost unequalled partiality, and fondness on her side ; and affection, gratitude, admiration, and sincerity on that of 'F. B., who could only conjecture the cessation to be caused by the resentment of Piozzi, when informed of her constant opposition to the union.

A HAPPY HOME.

Friday, Oct. 8.-I set off with my dear father for Chesington, where we passed five days very comfortably ; my father was all good humour, all himself,—such as you and I mean by that word. The next day we had the blessing of your Dover letter[180]and on Thursday, Oct.:14, I arrived at dear Norbury Park 'at about seven o'clock, after a pleasant ride in the dark. Locke most kindly and cordially welcomed me; he came out upon the steps to receive me, and his beloved Fredy[181]waited for me in the vestibule. Oh, with what tenderness did she take me to her bosom! I felt melted with her kindness, but I could not express a joy like hers, for my heart was very fullfull of my dearest Susan, whose image seemed before me upon the spot where we had so lately been together. They told me that Madame de la Fite, her daughter, and Mr. Hinde, were in the house; but as I am now, I hope, come for a long time, I did not vex at hearing this. Their first inquiries were if I had not heard from Boulogne. [182]

Saturday.-I fully expected a letter, but none came; but Sunday I depended upon one. The post, however, did not arrive before we went to church. Madame de la Fite, seeing my sorrowful looks, good naturedly asked Mrs. Locke what could be set about to divert a little la pauvre Mademoiselle Beurney? and proposed reading a drama of Madame de Genlis. I approved it much, preferring it greatly to conversation and accordingly, she and her daughter, each taking characters to themselves, read "La Rosire de Salency." It is a very interesting and touchingly simple little drama. I was so much pleased that they afterwards regularly read one every evening while they stayed.

Next morning I went up stairs as usual, to treat myself with a solo of impatience for the post, and at about twelve o'clock I heard Mrs. Locke stepping along the passage. I was sure of good news, for I knew, if there was bad, poor Mr. Locke would have brought it. She came in, with three letters in her hand, and three thousand dimples in her cheeks and chin! Oh, my dear Susy, what a sight to me was your hand ! I hardly cared for the letter; I hardly desired to open it ; the direction alone almost satisfied me sufficiently. How did Mrs. Locke embrace me! I half kissed her to death. O Then came dear Mr. Locke, his eyes brighter than ever—"Well, how does she do?"

This question forced me to open my letter; all was just as I could wish, except that I regretted the having written the day before such a lamentation. I was so congratulated! I shook hands with Mr. Locke; the two dear little girls came jumping to wish me joy and Mrs. Locke ordered a fiddler, that they might have a dance in the evening, which had been promised them from the time of Mademoiselle de la Fite's arrival, but postponed from day to day, by general desire, on account of my uneasiness.

Monday, Oct. 25-Mr. Hinde and Madame and Mademoiselle de la Fite all left us. They were all so good humoured and so happy, there was no being glad ; though how to be sorry at remaining alone with this family, I really know not. Both the De la Fites went away in tears. I love them for it.

Wednesday, Nov. 3-This day has brought ine another sweet letter from my Susy. What a set of broken-fortuned, brokencharactered people of fashion are about you at Boulogne. [183]The accounts are at once curious and melancholy to me.

Nothing can be more truly pleasant than our present lives. I bury all disquietudes in immediate enjoyment; an enjoyment more fitted to my secret mind than any I had ever hoped to attain. We are so perfectly tranquil, that not a particle of our whole frames seems ruffled or discomposed., Mr. Locke is gayer and more sportive than I ever have seen him; his Freddy seems made up of happiness; and the two dear little girls are in spirits almost ecstatic; and all from that internal contentment which Norbury Park seems to have gathered from all corners of the world into its own sphere. Our mornings, if fine, are to ourselves, as .Mr. Locke rides out; if bad, we assemble in the picture room. We have two books in public reading: Madame de S6vigne's "Letters," and Cook's last "Voyage." Mrs. Locke reads the French, myself the English.

Our conversations, too, are such as I could almost wish to last for ever. Mr. Locke has been all himself,-all instruction, information, and intelligence,—since we have been left alone; and the invariable sweetness, as well as judgment, of all he says, leaves, indeed, nothing to wish. They will not let me go while I can stay, and I am now most willing to stay till I must go. The serenity of a life like this, smoothes the whole internal surface of the mind. My own I assure you, begins to feel quite glossy. To see Mrs. Locke so entirely restored to total health, and to see her adoring husband lose all his torturing Solicitude, while he retains his Unparalleled tenderness-these are sights to anticipate a taste of paradise, if paradise has any felicity consonant to our now ideas.

Tuesday, Nov. 9.- This is Mr. William Locke's birthday; he is now seventeen. he came home, with his brothers, to keep it, three days ago. May they all be as long-lived and as happy as they are now sweet and amiable! This sweet place is beautiful even yet, though no longer of a beauty young and blooming, such as you left it; but the character Of the prospect is so 'grand that winter cannot annihilate its charms, though it greatly diminishes them. The variety of the grounds, and the striking form of the hills, always afford something new to observe, and contain something lasting to admire. Were 1, however, in a desert, people such as these would make it gay and cheery.

LADY F.'s ANGER AT MRS. PIOZZI'S MARRIAGE.
(FANNY BUrney to Mrs. Locke.) St. Martin's-st., Nov. 14.

. . . . . I had a very unpleasant morning after I left you. When the coach and I had waited upon my father, I made the visit I mentioned to you. O what a visit!—all that I pre-supposed of attack, inquiry, and acrimony, was nothing to what passed. Rage more intemperate I have not often seen ; and the shrill voice of feeble old age, screaming with unavailing passion is horrible. She had long looked upon Mrs. Thrale as a kind of prot6ge, whom she had fondled as a child, and whose fame, as she grew into notice, she was always proud to hear of, and help to exalt. She is a woman (I can well attest !) of most furious passions herself, however at liberty she thinks she may be to show no sort of mercy to those of another.

Once, had I been less disturbed, I could have laughed; for she declared with great vehemence, that if she had suspected "the wretch of any intention to marry the man, she would have ordered her own postchaise, and followed her to prevent it!"

Alas, poor Lady F.

She then called upon me, to hear my story ; which, most painfully to myself, I related. She expressed herself very sorry for me, till I came to an avowal of my letter after the marriage she then flew out into new choler. "I am amazed you would write to her, Miss Burney! I wonder you could think of it any more.

I told her, I had thought myself so much indebted to her patience with my opposition to all her views and wishes for the whole tine of her long conflict, that, although I was the first to acknowledge her last action indefensible, I should be the last to forget all that had made me love her before it was committed.

This by no means satisfied her, and she poured forth again a torrent of unrelenting abuse. Some company, at last, came in, and I hastily took my leave. She called after me to fix some day for a longer visit ; but I pretended not to hear, and ran down stairs, heartily resolving that necessity alone should ever force me into her presence again.

When I came home—before I could get upstairs—I was summoned to Miss Streatfield, whom I met with as little pleasure as Lady F., since I had never seen her, nor indeed anybody, from the time this cruel transaction has been published. Not that I dreaded her violence, for she is as gentle as a lamb but there were causes enough for dread of another nature. However fortunately and unexpectedly, she never named the subject, but prattled away upon nothing but her own affairs; and so, methinks, have I done too, and just as if I knew you wished to hear them. Do you?—I ask only for decency's sake.

DR. JOHNSON's FAILING HEALTH.
Norbury Park, Sunday, Nov. 28.-Last Thursday, my father set me down at

Bolt-court, while lie went on upon business. I was anxious to again see poor Dr. Johnson, who has had terrible health since his return from Lichfield. He let me in, though very ill. He was alone, which I much rejoiced at; for I had a longer and more satisfactory conversation with him than I have had for many months. He was in rather better spirits, too, than I had lately seen him. but he told me he was going to try what sleeping Out of town might do for him

"I remember," said he, "that my wife, when she was near her end, poor woman, was also advised to sleep out of town, and when she was carried to the lodgings that had been prepared for her, she complained that the staircase was in very bad condition—for the plaster was beaten off the wall in many places. 'Oh,' said the man of the house, 'that's nothing but by the knocks against it of the coffins of the poor souls that have died in the lodgings.'

He laughed, though not without apparent secret anguish, in telling me this. I felt extremely shocked, but, willing to confine my words at least to the literal story, I only exclaimed against the unfeeling absurdity of such a confession.

"Such a confession," cried he, "to a person then coming to try his lodgings for her health, contains, indeed, more absurdity than we can well lay our account for."

I had seen Miss Thrale the day before.

"So," said he, "did I."

I then said,—"Do you ever, sir, hear from her mother?"

"No," cried he, "nor write to her. I drive her quite from my mind. If I meet with one of her letters, I burn it instantly. I have burnt all I can find. I never speak of her, and I desire never to hear of her more. I drive her, as I said, wholly from my mind."

Yet, wholly to change this discourse, I gave him a history of the Bristol milk-woman, and told him the tales I had heard of her writing so wonderfully, though she had read nothing but Young and Milton "though those," I continued, "could never possibly, I should think, be the first authors with anybody. Would children understand them? and grown people who have not read are children in literature."

"Doubtless," said he; "but there is nothing so little comprehended among mankind as what is genius. They give to it all, when it can be but a part. Genius is nothing more than knowing the use of tools - but there must be tools for it to use: a man who has spent all his life in this room will give a very poor account of what is contained in the next." '

"Certainly, sir ; yet there is such a thing as invention. Shakspeare could never have seen a Caliban."

" No; but he had seen a man, and knew, therefore, how to vary him to a monster. A man who would draw a monstrous cow, must first know what a cow commonly is; or how can he tell that to give her an ass's head or an elephant's tusk will make her monstrous. Suppose you show me a man who is a very expert carpenter; another will say he was born to be a carpenter-but what if he had never seen any wood? Let two men, one with genius, the other with none, look at an overturned waggon ; he who has no genius, will think of the waggon only as he sees it, overturned, and walk on ; he who has genius, will paint it to himself before it was overturned-standing still, and moving on, and heavy loaded, and empty ; but both must see the waggon, to think of it at all."

He then animated, and talked on, upon this milk-woman, upon a once as famous shoemaker, and upon our immortal Shakspeare, with as much fire, spirit, wit, and truth of criticism and judgment, as ever yet I have heard him. How delightfully bright are his faculties, though the poor and infirm machine that contains them seems alarmingly giving way.

Yet, all brilliant as he was, I saw him growing worse, and offered to go, which, for the first time I ever remember, he did not oppose; but, most kindly pressing both my hands,—

"Be not," he said, in a voice of even tenderness, "be not longer in Coming again for my letting you go now."

I assured him I would be the sooner, and was running off. but he called me back, in a solemn voice, and, in a manner the most energetic, said,—

"Remember me in your prayers!"

I longed to ask him to remember me, but did not dare. I gave him my promise, and, very heavily indeed, I left him. Great, good, and excellent that he Is, how short a time will he be our boast! Ah, my dear Susy, I see he is going! This winter will never conduct him to a more genial season here! Elsewhere, who shall hope a fairer? I wish I had bid him pray for me, but it seemed to me presumptuous.

DR. JOHNSON DYING. His DEATH.

Wednesday, Dec. 8.-At night my father brought us the most dismal tidings of dear Dr. Johnson. Dr. Warren had seen him, and told him to take what opium he pleased! He had thanked and taken leave of all his physicians. Alas!—I shall lose him, and he will take no leave of me! [184]My father was deeply depressed ; he has himself tried in vain for admission this week. Yet some people see him—the Hooles, Mr. Sastres,

Mr. Langton;—but then they must be in the house, watching for one moment, whole hours. I hear from every one he is now perfectly resigned to his approaching fate, and no longer in terror of death. I am thankfully happy in hearing that he speaks himself now of the change his mind has undergone, from its dark horror—and says—"He feels the irradiation of hope," Good, and pious, and excellent Christian—who shall feel it if not he?

Dec. 11.-We had a party to dinner, by long appointment, for which, indeed, none of us were well disposed, the apprehension of hearing news only of death being hard upon us all. The party was, Dr. Rose, Dr. Gillies, Dr. Garthshore, and Charles.

The day could not be well—but mark the night.

My father, in the morning, saw this first of men! I had not his account till bed-time; he feared over-exciting me. He would not, he said, but have seen him for worlds! He happened to be better, and admitted him. He Was up, and very composed. He took his hand very kindly, asked after all his family, and then, in particular, how Fanny did? "I hope," he said, "Fanny did not take it amiss that I did not see her? I was very bad!"

Amiss!—what a Word! Oh that I had been present to have answered it! My father stayed, I suppose, half an hour, and then was coming away. He again took his hand, and encouraged him to come again to him ; and when he Was taking leave, said—"Tell Fanny to pray for me!"

Ah! dear Dr. Johnson! might I but have your prayers! After which, still grasping his hand, he made a prayer for himself,— the most fervent, pious, humble, eloquent, and touching, my father says, that ever was composed. Oh, would I had heard it! He ended it with Amen! in which my father joined, and was echoed by all present. And again, when my father was leaving him, he brightened up, something of his arch look returned, and he said- -"I think I shall throw the ball at Fanny yet!"

Little more passed ere my father came away, decided, most tenderly, not to tell me this till our party was done.

This most earnestly increased my desire to see him; this kind and frequent Mention of me melted me into double sorrow and regret. I would give the world I had but gone to him that day! It was, however, Impossible, and the day was over before I knew he had said what I look upon as a call to me. This morning, [185]after church time, I went. Frank[186]said he was very ill, and saw nobody; I told him I had understood by my father the day before that he meant 'to see me. He then let me in. I went into his room up stairs; he was in his bedroom. I saw it crowded, and ran hastily down. Frank told me his master had refused seeing even Mr. Langton. I told him merely to say I had called, but by no means to press my admission. His own feelings were all that should be consulted ; his tenderness, I knew, Would be equal, whether he was able to see me or not.

I went into the parlour, preferring being alone in the cold, to any company with a fire. Here I waited long, here and upon the stairs, which I ascended and descended to meet again with Frank, and make inquiries ; but I met him not. At last, upon Dr. Johnson's ringing his bell, I saw Frank enter his room, and Mr. Langton follow. "Who's that?" I heard him say; they answered, "Mr. Langton," and I found he did not return.

Soon after, all the rest went away but a Mrs. Davis, a good sort of woman, whom this truly charitable soul had sent for to take a dinner at his house. I then went and waited with her by the fire ; it was, however, between three and four o'clock before I got any answer. Mr. Langton then came himself. He could not look at me, and I turned away from him. Mrs. Davis asked how the doctor was? "Going on to death very fast!" was his mournful answer. "Has he taken," said she, "anything?" "Nothing at all! We carried him some bread and milk—he refused it, and said—'The less the better.'" She asked more questions, by which I found his faculties were perfect, his mind composed, and his dissolution was quick drawing on. . . .

I could not immediately go on, and it is now long since I have written at all; but I will go back to this afflicting theme, which I can now better bear.

Mr. Langton was, I believe, a quarter of an hour in the room before I suspected he meant to speak to me, never looking near me. At last he said—

"This poor man, I understand, ma'am, desired yesterday to see you."

"My understanding that, sir, brought me here to-day."

"Poor man! it is a pity he did not know himself better, and that you should have had this trouble."

"Trouble!" cried I; "I would have come a hundred times to see him the hundredth and first!"

"He hopes, now, you will excuse him ; he is very sorry not to see you; but he desired me to come and speak to you myself, and tell you he hopes you will excuse him, for he feels himself too weak for such an interview."

I hastily got up, left him my most affectionate respects, and every good wish I could half utter, and ran back to the coach. Ah, my Susy! I have never been to Bolt-court since! I then drove to poor Miss Strange, [187]to make inquiries of the maid but Andrew ran out to the coach door, and told me all hope was at an end. In short, the next day was fatal to both !-the same day!

December 20.-This day was the ever-honoured, ever-lamented Dr. Johnson committed to the earth. Oh, how sad a day to me! My father attended, and so did Charles. [188] I could not keep my eyes dry all day; nor can I now, in the recollecting it; but let me pass over what to mourn Is now so vain!

December 30.—In the evening I went to Mrs. Chapone. I was late, on account of the coach, and all her party was assembled. This was the first time I had seen any of them, except Mrs. Ord, since last spring. I was received with the utmost kindness by them all, but chiefly by Mrs. Chapone herself, who has really, I believe, a sincere regard for me. I had talk with all of them, except Mrs. Levison, with whom I have merely a courtesying acquaintance. But I was very sad within; the loss of dear Dr. Johnson—the flight of Mrs. Thrale, the death of poor Miss Kitty Cambridge, and of poor, good Miss Strange,—all these home and bosom strokes, which had all struck me since my last meeting this society, were revolving in my mind the whole time I stayed.

Sir Lucas Pepys talked to me a great deal of Mrs. Thrale, and read me a letter from her, which seems to shew her gay and happy. I hope it shews not false colours. No one else named her - but poor Dr. Johnson was discussed repeatedly. How melancholy will all these circumstances render these once so pleasant meetings.

| 153 | "Memoirs of Dr. Burney," vol. ii. p. 110. |

153   "Memoirs of Dr. Burney," vol. ii. p. 110.

154   The physician, afterwards Sir Lucas Pepys.-ED.

155   A character in "Cecilia."-ED.

156   The master of the ceremonies.

157   Philip Metcalf, elected member of Parliament for Horsham, together with Mr. Crutchley, in 1784.-ED.

158   Miss Burney had seen this gentleman a few days previously and thus speaks of him in her "Diary." -Mr. Kaye of the Dragoons,—a baronet's son, and a very tall, handsome, and agreeable-looking young man; and, is the folks say, it is he for whom all the belles here are sighing. I was

glad to see he seemed quite free from the nonchalance, impertinence of the times."-ED.

159 Afterwards Countess of Cork and Orrery.

160 The Thrales and Fanny were now again in London, whither they returned from Brighton, November 20. Mrs, Thrale had taken a house in Argyle-street,-ED.

161 Lady Margaret Cavendish Harley, daughter of Robert Harley, Earl of Oxford; married, in 1734, to the second Duke of Portland, She inherited from her father a taste for literature. She was the constant associate of Mrs. Delaney, and an old friend of Mr. Crisp. Of Mrs. Delany we shall give some account hereafter-ED. I

162 Mrs. Greville's maiden name was Frances Macartney.-ED.

163 The miserly guardian of Cecilia, in Fanny's novel. Among the "Fragments of the journal of Charlotte Anne Burney," appended to the "Early Diary," occurs the following passage, written at the end of 1782. "Fanny's Cecilia came out last summer, and is as much liked and read I believe as any book ever was. She had 250 pounds for it from Payne and Cadell. Most people say she ought to have had a thousand. It is now going into the third edition, though Payne owns that they printed 2,000 at the first edition, and Lowndes told me five hundred was the common number for a novel." ("Early Diary," vol. ii. P. 307. ED.

164 Richard Burke, the only son of the great Edmund. He died in 1794, before his father.-ED.

165 Sir Joshua Reynolds was then in his sixtieth year; he was born in 1723.-ED.

166 She copied pictures cleverly and painted portraits.-ED.

167 Probably the Hon. Thomas Erskine, afterwirds Lord Chancellor.-ED.

168 Richard Owen Cambridge, a gentleman admired for his wit in conversation, and esteemed as an author. "He wrote a burlesque poem called 'The Scribleriad,' and was a principal contributor to the periodical paper called 'The World.'" He died in 1802, at his villa on the banks of the Thames, near Twickenham, aged eighty-five years.-ED.

169 Mrs. Ord was a famous blue-stocking and giver of literary parties, and a constant friend of Fanny's-ED.

170 The Rev. George Owen Cambridge, second son of Richard Owen Cambridge, whose works he edited, and whose memoir he wrote. He died at Twickenham in 1841.-ED.

171 John Hoole, the translator of Tasso.-ED.

172 Frances Reynolds, the miniature painter,-Sir Joshua's sister-ED.

173 Soame Jenyns was one of the most celebrated of the "old wits." He was born in 1704; was for twenty-five years member of Parliament for Cambridgeshire; died in 1787. His principal works were "A Free Enquiry into the Origin of Evil," and "A View of the Internal Evidence of the Christian Religion." Boswell writes of him: "Jenyns was possessed of lively talents, and a style eminently pure and 'easy', and

could very happily play with a light subject, either in prose or verse; but when he speculated on that most difficult and excruciating question, 'The Origin of Evil,' he ventured far beyond his depth, and, accordingly, was exPosed by Johnson [in the 'Literary Magazine'both with acute argument and brilliant wit."-ED.

174 "Memoirs of Dr. Burney," vol. iii. p. 169.

175 Hester Mulso was born in 1727; she married, in 1760, an attorney named Chapone, who died within a year of the marriage. Among the many young ladies who surrounded and corresponded with Samuel Richardson, Hester was a first favourite. The great novelist's letters to his "dear Miss Mulso" are very pleasant to read. Mrs. Chapone enjoyed considerable esteem as an authoress. Her "Letters on the Improvement of the Mind," dedicated to Mrs. Montagu, went through several editions. We should like to praise them, but the truth must be owned— they are Vdecidedly commonplace and "goody-goody." Still, they are written in a spirit of tender earnestness, which raises our esteem for the writer, though it fails to reconcile us to the book. Mrs. Chapone died on Christmas-day, 18o1.-ED.

176 Truly said, "my dear Miss Mulso," but if they cannot feel the wonderful charm and reality of "Clarissa" in the very first volume, they may as well leave it alone.-ED.

177 In a corner of the nave of the quaint little church at Chesington is a large white marble tablet, marking the spot where Mr. Crisp lies buried. The following lines from the pen of Fanny's father inscribed on it do not, it must be confessed, exhibit the doctor's poetical talents by any means in a favourable light. "In memory Of SAMUEL CRISP, Esq., who died April 24, 1783, aged 76.

Reader, this cold and humble spot contains The much lamented, much rever'd remains Of one whose wisdom, learning, taste, and sense, Good-humour'd wit and wide benevolence Cheer'd and enlightened all this hamlet round, Wherever genius, worth, or want was found. To few it is that bounteous heav'n imparts Such depth of knowledge, and such taste in arts Such penetration, and enchanting pow'rs Of brit'ning social and convivial hours. Had he, through life, been blest by nature kind With health robust of body as of mind, With skill to serve and charm mankind, so great In arts, in science, letters, church, or state, His name the nation's annals had enroll'd And virtues to remotest ages told. "C. BURNEY."

177 Mr, Gibbon, "in stepping too lightly from, or to a boat of Mr. Cambridge's, had slipt into the Thames; whence, however, he was intrepidly and immediately rescued, with no other mischief than a wet jacket, by one of that fearless, water-proof race, denominated, by Mr. Gibbon, the amphibious family of the Cambridges." Memoir of Dr. Burney," vol. ii. P. 341. ED.

178   The "Essex Head" club, just founded by Dr. Johnson. The meetings were held thrice a week at the Essex Head, a tavern in Essex-street, Strand, kept by Samuel Greaves, an old servant of Mr. Thrale's. Among the rule's of the club, which were drawn up by Dr. Johnson, we find the following: "Every member present at the club shall spend at least sixpence; and every member who stays away shall forfeit threepence." He ought to have added, "to be spen by the company in punch." See Goldsmith's delightful essay on the London clubs. ED.

179   The Lockes, of Norbury Park, Surrey, were friends of Fanny's sister, Mrs. Phillips, and, subsequently, among the most constant and attached friends of Fanny herself.-ED.

180   It must be borne in mind that the , Diary " is addressed to Fanny's sister Susan Mrs. Phillips,-ED.

181   Mrs. Locke.-ED.

182   Mrs. Phillips had lately gone to live at Boulogne for the benefit of her health.-ED.

183   Mrs. Phillips returned in less than a twelvemonth from Boulogne, much recovered in health, and settled with her husband and family in a house at MickIcham, at the foot of Norbury Park.

184   Fanny had called upon Dr. Johnson the same day, but he was too ill to see her.-ED.

185   Sunday, December 12.-ED.

186   Frank Barber, Dr. Johnson's negro servant. -ED.

187   Mary Bruce Strange, daughter of Sir Robert Strange, the celebrated engraver. She died, as Fanny tells us, on the same day with Dr. Johnson, December 13, 1784, aged thirty-five. The Stranges were old and very intimate friends of the Burneys-ED. I

188   Her brother-ED.

SECTION 6 17856.)

MISS BURNEY IS FAVOURABLY NOTICED BY THE KING AND QUEEN.

[THE pleasantest portion of the following section of the Diary is that which relates to the growing intimacy between Fanny and Mrs. Delany. It was a friendship, however, which proved dear to Fanny in every sense of the word. On the one hand the mutual affection which subsisted between her and a lady in every way so worthy of her regard, was a source of continual gratification to both ; on the other hand it was the immediate cause of an event which may be, without exaggeration, described as the greatest misfortune of Fanny's life—her ill-starred appointment at Court. We fully share Macaulay's indignation at this absurd and singularly unsuitable appointment. Its consequences to Fanny were almost disastrous ; yet the reader will reap the reward of her suffering in perusing the brilliant pages in which her humour and penetration have invested with an interest not its own the frivolous tattle of her commonplace companions. Her account of the royal family is on the whole favourable. The princesses appear to have been really amiable and, so far as etiquette would permit, sensible young women. Of the king and queen we know few things which are more to their credit than that they should have been able to inspire Fanny with a regard so obviously sincere. But even Fanny, with all her loyal partiality, could make no more of them than a well-meaning couple, whose conversation never rose above the commonplace. After all, we can hardly help feeling that the whole of this CourtDiary, entertaining as it is, would be well exchanged for the description, in Fanny's animated style, of a few more dinnerparties at Sir joshua's, a few more conversations with Edmund Burke.

The burst of exultation with which Fanny's friends greeted the unhappy appointment says little for their common sense. Even Burke, who at least ought to have known better, fell in with the general infatuation, although he, if no one else felt that the honour was not all on Fanny's side. He called in St. Martin's-street, and finding Dr. Burney and his daughter from home, left a card on which he had written these words :—"Mr. Burke, to congratulate upon the honour done by the queen to Miss Burney,- -and to herself."

The office which Fanny shared with that "old hag," Mrs. Schwellenberg, was that of keeper of the robes, and she entered upon her new duties in the month Of July, 1786. Dress had always been one of the last subjects about which she troubled herself, and her want of experience in this all-important matter was graciously taken into consideration by the queen. The duties of the place were lightened, or, at least, altered in her favour. "The difficulties with respect to jewellery, laces, and Court habiliments, and the other routine business belonging to the dress manufactory appertained to her colleague, Mrs. Schwellenberg; the manual labours and cares devolved upon the wardrobewomen ; while from herself all that officially was required was assiduous attention, unremitting readiness for every summons to the dressing- room, not unfrequent long readings, and perpetual sojourn at the palace." [189]ED.]

ROYAL GENEROSITY TO MRs. DELANY.
(Fanny Burney to Dr. Burney. St. James's-place, Aug. 24.

I must tell you, dearest sir, a tale concerning Mrs. Delany, which I am sure you will hear with true pleasure. Among the many Inferior losses which have been included in her great and irreparable calamity, [190]has been that of a country house for the summer, which she ad in Bulstrode, and which for the half of every year was her constant home. The Duke of Portland behaved with the utmost propriety and feeling upon this occasion, and was most earnest to accommodate her to the best of his power, with every comfort to which she had been accustomed ; but this noblest of women declared she loved the memory of her friend beyond all other things, and would not suffer it to be tainted in the misjudging world by an action that would be construed into a reflection upon her will, as if deficient in consideration to her. She steadily, therefore, refused all offers, though made to her with even painful earnestness, and though solicited till her refusal became a distress to herself

This transaction was related, I believe, to their majesties and Lady Weymouth, the duchess's eldest daughter, was commissioned to wait upon Mrs. Delany with this message That the queen was extremely anxious about her health, and very apprehensive lest continuing in London during the summer should be prejudicial to it : she entreated her, therefore, to accept a house belonging to the king at Windsor, which she should order to be fitted up for her immediately ; and she desired Lady Weymouth to give her time to consider this proposal, and by no means to hurry her; as well as to assure her, that happy as it would make her to have one she so sincerely esteemed as a neighbour, she should remember her situation, and promise not to be troublesome to her. The king, at the same time, desired to be allowed to stand to the additional expenses incurred by the maintenance of two houses, and that Mrs. Delany would accept from him 3oo pounds a year.

It would be needless to tell you how Mrs. Delany was touched by this benevolence. Yet she dreaded accepting what she feared would involve her in a new course of life, and force her into notice and connexions she wished to drop or avoid. She took the time the queen so considerately gave her for deliberation, and she consulted with some of her old friends. They all agreed there must be no refusal, and Lady Weymouth was made the messenger of her majesty's offer being accepted.

The house, therefore, is now fitting up, and the king sees after the workmen himself.

A few days ago, Miss Planta[191]was sent from the queen, with very kind inquiries after Mrs. Delany's health, and information that she would receive a summons very soon. She told her, also, that as the house might still require a longer time in preparation than would suit Mrs. Delany to wait in London, the queen had ordered some apartments in the Castle, which lately belonged to Prince Edward, to be got ready with all speed, that she might reside in them till her own .house was finished.

This is the state of her affairs. I am now with her entirely. At first I slept at home ; but going after supper, and coming before breakfast, was inconvenient, and she has therefore contrived me a bed-room. . . .

(Fanny Burney to Mrs. Locke.)

St. James's-place, Aug. 29.

All our movements are at present uncertain ; Mrs. Delany,s Windsor house is still unfinished, but I suppose it will be fit for her reception by the beginning of next week, and I have the happiest reasons for hoping she will then be fit for it herself. Her maid has been to see what forwardness it is in, and this was her report:—She was ordered to wait Upon Miss Goldsworthy, [192]by the king's direction, who heard of her being sent to inspect the house; and there she received commands, in the name of both king and queen, to see that Mrs. Delany brought with her nothing but herself and clothes, as they insisted upon fitting up her habitation with everything themselves, including not only plate, china, glass, and linen, but even all sort of stores—wine, sweetmeats, pickles, etc. Their earnestness to save her every care, and give her every gratification in their power, is truly benevolent and amiable. They seem to know and feel her worth as if they had never worn crowns, or, wearing, annexed no value to them.

A VISIT TO MRS. DELANY.

Windsor, Saturday, Nov. 25—I got to Hounslow almost at the same moment with Mrs. Astley, my dear Mrs. Delany's maid, who was sent to meet me. As soon as she had satisfied my inquiries concerning her lady, she was eager to inform Tne that the queen had drunk tea with Mrs. Delany the day before, and had asked when I should come, and heard the time; and that Mrs. Delany believed she would be with her again that evening, and desire to see me. This was rather fidgetting intelligence. I rather, in my own mind, thought the queen would prefer giving me the first evening alone with my dear old friend. I found that sweet lady not so well as I had hoped, and strongly affected by afflicting recollections at sight of me. With all her gentleness and resignation, bursts of sorrow break from her still whenever we are alone together, for the Duchess of Portland was a boson' friend to her.

Miss Port, [193]who is a truly lovely girl, received me with her usual warmth of joy, and was most impatient to whisper me that " all the princesses intended to come and see me." She is just at the age to doat upon an ado, and nothing so much delights her as the thought of my presentations.

Mrs. Delany acquainted me that the queen, in their first Interview, upon her coming to this house, said to her, " Why did not you bring your friend Miss Burney with you?"

My dear Mrs. Delany was very much gratified by such an attention to whatever could be thought interesting to her, but, with her usual propriety, answered that, in coming to a house of her majesty's, she could not presume to ask anybody without immediate and express permission. "The king, however," she added, "made the very same inquiry when I saw him next."

Sunday, Nov. 26.-So now the royal encounters, for a while at least, are out of all question. Nobody came last night, though Mrs. Delany I saw, and Miss Port I heard, in continual expectation; but this morning, Mr. Battiscombe, apothecary to the household, called, and said that an express arrived from Germany yesterday afternoon, with an account of the death of the queen's youngest brother.

The queen, -whose domestic virtues rise upon me every hour, is strongly attached to all her family, and in much affliction at this news ; for though this brother was quite a boy when she left Germany, he has twice been to visit her in, England. None of the royal family will appear till the mourning takes place ; the queen, perhaps, may shut herself up still longer.

At night, quite incog, quite alone, and quite privately, the king came, and was shut up with Mrs. Delany for an hour. It is out of rule for any of the family to be seen till in mourning, but he knew she was anxious for an account of the queen. I had a very narrow escape of being surprised by him, which would have vexed me, as he only meant to see Mrs. Delany by herself, though she says he told her he was very glad to hear I was come.

ROYAL CURIOSITY ABOUT Miss BURNEY.

Thursday, Dec. 1.-To-day the queen sent Miss Planta to tell Mrs. Delany that if she would not yet venture to the Lodge, she would come to her in the evening. Mrs. Delany accepted the gracious offer, and, at tea-time, she came, as well as the king, and spent two hours here.

Mrs. Delany told me afterwards, that the queen was very low-spirited, and seemed to wish for nothing but the solace of sitting perfectly quiet. She is a sweet woman, and has all the domestic affections warm and strong in her heart.

Nevertheless they talked of me, she says, a good deal - and the king asked many questions about me. There is a new play, he told Mrs. Delany, coming out ; "and it is said to be Miss Burney's!" Mrs. Delany immediately answered that she knew the report must be untrue. "But I hope she is not idle?" cried the king. "I hope she is writing something?

What Mrs. Delany said, I know not; but he afterwards inquired what she thought of my writing a play?

"What," said he, "do you wish about it, Mrs. Delany?"

Mrs. Delany hesitated, and the queen then said,

"I wish what I know Mrs. Delany does—that she may not; for though her reputation is so high, her character, by all I hear, is too delicate to suit with writing for the stage."

Sweet queen! I could have kissed the hem of her garment for that speech, and I could not resist writing it.

Mrs. Delany then said,

" Why My opinion is what I believe to be Miss Burney's own ; that It is too public and hazardous a style of writing for her quiet and fearful turn of mind."

I have really the grace to be a little ashamed of scribbling this, but I know I can scribble nothing my dear father will be more curious to hear.

Saturday, Dec- 3-This morning we had better news of the princess - and Mrs. Delany went again to the Lodge in the evenin, to the queen. When Mrs. Delany returned, she confirmed the good accounts of the Princess Elizabeth's amendment. She had told the queen I was going to-morrow to Thames Ditton, for a week; and was asked many questions about my coming back, which the queen said she was sure I should be glad to do from Mrs. Walsingham to Mrs. Delany. O most penetrating queen!

She gratified Mrs. Delany by many kind speeches, of being sorry I was going, and glad I was returning, and so forth. Mrs. Delany then told her I had been reading "The Clandestine Marriage" to her, which the queen had recommended, and she thanked her majesty for the very great pleasure she had received from it.

"O then," cried the queen, "if Miss Burney reads to you, what a pleasure you must have to make her read her own works!"

Mrs. Delany laughed, and exclaimed,

"O ma'am! read her own works!—your majesty has no notion of Miss Burney! I believe she would as soon die!"

This, of course, led to a great deal of discussion, in the midst of which the queen said,

"Do you know Dr. Burney, Mrs. Delany?

"Yes, ma'am, extremely well," answered Mrs. Delany.

"I think him," said the queen, "a very agreeable and entertaining man."

There, my dear father! said I not well just now, O most penetrating queen?

So here ends my Windsor journal, part the first. Tomorrow morning I go for my week to Thames Ditton.

AN ANTICIPATED ROYAL INTERVIEW.

Windsor, Wednesday, Dec. 14-Yesterday I returned to my dear Mrs. Delany, from Thames Ditton, and had the great concern of finding her very unwell. Mr. Bernard Dewes, one of her nephews, and his little girl, a sweet child of seven years old, were with her, and, of course, Miss Port. She had been hurried, though only with pleasure, and her emotion, first in receiving, and next in entertaining them, had brought on a little fever.

She revived in the afternoon, and I had the pleasure of reading to her a play of Shakspeare's, that she had not heard for forty years, and which I had never read since I was a child,—"The Comedy of Errors;"—and we found in it all the entertainment belonging to an excellent farce, and all the objections belonging to an indifferent play but the spirit with which she enters into every part of everything she hears, gives a sort of theatric effect to whatever is read to her; and my spirits rise in her presence, with the joy of exciting hers.

But I am now obliged, by what follows, to confess a little discussion I have had with my dear Mrs. Delany, almost all the time I spent with her at first, and now again upon my return, relative to the royal interview, so long in expectation.

Immediately upon my arrival, she had imagined, by what had preceded it, that a visit would instantly ensue here, and I should have a summons to appear ;

but the death of the queen's brother, which was known the very night I came, confined her majesty and all the family for some days to the Lodge ; and the dangerous illness of the Princess Elizabeth nexttook place, in occupying all their thoughts, greatly to their credit. My dear old friend, however, earnest I Should have an honour which her grateful reverence for their majesties makes her regard very highly, had often wished me to stay in the room when they came to see her, assuring me that though they were so circumstanced as not to send for a stranger, she knew they would be much pleased to meet with me. This, however, was more than I could assent to, without infinite pain, and that she was too kind to make a point of my enduring.

Yesterday, upon my return, she began again the same reasoning; the Princess Elizabeth had relapsed, and she knew, during her being worse, there was no chance the queen would take any active step towards a meeting. "But she inquires," continued Mrs. Delany, "so much about you, and is so earnest. that you should be with me, that I am sure she wants to see and converse with you. You will see her, too, with more ease to yourself by being already in the room, than from being summoned. I would not for the world put this request to you, if I were not sure she wishes it."

There was no withstanding the word "request" from Mrs. Delany, and little as I liked the business, I could not but comply. What next was to be done, was to beg directions for the rencounter.

Now though you, my dear father, have had an audience, and you, my dear Susan, are likely enough to avoid one, yet I think the etiquettes on these occasions will be equally new to you both ; for one never inquired into them, and the other has never thought of them. Here, at Windsor, where more than half the people we see are belonging to the Court, and where all the rest are trying to be in the same predicament, the intelligence I have obtained must be looked upon as accurate, and I shall, therefore give it., in full confidence you will both regard it as a valuable addition to your present stock of Court knowledge, and read it with that decent awe the dignity of the topic requires!

DIRECTIONS FOR A PRIVATE ENCOUNTER WITH THE ROYAL FAILY.

. . . . . TO come, then, to those particular instructions I received myself, and which must not be regarded as having anything to do with general rules.

"I do beg of you," said dear Mrs. Delany, "When the queen or the king speak to you, not to answer with mere monosyllables. The queen often complains to me of the difficulty with which she can get any conversation, as she not only always has to start the subjects, but, commonly, entirely to support them: and she says there is nothing she so much loves as conversation, and nothing she finds so hard to get. She is always best pleased to have the answers that are made her lead on to further discourse. Now, as I know she wishes to be acquainted with you, and converse with you, I do really entreat you not to draw back from her, nor to stop conversation with only answering 'Yes,' or 'No.'"

This was a most tremendous injunction; however, I could not but promise her I would do the best I could.

To this, nevertheless, she readily agreed, that if upon entering the room, they should take no notice of me, I might quietly retire. And that, believe me, will not be very slowlv ! They cannot find me in this house without knowing who I am, and therefore they can be at no loss whether to speak to me or not, from incertitude.

A PANIC.

In the midst of all this, the queen came!

I heard the thunder at the door, and, panic struck, away flew all my resolutions and agreements, and away after them flew I!

Don't be angry, my dear father—I would have stayed if I could, and I meant to stay - but, when the moment came, neither my preparations nor intentions availed, and I arrived at my own room, ere I well knew I had left the drawing-room, and quite breathless between the race I ran with Miss Port and the joy of escaping,

Mrs. Delany, though a little vexed at the time, was not afterwards, when she found the queen very much dispirited by a relapse of the poor Princess Elizabeth. She inquired if I was returned, and hoped I now came to make a longer stay.

Friday, Dec. 16.-Yesterday morning we had a much better account of the Princess Elizabeth; and Mrs. Delany said to me,

"Now you will escape no longer, for if their uneasiness ceases, I am sure they will send for you, when they come next."

To be sent for, I confessed to her, would really be more formidable than to be surprised; but to pretend to be surprise, would answer no purpose in making the meeting easy to me. and therefore I preferred letting the matter take its chance.

"THE KING! AUNT, THE KING!"

After dinner, while Mrs. Delany was left alone, as usual, to take a little rest,—for sleep it but seldom proves,—Mr. B. Dewes, his little daughter, Miss Port, and myself, went into the drawing-room. And here, while, to pass the time, I was amusing the little girl with teaching her some Christmas games, in which her father and cousin joined, Mrs. Delany came in. We were all in the middle of the room, and in some confusion ;—but she had but just come up to us to inquire what was going forwards, and I was disentangling myself from Miss Dewes, to be ready to fly off if any one knocked at the streetdoor, when the door of the drawing-room was again opened, and a large man, in deep mourning, appeared at it, entering, and shutting it himself without speaking.

A ghost could not more have scared me, when I discovered, by its glitter on the black, a star! The general disorder had prevented his being seen, except by myself, who was always on the watch, till Miss Port, turning round, exclaimed, "The king!— aunt, the king!"

O mercy! thought I, that I were but out of the room! which way shall I escape? and how pass him unnoticed? There is but the single door at which he entered, in the room! Every one scampered out of the way: Miss Port, to stand next the door; Mr. Bernard Dewes to a corner opposite it; his little girl clung to me; and Mrs. Delany advanced to meet his majesty, who, after quietly looking on till she saw him, approached, and inquired how she did,

He then spoke to Mr. Bernard, whom he had already met two or three times here.

I had now retreated to the wall, and purposed gliding softly, though speedily, out of the room ; but before I had taken a single step, the king, in a loud whisper to Mrs. Delany, said, " Is that Miss Burney ? "-and on her answering, " Yes, sir," he bowed, and with a countenance of the most perfect good humour, came close up to me.

A most profound reverence on my part arrested the progress of my intended retreat.

"How long have you been come back, Miss Burney?"

"Two days, sir."

Unluckily he did not hear me, and repeated his question and whether the second time he heard me or not, I don't know, but he made a little civil inclination of his head, and went back to Mrs. Delany.

He insisted she should sit down, though he stood himself, and began to give her an account of the Princess Elizabeth, who once again was recovering, and trying, at present, James's powders. She had been blooded, he said, twelve times in this last fortnight, and had lost seventy-five ounces of blood, besides undergoing blistering and other discipline. He spoke of her illness with the strongest emotion, and seemed quite filled with concern for her danger and suffering.

Mrs. Delany next inquired for the younger children. They had all, he said, the whooping-cough, and were soon to be removed to Kew.

"Not," added he, " for any other reason than change of air for themselves ; though I am pretty certain I have never had the distemper myself, and the queen thinks she has not had it either :—we shall take our chance. When the two eldest had it, I sent them away, and would not see them till it was over; but now there are so many of them that there would be no end to separations, so I let it take its course."

Mrs. Delany expressed a good deal of concern at his running this risk, but he laughed at it, and said, he was much more afraid of catching the rheumatism, which has been threatening one of his shoulders lately, However, he added, he should hunt, the next morning, in defiance of it.

A good deal of talk then followed about his own health, and the extreme temperance by which he preserved it. The fault of his constitution, he said, was a tendency to excessive fat, which e kept, however, in order, by the most vigorous exercise and the strictest attention to a simple diet.

Mrs. Delany was beginning to praise his forbearance, but he stopped her.

"NO, no," he cried, " 'tis no virtue ; I only prefer eating plain and little to growing diseased and infirm."

During this discourse, I stood quietly In the place where he had first spoken to me. His quitting me so soon, and conversing freely and easily with Mrs. Delany, proved so delightful a relief to me, that I no longer wished myself away; and the moment my first panic from the surprise was over, I diverted myself with a thousand ridiculous notions, of my own Situation.

The Christmas games we had been showing Miss Dewes, it seemed as if we were still performing, as none of us thought it proper to move, though our manner of standing reminded one of "Puss in the corner." Close to the door was posted Miss Port; opposite her, close to the wainscot, stood Mr. Dewes; at just an equal distance from him, close to a window, stood myself Mrs. Delany, though seated, was at the opposite side to Miss Port; and his majesty kept pretty much in the middle of the room. The little girl, who kept close to me, did not break the order, and I could hardly help expecting to be beckoned, with a PUSS! PUSS! PUSS! to change places with one of my neighbours.

This idea, afterwards, gave way to another more pompous. It seemed to me we were acting a play. There is something so little like common and real life, in everybody's standing, while talking, in a room full of chairs, and standing, too, so aloof from each other, that I almost thought myself upon a stage, assisting in the representation of a tragedy,—in which the king played his own part, of the king; Mrs. Delany that of a venerable confidante; Mr. Dewes, his respectful attendant;Miss Port, a suppliant Virgin, waiting encouragement to bring forward some petition; Miss Dewes, a young orphan, intened to move the royal compassion; and myself,—a very solemn, sober, and decent mute.

These fancies, however, only regaled me while I continued a quiet spectator, and without expectation of being called into play. Butt the king, I have reason to think, meant only to give me time to recover from my first embarrassment; and I feel infinitely obliged to his good breeding and consideration, which perfectly answered, for before he returned to me, I was entirely recruited,

To go back to my narration.

When the discourse upon health and strength was over, the king went up to the table, and looked at a book of prints, from Claude Lorraine, which had been brought down for Miss Dewes; but Mrs. Delany, by mistake, told him they were for me. He turned over a leaf or two, and then said—

"Pray, does Miss Burney draw, too?"

The too was pronounced very civilly.

"I believe not, Sir," answered Mrs. Delany "at least, she does not tell."

"Oh!" cried he, laughing, "that's nothing; she is not apt to tell! she never does tell, you know!—Her father told me that himself. He told me the whole history of her 'Evelina.' And I shall never forget his face when he spoke of his feelings at first taking up the book!—he looked quite frightened, just as if he was doing it that moment! I never can forget his face while I live!"

THE KING CATEGORICALLY QUESTIONS Miss BURNEY.

Then coming up close to me, the king said-

"But what?—what?—how was it?"

"Sir"—cried I, not well understanding him.

"How came you—how happened it—what?—what?"

"I—I only wrote, Sir, for my own amusement,—only in some odd, idle hours."

"But your publishing—your printing,—how was that?

"That was only, sir,—only because—"

I hesitated most abominably, not knowing how to tell him a long story, and growing terribly confused at these questions;— besides,—to say the truth, his own "what? what? " so reminded me of those vile "Probationary Odes," that, in the midst of all my flutter, I was really hardly able to keep my countenance.

The What! was then repeated, with so earnest a look, that, forced to say something, I stammeringly answered—

"I thought-sir-it would look very well in print!" '

I do really flatter myself this is the silliest speech I ever made! I am quite provoked with myself for it; but a fear of laughing made me eager to utter anything, and by no means conscious, till I had spoken, of what I was saying. He laughed very heartily himself,—well he might—and walked away to enjoy it, crying out,

"Very fair indeed! that's being very fair and honest

Then, returning to me again, he said,

"But your father—how came you not to show him what you wrote?"

"I was too much ashamed of it, sir, seriously."

Literal truth that, I am sure.

"And how did he find it out?

"I don't know myself, sir. He never would tell me."

Literal truth again, my dear father, as you can testify.

"But how did you get it printed?"

"I sent it, sir, to a bookseller my father never employed, and that I never had seen myself, Mr. Lowndes, in full hope by that means he never would hear of it."

"But how could you manage that?"

"By means of a brother, sir."

"O!—you confided in a brother, then?"

"Yes, sir,—that is, for the publication."

"What entertainment you must have had from hearing people's conjectures, before you were known! Do you remember any of them?"

"Yes, sir, many."

"And what?"

"I heard that Mr. Baretti [194] laid a wager it was written by a man for no woman, he said, could have kept her own counsel."

This diverted him extremely.

"But how was it," he continued, "you thought most likely for your father to discover you?"

"Sometimes, sir, I have supposed I must have dropt some of the manuscript; sometimes, that one of my sisters betrayed me."

"O! your sister?—what, not your brother?"

"No, sir; he could not, for—"

I was going on, but he laughed so much I could not be heard, exclaiming,

"Vastly well! I see you are of Mr. Baretti's'mind, and think your brother could keep your secret, and not your sister?"

"Well, but," cried he presently, "how was it first known to you, you were betrayed?"

"By a letter, sir, from another sister. I was very ill, and in the country; and she wrote me word that my father had taken up a review, in which the book was mentioned, and had put his finger upon its name, and said—'Contrive to get that book for me.'"

"And when he got it," cried the king, "he told me he was afraid of looking at it! and never can I forget his face when he mentioned his first opening it. But you have not kept your pen unemployed all this time?"

"Indeed I have, sir."

"But why?"

"I—I believe I have exhausted myself, sir."

He laughed aloud at this, and went and told it to Mrs. Delany, civilly treating a plain fact as a mere bon mot.

Then, turning to me again, he said, more seriously, "But you have not determined against writing, any more?"

"N-o, sir"

"You have made no vow—no real resolution of that sort?"

"No, sir."

"You only wait for inclination"'"

"No, sir."

A very civil little bow spoke him pleased with this answer, and he went again to the middle of the room, where he chiefly stood, and, addressing us in general, talked upon the different motives of writing, concluding with,

"I believe there is no constraint to be put upon real genius; nothing but inclination can set it to work. Miss Burney, however, knows best." And then, hastily returning to me, he cried, "What? what?"

"No, sir, I—I-believe not, certainly," quoth I, very awkwardly, for I seemed taking a violent compliment only as my due; but I knew not how to put him off as I would another person.

He then made some inquiries concerning the pictures with which the room is hung, and which are all Mrs. Delany's own painting and a little discourse followed, upon some of the masters whose pictures she has copied. This was all with her; for nobody ever answers him without being immediately addressed by him.

He then came to me again, and said,

"Is your father about anything at present?"

"Yes, sir, he goes on, when he has time, with his history."

"Does he write quick?"

"Yes, sir, when he writes from himself; but in his history he has so many books to consult, that sometimes he spends' three days in finding authorities for a single passage."

"Very true ; that must be unavoidable." He pursued these inquiries some time, and then went again to his general station before the fire, and Mrs. Delany inquired if he meant to hunt the next day. "Yes," he answered; and, a little.pointedly, Mrs. Delany said,

"I would the hunted could but feel as much pleasure as the hunter."

The king understood her, and with some quickness, called out, "Pray what did you hunt ?"

Then, looking round at us all,—

"Did you know," he said, "that Mrs. Delany once hunted herself?— and in a long gown, and a great hoop?"

It seems she had told his majesty an adventure of that sort which had befallen her in her youth, from some accident in which her will had no share.

THE QUEEN APPEARS UPON THE SCENE.

While this was talking over, a violent thunder was made at the door. I was almost certain it was the queen. Once more I would have given anything to escape ; but in vain. I had been informed that nobody ever quitted the royal presence, after having been conversed with, till motioned to withdraw.

Miss Port, according to established etiquette on these occasions, opened the door which she stood next, by putting her hand behind her, and slid out, backwards, into the hall, to light the queen 'In. The door soon opened again, and her majesty entered.

Immediately seeing the king, she made him a low curtsey, and cried,—

"Oh, your majesty is here."

"Yes," he cried, "I ran here, without speaking to anybody."

The queen had been at the lower Lodge, to see the Princess Elizabeth, as the king had before told us.

She then, hastened up to Mrs. Delany, with both her hands held out, saying, "My dear Mrs. Delany, how are you?"

Instantly after, I felt her eye on my face. I believe, too, she curtsied to me; but though I saw the bend, I was too near-sighted to be sure it was intended for me. I was hardly ever in a situation more embarrassing - I dared not return what I was not certain I had received, yet considered myself as appearing quite a monster, to stand stiff-necked, if really meant.

Almost at the same moment, she spoke to Mr. Bernard Dewes, and then nodded to my little clinging girl.

I was now really ready to sink, with horrid uncertainty of what I was doing, or what I should do,—when his majesty, who I fancy saw my distress, most good-humouredly said to the queen something, but I was too much flurried to remember what, except these words,—"I have been telling Miss Burney—"

Relieved from so painful a dilemma, I immediately dropped a curtsey. She made one to me in the same moment, and, with a very smiling countenance, came up to me; but she could not speak, for the king went on talking, eagerly, and very gaily, repeating to her every word I had said during our conversation upon "Evelina," its publication, etc. etc.

Then he told her of Baretti's wager, saying,—"But she heard of a great many conjectures about the author, before it was known, and of Baretti, an admirable thing !-he laid a bet it must be a man, as no woman, he said, could have kept her own counsel!"

The queen, laughing a little, exclaimed-

"Oh, that is quite too bad an affront to us !-Don't you think so?" addressing herself to me, with great gentleness of voice and manner.

I assented; and the king continued his relation, which she listened to with a look of some interest; but when he told her some particulars of my secrecy, she again spoke to me.

"But! your sister was your confidant, was she not?"

"Yes, ma'am."

My sisters, I might have said, but I was always glad to have done.

"Oh, yes!" cried the king, laughing "but I assure you she is of Baretti's opinion herself; for I asked her if she thought it was her sister or her brother that betrayed her to her father?—and she says her sister, she thinks."

Poor Esther !-but I shall make her amends by what follows; for the queen, again addressing me, said—

"But to betray to a father is no crime-don't you think so ?"

I agreed ; and plainly saw she thought Esther, if Esther it was, had only done right.

The king then went on, and when he had finished his narration the queen took her seat. She made Mrs. Delany sit next her, and Miss Port brought her some tea.

"Miss BURNEY PLAYS-BUT NOT TO ACKNOWLEDGE IT."

The king, meanwhile, came to me again, and said,—"Are you musical?"

"Not a performer, sir."

Then, going from me to the queen, he cried,—"She does not play." I did not hear what the queen answered - she spoke in a low voice, and seemed much out of spirits.

They now talked together a little while, about the Princess Elizabeth, and the king mentioned having had a very promising account from her physician, Sir George Baker and the queen soon brightened up.

The king then returned to me and said,-

"Are you sure you never play?—never touch the keys at all."

"Never to acknowledge it, sir."

"Oh ! that's it ! " cried he; and flying to the queen, cried, "She does play-but not to acknowledge it!"

I was now in a most horrible panic once more ; pushed so very home, I could answer no other than I did, for these categorical questions almost constrain categorical answers; and here, at Windsor, it seems an absolute point that whatever they ask must be told, and whatever they desire must be done.

Think but, then, of my consternation, in expecting their commands to perform! My dear father, pity me!

The eager air with which he returned to me fully explained what was to follow. I hastily, therefore, spoke first, in order to stop him, crying-" I never, sir, played to anybody but myself!— never!"

"No ?" cried he, looking incredulous; "what, not to

"Not even to me, sir! " cried my kind Mrs. Delany, who saw what was threatening me.

"No?—are you sure?" cried he, disappointed; "but—but you'll—"

"I have never, sir," cried I, very earnestly, "played in my life, but when I could hear nobody else-quite alone, and from a mere love of any musical sounds."

He repeated all this to the queen, whose answers I never heard; but when he once more came back, with a face that looked unwilling to give it up, in my fright I had recourse to dumb show, and raised my hands in a supplicating fold, with a most begging countenance to be excused. This, luckily, succeeded; he understood me very readily, and laughed a little, but made a sort of desisting, or rather complying, little bow, and said no more about it.

I felt very much obliged to him, for I saw his curiosity was all alive, I wished I could have kissed his hand. He still, however, kept me in talk, and still upon music.

"To me," said he, " it appears quite as strange to meet with people who have no ear for music, and cannot distinguish one air from another, as to meet with people who are dumb. Lady Bell Finch once told me that she had heard there was some difference between a psalm, a minuet, and a country dance, but she declared they all sounded alike to her! There are people who have no eye for difference of colour. The Duke of Marlborough actually cannot tell scarlet from green!"

He then told me an anecdote of his mistaking one of those colours for another, which was very laughable, but I do not remember it clearly enough to write it. How unfortunate for true virtuosi that such an eye should possess objects worthy the most discerning—the treasures of Blenheim! " I do not find, though," added his majesty, "that this defect runs in his family, for Lady Di Beauclerk, draws very finely."

He then went to Mr. Bernard Dewes.

Almost instantly upon his leaving me, a very gentle voice called out-" Miss Burney!"

It was the queen's. I walked a little nearer her, and a gracious inclination of her head made me go quite up to her.

"You have been," she said, "at Mrs. Walsingham's?"

"Yes, ma'am."

"She has a pretty place, I believe?"

"Yes, ma'am."

"Were You ever there before?"

"Yes, ma'am."

Oh, shocking! shocking ! thought I ; what will"Mrs. Delany say to all these monosyllables ?

"Has not she lately made some improvements?"

"Yes, ma'am; she has built a conservatory."

Then followed some questions about its situation, during which the king came up to us; and she then, ceasing to address me in particular, began a general sort of conversation, with a spirit and animation that I had not at all expected, and which seemed the result of the great and benevolent pleasure she took in giving entertainment to Mrs. Delany.

A DRAWING-ROOM DURING A FOG.

The subject was the last Drawing-room, which she had been in town to keep on Thursday, during the dense fog.

"I assure you, ma'am," cried she to Mrs. Delany, "it was so dark, there was no seeing anything, and no knowing any body. And Lady Harcourt could be of no help to tell me who people were, for when it was light, she can't see and now it was dark, I could not see myself. So it was in vain for me to go on in that manner, without knowing which I had spoken to, and which was waiting for me; so I said to Lady Harcourt, 'We had better stop, and stand quite still, for I don't know anybody, no more than you do. But if we stand still, they will all come up in the end, and we must ask them who they are, and if I have spoken to them yet, or not: for it is very odd to do it, but what else can we manage?'"

Her accent is a little foreign, and very prettily so ; and her emphasis has that sort of changeability, which gives an interest to everything she utters. But her language is rather peculiar than foreign.

"'Besides,'" added she, with a very significant look, "'if we go on here in the dark, maybe I shall push against somebody, or somebody will push against me—which is the more likely to happen.'"

She then gave an account of some circumstances which attended the darkness, in a manner not only extremely lively, but mixed, at times, with an archness and humour that made it very entertaining. She chiefly addressed herself to Mrs. Delany ; and to me, certainly, she would not, separately, have been so communicative; but she contrived, with great delicacy, to include me in the little party, by frequently looking at me, and always with an expression that invited my participation in the conversation. And, indeed, though I did not join in words, I shared very openly in the pleasure of her recital.

"well," she continued, "so there was standing by me a man that I could not see in the face; but I saw the twisting of his bow; and I said to Lady Harcourt, 'I am sure that must be nobody but the Duke of Dorset.'—'Dear,' she says, 'how can you tell that?'—'Only ask,' said I; and so it proved he."

"Yes," cried the king, "he is pretty well again; he can smile again, now!"

It seems his features had appeared to be fixed, or stiffened. It is said, he has been obliged to hold his hand to his mouth, to hide it, ever since his stroke,—which he refuses to acknowledge was paralytic.

The queen looked as if some comic notion had struck her, and, after smiling a little while to herself, said, with a sort of innocent archness, very pleasing,

"To be sure, it is very wrong to laugh at such things,—I know that; but yet, I could not help thinking, when his mouth was in that way, that it was very lucky people's happiness did not depend upon his smiles!"

Afterwards, she named other persons, whose behaviour and manners pointed them out to her, in defiance of obscurity.

"A lady," said she, "came up to me, that I could not see, so I was forced to ask who she was; and immediately she burst into a laugh. 'O,' says I, 'that can be only Mrs. De Rolles!'—and so it proved."

Methinks, by this trait, she should be a near relation to my Miss Larolles! [195]

WILL Miss BURNEY WRITE ANY MORE?

When these, and some more anecdotes which I do not so clearly remember, were told, the king left us, and went to Mr. Bernard Dewes. A pause ensuing, I, too, drew back, meaning to return to my original station, which, being opposite the fire, was never a bad one. But the moment I began retreating, the queen, bending forward, and speaking in a very low voice, said, "Miss Burney!"— and, upon my coming up to her, almost in a whisper, cried, "But shall we have no more—nothing more?"

I could not but understand her, and only shook my head. The queen then, as if she thought she had said too much, with great sweetness and condescension, drew back herself, and, very delicately, said,

"To be sure it is, I own, a very home question, for one who has not the pleasure to know you."

I was quite ashamed of this apology, but did not know what to say to it. But how amiable a simplicity in her speaking of herself in such a style,- for one who has not the ,pleasure to know you."

"But, indeed," continued she, presently, "I would not say it, only that I think from what has been done, there is a power to do so much good—and good to young people, which is so very good a thing—that I cannot help wishing it could be."

I felt very grateful for this speech, and for the very soft manner in which she said it ; and I very much wished to thank her and was trying to mutter something, though not very intelligibly, when the king suddenly coming up to us, inquired what was going forward.

The queen readily repeated her kind speech.

The king eagerly undertook to make my answer for me, crying, "O, but she will write!—she only waits for inclination—she told me so." Then, speaking to me, he said, "What—is it not so?"

I only laughed a little; and he again said to the queen,

"She will write. She told me, just now, she had made no vow against It."

"No, no," cried the queen, "I hope not, indeed."

"A vow!" cried dear Mrs. Delany, "no, indeed, I hope she would not be so wicked—she who can so do what she does!"

"But she has not," said the king, earnestly; "she has owned that to me already."

What excessive condescension, my dear padre!

"I only wish," cried Mrs. Delany, "it could be as easily done, as it is earnestly and universally desired."

"I doubt it not to be so desired," said the queen.

I was quite ashamed of all this, and quite sorry to make no icknowledgment of their great condescension in pressing such subject, and pressing it so much in earnest. But I really could get out nothing, so that's the truth; and I wish I could give a better account of my eloquence, my dear padre and I cannot, however, in justice any more than in inclination, go on, till I stop to admire the sweetness of the queen, and the consideration of the king, in each making me a party in their general conversation, before they made any particular address to me.

A MUSICIAN, WITH A PROBOSCIS.

They afterwards spoke of Mr. Webb, a Windsor musician, who is master to the young princesses, and who has a nose, from some strange calamity, of so enormous a size that it covers all. the middle of his face. I never saw so frightful a deformity. Mrs. Delany told the queen I had met with him, accidentally, when he came to give a lesson to Miss Port, and had been quite startled by him.

"I dare say so," said her majesty. "I must tell Miss Burney a little trait of Sophia, about Mr. Webb."

A small table was before the queen, who always has it brought when she is seated, to put her tea or work upon, or, when she has neither, to look comfortable, I believe ; for certainly it takes off much formality in a standing circle. And close to this, by the gracious motion of her head, she kept me.

"When first," continued she, "Mr. Webb was to come to Sophia, I told her he had had some accident to disfigure his whole face, by making him an enormous nose; but I desired her to remember this was a misfortune, for which he ought to be pitied, and that she must be sure not to laugh at it, nor stare at it. And she minded this very well, and behaved always very properly. But, while Lady Cremorne was at the Lodge, she Was with Sophia when Mr. Webb came to give her a lesson. As soon as he was named, she coloured very red, and ran up to Lady Cremorne, and said to her in a whisper, 'Lady Cremorne, Mr. Webb has got a very great nose, but that is only to be pitied —so mind you don't laugh.'"

This little princess is just nine years old !

The king joined us while the queen was telling this, and added, "Poor Mr. Webb was very much discountenanced when he first saw me, and tried to hide his nose, by a great nosegay, or I believe only a branch, which he held before it: but really that had so odd a look, that it was worse, and more ridiculous, than his nose. However, I hope he does not mind me, now, for I have seen him four or five times."

GENERAL CONVERSATION: ROYALTY DEPARTS.

After this, Mrs. Delany mentioned Madame de la Fite and her son.

The queen said, "He is a pretty little boy; and when be goes to school, it will do him 'good,"

"Where will she send him ? " said the king.

The queen, looking at me, with a smile answered, "To the school where Mr. Locke puts his sons. I know that!"

"And where is that?"

"Indeed I don't know; where is it, Miss Burney?"

"At Cheam, ma'am."

"Oh, at young Gilpin's?" cried the king. "Is it near Mr. Locke's?"

"Yes, sir; within about six miles, I believe."

The queen, then, with a little arch smile, that seemed to premise she should make me stare, said,

"It was there, at Mr. Locke's, your sister[196]laid in?"

"O yes, ma'am!" cried I, out of breath with surprise.

The king repeated my "O yes!" and said, "I fancy—by that O —you were frightened a little for her? What?"

I could not but assent to that; and the king, who seemed a good deal diverted at the accident—for he loves little babies too well to look upon it, as most people would, to be a shocking business—questioned me about it.

"How was it?" said he,—"how happened it? Could not she get home?"

"It was so sudden, sir, and so unexpected, there was no time."

"I dare say," said the sweet queen, "Mrs. Locke was only veryhappy to have it at her house."

"Indeed, ma'am," cried I, "her kindness, and Mr. Locke's would make anybody think so but they are all kindness and ggoodness."

"I have heard indeed," said the queen, "that they are all sensible, and amiable, and ingenuous, in that family."

"They are indeed," cried I, "and as exemplary as they are accomplished."

"I have never seen Mrs. Locke," said the king, "since she was that high;"— pointing to little Miss Dewes.

"And I," said the queen "I have never seen her in my life; but for all that, from what I hear of her, I cannot help feeling interested whenever I only hear her name."

This, with a good deal of animation, she said directly to me.

"Mr. William Locke, ma'am," said Mrs. Delany, "I understand from Miss Burney, is now making the same wonderful progress in painting that he had done before in drawing,"

"I have seen some of his drawings," said the queen, "which were charming."

"How old is he?" cried the king.

"Eighteen, sir."

"Eighteen!" repeated the king—"how time flies!"

"Oh! for me," cried the queen, "I am always quarrelling with time! It is so short to do something, and so long to do nothing."

She has now and then something foreign to our idiom, that has a very pretty effect.

"Time," said the king, "always seems long when we are young, and short when we begin to grow old."

"But nothing makes me so angry," said the queen, "as to hear people not know what to do! For me, I never have half time enough to do things. But what makes me most angry still, is to see people go up to a window and say, 'what a bad day!—dear, what shall we do such a day as this?' 'What?' I say; 'why, employ yourselves; and then what signifies the bad day?'"

Afterwards, there was some talk upon sermons, and the queen wished the Bishop of Chester would publish another volume.

"No, no," said the king, "you must not expect a man, while he continues preaching, to go on publishing. Every sermon printed, diminishes his stock for the pulpit."

"Very true," said the queen, "but I believe the Bishop of Chester has enough to spare."

The king then praised Carr's sermons, and said he liked none but what were plain and unadorned.

"Nor I neither," said the queen; "but for me, it is, I suppose, because the others I don't understand."

The king then, looking at his watch, said, "It is eight o'clock, and]If we don't go now, the children will be sent to the other house."

"Yes, your majesty," cried the queen, instantly rising.

Mrs. Delany put on her majesty's cloak, and she took a very kind leave of her. She then curtsied separately to us all, and the king handed her to the carriage.

It is the custom for everybody they speak to to attend them out, but they would not suffer Mrs. Delany to move. Miss Port, Mr. Dewes, and his little daughter, and myself, all accompanied them, and saw them in their coach, and received their last gracious nods.

When they were gone, Mrs. Delany confessed she had heard the king's knock at the door before she came into the drawinroom, but would not avow it, that I might not run away. Well ! being over was so good a thing, that I could not but be content.

The queen, indeed, is a most charming woman. She appears to me full of sense and graciousness, mingled with delicacy of mind and liveliness of temper. She speaks English almost perfectly well, with great choice and copiousness of language, though now and then with foreign idiom, and frequently with a foreign accent. Her manners have an easy dignity, with a most engaging simplicity, and she has all that fine high breeding which the mind, not the station, gives, of carefully avoiding to distress those who converse with her, or studiously removing the embarrassment she cannot prevent.

The king, however he may have power, in the cabinet, to command himself, has, in private, the appearance of a character the most open and sincere. He speaks his opinions without reserve, and seems to trust them intuitively to his hearers, from a belief they will make no ill use of them. His countenance is full of inquiry, to gain information without asking it, probably from believing that to be the nearest road to truth. All I saw of both was the most perfect good humour, good spirits, ease, and pleasantness.

Their behaviour to each other speaks the most cordial confidence and happiness. The king seems to admire as much as he enjoys her conversation, and to covet her participation in everything he either sees or hears. The queen appears to feel the most grateful regard for him, and to make it her chief study to raise his consequence with others, by always marking that she considers herself, though queen to the nation, only to him, the first and most obedient of subjects. Indeed, in their different ways, and allowing for the difference of their characters, they left me equally charmed both with their behaviour to each other and to myself.

THE KING AGAIN: TEA TABLE ETIQUETTE.

Monday, Dec. 19-In the evening, while Mrs. Delany, Miss Port, and I were sitting and working together in the drawing-room, the door was opened, and the king entered.

We all started up; Miss Port flew to her modest post by the door, and I to my more comfortable one opposite the fire, which caused me but a slight and gentle retreat, and Mrs. Delany he immediately commanded to take her own place again.

He was full of joy for the Princess Elizabeth. He had been to the lower Lodge, and found her in a sweet sleep, and she was now, he said, in a course of James's powders, from which he hoped her perfect restoration. I fear, however, it is still but precarious.

Mrs. Delany congratulated him, and then inquired after the whooping-cough. The children, he said, were better, and were going to Kew for some days, to change the air. He and the queen had been themselves, in the morning, to Kew, to see that their rooms were fit for their reception. He could not, he said, be easy to take any account but from his own eyes, when they were sick. He seems, indeed, one of the most tender fathers in the world.

I cannot pretend to write this meeting with the method and minuteness of the first ; for that took me so long, that I have not time to spare for such another detail. Besides the novelty is now over, and I have not the same inducement to be so very circumstantial. But the principal parts of the conversation I will write, as I recollect.

Our party being so small, he made all that passed general; for though he principally addressed himself to Mrs. Delany, he always looked round to see that we heard him, and frequently referred to us.

I should mention, though, the etiquette always observed upon his entrance, which, first of all, is to fly off to distant quarters - and next, Miss Port goes out, walking backwards, for more candles, which she brings in, two at a time, and places upon the tables and pianoforte. Next she goes out for tea, which she then carries to his majesty, upon a large salver, containing sugar, cream, and bread and butter, and cake, while she hangs a napkin over her arm for his fingers.

When he has taken his tea, she returns to her station, where she waits till he has done, and then takes away his cup, and fetches more. This, it seems, is a ceremony performed in other places always by the mistress of the house; but here neither of their majesties will permit Mrs. Delany to attempt it.

Well; but to return. The king said he had just been looking over a new pamphlet, of Mr. Cumberland's, upon the character of Lord Sackville,

I have been asking Sir George Baker," he said, "if he had read it, and he told me, yes, but that he could not find out why Cumberland had written it. However, that, I think, I found out in the second page. For there he takes an opportunity to give a high character of himself."

He then enlarged more upon the subject, very frankly declaring in what points he differed from Mr. Cumberland about Lord Sackville; but as I neither knew him, nor had read the pamphlet, I could not at all enter into the subject.

Mrs. Delany then mentioned something of Madame de Genlis, [197]upon which the king eagerly said to me,

"Oh, you saw her while she was here?"

"Yes, sir."

"And—did she speak English?"

"Yes, sir."

"And how?"

"Extremely well, sir; with very great facility."

"Indeed? that always surprises me in a foreigner that has not lived here."

Her accent is foreign, however ; but her language is remarkably ready.

He then spoke of Voltaire, and talked a little of his works, concluding with this strong condemnation of their tendency:—

"I," cried he, "think him a monster, I own it fairly."

Nobody answered. Mrs. Delany did not quite hear him, and I knew too little of his works to have courage to say anything about them.

He next named Rousseau, whom he seemed to think of with more favour, though by no means with approbation, Here, too, I had read too little to talk at all, though his majesty frequently applied to me. Mrs. Delany told several anecdotes which had come to her immediate knowledge of him while he was in England, at which time he had spent some days with her brother, Mr. Granville, at Calwich. The king, too, told others, which had come to his own ears, all charging him with savage pride and Insolent ingratitude.

Here, however, I ventured to interfere ; for, as I knew he had had a pension from the king, I could not but wish his majesty should be informed he was grateful to him. And as you, my dear father, were my authority, I thought it but common justice to the memory of poor Rousseau to acquaint the king of his personal respect for him.

"Some gratitude, sir," said I, "he was not without. When my father was in Paris, which was after Rousseau had been in England, he visited him in his garret, and the first thing he showed him was your majesty's portrait over his chimney."

The king paused a little while upon this ; but nothing more was said of Rousseau.

GEORGE III. ON PLAYS AND PLAYERS.

Some time afterwards, the king said he found by the newspapers, that Mrs. Clive[198]was dead.

Do you read the newspapers? thought I. O, king! you must then have the most unvexing temper in the world, not to run wild.

This led on to more players. He was sorry, he said, for Henderson, [199]and the more as Mrs. Siddons had wished to have him play at the same house with herself. Then Mrs. Siddons took her turn, and with the warmest praise.

"I am an enthusiast for her," cried the king, "quite an enthusiast, I think there was never any player in my time so excellent—not Garrick himself—I own it!"

Then, coming close to me, who was silent, he said,—"What? what?"— meaning, what say you? But I still said nothing; I could not concur where I thought so differently, and to enter into an argument was quite impossible; for every little thing I said, the king listened to with an eagerness that made me always ashamed of its insignificancy. And, indeed, but for that I should have talked to him with much greater fluency, as well as ease.

From players he went to plays, and complained of the great want of good modern comedies, and of the extreme immorality of most of the old ones.

And they pretend," cried he, " to mend them; but it is not possible. Do you think it is?—what?"

"No, sir, not often, I believe;-the fault, commonly, lies in the very foundation."

"Yes, or they might mend the mere speeches —but the characters are all bad from the beginning to the end."

Then he specified several; but I had read none of them, and consequently could say nothing about the matter -till, at last, he came to Shakspeare.

"Was there ever," cried he, "such stuff as great part of Shakspeare only one must not say so! But what think you?— What?—Is there not sad stuff? what?— what?"

"Yes, indeed, I think so, sir, though mixed with such excellences, that———"

"O!" cried he, laughing good-humouredly, "I know it is not to be said! but it's true. Only it's Shakspeare, and nobody dare abuse him."

Then he enumerated many of the characters and parts of plays that he objected to - and when he had run them over, finished with again laughing, and exclaiming,

"But one should be stoned for saying so!"

"Madame de Genlis, sir," said I, "had taken such an impression of the English theatre, that she told me she thought no woman ought to go to any of our comedies."

This, which, indeed, is a very overstrained censure of our dramas, made him draw back, and vindicate the stage from a sentence so severe ; which, however, she had pronounced to me, as if she looked upon it to be an opinion in which I should join as a thing past dispute.

The king approved such a denunciation no more than his little subject; and he vindicated the stage from so hard an aspersion, with a warmth not wholly free from indignation.

This led on to a good deal more dramatic criticism; but what was said was too little followed up to be remembered for writing. His majesty stayed near two hours, and then wished Mrs. Delany good night, and having given me a bow, shut the door himself, to prevent Mrs. Delany, or even me, from attending him out, and, with only Miss Port to wait upon him, put on his own great coat in the passage, and walked away to the lower Lodge, to see the Princess Elizabeth, without carriage or attendant. He is a pattern of modest, but manly superiority to'rank. I should say more of this evening, and of the king, with whose unaffected conversation and unassuming port and manner I was charmed, but that I have another meeting to write,-a long, and, to me, very delightful private conference with the queen. It happened the very next morning.

LITERARY TALK WITH THE QUEEN.
Tuesday, Dec. 20.-1st, summons; 2ndly, entr6e.
" Miss Burney, have you heard that Boswell is going to publish a life of your friend Dr. Johnson?"
"No, ma'am."
"I tell you as I heard. I don't know for the truth of it, and I can't tell what he will do. He is so extraordinary a man, that perhaps he will devise something extraordinary. What do you think of Madame de Genlis' last work?"
"I have not read it, ma'am."
" Not read it?"
(I believe she knew my copy, which lay on the table.)
I said I had taken it to Norbury, and meant to read it with Mrs. Locke, but things then prevented.
"Oh! (looking pleased) have you read the last edition of her 'Ad`ele?"'[200]
"No, ma'am."
"Well, it is much improved; for the passage, you know, Mrs. Delany, of the untruth, is all altered - fifteen pages are quite new ; and she has altered it very prettily. She has sent it to me. She always sends me her works ; she did it a long while ago, when I did not know there was such a lady as Madame de Genlis. You have not seen 'Ad`ele,' then?"
"No, ma'am."
"You would like to see it. But I have it not here. Indeed, I think sometimes I have no books at all, for they are at Kew, or they are in town, and they are here ; and I don't know which is which. Is Madame de Genlis about any new work?"
"Yes, ma'am - one which she intends 'pour le peuple.'"
"AH, that will be a good Work. Have you heard of—" (mentioning some German book, of which I forget the name
"No, ma'am."
"O, it will be soon translated; very fine language,—very bad book. They translate all our worst 1 And they are so improved in language; they write so

finely now, even for the most silly books, that it makes one read on, and one cannot help it. O, I am very angry sometimes at that ! Do you like the 'Sorrows of Werter?'"

"I—I have not read it, ma'am, only in part."

"No? Well, I don't know how it is translated, but it is very finely writ in German, and I can't bear it.'"

"I am very happy to hear that, for what I did look over made me determine never to read it. It seemed only writ as a deliberate defence of suicide."

"Yes; and what is worse, it is done by a bad man for revenge."

She then mentioned, with praise, another book, saying,

"I wish I knew the translator."

"I wish the translator knew that."

"O—it is not—I should not like to give my name, for fear I have judged ill: I picked it up on a stall. O, it is amazing what good books there are on stalls."

"It is amazing to me," said Mrs. Delany, "to hear that."

"Why, I don't pick them up myself; but I have a servant very clever; and if they are not to be had at the booksellers', they are not for me any more than for another."

She then spoke of Klopstock's "Messiah," saying it contained four lines most perfect on religion.

"How I should like to see it. Is it translated?" asked Mrs. Delany, turning to me.

"In it," said her majesty: " there is a story of Lazarus and the Centurion's daughter; and another young lady, Asyddel, he calls her; and Lazarus is in love;—a very pretty scene— no stopping;—but it is out of place;—I was quite angry to read it. And a long conversation between Christ and Lazarus—very strange!"

" "Yet Milton does that."

"Yes."

THE QUEEN ON ROMAN CATHOLIC SUPERSTITIONS.

And then she went on discussing Milton; this led to Wickliffe and Cranmer; and she spoke of the Roman Catholic superstitions.

"O, so odd! Can it signify to God Almighty if I eat a piece of fish or a piece of meat? And one of the Queen of France's sisters wears the heel of her shoe before for a penance; as if God Almighty could care for that!'"

"It is supposing in Him the caprice of a fine lady."

"Yes, just so. Yet it is amusing, and pretty too, how sincere the lower people are, of the Catholics. I was with my mother at —, a Catholic town, and there was a lady we knew, had a very bad tooth-ache; she suffered night and day, and we were very sorry. But, over the river there was a Virgin Mary of great fame for miracles, and, one morning, when I wanted to get up, our maid did not come, and nobody knew where she was, and she could not be found. At last she came back with a large bouquet, which she had carried over the river in the night and got it blessed, and gave it to the lady to cure her tooth-ache. But we have

Protestant nunneries in Germany. I belonged to one which was under the Imperial protection ; there is one for royal families-one for the noblesse,- the candidates' coats of arms are put up several weeks to be examined, and if any flaw is found, they are not elected. These nunneries are intended for young ladies of little fortunes and high birth. There is great licence in them. They have balls, not at home, but next door; and there is no restriction but to go to prayers at eight, at nine, and at night,-that is very little, you know,- and wear black or white, The dress consists of three caps, one over the forehead, one for the back, one up high, and one lower, for the veil; very pretty; and the gown is a vest, and the skirt has I don't know how many hundred plaits. I had the cross and order, but I believe I gave it away when I came to England —for you may transfer; so I gave it to the Countess of a friend of mine."

I could not help saying, how glad we all were that she was no nun!

"Once," she continued, "I wanted to go to a chapel in that Catholic town, and my mother said I should go if I would be sure not to laugh at anything; and I promised I would not; so, I took care to keep my eyes half shut, half open, thus, for fear I should see something to make me laugh, for my mother told me I should not come out all day if I laughed. But there was nothing ridiculous."

[The memorandum of the above conversation breaks off abruptly.]

ON BEING PRESENTED.
(FANNY BUrney to Mrs. Burney. Windsor, Dec. 17

My dearest Hetty, I am sorry I could not more immediately write; but I really have not had a moment since your last.

Now I know what you next want is, to hear accounts of kings, queens, and such royal personages. O ho! do you so? Well.

Shall I tell you a few matters of fact?—or, had you rather a few matters of etiquette? Oh, matters of etiquette, you cry! for matters of fact are short and stupid, and anybody can tell, and everybody is tired with them.

Very well, take your own choice.

To begin, then, with the beginning.

You know I told you, in my last, my various difficulties, what sort of preferment to turn my thoughts to, and concluded with just starting a young budding notion of decision, by suggesting that a handsome pension for nothing at all would be as well as working night and day for a salary.

This blossom of an idea, the more I dwelt upon, the more I liked. Thinking served it for a hothouse, and it came out into full blow as I ruminated upon my pillow. Delighted that thus all my contradictory and wayward fancies were overcome, and my mind was peaceably settled what to wish and to demand, I gave over all further meditation upon choice of elevation, and had nothing more to do but to make my election known.

My next business, therefore, was to be presented. This could be no difficulty; my coming hither had been their own desire, and they had earnestly pressed its execution. I had only to prepare myself for the rencounter.

You would never believe—you, who, distant from Courts and courtiers, know nothing of their ways—the many things to be studied, for appearing with a proper propriety before crowned heads. Heads without crowns are quite other sort of rotundas.

Now, then, to the etiquette. I inquired into every particular, that no error might be committed. And as there is no saying what may happen in this mortal life, I shall give you those instructions I have received myself, that, should you find yourself in the royal presence, you may know how to comport yourself.

DIRECTIONS FOR COUGHING, SNEEZING, OR MOVING BEORE THE KING AND QUEEN.

In the first place, you must not cough. If you find a cough tickling in your throat, you must arrest it from making any sound; if you find yourself choking with the forbearance, you must choke—but not cough.

In the second place, you must not sneeze. If you have a vehement cold, you must take no notice of it; if your nose membranes feel a great irritation, you must hold your breath; if a sneeze still insists upon making its way, you must oppose it, by keeping your teeth grinding together; if the violence of the repulse breaks some blood-vessel, you must break the blood-vessel—but not sneeze.

In the third place, you must not, upon any account, stir either hand or foot. If, by chance, a black pin runs into your head, you must not take it out. If the pain is very great, you must be sure to bear it without wincing; if it brings the tears into your eyes, you must not wipe them off; if they give you a tingling by running down your cheeks, you must look as if nothing was the matter. If the blood should gush from your head by means of the black pin, you must let it gush; if you are uneasy to think of making such a blurred appearance, you must be uneasy, but you must say nothing about it. If, however, the agony is very great, you may, privately, bite the inside of your cheek, or of your lips, for a little relief; taking care, meanwhile, to do it so cautiously as to make no apparent dent outwardly. And, with that precaution, if you even gnaw a piece out, it will not be minded, only be sure either to swallow it, or commit it to a corner of the inside of your mouth till they are gone- for you must not spit.

I have many other directions but no more paper; I will endeavour, however, to have them ready for you in time. Perbaps, meanwhile, you would be glad to know if I have myself had opportunity to put in practice these receipts?

DR. BURNEY is DISAPPOINTED OF A PLACE.

Sunday, May 21, 1786.-I have now quite a new business to write upon. Late on Saturday night news reached my father of the death of the worthy Mr. Stanley, who has been long in a declining state of health. His place of master of the king's band my dear father had been promised formerly.

Now he was once more to apply for it; and early on Sunday morning he went to Mr. Smelt, to beg his advice what way to proceed.

just as I was at the door, and going to church, my father returned, and desired me to come back, as he had something to communicate to me. Mr. Smelt, he then told me, had counselled him to go instantly to Windsor, not to address the king, but to be seen by him. "Take your daughter," he said, "in your hand, and walk upon the Terrace. The king's seeing you at this time he will understand, and he is more likely to be touched by a hint of that delicate sort than by any direct application."

My father determined implicitly to follow this advice. But let me not omit a singular little circumstance, which much enlivened and encouraged our expedition. While I was changing my dress for the journey, I received a letter from Miss Port, which was sent by a private hand, and ought to have arrived sooner, and which pressed my visit to my dear Mrs. Delany very warmly, and told me it was by the queen's express wish. This gave me great spirits for my dear father's enterprise, and I was able to help him on the road, from so favourable a symptom.

When we got to Windsor, my father saw me safe to Mrs. Delany's, and then went himself to Dr. Lind's. With what joy did I fly into the dear, open arms of this most venerable of women ! Her reception had all the warm liveliness of pleasant surprise, added to its unfailing kindness.

Miss Port, with her usual partiality, was in high glee from the surprise. I dined and drank tea with them. Mrs. Delany related to me the most flattering speech made to her by the queen, about my coming to her as " the friend best suited to solace her in her disturbances," and assured me she had quite interested herself in pressing Mrs. Delany to hasten me.

'Tis very extraordinary what a gracious disposition towards me this sweet queen always manifests, and what peculiar elegance there is in the expressions she makes use of in my favour. They were now particularly well-timed, and gave me most pleasant hopes for my dear father. He came to tea at Mrs. Delany's, and, at the proper hour, went to the Terrace, with the good-natured Dr. Lind, who is always ready to oblige. I waited to go with a female party, which was arranged for me by Mrs. Delany, and soon followed.

All the royal family were already on the Terrace before we arrived. The king and queen, and the Prince of Mecklenburg, and her majesty's mother -walked together. Next them the princesses and their ladies, and the young princesses, making a very gay and pleasing procession, of one of the finest families in the world. Every way they moved, the crowd retired to stand up against the wall as they passed, and then closed in to follow. When they approached towards us, and we were retreating, Lady Louisa Clayton placed me next herself, making her daughters stand below-a politeness and attention without which I had certainly not been seen; for the moment their majesties advanced, I involuntarily looked down, and drew my hat over my face. I could not endure to stare at them, and, full of our real errand, I felt ashamed , even of being seen by them. The very idea of a design, however far from illaudable is always distressing and uncomfortable. Consequently, I should have stood in the herd, and unregarded; but Lady Louisa's kindness and good breeding put me in a place too conspicuous to pass unnoticed. The moment the queen had spoken to her, which she stopped to do as soon as she came up to her, she inquired, in a whisper, who was with her; as I know by hearing my own name given for the answer. The queen then instantly stepped nearer me, and asked me how I did; and then the king came forward, and, as soon as he had repeated the same question, said, "Are you come to stay?"

"No, sir, not now."

"No; but how long shall you stay?"

"I go to-night, sir."

"I was sure," cried the queen, "she was not come to stay, by seeing her father."

I was glad by this to know my father had been observed.

"And when did you come?" cried the king.

"About two hours ago, sir."

"And when do you return again to Windsor?"

"Very soon, I hope, sir."

"And—and—and—" cried he, half laughing, and hesitating, significantly, "pray, how goes on the Muse?"

At first I only laughed, too; but he repeated the inquiry, and then I answered, "Not at all, sir."

"No? But why?—why not?"

"I—I—I am afraid sir," stammered I, and true enough, I am sure.

"And why?" repeated he, "of what?"

I spoke something,—I hardly know what myself,—so indistinctly, that he could not hear me, though he had put his head quite under my hat, from the beginning of the little conference and, after another such question or two, and no greater satisfaction in the answer, he smiled very good humouredly, and walked on, his charming queen by his side. His condescension confuses, though it delights me.

We stayed some time longer on the Terrace, and my poor father occasionally joined me; but he looked so conscious and depressed, that it pained me to see him. There is nothing that I know so very dejecting, as solicitation. I am sure I could never, I believe, go through a task of that sort. My dear father was not spoken to, though he had a bow every time the king passed him, and a curtsey from the queen. But it hurt him, and he thought it a very bad prognostic ; and all there was at all to build upon was the graciousness shewn to me, which, indeed, in the manner I was accosted, was very flattering, and, except to high rank, I am told, very rare.

We stayed but a very short time with my sweet Mrs. Delany, whose best wishes you are sure were ours. I told her our plan, and our full conviction that she could not assist in it; as the obligations she herself owes are so great and so weighty, that any request from her would be encroaching and improper.

We did not get home till past eleven o'clock. We were then informed that Lord Brudenel had called to say Mr. Parsons had a promise of the place from the lord chamberlain. This was not very exhilarating.

A VISIT TO WARREN HASTINGS AND HIS WIFE.

I HAD BEen invited by Mr. Cambridge to pass a day at Twickenham with

Mr. and Mrs. Hastings, who had proposed to carry me with them : accordingly, on May 24th, MrsHastings sent her carriage here before ten o'clock. I made her and Mr. Hastings a visit of about half an hour previously to our journey. I am quite charmed with Mr. Hastings, and, indeed, from all I can gather, and all I can observe,-both which are but little,-he appears to me to be one of the greatest men now living, as a public character; while as a private one, his gentleness, candour, soft manners, and openness of disposition, make him one of the most pleasing.

The little journey was extremely agreeable. He spoke with the utmost frankness of his situation and affairs, and with a noble confidence in his certainty of victory over his enemies,

from his consciousness of integrity and honour, that filled me with admiration and esteem for him. Mrs. Hasting's is lively, obliging, and entertaining, and so adored by her husband, that, in her sight and conversation he seems to find a recompense, adequate to all his wishes, for the whole of his toils, and long disturbances and labours. How rare, but how sweet and pleasant, the sight of such unions. [201]

A PROPOSAL FROM THE QUEEN.

[JUNE, 1786.-A vacancy at this time occurred in the royal household, from the resignation of Madame Haggerdorn, one of the queen's German attendants who, together with Madame Schwellenberg, held the office of keeper of the robes. The place was much sought after, but her majesty had been so well pleased with what she saw of Miss Burney, that she graciously empoWered Mr. Smelt to offer her this situation, allowing her time to consider and weigh its advantages.

Miss Burney, though deeply grateful for such a distinction, foresaw with alarm the separation from her family and the total confinement it would occasion; and, in her perplexity how to decide, she wrote to her friend, Miss Cambridge, in the following terms.]

Monday, June, 1786.

. . . . Yesterday evening, while I was with Mrs. Delany, Mr. Smelt arrived from Windsor, and desired a private conference with her; and, when it was over, a separate one with me: surprising me not a little, by entreating me to suffer some very home questions from him, relative to my situation, my views, and even my wishes, with respect to my future life. At first, I only laughed: but my merriment a little failed, me, when he gave me to understand he was commissioned to make these inquiries by a great personage, who had conceived so favourable an opinion of me as to be desirous of undoubted information, whether or not there was a probability she might permanently attach me to herself and her family.

You cannot easily, my dear Miss Cambridge, picture to yourself the consternation with which I received this intimation. It was such that the good and kind Mr. Smelt, perceiving it, had the indulgence instantly to offer me his services, first, in forbearing to mention even to my father his commission, and next in fabricating and carrying back for me a respectful excuse. And I must always consider myself the more obliged to him, as I saw in his own face the utmost astonishment and disappointment at this reception of his embassy.

I could not, however, reconcile to myself concealing from my dear father a matter that ought to be settled by himself; yet I frankly owned to Mr. Smelt that no situation of that sort was suited to my own taste, or promising to my own happiness.

He seemed equally sorry and surprised ; he expatiated warmly upon the sweetness of character of all the royal family, and then begged me to consider the very peculiar distinction shown me, that, unsolicited, unsought, I had been marked out with such personal favour by the queen herself, as a person with whom she had been so singularly pleased, as to wish to settle me with one of the princesses, in preference to the thousands of offered candidates, of high birth and rank, but small fortunes, who were waiting and supplicating for places in the new-forming establishment. Her majesty proposed giving me apartments in the palace ; making me belong to the table of Mrs. Schwellenberg, with whom all her own visitors—bishops, lords, or commons— always dine; keeping me a footman, and settling on me 200 pounds a year. "And in such a situation," he added, "so respectably offered, not solicited, you may have opportunities of serving your particular friends,—especially your father,—such as scarce any other could afford you."

My dear Miss Cambridge will easily feel that this was a plea not to be answered. Yet the attendance upon this princess was to be incessant,—the confinement to the court continual; I was scarce ever to be spared for a single visit from the palaces, nor to receive anybody but with permission,—and, my dear Miss Cambridge, what a life for me, who have friends so dear to me, and to whom friendship is the balm, the comfort, the very support of existence!

Don't think me ungrateful, meanwhile, to the sweet queen, for thus singling out and distinguishing an obscure and most unambitious individual. No indeed, I am quite penetrated with her partial and most unexpected condescension ; but yet, let me go through, for her sake, my tasks with what cheerfulness I may, the deprivations I must suffer would inevitably keep me from all possibility of happiness.

Though I said but little, my dear Mrs. Delany was disturbed and good Mr. Smelt much mortified, that a proposition which had appeared to them the most flattering and honourable, should be heard only with dejection. I cast, however, the whole into my father's disposal and pleasure.

But I have time for no more detail, than merely to say, that till the offer comes in form, no positive answer need be given, and therefore that I am yet at liberty. Write to me, then, my dearest Miss Cambridge, with all your fullest honesty, and let me know which you wish to strengthen—my courage in making my real sentiments openly known, or my fortitude in concealing what it may be right I should endure. . . .

Monday Night,

I have now to add, that the zealous Mr. Smelt is just returned from Windsor, whither he went again this morning, purposely to talk the matter over with her majesty. What passed I know not,-but the result is, that she has desired an interview with me herself; it is to take place next Monday, at Windsor. I now see the end—I see it next to inevitable. I can suggest nothing upon earth that I dare say for myself, in an audience so generously meant. I cannot even to my father utter my reluctance,—I see him so much delighted at the prospect of an establishment he looks upon as so honourable. But for the queen's own word "permanent,"—but for her declared desire to attach me entirely to herself and family!—I should share in his pleasure; but what can make me amends for all I shall forfeit? But I must do the best I can,

Write me a comforting and strengthening letter, my dearest Miss Cambridge. I have no heart to write to Mickleham, or Norbury. I know how they will grieve:—they have expected me to spend the whole summer with them. My greatest terror is, lest the queen, from what Mr. Smelt hinted, should make me promise myself to her for a length of years. What can I do to avoid that? Anything that has a period is endurable but what can I object that will not sound ungrateful, to the honour she is doing me and meaning me? She has given the most highly flattering reasons for making this application, in preference to listening to that of others; she has put it upon terms of commendation the most soothing; she is, indeed, one of the sweetest characters in the world. Will you, too, condemn me, then, that I feel thus oppressed by her proposal? I hope not,-I think not ;-but be very honest if you really do. I wish I could see you! It is not from nervousness;—I have always and uniformly had a horror of a life of attendance and dependence. . . .

Miss BURNEY ACCEPTS THE QUEEN'S OFFER.

[How Miss Cambridge replied is not known; but Miss Burney's appreciation of the queen's kindness, and the desire avowed by Dr. Burney and Mrs. Delany that so honourable and advantageous an offer should not be declined, induced her to accept it ; and the following letters to her father show the final result of her deliberations, and her affectionate care to prevent him from perceiving her uneasiness.]

Fanny Burney to Dr. Burney.

Monday, June 19.

How great must have been your impatience, dearest sir but my interview has only this morning taken place. Everything is settled, and to-morrow morning I go to the queen's Lodge, to see the apartments, and to receive my instructions.

I must confess myself extremely frightened and full of alarms at a change of situation so great, so unexpected, so unthought-of. Whether I shall suit it or not, heaven only knows, but I have a thousand doubts. Yet nothing could be sweeter than the queen,—more encouraging, more gentle, or more delicate. She did not ask me one question concerning my qualifications for the charge; she only said, with the most condescending softness, "I am sure, Miss Burney, we shall Suit One another very well." And, another time, "I arn sure we shall do very well together."

And what is itl dear Sir, you suppose to be my business? Not to attend any of the princesses—but the queen herself! This, indeed, was a delightful hearing, reverencing and admiring her as I have so sincerely done ever since I first saw her. And in this, my amazement is proportioned to my satisfaction; for the place designed me is that of Mrs. Haggerdorn, who came with her from Germany, and it will put me more immediately and more constantly in her presence than any other place, but that of Mrs. Schwellenberg, in the Court.

The prepossession the queen has taken in my favour is truly extraordinary, for it seems as if her real view was, as Mr. Smelt hinted, to attach me to her person. She has been long, she told Mrs. Delany, looking out for one to supply the place of Mrs. Haggerdorn, whose ill health forces her back to Germany; "and I was led to think of Miss Burney, first by her books ; then by Seeing her - then by always hearing how she was loved by her friends; but chiefly by your friendship for her."

I fancy my appointment will take place very soon.

Windsor, June 20.

Most dear Sir, I am sure you will be (glad to hear I have got one formality over, that was very disagreeable to my expectations. I have been introduced to Mrs. Haggerdorn whom I am to succeed, and to Mrs, Schwellenberg, whom I am to accompany. This passed at the queen's Lodge, in their own apartments, this morning. I cannot easily describe the sensation with which I entered that dwelling,—the thoughts of its so soon becoming my habitation,— -and the great hazard of how all will go on in it—and the sudden change!

Everything was perfectly civil and easy; the queen had herself prepared them to receive me, and requested me to go. They made no use of the meeting in the way of business it was merely a visit of previous ceremony. . . .

The utmost astonishment will take place throughout the Court when they hear of my appointment. Everybody has settled some successor to Mrs. Haggerdorn; and I have never,

I am very sure, been suspected by a single person. I saw, this morning, by all that passed with Mrs. S., how unexpected a step her majesty has taken. The place, she told me, has been solicited, distantly, by thousands and thousands of women of fashion and rank. . . .

(Fanny Burney to Mrs. Francis. [202])

St. Martin's-street, June 27.

. . . Her majesty has sent me a message, express, near a fortnight ago, with an offer of a place at Court, to succeed Mrs. Haggerdorn, one of the Germans who accompanied her to England, and who is now retiring into her own country. 'Tis a place of being constantly about her own person, and assisting in her toilette,-a place of much confidence, and many comforts; apartments in the palace; a footmnan kept for me; a coach in common with Mrs. Schwellenberg; 200 pounds a-year, etc.

I have been in a state of extreme disturbance ever since, from the reluctance I feel to the separation it will cause me from all my friends. Those, indeed, whom I most love, I shall be able to invite to me in the palace - but I see little or no possibility of being able to make what I most value, excursions into the country. . . . I repine at losing my loved visits to Mickleham, Norbury, Chesington, Twickenham, and Ayle sham ; all these I must now forego. . . .

You may believe how much I am busied. I have been presented at the queen's Lodge in Windsor, and seen Mrs. Haggerdorn in office, and find I have a place of really nothing to do, but to attend; and on Thursday I am appointed by her majesty to go to St. James's, to see all that belongs to me there. And I am now "fitting Out" just as you were, and all the maids and workers suppose I am going to be married, and snigger every time they bring in any of My new attire. I do not care to publish the affair till it is made known by authority ; so I leave them to their conjectures, and I fancy their greatest wonder is, who and where is the sposo; for they must think it odd he should never appear!

---

189   "Memoirs of Dr. Burney," vol. iii. p. 87. Fanny had, however, to assist in dressing the queen. See postea, P- 345.

190   The death of the Duchess dowager of Portland.

191   Miss Planta was English teacher to the two eldest princesses.-ED.

192   One of the governesses to the princesses.-ED.

193   Georgina Mary Anne Port, grandniece of Mrs. Delany, by whom she was brought up from the age of seven until Mrs. Delany's death. She was born in 1771, and mairied, in 1789, Mr. Waddington, afterwards Lord Llanover. She was for many years on terms of friendship with Fanny, but after Madame D'Arblay's death, Lady Llanover seized the opportunity of publishing, in her edition of Mrs. Delany's Correspondence, an attack upon her former friend, of which the ill-breeding is only equalled by the inaccuracy. The view which she there takes of Fanny is justly characterised by Mr. Shuckburgh as "the lady-in-waiting's lady's-maid's view." (See Macmillan's magazine for February, 1890.)-ED.

194   Joseph Baretti, author of an Italian and English Dictionary, and other works; the friend Of JOhnson, well known to readers of Boswell. He had long been acquainted wifh the Burneys. Fanny writes in her "Early Diary" March, 1773 "Mr. Baretti appears to be very facetious; he amused himself very much with Charlotte, whom he calls churlotte, and kisses whether she will or no, always calmly saying, 'Kiss A me, Churlotte!'" Charlotte Burney was then about fourteen; she was known after this in the family as Mrs. Baretti.-ED.

195   A character in "Cecilia."-ED.

196   Mrs. Phillips (Susan)-ED.

197   Madame de Genlis had visited England during the spring of 1785, and made the acquaintance of Dr. Burney and his daughter Fanny. In July Fanny writes of her as "the sweetest as well as the most accomplished Frenchwoman I ever met with," and in the same month Madame de Genlis writes to Fanny: "Je vous aime depuis l'instant o`u j'ai lu Evelina et Cecilia, et le bonheur de vous entendre et de vous conn6itre

personellement a rendu ce sentiment aussi tendre qu'il est bien fond6."
The acquaintance, however, was not kept up.-ED.

198   The famous actress, Kitty Clive. She had quitted the stage in 1760. Genest says of her, "If ever there was a true Comic Genius, Mrs. Clive was one."—ED.

199   John Henderson was by many people considered second only to Gairick, especially in Shakspearean parts. He too was lately dead, having made his last appearance on the stage on the 8th of November, 1785, within less than a month of his death.-ED.

200   "Ad`ele et Th`eodore, ou Lettres sur l'`education" by Madame de Genlis, ffirst published in 1782.-ED.

201   We shall hear again of 'Mr, and Mrs. Hastings, and of the scandal which was caused by the lady's reception at Court. She was bought by Hastings of her former husband for 10,000 pounds. The story is briefly as follows:—

Among the fellow-passengers of Hastings on the ship which conveyed him to India in 1769, were a German portrait-painter, named Imhoff, and his wife, who were going out to -Madras in the hope of bettering their circumstances. During the voyage a strong attachment sprang up between Hastings and the lady, who nursed him through an illness. The husband, it seems, had as little affection for his wife as she had for him, and was easily prevailed upon to enter into an amicable arrangement, by virtue of which Madame Imhoff instituted proceedings for divorce against him in the German courts. Pending the result, the Imhoffs continued to live together ostensibly as man and wife to avoid scandal. The proceedings- were long protracted, but a decree of divorce was finally procured in 1772, when Hastings married the lady and paid to the complaisant husband a sum, it Is said, exceeding, 10,000 pounds.

The favourable reception accorded by the queen to Mrs. Hastings, when, in 1784, she returned to England as wife of the Governor- general of Bengal, passed not without public comment. Her husband, however, was in high esteem at Court from his great services, and she had an additional recommendation to the queen's favour in the friendship of Mrs. Schwellenberg, the keeper of the robes, whom she had known before her voyage to -India.-ED.

202   Fanny's sister Charlotte, who had mairied Clement Francis, Feb. 11, 1786. They were now settled at Aylesham, in Norfolk, where Mr. Francis was practising as a surgeon.-ED.

SECTION 7 (1786)

MISS BURNEY ENTERS UPON HER COURT DUTIES.

[The original editor of Madame D'Arblay's Diary intimates that fictitious names have been given to one or two of the persons spoken of in the following portion of the work. These names we retain in the present text, but the following persons have been identified :-
"Col. Fairly," with Col. the Hon. Stephen Digby; "Col. Wellbred," with Col. Greville; "Mr. Turbulent," with the Rev. Charles de Guiffardi`ere; and "Miss Fuzilier" with Miss Gunning-ED.]

THE QUEEN'S SUMMONS.
Queen's Lodge, Windsor, Monday, July 17-
With what hurry of mind and body did I rise this morning! Everything had already been arranged for Mrs. Ord's carrying us to Windsor, and my father's carriage was merely to go as baggage-waggon for my clothes. But I wept not then. I left no one behind me to regret; my dear father accompanied me, and all my dear sisters had already taken their flight, never more to return. Even poor little Sarah. [203]whom I love very dearly, was at Chesington.

Between nine and ten o'clock we set off. W e changed carriage in Queen Ann-street, and Mrs. Ord conveyed us thence to Windsor. With a struggling heart, I kept myself tolerably tranquil during the little journey. My dear father was quite happy, and Mrs. Ord felt the joy of a mother in relinquishing me to the protection of a queen so universally reverenced. Had I been in better spirits, their ecstasy would have been unbounded ; but alas !-what I was approaching was not in my mind - -what I was leaving had taken Possession of it solely.

Miss Port flew out to us as the carriage stopped-the youthful blush of pleasure heightening her complexion, and every feature shewing her kind happiness. Mrs. Delany, she said, was gone out with the queen. I took leave of my good Mrs. Ord, whose eyes overflowed with maternal feelings-chiefly of contentment. Mrs. Delany came home in about An hour. A chastened satisfaction was hers; she rejoiced in the prospect before me; she was happy we ,should now be so much united, but she felt for my deprivations, she saw the hard conflict within me, and the tenderest pity checked her delight.

It was now debated whether I was immediately to go to the Lodge, or wait for orders. The accustomed method for those who have their majesties' commands to come to them is, to present themselves to the people in waiting, and by them to be announced. My heart, however, was already sinking, and my spirits every moment were growing more agitated, and my sweet Mrs. Delany determined to spare me the additional task of passing through such awe-striking formalities. She therefore employed my dear father-delighted with the employment-to write a note, in her name.

" Mrs. Delany presents her most humble duty to the queen; she found Dr. Burney and his daughter at her house. Miss Burney waits the honour of her majesty's commands."

This, though unceremonious and unusual, she was sure the queen would pardon. A verbal answer came that I was to go to the Lodge immediately.

O, my dear Susan! in what an agony of mind did I obey the summons! I was still in my travelling dress, but could not stay to change it. My father accompanied me. Mrs. Delany, anxiously and full of mixed sensations, gave me her blessing. We walked; the queen's Lodge is not fifty yards from Mrs. Delany's door. My dear father's own courage all failed him in this little step; for as I was now on the point of entering—probably for ever-into an entire new way of life, and of foregoing by it all my most favourite schemes, and every dear expectation my fancy had ever indulged of happiness adapted to its taste—as now all was to be given up—I could disguise my trepidation no longer—indeed I never had disguised, I had only forborne proclaiming it. But my dear father now, sweet soul ! felt it all, as I held by his arm, without power to say one word, but that if he did not hurry along I should drop by the way. I heard in his kind voice that he was now really alarmed ; he would have slackened his pace, or have made me stop to breathe; but I could not; my breath seemed gone, and I could only hasten with all my might, lest my strength should go too.

A page was in waiting at the gate, who shewed us 'Into Mrs. Haggerdorn's room, which was empty. My dear father endeavoured here to compose my spirits; I could have no other command over them than to forbear letting him know the afflicted state of all within, and to suffer him to keep to his own conclusions, that my emotion was all from fear of the approaching audience.

The page came in a minute or two to summon me to the queen. The queen was in her dressing-room. Mrs. Schwellenberg was standing behind her : nobody else present.

She received me with a most gracious bow of the head, and a smile that was all sweetness. She saw me much agitated, and attributed it, no doubt, to the awe of her presence. O, she little knew my mind had no room in it for feelings of that sort! She talked to me of my journey, my father, my sisters, and my brothers; the weather, the roads, and Mrs. Delany, any, every thing she could suggest, that could best tend to compose and to make me easy; and when I had been with her about a quarter of an hour, she desired Mrs. Schwellenberg to shew me my apartment, and, with another graceful bow, motioned my retiring.

Not only to the sweet queen, but to myself let me here do justice, in declaring that though I entered her presence with a heart filled with everything but herself, I quitted it with sensations much softened. The condescension of her efforts to quiet me, and the elegance of her receiving me, thus, as a visitor, without naming to me a single direction, without even the most distant hint of business, struck me to shew so much delicacy, as well as graciousness, that I quitted her with a very deep sense of her goodness, and a very strong conviction that she merited every exertion on my part to deserve it.

Mrs. Schwellenberg left me,—at the room door, where my dear father was still waiting for me, too anxious to depart till he again saw me.

We spent a short time together, in which I assured him I would from that moment take all the happiness in my power, and banish all the regret. I told him how gratifying had been my reception, and I omitted nothing I could think of to remove the uneasiness that this day seemed first to awaken in him Thank God ! I had the fullest success; his hopes and gay expectations were all within call, and they ran back at the first beckoning.

This settled, and his dear countenance all fresh illumined with returning content, we went together to Mrs. Schwellenherg, where we made a visit of about an hour, in which I had the pleasure of seeing them upon very amicable terms ; and then we had one more t`ete-`a-t`ete all in the same cheering style, and he left me to drest, and went to dine with Mrs. Delany.

Left to myself, I did not dare stop to think, nor look round upon my new abode, nor consider for how long I was taking possession; I rang for my new maid, and immediately dressed for dinner. I now took the most vigorous resolutions to observe the promise I had made my dear father. Now all was filially settled, to borrow my own words, I needed no monitor to tell me it would be foolish, useless, even wicked, not to reconcile myself to my destiny.

The many now wishing for just the same—O! could they look within me. I am married, my dearest Susan—I look upon it In that light—I was averse to forming the union, and I endeavoured to escape it; but my friends interfered— they prevailed—and the knot is tied. What then now remains but to make the best wife in my power? I am bound to it in duty, and I will strain every nerve to succeed.

A MILITARY GOURMAND.

When summoned to dinner, I found Mrs. Schwellenberg and a German officer, Colonel Polier, who is now an attendant of Prince Charles of Mecklenburg, the queen's brother, who is on a visit to their majesties. I was introduced to himpand we took our places. I was offered the seat of Mrs. Haggerdorn, which was at the head of the table; but that was an undertaking I could not bear. I begged leave to decline it; and as Mrs. Schwellenberg left me at my own choice, I planted myself quietly at one side.

Colonel Polier, though a German officer, is of a Swiss family.

He is a fat, good-humoured man, excessively fond Of eating and drinking. His enjoyment of some of the fare, and especially of the dessert, was really laughable; he could never finish a speech he had begun, if a new dish made its appearance, without stopping to feast his eyes upon it, exclaim something in German, and suck the inside of his mouth; but all so openly, and with such perfect good-humour, that it was diverting without anything distasteful.

After dinner we went upstairs into Mrs. Schwellenber,-'s room, to drink coffee. This is a daily practice. Her rooms are exactly over mine ; they are the same size, and have the same prospect, but they are much more sumptuously fitted up.

A SUCCESSION OF VISITORS.

Colonel Polier soon left us, to attend Prince Charles. Mrs. Schwellenberg and I had then a long t`ete-`a-t`ete, in which I found her a woman of understanding, and fond of conversation. I was called down afterwards to Miss Port, who was eager to see me in my new dwelling, and dying with impatience to know, hear, and examine everything about me. She ran about to make all the inquiries and discoveries she could for me, and was so highly delighted with my situation, it was impossible not to receive some pleasure even from looking at her. She helped me to unpack, to arrange, to do everything that came in the way.

In a short time Madame de la Fite entered, nearly as impatient as herself to be my first visitor. She was quite fanciful and entertaining about my succeeding to Mrs. Haggerdorn, and repeatedly turned round to look at me fresh and fresh, to see if it was really me, and me in that so long differently appropriated apartment.

She had but just left me, when who should enter but my dear Mrs. Delany herself. This was indeed a sweet regale to me. She came to welcome me in my own apartment, and I am sure to teach me to love it. What place could I see her in and hate ? I could hardly do anything but kiss her soft cheeks, and dear venerable hands, with gratitude for her kindness, while she stayed with me, which was till the royal family came home from the Terrace, which they walk upon every fine evening. She had already been invited to the king's concert, which she then attended.

Miss Port and I now planned that we would drink t together. It was, indeed, my dearest Mrs. Locke's injunctions that determined me upon making that trial; for I knew nothing could more contribute to my future chance of some happy hours than securing this time and this repast to imself. Mrs, Delany had the same wish, and encouraged me in the attempt.

As I knew not to whom to speak, nor how to give a positive order, in my ignorance whether the measure I desired to take was practicable or not, Miss Port undertook to be my agent. She therefore ran out, and scampered up and down the stairs and passages in search of some one to whom she could apply. She met at last Mrs. Schwellenberg's man, and boldly bid him " bring Miss Burney's tea." "It is ready," he answered, "in the dining parlour." And then he came to me, with his mistress's compliments, and that she was come down to tea, and waited for me.

To refuse to go was impossible it would have been an opening so offensive, with a person destined for my principal companion, and who had herself begun very civilly and attentively, that I could not even hesitate. I only felt heavyhearted, and Miss Port made a thousand faces, and together we went to the eating-room.

THE TEA TABLE OF THE KEEPER OF THE ROBES.

Mrs. Schwellenberg had already made the tea; and four gentlemen were seated at the table. The Bishop of Salisbury, as I afterwards found he was, came up to congratulate me, and spoke very kindly of my father, whom he said he had just seen on the Terrace. This is a brother of Lord Barrington's: I had never met him before.

Next him sat a young clergyman, Mr. Fisher, whom I did not recollect, but who said he had seen me once at Mrs. Ord's, and spoke to me of her, and of Mrs. Thrale, whom he had lately left in Italy, where he has been travelling.

And next was Major Price, the equerry of the king at present in waiting. He is the same that all the Barborne family so adored when a captain. He mentioned them all to me, with high praise and great good-breeding. I am very much pleased with him, and happy he should be the equerry in waiting on my first arrival. Colonel Polier was also of the party.

I find it has always belonged to Mrs. Schwellenberg and Mrs. Haggerdorn to receive at tea whatever company the king or queen invite to the Lodge, as it is only a very select few OF them that can eat with their majesties, and those few are only ladies; no men, of what rank soever, being permitted to sit in the queen's presence. I mean and hope to leave this business wholly to Mrs. Schwellenberg, and only to succeed Mrs. Haggerdorn in personal attendance upon the queen.

During tea the door opened, and a young lady entered, upon whose appearance all the company rose, and retreated a few paces backward, with looks of high respect. She advanced to Mrs. Schwellenberg, and desired her to send a basin of tea into the music-room for Mrs. Delany : then walking up to me, with a countenance of great sweetness, she said, "I hope you are very well, Miss Burney?" I only curtseyed, and knew not till she left the room, which was as soon as she had spoken a few words to Major Price, that this was the Princess Elizabeth.

Immediately after the concert began; the band being very full, and the performance on the ground-floor, as is the eating-room. I heard it perhaps better, because softer, than if I had been in the music-room. I was very glad of this circumstance. Nothing was played but Handel; but I was pleased to hear any music, so much had I persuaded myself I should hear no more.

EVENING CEREMONIAL IN THE QUEEN's DRESSING **ROOM**.

At night I was summoned to the queen's apartment. Mrs. Schwellenberg was there, waiting. We sat together some time. The queen then arrived, handed into her dressing-room by the king, and followed by the princess royal and Princess Augusta. None other of the princesses slept in the queen's Lodge. The lower Lodge, which is at the further end of the garden, is the dwelling-place of the four younger princesses.

The king, with a marked appearance of feeling for the-no doubt evident-embarrassment of my situation, on their entrance, with a mild good-breeding inquired of me how I had found Mrs. Delany : and then, kissing both his daughters, left the room. The two princesses each took the queen's hand, which they respectfully kissed, and wishing her good night, curtseyed condescendingly to her new attendant, and retired.

The queen spoke to me a little of my father, my journey, and Mrs. Delany, and then entered into easy conversation, in German, with Mrs. Schwellenberg, who never speaks English but by necessity. I had no sort of employment given me. The queen was only waited upon by Mrs. Schwellenberg and Mrs. Thielky, her wardrobe woman ; and when she had put on her night dishabille, she wished me good night.

This consideration to the perturbed state of my mind, that led her majesty to permit my presence merely as a spectatress, by way of taking a lesson of my future employment for my own use, though to her, doubtless, disagreeable, was extremely gratifying to me, and sent me to bed with as much ease as I now could hope to find.

THE QUEEN'S TOILETTES.

Monday, July 8.-I rose at six, and was called to the queen soon after seven. Only Mrs. Schwellenberg was with her, and again she made me a mere looker-on; and the obligation I felt to her sent me somewhat lighter hearted from her presence.

When she was dressed, in a simple morning gown, she had her hat and cloak put on, to go to prayers at eight o'clock, at the king's chapel in the Castle; and I returned to my room.

At noon came my dear father, and spent an hour or two with me—so happy! so contented! so big with every pleasant expectation!—I rejoice to recollect that I did nothing, said nothing this morning to check his satisfaction; it was now, suddenly and at once, all my care to increase his delight. And so henceforward it must invariably continue.

We parted cheerfully on* both sides; yet I saw a little pang in his last embrace, and felt it in his dear hands :-but I kept myself well up, and he left me, I really believe, without a wish ungratified.

At dressing-time the same quiet conduct was still observed by the queen—fixed in her benign determination to permit me to recover breath and ease, ere she gave me any other trial than merely standing in her presence.

At dinner we—I mean Mrs. Schwellenberg and myself-had Miss Planta and Colonel Polier; and I was happy to be again diverted with the excess of his satisfaction at sight of turtle upon the table.

CONGRATULATORY VISITS FROM COURT OFFICIALS.

in the evening I had a visit from Lady Elizabeth Waldegrave, who brought her sister, Lady Caroline Waldegrave, both to pay congratulatory compliments. Lady Elizabeth is lady of the bedchamber to the princess royal, and lives in this Lodge.

Her sister, by the queen's, goodness, is permitted to spend .some months of every year with her. They were left orphans at about sixteen: the queen instantly took them both under her protection. They are gentle and well bred, and seem very amiable. They stayed with me till it was time for them to go into waiting for the princess royal, whom they attend to the Terrace.

My dearest Mrs. Delany came again, to visit me wholly, and drink tea with me. We had a thousand things to discuss, but were scarce a moment together before we were interrupted by Madame de la Fite, who, however, only stayed to give and receive from Mrs. Delany congratulations on meeting in my room at Windsor, and then she pretty soon took leave.

We had but again arranged ourselves to a little comfort, when a tat-tat at my door followed, and a lady entered whom I had never seen before, with a very courteous air and demeanour, saying, "I could not defer paying my compliments to Miss Burney, and wishing her much joy, which we must all feel in such an accession to our society: I must get my daughter to introduce me." And then advanced Mrs. Fielding, and I found this was Lady Charlotte Finch.

Mrs. Fielding is one of the women of the bedchamber. She lives with her mother, Lady Charlotte, and her three daughters, girls from ten to fifteen years of age.

When she also wished me joy, I saw in her face a strong mark of still remaining astonishment at my appointment. Indeed all the people in office here are so evidently amazed that one so unthought of amongst them should so unexpectedly fill a place to which they had all privately appropriated some acquaintance, that I see them with difficulty forbear exclaiming, "How odd it is to see you here!"

Lady Charlotte's visit was short and very civil; she was obliged to hasten to the Castle, to attend the younger princesses till they went to the Terrace. They are sent to wait in an apartment of the Castle, till the king and queen and the elders walk out, and then they are called to join them, when the crowd is not great, and when the weather is fine.

My Windsor apartment is extremely comfortable. I have a large drawing-room, as they call it, which is on the ground floor, as are all the queen's rooms, and which faces the Castle and the venerable round tower, and opens at the further side, from the windows, to the little park. It is airy, pleasant, clean, and healthy, My bed-room is small, but neat and comfortable; its entrance is only from the drawing-room, and it looks to the garden. These two rooms are delightfully independent of all the rest of the house, and contain everything I can desire'for my convenience and comfort.

In her way to my room, Mrs. Delany had met the king; she -was alittle shocked, and feared she came at an improper hour, or ought to have come in the back Way. I know not if he had perceived her distress; but he soon removed It, for when he went out to go to the Terrace he looked towards my windows, and seeing her there, advanced a few steps to ask her how she did. The queen turned round and curtseyed to her, and the Princess Augusta ran up to speak to her.

I had retired behind her; but when they moved on, Miss Goldsworthy, the sub-governess, stole from her charges, and came to the window to desire Mrs. Delany to introduce' her to me.

Sweet Mrs. Delany, thwarted in her kind private views of an interesting confabulation, grew fatigued, and went home; and then Mrs. Fielding rose to accompany her. Miss Port made a second attempt for tea, but received for answer that Mrs. Schwellenberg would come down and make it as soon as the king and queen came from the Terrace.

The ceremony of waiting tea till the royal family return from the Terrace, is in order to make it for any company they may invite to it. . . .

To-night, like the rest of my attendance, I was merely treated as if an accidental visitor. Sweet queen !,;z-she seems as fearful of employing me as I am myself of being employed.

INOPPORTUNE VISITORS.

July 20.-This morning the queen enquired of me if I loved walking? I answered yes; and she then told me I had better not leave off that exercise, but walk out every morning.

I called at my dear Mrs. Delany's, and took Miss Port with me. We went together to Lady Louisa Clayton. We next went to Lady Charlotte Finch, who is one of 'her sisters, and governess to the princesses.

I called also at Madame de la Fite's; but she was so urgent with me to prolong my stay, that I returned too late to dress for my noon attendance, and just as I was in the midst of my hair dishevelling, I was summoned.

I was obliged to slip on my morning gown, and a large morning cap, and run away as fast as possible. The queen, who was only preparing for her own hair-dresser, was already en peignoir: she sat down, the man was called in, and then, looking at me with a smile, she said "Now, Miss Burney, you may go and finish your dress."

Away I gallopped as fast as possible, to be ready against her hair-dresser departed : but when I came pretty near my own apartment, I was stopped in the gallery by a lady, who coming up to me, said "Miss Burney?"

I started and looked at her; but finding her a perfect stranger to me, I only said "Ma'am!"—and my accent of surprise made her beg my pardon and walk on. I was too much in haste to desire any explanation, 'and was only quickening my pace, when I was again stopped by a gentleman with a star and red ribbon, who, bowing very civilly, said "Miss Burney, I presume?"

"Sir!—" was again all my answer and again, like the lady, he begged my pardon, and retreated and I was too seriously earnest to pursue my business to dare lose a moment. On, therefore, I again hurried; but, at the very door of my room, which is three steps down and three up place out of the even line of the gallery, I was once more stopped, by a very fat lady: who, coming up to me, also said "Miss Burney, I believe?"

"Yes, ma'am."

"We have just," cried she, "been to wait upon you,—but I could find nobody to introduce me; I believe I must introduce myself,-Lady Effingham."

I thanked her for the honour she did me,—but when she proposed returning with me to my room, in order to finish her visit, I was quite disconcerted; and hesitated so much that she said "Perhaps it is not convenient to you?-"

"Ma'am—I—I was just going to dress—" cried I; I meant to add, and ought to have added, to " wait upon the queen," but I was so unused to such a plea, that it sounded as a liberty to my vmind's voice, and I could not get it out.

She desired she might be no impediment to me,-and we parted I was forced to let her go and to run into my own room, and fly - to my toilette Not quite the sort of flight I have been used to making. However, all is so new here that it makes but a part in the general change of system.

The lady who had met me first was her daughter, Lady Frances Howard; and the gentleman, her second husband, Sir George Howard.

I afterwards saw her ladyship in the queen's dressing-room, where her majesty sent for her as soon as she was dressed, and very graciously kept me some time, addressing me frequently while I stayed, in the conversation that took place, as if with a sweet view to point out to this first lady of her bedchamber I have yet seen, the favourable light in which she considers me,

MAJOR PRICE AND COLONEL POLIER.

The Duke de Saxe-Gotha, first cousin to the king, came to Windsor to-day, to spend some time. Major Price, who had the honours to do to his chief attendant, Baron ——, missed us therefore at coffee ; but at tea we had them both, and my dear 'Mrs. Delany, as well as the jovial gourmand colonel, with whom I became prodigiously well acquainted, by making him 'teach me a few German phrases, which he always contrives, let me ask what question I may, to turn into some expression relating to eating and drinking.

When all were gone, except the Duke de Saxe-Gotha's baron and Major Price, I had a very long conversation with the major, while Mrs. Schwellenberg was entertaining the baron in German. I find, my dearest Susan, he has seen you often at Lady Clarges's; Sir Thomas[204] was his first cousin. He knows my dearest Mrs. Locke, also, by another cousin, Lady Templetown; and he knows me my own self by my cousins of Worcester. These mutual acquaintances have brought us into almost an intimacy at once, and I was quite glad of this opportunity of a little easy and natural conversation.

Sunday, July 23—Charles Wesley played the organ; and after the service was over he performed six or seven pieces by the king's order. They were all of Handel, and so well suited to the organ, and so well performed on a remarkably good instrument, that it was a great regale to me to hear them. The pleasure I received from the performance led me into being too late for the queen. I found I had already been enquired for to attend at the queen's toilette.

When I came back the tea-party were all assembled in the eating-parlour. Colonel Polier was in the highest spirits : the king had just bestowed some appointment upon him in Hanover. He was as happy as if just casting his eyes upon pine-apple, melon, and grapes. I made Mrs. Schwellenberg teach me how to wish him joy in German : which is the only phrase I have yet got that has no reference to eating or drinking.

MISS BURNEY'S DAILY ROUTINE AT WINDSOR.

Monday, July 24-Having now journalized for one complete week, let me endeavour to give you, more connectedly, a concise abstract of the general method of passing the day, that then I may only write what varies, and occurs occasionally.

I rise at six o'clock, dress in a morning gown and cap, and wait my first summons, which is at all times from seven to near eight, but commonly in the exact half hour between them.

The queen never sends for me till her hair is dressed. This, in a morning, is always done by her wardrobe-woman, Mrs. Thielky, a German, but who speaks English perfectly well.

Mrs. Schwellenberg, since the first week, has never come down in a morning at all. The queen's dress is finished by Mrs. Thielky and myself. No maid ever enters the room while the queen is in it. Mrs. Thielky hands the things to me, and I put them on. 'Tis fortunate for me I have not the handing them! I should never know which to take first, embarrassed as I am, and should run a prodigious risk of giving the gown before the hoop, and the fan before the neckkerchief.

By eight o'clock, or a little after, for she is extremely expeditious, she is dressed. She then goes out to join the king, and be joined by the princesses, and they all proceed to the king's chapel in the Castle, to prayers, attended by the governesses of the princesses, and the king's equerry. Various others at times attend, but only these indispensably.

I then return to my own room to breakfast. I make this meal the most pleasant part of the day; I have a book for my companion, and I allow myself an hour for it. At nine O'clock I send off my breakfast things, and relinquish my book, to make a serious and steady examination of everything I have upon my hands in the way of business-in which preparations for dress are always included, not for the present day alone, but for the Court-days, which require a particular dress; for the next arriving birthday of any of the royal family, every one of which requires new apparel; for Kew, where the dress is plainest; and for going on here, where the dress very pleasant to me, requiring no shew nor finery, but merely to be neat, not inelegant, and moderately fashionable.

That over, I have my time at my own disposal till a quarter before twelve, except on Wednesdays and Saturdays, when I have it only to a quarter before eleven. My rummages and business sometimes occupy me uninterruptedly to those hours. When they do not, I give till ten to necessary letters of duty, ceremony, or long arrears ;-and now, from ten to the times I have mentioned, I devote to walking. These times mentioned call me to the irksome and quick-returning labours of the toilette. The hour advanced on the Wednesdays and Saturdays is for curling and craping the hair, which it now requires twice a week.

A quarter before one is the usual time for the queen to begin dressing for the day. Mrs. Schwellenberg then constantly attends; so do I; Mrs. Thielky, of course, at all times. We help her off with her gown, and on with her powdering things, and then the hair-dresser is admitted. She generally reads the newspaper during that operation.

When she observes that I have run to her but half dressed, she constantly gives me leave to return and finish -as soon as she is seated. If she is grave, and reads steadily on, she dismisses me, whether I am dressed or not; but at all times she never forgets to send me away while she is powdering, with a consideration not to spoil my clothes, that one would not expect belonged to her high station. Neither does she ever detain me without making a point of reading here and there some little paragraph aloud.

When I return, I finish, if anything is undone, my dress, and then take Baretti's "Dialogues," my dearest Fredy's "Tablet of Memory," or some such disjointed matter, for the few minutes that elapse ere I am again summoned.

I find her then always removed to her state dressing-room. if any room in this private mansion can have the epithet of state. There, in a very short time, her dress is finished. She then says she won't detain me, and I hear and see no more of her till bed-time.

It is commonly three o'clock when I am thus set at large. And I have then two hours quite at my disposal: but, in the natural course of things, not a moment after! These dear and quiet two hours, my only quite sure and undisturbed time in the whole day, after breakfast is over, I shall henceforth devote to thus talking with my beloved Susan, my Fredy, and my other sisters, my dear father, or Miss Cambridge; with my brothers, cousins, Mrs. Ord, and other friends, in such terms as these two hours will occasionally allow me. Henceforward, I say; for hitherto dejection of spirits, with uncertainty how long my time might last, have made me waste moment after moment as sadly as unprofitably.

At five, we have dinner. Mrs. Schwellenberg and I meet in the eating-room. We are commonly t`ete-`a-t`ete: when there is anybody added, it is from her invitation only. Whatever right my place might afford me of also inviting my friends to the table I have now totally lost, by want of courage and spirits to claim it originally.

When we have dined, we go upstairs to her apartment, which is directly over mine. Here we have coffee till the "terracing" is over: this is at about eight o'clock. Our t`ete-`a-t`ete then finishes, and we come down again to the eating-room. There the equerry, whoever he is, comes to tea constantly, and with him any gentleman that the king or queen may have invited for the evening; and when tea is over, he conducts them, and goes himself, to the concert-room. This is commonly about nine o'clock.

From that time, if Mrs. Schwellenberg is alone, I never quit her for a minute, till I come to my little supper at near eleven. Between eleven and twelve my last summons usually takes place, earlier and later occasionally. Twenty minutes is the customary time then spent with the queen: half an hour, I believe, is seldom exceeded.

I then come back, and after doing whatever I can to forward MY dress for the next morning, I go to bed-and to sleep, too, believe me : the early rising, and a long day's attention to new affairs and occupations, cause a fatigue so bodily, that nothing mental stands against it, and to sleep I fall the moment I have put Out my candle and laid down my head.

Such is the day to your F. B. in her new situation at Windsor; such, I mean, is its usual destination, and its intended course. I make it take now and then another channel, but never stray far enough not to return to the original stream after a little meandering about and about it.

I think now you will be able to see and to follow me pretty closely.

With regard to those summonses I speak of, I will now explain myself. My summons, upon all regular occasionsthat is, morning, noon, and night toilets-is neither more nor less than a bell. Upon extra occasions a page is commonly sent. At first, I felt inexpressibly discomfited by this mode of call. A bell!—it seemed so mortifying a mark of servitude, I always felt myself blush, though alone, with conscious shame at my own strange degradation. But I have philosophized myself now into some reconcilement with this manner of summons, by reflecting that to have some person always sent would b often very inconvenient, and that this method is certainly less an interruption to any occupation I may be employed in, than the entrance of messengers so many times in the day. It is, besides, less liable to mistakes. So I have made up my mind to it as well as I can ; and now I only feel that proud blush when somebody is by to revive my original dislike of it.

THE PRINCEss ROYAL.

Tuesday, july 25.-I now begin my second week, with a scene a little, not much, different. We were now to go to Kew, there to remain till Friday.

I had this morning, early, for the first time, a little visit from one of the princesses. I was preparing for my journey, when a little rap at my room-door made me call out " Come in and who should enter but the princess royal!

I apologised for my familiar admittance, by my little expectation of such an honOUr. She told me she had brought the queen's snuff-box, to be filled with some snuff which I had been directed to prepare. It is a very fine-scented and mild snuff, but requires being moistened from time to time, to revive its smell. The princess, with a very sweet smile, insisted upon holding the box while I filled it; and told me she had seen Mrs. Delany at the chapel, and that she was very well; and then she talked on about her, with a visible pleasure in having a subject so interesting to me to open upon,

When the little commission was executed, she took her leave with an elegant civility of manner as if parting with another king's daughter. I am quite charmed with the princess royal unaffected condescension and native dignity are so happily blended in her whole deportment.

She had left me but a short time before she again returned. "Miss Burney," cried she, smiling with a look of congratulation, "Mamma says the snuff is extremely well mixed; and she has sent another box to be filled."

I had no more ready. She begged me not to mind, and not to hurry myself, for she would wait till it was done.

THE COURT AT KEW: A THREE YEAR OLD PRINCESS.

Mrs. Schwellenberg, Miss Planta, and myself travelled to Kew together. I have two rooms there; both small, and up two pair of stairs; but tidy and comfortable enough. Indeed all the apartments but the king's and queen's, and one of Mrs. Schwellenberg's, are small, dark, and old-fashioned. There are staircases in every passage, and passages to every closet. I lost myself continually, only in passing from my own room to the queen's. just as I got upstairs, shown the way first by Miss Planta, I heard the king's voice. I slipped into my room ; but he saw me, and following, said,

"What! is Miss Burney taking possession?"

And then he walked round the room, as if to see if it were comfortable for me, and smiling very good-humouredly, walked out again. A surveyor was with him,— I believe he is giving orders for some alterations and additions. . . .

When I went to the queen before dinner, the little Princess Amelia was with her; and, though shy of me at first, we afterwards made a very pleasant acquaintance. She is a most lovely little thing, just three years old, and full of sense, spirit, and playful prettiness: yet decorous and dignified when called upon to appear en princesse to any strangers, as if conscious of her high rank, and of the importance of condescendingly sustaining it. 'Tis amazing what education can do, in the earliest years, to those of quick understandings. [205]This little princess, thus in infancy, by practice and example, taught her own consequence, conducts herself, upon all proper occasions, with an air of dignity that is quite astonishing, though her natural character seems all sport and humour.

When we became a little acquainted, the queen desired me to take her by the hand, and carry her downstairs to the king, who was waiting for her in the garden. She trusted herself to me with a grave and examining look, and shewed me, for I knew it not, the way. The king, who dotes upon her, seemed good-humouredly pleased to see me bring her. He took her little hand and led her away.

A DRAWING-ROOM AT ST. JAMES'S.

Thursday, July 27-This being a Court-day, we went to town. The queen dresses her head at Kew, and puts on her Drawing-room apparel at St. James's. Her new attendant dresses all at Kew, except tippet and long ruffles, which she carries in paper, to save from dusty roads. I forgot to tell you, I believe, that at St. James's I can never appear, even though I have nothing to do with the Drawing-room, except in a sacque: 'tis the etiquette of my place.

Mrs. Schwellenberg, Miss Planta, and myself went about an hour before the king and queen. Mrs. Schwellenberg went to the queen's dressing-room to give orders about the dress, Miss Planta went to the princesses' room for the same purpose, and I was shewn to mine for no purpose.

Mine are two small rooms, newly and handsomely furnished, one of which has a view of the park, over the stable-yard, and the other only of the passage to the park from St. James'sstreet. I had now the great satisfaction to find that there was a private staircase, from that same passage, that leads straight up to my apartments, and also that I may appoint any friend to meet me in them on the court-days. I hope never to be there again without making use of this privilege.

Having now neither companion nor book, I sent John, who came with me to town, to borrow some writing implements of one of the pages, and I employed myself in answering some letters, till the queen arrived, and I was summoned, by Mrs. Leverick, the town wardrobe woman, to the dressing-room. There the queen put on her court dress, and as soon as she was attired sent for the princesses royal and Augusta, who came to attend her to the Drawing-room.

Mr. Nicolay, the page in waiting, then came to beg a little audience for the Duchess ofAncaster.. The queen went to her in the ante-room - The moment I was left with the princesses, they both came up to me, and began conversing in the most easy, unaffected, cheerful, and obliging manner that can be conceived.

When the queen returned, the bell was rung for the bedchamber woman; the etiquette of court-days requiring that one of them should finish her dress.

It happened now to be my acquaintance, Mrs. Fielding. She only tied on the necklace, and handed the fan and gloves. The queen then leaves the dressing.room, her train being carried by the bedchamber woman. The princesses follow. She goes to the ante-room, where she sends for the lady of the bedchamber in waiting, who then becomes the first train-bearer, and they all proceed to the Drawing-room.

We returned to Kew to dinner, very late.

ABSENCE OF STATE AT KEW.

Friday, July 28.-The Kew life, you will perceive, is different from the Windsor. As there are no early prayers, the queen rises later; and as there is no form or ceremony here of any sort, her dress is plain, and the 'hour for the second toilette extremely uncertain. The royal family are here always in so very retired a way, that they live as the simplest country gentlefolks. The king has not even an equerry with him, nor the queen any lady to attend her when she goes her airings.

Miss Planta belongs here to our table; so does anybody that comes, as there is no other kept. There is no excuse for parting after dinner, and therefore I live unremittingly with Mrs. Schwellenberg after the morning.

It is a still greater difficulty to see company here than at Windsor, for as my apartments are upstairs, there is a greater danger of encountering some of the royal family ; and I find all the household are more delicate in inviting or admitting any friends here than elsewhere, on account of the very easy and unreserved way in which the family live, running about from one end of the house to the other, without precaution or care.

Miss BURNEY'S FIRST EVENING OUT.

Windsor, July 28.-To-day I made my first evening visit, and for the first time failed Mrs. Schwellenberg's tea-table entirely. You will be surprised to hear for whom I took this effort —Lady Effingham! But I found from Mrs. Delany

She had been a little hurt by the passage-scene, and seemed to think I meant to avoid her future visits and civilities. -Mrs. Delany, therefore, advised me to go to Stoke, her country-seat, by way of apologizing, and to request the queen's permission, Promising to carry me herself.

I never hesitate where she counsels. I thought it, too, a good opportunity of trying my length of liberty, as Lady Effingham is one of the ladies of the bedchamber, and is frequently at the Lodge as a private visitor.

It was inexpressibly awkward to me to ask leave to go out, and awkwardly enough I believe I did it, only saying that if her majesty had no objection, Mrs. Delany would carry me in the evening to Stoke. She smiled immediate approbation, and nothing more passed.

I had then to tell my intention to Mrs. Schwellenberg who was, I believe, a little surprised. Fortunately, Major Price came upstairs to coffee. A little surprised, too, I am sure, was Major Price, when I made off for the whole evening. Everybody had taken it for granted I must necessarily pursue the footsteps of Mrs. Haggerdorn, and never stir out. But, thank God, I am not in the same situation ; she had no connections—I have such as no one, I believe, ever had before.

The evening was rainy; but, my leave asked and obtained, my kind Mrs. Delany would not defer the excursion. Stoke is about three miles off.

We were received in the civilest manner possible by Lady Effingham, and Sir George Howard and Lady Frances. There were also several of their relations with them. Lady Effingham seems a mighty good-humoured, friendly woman. Sir George is pompous, yet he, too, is as good-humoured in his manners as his Lady.

CASUAL CALLERS TO BE KEPT OFF: A NEw ARRIVAL.

July 31.-I had a very pleasant visit from Mrs. Hastings[206]this morning, whose gay good-humour is very enlivening : but she detained me from my dress, and I was not ready for the queen ; and I have now adopted the measure of stationing John in the gallery while I am at that noble occupation, and making him keep off all callers, by telling them I am dressing for the queen. I have no other way ; and being too late, or even the fear of being too late, makes me nervous and ill.

Every little failure of this sort, though always from causes unknown to her majesty, she has borne without even a look of surprise or of gravity ; though she never waits an instant, for if Mrs. Schwellenberg is not with her, she employs Mrs. Thielky, or goes on with her dress or her undress without either.

This graciousness, however, makes me but the more earnest to grow punctual; especially as I am now always employed, when present and in time.

I went in the afternoon to Mrs. de Luc. When I returned here, to the conclusion of the tea-drinking, I found a new gentleman, dressed in the king's Windsor uniform-which is blue and gold, turned up with red, and worn by all the men who belong to his majesty, and come into his presence at Windsor.

Major Price immediately presented us to each other. It was General Bud`e: what his post may be I have not yet learned, but he is continually, I am told, at Windsor, and always resides in this Lodge, and eats with the equerries.

I do not quite know what to say of General Bud`e; except that his person is tall and showy, and his manners and appearance are fashionable. But he has a sneer in his smile that looks sarcastic, and a distance in his manner that seems haughty.

THE ROYAL PRINCESSES.

Wednesday, 2.—This morning, for the first time, I made a little sort of acquaintance with the two younger princesses. I was coming from the queen's room, very early, when I met the Princess Mary, just arrived from the lower Lodge: she was capering upstairs to her elder sisters, but instantly stopped at sight of me, and then coming up to me, inquired how I did, with all the elegant composure of a woman of maturest age. Amazingly well are all these children brought up. The readiness and the grace of their civilities, even in the midst of their happiest wildnesses and freedom, are at once a surprise and a charm to all who see them.

The queen, when she goes to early prayers, often leaves me the charge of her little favourite dog, Badine. To-day, after her return, she sent her page for him ; and presently after, I had a rap again at the door, and the little Princess Sophia entered. "Miss Burney," cried she, curtseying and colouring, "Mamma has sent me for the little dog's basket."

I begged her permission to carry it to the queen's room but she would not suffer me, and insisted upon taking it herself, with a mingled modesty and good breeding extremely striking in one so young.

About half an hour after she returned again, accompanying the princess royal. The queen had given me a new collection of German books, just sent over, to cut open for her; and she employed the princess royal to label them. She came most smilingly to the occupation, and said she would write down their names, " if I pleased," in my room. You may believe I was not much displeased. I gave her a pencil, and she seized a piece of whity-brown paper, inquiring "if she might have it?"—I would fain have got her better, but she began writing immediately, stooping to the table.

I was now in a momentary doubt whether or not 'It Would b(' - proper, or too great a liberty, to ask her royal highness to be seated ; but, after a moment's hesitation, I thought it best to place her a chair, and say nothing.

I did ; and she turned about to me with a most graceful curtsey, and immediately accepted it, with a most condescending apology for my trouble. I then, thus encouraged, put another chair for the little Princess Sophia, who took it as sweetly.

"Pray sit down too," cried the princess royal: "I beg you will, Miss Burney!"

I resisted a little while; but she would not hear me, insisting, with the most obliging earnestness, upon carrying her point.

She writes German with as much facility as I do English and therefore, the whole time she was taking down the titles of the books, she kept up a conversation, Mrs. Delany her well and kindly chosen subject. When she had done her task, she quitted me with the same sweetness, and the Princess Mary ran in for her little sister.

The princess royal, not long after, again returned:—"There is no end to me, you will think, this morning," cried she, on entering; and then desired to have all the books I had cut open; nor would she suffer me to carry one for her, though they were incommodious, from their quantity, for herself.

Such has been the singular 'condescension of the queen, that every little commission with which she has yet intrusted me she has contrived to render highly honourable, by giving the princesses some share in them.

ALARMING NEWS.

In the evening I had no little difficulty how to manage to go to Mrs. Delany,—for I have here to mention the worst thing that has happened to me at Windsor,-the desertion of Major Price from the coffee. The arrival of General Bud`e, who belongs to the equerries' table, has occasioned his staying to do the honours to him till terrace time. At tea, they belong to Mrs. Schwellenberg.

This has not only lost me some of his society, the most pleasant I had had in the Lodge, but has trebled my trouble to steal away. While I left him behind, the absconding from a beau was apology all-sufficient for running away from a belle; but now I am doubly wanted to stay, and too-doubly earnest to go! . . .

I went into my own room for my cloak, and, as usual, .found Madame de la Fite just waiting for me. She was all emotion,—she seized my hand,—"Have you heard?—O mon Dieu!—O le bon Roi! O Miss Burney!—what an horrreur!"

I was very much startled, but soon ceased to wonder at her perturbation ;- she had been in the room with the Princess Elizabeth, and there heard, from Miss Goldsworthy, that an attempt had just been made upon the life of the king!

I was almost petrified with horror at the intelligence. If this king is not safe,- good, pious, beneficent as he is,.-if his life is in danger, from his own subjects, what is to guard the throne? and which way is a monarch to be secure?

Madame de la Fite had heard of the attempt only, not the particulars; but I was afterwards informed of them in the most interesting manner,—namely, how they were related to the queen. And as the newspapers will have told you all else, I shall only and briefly tell that.

No information arrived here of the matter before his majesty's return, at the usual hour in the afternoon, from the levee. The Spanish minister had hurried off instantly to Windsor, and was in waiting, at Lady Charlotte Finch's, to be ready to assure her majesty of the king's safety, in case any report anticipated his return.

The queen had the two eldest princesses, the Duchess of Ancaster, and Lady Charlotte Bertie with her when the king came in. He hastened up to her, with a countenance of striking vivacity, and said, " Here I am !-safe and well,-as you see !-but I have very narrowly escaped being stabbed!"

His own conscious safety, and the pleasure he felt in thus personally shewing it to the queen, made him not aware of the effect of so abrupt a communication. The queen was seized with a consternation that at first almost stupefied her, and after a most painful silence, the first words she could articulate were, in looking round at the duchess and Lady Charlotte, who had both burst into tears,-" I envy you !-I can't cry!"

The two princesses were for a little while in the same state but the tears of the duchess proved infectious, and they then' wept even with violence.

THE ATTEMPT AGAINST THE KING.

The king, with the gayest good-humour, did his utmost to comfort them ; and then gave a relation of the affair, with a calmness and unconcern that, had any one but himself been his hero, would have been regarded as totally unfeeling.

You may have heard it wrong; I will concisely tell it right. His carriage had just stopped at the garden-door at St. James's, and he had just alighted from it, when a decently-dressed woman, who had been waiting for him some time, approached him, with a petition. It was rolled up, and had the usual superscription— "For the king's most excellent majesty." She presented it with her right hand; and at the same moment that the king bent forward to take it, she drew from it, with her left hand, a knife, with which she aimed straight at his heart.

The fortunate awkwardness of taking the instrument with the left hand made her design perceived before it could be executed;—the king started back, scarce believing the testimony of his own eyes; and the woman made a second thrust, which just touched his waistcoat before he had time to prevent her;—and at that moment one of the attendants, seeing her horrible intent, wrenched the knife from her hand.

"Has she cut my waistcoat?" cried he, in telling it,—Look! for I have had no time to examine."

Thank heaven, however, the poor wretch had not gone quite so far. "Though nothing," added the king, in giving his relation, "could have been sooner done, for there was nothing for her to go through but a thin linen, and fat."

While the guards and his own people now surrounded the king, the assassin was seized by the populace, who were tearing her away, no doubt to fall the instant sacrifice of her murtherous purpose, when the king, the only calm and moderate person then present, called aloud to the mob, "The poor creature is mad!—Do not hurt her! She has not hurt me!"

He then came forward, and showed himself to all the people, declaring he was perfectly safe and unhurt; and then gave positive orders that the woman should be taken care of, and went into the palace, and had his levee. [207]

There is something in the whole of his behaviour upon this occasion that strikes me as proof indisputable of a true and noble courage : for in a moment so extraordinary-an attack, in this country, unheard of before-to settle so instantly that it was the effect of insanity, to feel no apprehension of private plot or latent conspiracy-to stay out, fearlessly, among his people, and so benevolently to see himself to the safety of one who had raised her arm against his life,—these little traits, all impulsive, and therefore to be trusted, have given me an impression of respect and reverence that I can never forget, and never think of but with fresh admiration.

If that love of prerogative, so falsely assigned, were true, what an opportunity was here offered to exert it! Had he instantly taken refuge in his palace, ordered out all his guards, stopped every avenue to St. james's, and issued his commands that every individual present at this scene should be secured and examined,-who would have dared murmur, or even blame such measures? The insanity of the woman has now fully been proved ; but that noble confidence which gave that instant excuse for her was then all his own.

AGITATION OF THE QUEEN AND PRINCESSES.

Nor did he rest here; notwithstanding the excess of terror for his safety, and doubt of further mischief, with which all his family and all his household were seized, he still maintained the most cheerful composure, and insisted upon walking on the terrace, with no other attendant than his single equerry.

The poor queen went with him, pale and silent,-the princesses followed, scarce yet commanding their tears. In the evening, just as usual, the king had his concert : but it was an evening of grief and horror to his family: nothing was listened to, scarce a word was spoken ; the princesses wept continually; the queen, still more deeply struck, could only, from time to time, hold out her hand to the king, and say, "I have you yet!"

The affection for the king felt by all his household has been at once pleasant and affecting to me to observe : there has not been a dry eye in either of the Lodges, on the recital of his danger, and not a face but his own that has not worn marks of care ever since.

I put off my visit to my dear Mrs. Delany; I was too much horror-struck to see her immediately; and when, at night, I went to her, I determined to spare her the shock of this event till the next day. . . . General Bud`e and Major Price were with Mrs. Schwellenberg at my return; and not a word was uttered by either of them concerning the day's terrific alarm. There seemed nothing but general consternation and silence.

When I went to the queen at night she scarce once opened her lips. Indeed I could not look at her without feeling the tears ready to start into my eyes. But I was very glad to hear again the voice of the king, though only from the next apartment, and calling to one of his dogs.

August 3-The poor queen looked so ill that it was easy to see how miserable had been her night. It is unfortunately the unalterable opinion of Mrs. Schwellenberg that some latent conspiracy belongs to this attempt, and therefore that it will never rest here. This dreadful suggestion preys upon the mind of the queen, though she struggles to conquer or conceal it. I longed passionately this morning, when alone with her, to speak upon the matter, and combat the opinion.; but as she still said nothing, it was not possible.

When she was dressed for the chapel, she desired me to keep little Badine; but he ran out after her: I ran too, and in the gallery, leading from the queen's room to mine, all the princesses, and their governesses, were waiting for the queen. They all looked very ill, the princess royal particularly.—O well indeed might they tremble! for a father more tender, more kind, more amiable, I believe has scarcely ever had daughters to bless. . . .

I then passed on to my own room, which terminates this gallery. But I have since heard it is contrary to rule to pass even the door of an apartment in which any of the royal family happen to be, if it is open. However, these little formalities are all dispensed with to the ignorant - and as I learn better I shall observe them more. I am now obliged to feel and find my way as I can, having no friend, adviser, nor informer in the whole house. Accident only gives me any instruction, and that generally arrives too late to save all error. My whole dependence is upon the character of the queen ; her good sense and strong reason will always prevent the unnecessary offence of ranking mistakes from inexperience, with disrespect or inattention. I have never, therefore, a moment's uneasiness upon these points. Though there is a lady who from time to time represents them as evils the most heinous. [208]

I had afterwards a letter from my poor Mrs. Delany, written with her own hand, and with a pencil, as she is now too indistinct of sight to see even a word. She writes therefore only by memory, and, if with pen and ink, cannot find her place again when she leaves it, to dip the pen in the inkstand.

She had escaped the news at the chapel, but had been told it afterwards by Lady Spencer, lest it should reach her ears in any worse manner. You may imagine how greatly it shocked her.

I ran to answer her note in person, determining, upon such an occasion, to risk appearing before the queen a second time in my morning dress, rather than not satisfy my dear Mrs. Delany by word of mouth. I gave her all the comfort in my power, and raised her agitated spirits by dwelling upon the escape, and slightly passing by the danger.

The queen was so late before her second summons that I was still in time. I found her with her eyes almost swollen out of her head, but more cheerful and easy, and evidently relieved by the vent forced, at length, to her tears.

She now first spoke upon the subject to me; inquiring how Mrs. Delany had borne the hearing it. I told her of the letter sent me in the morning, and half proposed shewing it, as it expressed her feelings beyond the power of any other words. She bowed her desire to see it, and I ran and brought it. She read it aloud, Mrs. Schwellenberg being present, and was pleased and soothed by it.

A PRIVILEGE IS SECURED.

A LITTLE incident happened afterwards that gave me great satisfaction in perspective. While I was drinking coffee with Mrs. Schwellenberg, a message was brought to me, that Mrs. and Miss Heberden[209] desired their compliments, and would come to drink tea with me if I was disengaged.

To drink tea with me! The words made me colour. I hesitated,—I knew not if I might accept such an offer. With regard to themselves, I had little or no interest in it, as they were strangers to me, but with regard to such an opening to future potentiality,—there, indeed, the message acquired consequence. After keeping the man some minutes, I was so much at a loss, still, to know what step I had power to take, that I was induced to apply to Mrs. Schwellenberg, asking her what I must do.

"What you please!" was her answer; and I waited nothing more explicit, but instantly sent back my compliments, and that I should be very glad of their company.

This was a most happy event to me : it first let me know the possibility of receiving a friend in my own room to tea.

They left me before the tea-party assembled in our common room. It was very much crowded, everybody being anxious to hear news of the queen. When they were all gone but Mrs. Delany, Mrs. Schwellenberg made us both very happy by a private communication that the Prince of Wales was actually then in the Lodge, whither he rode post haste, on the first news of the alarm given to the queen.

THE QUEEN CONTINUES ANXIOUS.

Friday, Aug. 4-This was an extremely arduous morning to the poor queen. The king again went to town ; and her anxiety in his absence, and fear how it might end, oppressed her most painfully. She could not take her usual airing. She shut herself up with the Princess Augusta ; but, to avoid any rumours of her uneasiness, the carriage and usual horsemes were all at the door at the customary time ; and the princess royal, attended by the Duchess of Ancaster, went out, and passed, driving quick through the town, for the queen herself, to most of the people.

At her toilette, before dinner, Lady Effingham was admitted. The queen had her newspapers as usual, and she read aloud, while her hair was dressing, several interesting articles concerning the attack, the noble humanity of the king, his presence of mind, and the blessing to the whole nation arising from his preservation. The spirit of loyalty, warmth, and zeal with which all the newspapers are just now filled seemed extremely gratifyin- to her ; she dwelt upon several of the strongest expressions with marked approbation, exclaiming from time to time, as she read particular praises of his majesty's worth and importance, "That is true!- -That is true, indeed!" But suddenly, afterwards, coming upon a paragraph beginning with the words of the coronation anthem, "Long live the king! May the king live for ever!" her tears flowed so fast that they blinded her, and to hear her read such words was so extremely affecting, that I was obliged to steal behind her chair to hide myself; while Lady Effingham took out her handkerchief, and cried in good earnest. I believe her to be warmly and gratefully attached both to the king and queen and she has received from the queen very uncommon assistance, I am informed, in some very distressful Situations.

The queen, however, read on; dispersing her tears as she could, and always smiling through them when the praise, not the danger, drew them forth.

Nothing could be more gracious than her manner to me the whole time - she (lid not, as usual, dismiss me, either for her hair-dressing, or for Lady Effingham; she was sure I must be interested in what was going forward, and she looked at us alternately, for our comments, as she went on.

I rejoiced she had not set me to read these papers. I expected, for the first week, every summons would have ended in a command to read to her. But it never happened, and I was saved an exertion for which I am sure I should have had no voice.

SNUFF PREPARER-IN- CHIEF.

Sunday, Au,-. 6-This morning, before church, Miss Planta was sent to me by the queen, for some snuff, to be mixed as before : when I had prepared it, I carried it, as directed, to her majesty's dressing-room. I turned round the lock, for that, not rapping at the door, is the mode of begging admission; and she called out to me to come in.

I found her reading, aloud, some religious book, but I could not discover what, to the three eldest princesses. Miss Planta was in waiting. She continued after my entrance, only motioning to me that the snuff might be put into a box on the table.

I did not execute my task very expeditiously: for I was glad of this opportunity of witnessing, the maternal piety with which she enforced, in voice and expression, every sentence that contained any lesson that might be useful to her royal daughters. She reads extremely well, with great force, clearness, and meaning.

just as I had slowly finished my commission, the king entered. She then stopped, and rose ; so instantly did the princesses. He had a letter in his hand open: he said something to the queen in German, and they left the room together but he turned round from the door, and first spoke to me, with a good-humoured laugh, saying, "Miss Burney, I hear you cook snuff very well!"

"Cook snuff!" repeated the Princess Augusta, laughing and coming up to me the moment they left the room. "Pray, Miss Burney, let me have one pinch!" The Princess Elizabeth ran up to me, also, exclaiming, "Miss Burney, I hope you hate snuff? I hope you do, for I hate it of all things in the world!"

A SUPPER MYSTERY.

After tea, one of Mrs. Schwellenberg's domestics called me out of the room. John waited to speak to me in the gallery. "What time, ma'am," cried he, "shall you have your Supper?"

"What supper?" cried I. "I only eat fruit, as usual."

"Have not you ordered supper, ma'am, for to-night?

"No."

"There is one cooking for you—a fowl and peas."

"It's some great mistake; run down and tell them so."

I returned to the company, and would have related the adventure, had I been in spirits; but voluntary speech escaped me not. Where I am not happy, or forced to it, it never does. Presently I was called out again.

"Ma'am," cried John, "the supper is ordered in your name. I saw the order—the clerk of the kitchen gave it in."

This was the most ridiculous thing I ever heard. I desired him to run down forthwith, and inquire by whose directions all this was done. He came back, and said, "By Sir Francis Drake's." Sir Francis Drake is, I think, steward of the housebold. I then desired John to interfere no more, but let the matter be pursued in their own way.

As soon as the company was gone, all but a Miss Mawer, who is on a visit to Mrs. Schwellenberg, I told my tale. Mrs.Schwellenberg said the orders had been hers, that a hot supper belonged to my establishment, and that sometimes she might come and eat it with me.

I had now not a word to add. At ten o'clock both she and Miss Mawer accompanied me to my room. Miss Mawer is an old maid; tall, thin, sharp-featured, hurrying and disagreeable in her manner, but, I believe, good-natured and good-hearted, from all I have observed in her. The smell of the meat soon grew offensive to Mrs. Schwellenberg, who left me with Miss Mawer. As I never eat any myself at night, all I could devise to make the perfume tolerable was to consider it as an oppor'tunity for a lesson in carving: so I went to work straightforward to mangle my unbidden guest, for the use and service of Miss Mawer.

Soon after, I was delighted and surprised by the entrance of Mrs. Delany, ushered to my room by Major Price. The concert being over, and the royal family retired to supper, she would not go away without seeing me. I thanked the major for bringing me so sweet a guest, but I almost fear he expected to be invited in with her. I am sure I could have had nothing but pleasure from his joining us; but I had made a rule, on my thus first setting up for myself, to invite no man whatsoever, young, old, married, single, acquaintance or stranger, till I knew precisely the nature of my own situation : for I had been warned by an excellent friend, Mrs. de Luc, on my first entrance into office that there was no drawing back in a place such as this; and that therefore I ought studiously to keep back, till I felt my way, and knew, experimentally, what I could do, and what I should wish to leave alone. This advice has been of singular use to me, in a thousand particulars, from the very first to the present day of my abode in this Lodge.

LITTLE PRINCESs AMELIA's BIRTHDAY.

Monday, Aug. 7-This has been the first cheerful day since the memorable and alarming attack of the 2nd of August. It was the birthday of the little Princess Amelia : and the fond ness of the whole family for that lovely child, and her own infantine enjoyment of the honours paid her, have revived the spirits of the whole house.

The manner of keeping the birth-days here is Very simple. All the royal family are new-dressed; so—at least so they appear- -are all their attendants. The dinners and desserts are unusually sumptuous ; and some of the principal officers of state, and a few of the ladies of the Court, come to Windsor to make their compliments; and at night there is a finer concert, by an addition from town of the musicians belonging to the queen's band. If the weather is fine, all the family walk upon the Terrace, which is crowded with people of distinction, who take that mode of showing respect, to avoid the trouble and fatigue of attending at the following Drawing-room.

Another method, too, which is taken to express joy and attachment upon these occasions, is by going to the eight o'clock prayers at the royal chapel. The congregation all assemble, after the service, in the opening at the foot of the great stairs which the royal family descend from their gallery, and there those who have any pretensions to notice scarce ever fail to meet with it.

To-day, this staircase Drawing-room, as it is named by Major Price, was very much crowded; and it was a sweet sight to me, from my windows, to see that the royal group-respectfully followed by many people of distinction, who came on the occasion, and, at a still greater distance, encircled by humbler, but not less loyal congratulators-had their chief attention upon my dear, aged, venerable Mrs. Delany, who was brought in by the king and queen, to partake with them the birth-day breakfast.

In the evening, for the first time since my arrival, I went upon the Terrace, under the wing and protection of my dear Mrs. Delany, who was tempted to walk there herself, in order to pay her respects on the little princess's birth-day. She was carried in her chair to the foot of the steps. Mrs. Delany was desirous to save herself for the royal encounter : she thereFore sat down on the first seat till the royal party appeared 'In sight: we then, of course, stood up.

It was really a mighty pretty procession. The little princess, just turned of three years old, in a robe-coat covered with fine muslin, a dressed close cap, white gloves, and a fan, walked on alone and first, highly delighted in the parade, and turning from side to side to see everybody as she passed : for all the terracers stand up against the walls, to make a clear passage for the royal family, the moment they come in sight. Then followed the king and queen, no less delighted themselves with the joy of their little darling. The princess royal, leaning on Lady Elizabeth Waldegrave, followed at a little distance. This princess, the second female in the kingdom, shews, I think, more marked respect and humility towards the king and queen than any of the family.

Next the Princess Augusta, holding by the Duchess of Ancaster; and next the Princess Elizabeth, holding by Lady Charlotte Bertie. Office here takes place of rank, which occasioned Lady Elizabeth Waldegrave, as lady of her bedchamber, to walk with the princess royal.

Then followed the Princess Mary with Miss Goldsworthy, and the Princess Sophia with Mademoiselle Monmoulin and Miss Planta then General Bud`e and the Duke of Montagu and, lastly, Major Price, who, as equerry, always brings up the rear, walks at a distance from the group, and keeps off all crowd from the royal family.

On sight of Mrs. Delany, the king instantly stopped to speak to her. The queen, of course, and the little princess, and all the rest, stood still, in their ranks. They talked a good while with the sweet old lady; during which time the king once or twice addressed himself to me. I caught the queen's eye, and saw in it a little surprise, but by no means any displeasure, to see me of the party.

The little princess went up to Mrs. Delany, of whom she is very fond, and behaved like a little angel to her: she then, with a look of inquiry and recollection, slowly, of her own accord, came behind Mrs. Delany to look at me.

"I am afraid," said I, in a whisper, and stooping down, "your royal highness does not remember me?"

What think you was her answer? An arch little smile, and a nearer approach, with her lips pouted out to kiss me. I could not resist so innocent an invitation, but the moment I had accepted it, I was half afraid it might seem, in so public a place, an improper liberty: however, there was no help for it. she then took my fan, and, having looked at it on both sides, gravely returned it me, saying, "O! a brown fan!"

The king and queen then bid her curtsey to Mrs. Delany which she did most gracefully, and they all moved on; each of the princesses speaking to Mrs. Delany as they passed, and condescending to curtsey to her companion.

THE CIPHER BECOMES A NUMBER.

Mrs. Delany was too much fatigued to return to the Lodge to tea; but Mrs. Fielding and her three daughters, L ord Courtown, Mr. Fisher, the general, and the major, made up our set.

Mrs. Schwellenberg was very ill. She declined making tea, and put it into the hands of' the general. I had always kept back from that office, as well as from presiding at the table, that I might keep the more quiet, and be permitted to sit silent; which, at first, was a repose quite necessary to my depressed state of spirits, and which, as they grew better, I found equally necessary to keep off the foul fiends of Jealousy and Rivalry in my colleague; who, apparently, never wishes to hear my voice but when we are t`ete-`a-t`ete, and then never is in good-humour when it is at rest. I could not, however, see this feminine occupation in masculine hands, and not, for shame, propose taking it upon myself. The general readily relinquished it, and I was fain to come forth and do the honours.

Lord Courtown sat himself next me, and talked with me the whole time, in well-bred and pleasant discourse. The Major waited upon me as assiduously as if he had been as much my equerry as the king's, and all went smooth, well, and naturally, except that the poor sick lady grew evidently less and less pleased with the arrangement of things, and less and less in humour with its arrangers: so obvious, indeed, was the displeasure that the cipher should become a number, that had my own mind been easy, I should have felt much vexed to observe what a curb was placed over me: for hitherto, except when she had been engaged herself, and only to Major Price and Mr. Fisher, that cipher had "word spoke never one." 'Tis wonderful, my dearest Susan, what wretched tempers are to be met with—wretched in and to themselves— wretched to and for all that surround them. However, while only to be Stupid and silent will do, we shall not be at variance. Were I happier, perhaps I might comply with more difficulty; so be not sorry, my Susan, nor you, my sweet Fredy, if, bye-and-bye, You should hear me complain. It will be a very good sign.

DISPLAY OF LOYALTY AT LITTLE KEW.

Aug. 8.-An exceedingly pretty scene was exhibited to-day to their majesties.

We came, as usual on every alternate Tuesday, to Kew. The queen's Lodge is at the end of a long meadow, surrounded with houses, which is called Kew green ; and this was quite filled with all the inhabitants of the place— the lame, old, blind, sick, and infants, who all assembled, dressed in their Sunday garb, to line the sides of the roads through which their majesties passed, attended by a band of musicians, arranged in the front, who began "God save the King!" the moment they came upon the green, and finished it with loud huzzas. This was a compliment at the expense of the better inhabitants, who paid the musicians themselves, and mixed in with the group, which indeed left not a soul, I am told, in any house in the place.

This testimony of loyal.satisfaction in the king's safe return, after the attempted assassination, affected the queen to tears : nor were they shed alone; for almost everybody's flowed that witnessed the scene. The queen, speaking of it afterwards, said,

"O! I shall always love little Kew for this!"

MISS BERNAR, THE QUEEN WILL GIVE YOU A GOWN.

At the second toilette to-day, Mrs. Schwellenberg, who left the dressing-room before me, called out at the door, "Miss Bernar, when you have done from the queen, come to my room."

There was something rather more peremptory in the order than was quite pleasant to me, and I rather drily answered, "Very well, Mrs. Schwellenberg."

The queen was even uncommonly sweet and gracious in her manner after this lady's departure, and kept me with her some time after she was dressed. I never go rom her presence till I am dismissed; no one does, not even when they come in only with a hurried message,—except the pages, who enter merely as messengers, and Mrs. Schwellenberg, whose place and illness together have given her that privilege.

The general form of the dismission, which you may perhap's be curious to hear, is in these words, "Now I Will let You go," which the queen manages to speak with a grace that takes from them all air of authority.

At first, I must confess, there was something inexpressibly awkward to me, in waiting to be told to go, instead of watching an opportunity, as elsewhere, for taking leave before I thought myself de trop: but I have since found that this is, to me, a mark of honour; as it is the established custom to people of the first rank, the princesses themselves included, and only not used to the pages and the wardrobe-women, who are supposed only to enter for actual business, and therefore to retire when it is finished, without expectation of being detained to converse, or beyond absolute necessity.

I give you all these little details of interior royalty, because they are curious, from opening a new scene of life, and can only be really known by interior residence.

When I went to Mrs. Schwellenberg, she said, "You might know I had something to say to you, by my calling you before the queen." She then proceeded to a long prelude, which I could but ill comprehend, save that it conveyed much of obligation on my part, and favour on hers; and then ended with, "I might tell you now, the queen is going to Oxford, and you might go with her; it is a secret—you might not tell it nobody. But I tell you once, I shall do for you what I can; you are to have a gown."

I stared, and drew back, with a look so undisguised of wonder and displeasure at this extraordinary speech, that I saw it was understood, and she then thought it time, therefore, to name her authority, which with great emphasis, she did thus: "The queen will give you a gown! The queen says you are not rich," etc.

There Was something in the manner of this quite intolerable to me, and I hastily interrupted her with saying, "I have two new gowns by me, and therefore do not require another."

Perhaps a proposed present from her majesty was never so received before; but the grossness of the manner of the messenger swallowed up the graciousness of the design in the principal: and I had not even a wish to conceal how little it was to my taste.

The highest surprise sat upon her brow; she had imagined that a gown—that any present-would have been caught at with obsequious avidity,—but indeed she was mistaken.

Seeing the wonder and displeasure now hers, I calmly added, "The queen is very good, and I am very sensible of her majesty's graciousness; but there is not, in this instance, the least occasion for it."

"Miss Bernar," cried she, quite angrily, "I tell you once, when the queen will give you a gown, you must be humble, thankful, when you are Duchess of Ancaster."

She then enumerated various ladies to whom her majesty had made the same present, many of them of the first distinction, and all, she said, great secrets. Still I only repeated again the same speech.

I can bear to be checked and curbed in discourse, and would rather be subdued into silence-and even, if that proves a gratification that secures peace and gives pleasure, into apparent insensibility ; but to receive a favour through the vehicle of insolent ostentation—no! no! To submit to ill humour rather than argue and dispute I think an exercise of patience, and I encourage myself all I can to practice it : but to accept even a shadow of an obligation upon such terms I should think mean and unworthy ; and therefore I mean always, in a Court as I would elsewhere, to be open and fearless in declining such subjection.

When she had finished her list of secret ladies, I told her I must beg to speak to the queen, and make my own acknowledgments for her gracious intention.

This she positively forbid ; and said it must only pass through her hands. "When I give you the gown," she added, "I will tell you when you may make your curtsey."

I was not vexed at this prohibition, not knowing what etiquette I might offend by breaking it; and the conversation concluded with nothing being settled.

How little did the sweet queen imagine that this her first mark of favour should so be offered me as to raise in me my first spirit of resistance ! How differently would she have executed her own commission herself! To avoid exciting jealousy was, I doubt not, her motive for employing another.

A CROWDED DRAWING-ROOM.

Aug. 10.-I journeyed to town, with Mrs. Schwellenberg and Miss Planta; and this morning I was employed for the first time on a message to the queen. I was in the ante-room, when Mr. Nicolay, her majesty's page at St. James's, came and told me the Duchess of Ancaster sent her humble duty to the queen, and begged an audience before the Drawing-room. I told the queen, who, when dressed, all but her necklace, received the duchess in the ante-room.

I mention all these little ceremonies as they occur, that hereafter I may have no occasion, when they lead to other matters,, to explain them.

The bedchamber woman was rung for on the queen's return. So you see I am not the only one to answer a bell. It was Mrs. Fielding, who looked at me with an attention that will not leave her much in doubt as to my dress, at least, though she could not speak. I have told you, I believe, that no one, not even the princesses, ever speak in the presence of the king and queen, but to answer what is immediately said by themselves. There are, indeed, occasions in which this is set aside, from particular encouragement given at the moment; but it is not less a rule, and it is one very rarely infringed.

When the Drawing-room began, I went to my own room and there I had the great happiness of finding my father, who had contrived to be in town purposely, and to whom I had sent John, in St. Martin's-street, that he might be shown the straight way to my apartment. He had determined upon going to the Drawing-room himself, to manifest, amongst the general zeal of the times, his loyal joy in his majesty's safety.

The drawing-room was over very late indeed. So anxious has been the whole nation to show their affectionate attachment to the king, that this, the first Drawing-room since his danger, was as splendid, and as much crowded, as upon a birthday. When the queen summoned me, upon returning to her dressing-room, and mentioned how full and how hot it had been, I ventured to say, " I am very glad of it, ma'am; it was an honest crowd to-day."

THE KEEPER OF THE ROBES IS VERY MUCH PUT OUT.

At tea I found a new uniform. Major Price, immediately introduced me to him; he was Colonel Fairly. [210]He is a man of the most scrupulous good-breeding, diffident, gentle, and sentimental in his conversation, and assiduously attentive in his manners. He married Lady ——, and I am told he is a most tender husband to her.

A very unfortunate subject happened to be started during our tea; namely, the newspaper attacks upon Mrs. Hastings. The colonel, very innocently, said he was very sorry that lady was ever mentioned in the same paragraph with her majesty. Mrs. Schwellenberg indignantly demanded "Why?—where?—when? and what?"

Unconscious of her great friendship for Mrs. Hastings, the colonel, unfortunately, repeated his concern, adding, "Nothing has hurt me so much as the queen's being ever named in such company."

The most angry defence was now made, but in so great a storm. of displeasure, and confusion of language, that the colonel, looking utterly amazed, was unable to understand what was the matter. Major Price and myself were both alarmed; Miss Port longed to laugh; Miss Mawer sat perfectly motionless; Mrs. Fisher decidedly silent. No one else was present. The colonel, whenever he could be heard, still persisted in his assertion, firmly, though gently, explaining the loyalty of his motives.

This perseverance increased the storm, which now blew with greater violence, less and less distinct as more fierce. Broken sentences were all that could be articulated. "You might not say such thing!"—"Upon my vord!"—"I tell you once!"—"colonel what-you-call, I am quite warm!"—"Upon my vord!—I tell you the same!"—"You might not tell me such thing!"—"What for you say all that?"

As there was nothing in this that could possibly clear the matter, and the poor colonel only sunk deeper and deeper, by not understanding the nature of his offence, Major Price now endeavoured to interfere ; and, as he is a great favourite, he was permitted not only to speak, but to be heard.

"Certainly," said he, "those accounts about Mrs. Hastings, and the history of her divorce, are very unpleasant anecdotes in public newspapers; and I am sorry, too, that they should be told in the same paragraph that mentions her being received by the queen."

Nothing could equal the consternation with which. this unexpected speech was heard. "Upon my vord! You sorprise me!" was all that could now be got out.

As I found them now only running further from general comprehension, I felt so sorry that poor Mrs. Hastings, whom I believe to be a most injured woman, should so ill be defended even by her most zealous friend, that I compelled myself to the exertion of coming forward, now, in her behalf myself, and I therefore said, it was a thousand pities her story should' not be more accurately made known: as the mode of a second marriage from a divorce was precisely the contrary here of what it was in Germany; since here it could only take place upon misconduct, and there, I had been told, a divorce from misconduct prohibited a second marriage, which could only be permitted where the divorce was the mere effect of disagreement from dissimilar tempers. Mrs. Hastings, therefore, though acquitted of ill-behaviour by the laws of her own country seemed, by those of England, convicted; and I could not but much regret that her vindication was not publicly made by this explanation.

"So do I, too," cried Major Price "for I never heard this before."

"Nor I," cried the colonel "and indeed it ought to be made known, both for the sake of Mrs. Hastings, and because she has been received at Court, which gave everybody the greatest surprise, and me, in my ignorance, the greatest concern, on account of the queen."

This undid all again, though my explanation had just stilled the hurricane; but now it began afresh.

"You might not say that, Colonel Fairly; you might not name the queen!— O, I can't bear it!—I tell you once it is too moch!— What for you tell me that?"

"Ma'am, I—I only said—It is not me, ma'am, but the newspapers."

"What for you have such newspapers?—I tell you the same—it is- -what you call—I don't like such thing!"

"But, ma'am—"

"O, upon my vord, I might tell you once, when you name the queen, it is— what you call—I can't bear it!—when it is nobody else, with all my heart! I might not care for that—but when it is the queen,—I tell you the same, Colonel Fairly—it makes me—what you call—perspire."

The major again interfered, saying it was now all cleared up, by the account of the difference of the German customs, and therefore that it was all very well. A certain quiet, but yet decisive way, in which he sometimes speaks, was here very successful ; and as the lady stopped, the colonel saw all explanation too desperate to aim at further argument.

---

203   Dr. Burney's daughter by his second wife-ED.

204   Sir Thomas Clarges, whose wife was a dear friend of Susan Burney. Sir Thomas died in December, 1782. In the "Early Diary" he is mentioned once or twice, as a visitor at Dr. Burney's. Fanny writes of him in May, 1775, as "a young baronet, who was formerly so desperately enamoured of Miss Linley, now Mrs. Sheridan, that his friends made a point of his going abroad to recover himself: he is now just returned from italy, and I hope cured. He still retains all the schoolboy English mauvaise honte; scarce speaks but to make an answer, and is as shy as if his last residence had been at Eton instead of Paris.-ED.

205   'Tis amazing what nonsense sensible people can write, when their heads are turned by cunsiderations of rank and flummery!-ED.

206   The wife of Warren Hastings. Fanny had made the acquaintince of Mr. and Mrs. Hastings from her friend Mr. Cambridge, some months previously. (See note [201], ante, P. 327.-ED.

207   The name of the poor woman was Margaret Nicholson. She was, of course, insane, and had, a few days previously, presented a petition, which had probably been left unread at the time, but which turned out on investigation to be full of incoherent nonsense. On her examination before the Privy Council she declared that "the crown was hers, and that if she had not her rights England would be deluged with blood." She was ultimately consigned to Bedlam.-ED.

208   Fanny's bitter experience of Mrs. Schwellenberg is now commencing.-ED.

209   The wife and daughter of Dr. William Heberden, an eminent physician, and author of "Medical Commentaries on the History and Cure of Disease." Fanny had met these ladies recently at Mrs. Delany's-ED.

210   "Colonel Fairly" is the name given in the "Diary" to the Hon. Stephen Digby. His first wife, Lady Lucy Strangwayes Fox, youngest daughter of Lord Ilchester, died in 1787. He married, in 1790, Miss Gunning, "Miss Fuzilier," of the "Diary."—ED.

SECTION 8 (1786)

ROYAL VISIT TO NUNEHAM, OXFORD AND BLENHEIM.
A JOB'S COMFORTER.

AUG. 12, Saturday.The Prince of Wales's birthday. How I grieve at whatever may be the cause which absents him from his family!—a family of so much love, harmony, and excellence, that to mix with them, even rarely, must have been the first of lessons to his heart; and here, I am assured, his heart is good, though, elsewhere, his conduct renders it so suspicious.

I come now to the Oxford expedition.

The plan was to spend one day at Lord Harcourt's, at Nuneham, one at Oxford, and one at Blenheim; dining and sleeping always at Nuneham.

I now a little regretted that I had declined meeting Lady Harcourt, when invited to see her at Mrs. Vesey's about three years ago. I was not, just then, very happy—and I was surfeited of new acquaintances; when the invitation, therefore, came, I sent an excuse. But now when I was going to her house, I wished I had had any previous knowledge of her, to lessen the difficulties of my first appearance in my new character, upon attending the queen on a visit. I said something of this sort to Mrs. Schwellenberg, in our conversation the day before the journey ; and she answered that it did not signify for, as I went with the queen, I might be sure I should be civilly treated.

Yes, I said, I generally had been; and congratulated myself that at least I knew a little of Lord Harcourt, to whom I had been introduced, some years ago, at Sir Joshua Reynolds', and whom I had since met two or three times. "O," she said, "it is the same,—that is nothing,—when you go With the queen, it is enough; they might be civil to you for that sake. You might go quite without no, what you call, fuss; you might take no gown but what you go in:—that is enough,—you might have no servant,—for what?—You might keep on your riding-dress. There is no need you might be seen. I shall do everything that I can to assist you to appear for nobody."

I leave you to imagine my thanks. But the news about the servant was not very pleasant, as I thought it most likely I could never more want one than in a strange house added to a strange situation. However, I determined upon assuming no competition in command, and therefore I left the matter to her own direction.

THE JOURNEY To NUNEHAM: UNGRACious RECEPTION.

Their majesties went to Nuneham to breakfast. Miss Planta and myself were not to follow till after an early dinner. Princess Elizabeth, in a whisper, after the rest left the room,- advised me to go and lie down again as soon as they were gone. And, indeed, I was sufficiently fatigued to be glad to follow the advice.

My dear Mrs. Delany came to sit with me while I packed up. What a pleasure to rne is her constant society, and the reciprocal confidence of all our conversations ! She intrusts me with every thing in the world-I intrust her with every thing that now happens to me.

Our early dinner was with Mrs. Schwellenberg and Miss Mawer. We set out at three o'clock, and took with us Mrs. Thielky, the queen's wardrobe woman, and the comfort of my life in the absence of Mrs. Schwellenberg, for she is the real acting person, though I am the apparent one : and she is also a very good sort of woman,-plain, sensible, clear-headed, mild-mannered, sedate, and steady. I found her in this journey of infinite service, for she not only did almost every thing for the queen, but made it her business to supply also the place of maid to me, as much as ever I would suffer her. How fortunate for me that the person so immediately under me should be so good a creature ! The other person we took was a Miss

Mhaughendorf, a dresser to the Princesses Royal and Augusta, a very pleasing young woman, gentle and in teresting, who is just come from the king ,s German dominions to this place, to which she has been recommended by her father, who is clerk of the kitchen to the Duke of York. The princesses have a German in this office, to assist their study of that language, which, in their future destinations, may prove essential to them.

Miss Planta's post in the Court-calendar is that of English teacher, but it seems to me, that of personal attendant upon the two eldest princesses. She is with them always when they sup, work, take their lessons, or walk.

We arrived at Nunebam at about six o'clock. The house is one of those straggling, half new, half old, half comfortable, and half forlorn mansions, that are begun in one generation and finished in another. It is very pleasantly situated, and commands, from some points of view, all the towers of Oxford.

In going across the park to the entrance, we saw not a creature. All were busy, either in attendance upon the royal guests, or in finding hiding-places from whence to peep at them. We stopped at the portico,-but not even a porter was there : we were obliged to get out of the carriage by the help of one of the postilions, and to enter the house by the help of wet grass, which would not suffer me to stay out of it, otherwise, I felt so strange in going in uninvited and unconducted, that I should have begged leave to stroll about till somebody appeared.

Miss Planta, more used to these expeditions, though with quite as little taste for them, led the way, and said we had best go and seek for our rooms. I was quite of the same opinion, but much at a loss how we might find them. We went through various passages, unknowing whither they might lead us, till at length we encountered a prodigious fine servant. Miss Planta, asked him for Lady Harcourt's maid; he bowed slightly, and passed on without making any answer.

Very pleasant this!—I then begged we might turn back, not caring for another adventure of the same sort. Miss Planta complied; and we met two more of the yellow-laced saunterers, with whom she had precisely the same success.

I think I never remember to have felt so much shame from my situation as at that time. To arrive at a house where no mistress nor master of it cared about receiving me; to wander about, a guest uninvited, a visitor unthought of; without even a room to go to, a person to inquire for, or even a servant to speak to! It was now I felt the real want of either a man or maid, to send forward, and find out what we were to do with ourselves ; and indeed I resolved, then, I would not another time be so passive to unauthorized directions.

The fault of this strange reception was certainly in the lady of the house, whose affair it was to have given orders, previous to our arrival, that some of her people should shew us to whatever apartment she destined for us. The queen herself had sent word that we were to attend her; and however impossible it was that she could receive us herself, which her own attendance upon their majesties made really impracticable, it was incumbent upon her to have taken care that we should not have been utterly neglected.

We strayed thus, backwards and forwards, for a full quarter of an hour, in these nearly deserted straggling passages ; and then, at length, met a French woman, whom Miss Planta immediately seized upon : it was Lady Harcourt's woman, and Miss Planta had seen her at Windsor.

"Pray shew us," cried Miss Planta, "where we are to go."

She was civil, and led us to a parlour looking very pleasantly upon the park, and asked if we would have some tea. Miss Planta assented. She told us the king and queen were in the park, and left us. As there was a garden-door to this room, I thought it very possible the royal party and their suite might return to the house that way. This gave great addition to my discomposure, for I thought that to see them all in this forlorn plight would be still the worst part of the business,- I therefore pressed Miss Planta to let us make another attempt to discover our own rooms.

Miss Planta laughed exceedingly at my disturbance, but complied very obligingly with my request. In this our second wandering forth we had no better success than in the first; we either met nobody, or only were crossed by such superfine men in laced liveries, that we attempted not to question them. My constant dread was Of meeting any of the royal party, while I knew not whither to run. Miss Planta, more inured to such situations, was not at all surprised by our difficulties and disgraces, and only diverted by my distress from them.

We met at last with Mhaughendorf, and Miss Planta eagerly desired to be conducted to the princesses' rooms, that she might see if every thing was prepared for them. When they had looked at the apartments destined for the princesses, Miss Planta proposed our sitting down to our tea in the Princess Elizabeth's room. This was extremely disagreeable to me, as I was sensible it must seem a great freedom from me, should her royal highness surprise us there; but it was no freedom for Miss Planta, as she had belonged to all the princesses these nine years, and is eternally in their sight. I could not, therefore, persuade her of the difference ; and she desired Mhaughendorf to go and order our tea upstairs.

A HASTY INTRODUCTION To LADY HARCOURT.

Miss Planta, followed by poor me, then whisked backwards and forwards, from one of the apartments to another, superintending all the preparations; and, as we were crossing a landing-place, a lady appeared upon the stairs, and Miss

Planta called out "It's Lady Harcourt," and ran down to meet her.

They talked together a few minutes. "I must get you, Miss Planta," said she, looking up towards me, "to introduce me to Miss Burney."

She then came up the stairs, said she was glad to see me, and desired I would order any thing I wanted, either for the queen or for myself. Cold enough was my silent curtsey.

She talked again to Miss Planta, who, already knowing her, from seeing her frequently when in waiting, as she is one of the ladies of the bedchamber, was much more sociable than myself. She afterwards turned to me, and said, "If there is anything you want, Miss Burney, pray speak for it." And she added, "My sisters will attend you presently;—you will excuse me,-I have not a moment from their majesties." And then she curtseyed, and left us.

We returned to the Princess Elizabeth's room, and there the tea followed, but not the promised sisters. I never saw Miss Planta laugh so heartily before nor since; but my dismay was possibly comical to behold.

APPARITION OF THE PRINCESSES.

The tea was just poured out, when the door opened, and in entered all the princesses. I was very much ashamed, and started up, but had no asylum whither to run. They all asked us how we did after our journey; and I made an apology, as well as I could, to the Princess Elizabeth, for my intrusion into her apartment - confessing I did not know where to find my own.

The princess royal, eagerly coming up to me, said, "I thought you would be distressed at first arriving, and I wanted to help you; and I enquired where your room was, and said I would look at it myself ; and I went round to it, but I found the king was that way, and so, you know, I could not go past him; but indeed I wished to have seen it for you."

There was hardly any thanking her for such infinite sweetness ;-they then desired us to go on with our tea, and went into the princess royal's room.

I was now a little revived ; and soon after the Princess Elizabeth came back, and asked if we had done, desiring us at the same time not to hurry.

Yes, we said; and ashamed of thus keeping possession of her room, I was gliding out, when she flew to me, and said, " "Don't go!— pray come and stay with me a little." She then flew to another end of the room, and getting a chair, brought it herself close up to me, and seating herself on another, said, "Come, sit down by me, Miss Burney."

You may suppose how I resisted and apologised,-truly telling her that I had not opposed her royal highness's design, from being ashamed of even suspecting it. She only laughed good-humouredly, and made me take the chair she had thus condescended to fetch me. . . . In a very few minutes, the other princesses - came for her. The princess royal then told me she was quite sorry to hear we had been so much distressed —and I found Miss Plantabad recounted our adventures.

I was not glad of this, though greatly gratified by the goodness of the princess. But I know how quickly complaints circulate, and I wish not even for redress by such means, which commonly, when so obtained, is more humiliating than the offence which calls for it.

FROM PILLAR TO POST.

When the princesses left us, we were again at a loss what to do with ourselves ; we saw several passing servants, maids as well as men, and Miss Planta applied to them all to shew me my room, which I was anxious to inhabit in peace and solitude: however, they all promised to send, some one else, but no one came. Miss Planta, in the midst of the diversion she received from my unavailing earnestness to get into some retreat, had the good-nature to say, "I knew how this would turn out, and wished the visit over before it began ; but it must really be very new to you, unused as you are to it, and accustomed to so much attention in other places."

At length she seized upon a woman servant, who undertook to conduct me to this wished-for room. Miss Planta accompanied me, and off we set. In descending the stairs, a door opened which led to one of the state rooms, in which were the royal family. We glided softly past ; but the princess royal, attended by the Duchess of Ancaster, came out to us. We soon found her royal highness had told our tale. "Miss Vernons," said the duchess, "will come to take care of you; you must both go and take possession of the eating-parlour, where you will sup; and the equerries will be of your party."

I said not a word, but of general thanks, still longing only to go to my own room. I whispered this to Miss Planta, who obligingly, though rather reluctantly, consented to pursue our first scheme. But when the duchess observed that we were turning off, she called out, "I see you do not know your way, so I'll come and show you to the eating-parlour." The princess royal said she would come with us also; and., according to direction, we were therefore necessitated to proceed.

When we got to the hall leading to this parlour, we were suddenly stopped by the appearance of the king, who just then came out of that very room. Lord Harcourt attended with a candle in his hand, and a group of gentlemen followed. We were advanced too far to retreat, and therefore only stood still. The king stopped, and spoke to the Duchess of Ancaster; and then spoke very graciously to Miss Planta and me, inquiring when we set out, and what sort of journey we had had. He then ascended the stairs, the princess royal accompanying him, and all the rest following; the duchess first pointing to the door of the eating-parlour, and bidding us go there and expect Miss Vernons.

Lord Harcourt, during this meeting, had contrived to slip behind the king, to make me a very civil bow; and when his majesty moved on, he slid nearer me, and whispered a welcome to his house in very civil terms. This was all he could do, so situated.

We now entered the eating-room. We sat down,—but no Miss Vernons! Presently the door opened,-I hoped they were coming,— but a clergyman, a stranger to us both, appeared. This gentleman, I afterwards found, was Mr. Hagget, chaplain to Lord Harcourt, and rector of a living in his lordship's gift and neighbourhood ; a young man, sensible, easy, and remarkably handsome, in very high favour with all the family. With nobody to introduce us to each other, we could but rise and bow, and curtsey, and sit down again.

In a few minutes, again the door gave hopes to me of Miss Vernons ;-but there only appeared a party of gentlemen. Major Price came foremost, and immediately introduced me to General Harcourt. The general is a very shy man, with an air of much haughtiness ; he bowed and retreated, and sat down, and was wholly silent. Colonel Fairly followed him, and taking a chair next mine, began some of the civilest speeches imaginable, concerning this opportunity of making acquaintance with me. just then came in a housemaid, and said she would show me my room. I rose hastily. Miss Planta, who knew everybody present except the clergyman, was now willing to have sat still and chatted ; but nothing short of compulsion Could have kept me in such a situation, and therefore I instantly accompanied the maid; and poor Miss Planta could not stay behind. The truth is the non-appearance of any of the ladies of the house struck me as being so extremely uncivil, that I desired nothing but to retire from all the party.

I felt quite relieved when I once took possession of a room that, for the time, I might call my own; and I could not possibly listen to Miss Planta's desire of returning to the company. I told her frankly that it was a situation so utterly disagreeable to me, that I must beg to decline placing myself in it again. She was afraid, she said, that, as the Duchess of Ancaster had taken the trouble to show us the room, and to tell us what to do, in the presence of the princess royal, the queen might hear of our absconding, and not be pleased with it.

"I must risk that," I answered - "I shall openly tell my reasons, If questioned, and I firmly believe they will be satisfactory, If not questioned, I shall say nothing ; and indeed I very much wish you would do the same."

She agreed,—consented, rather—and I was the more obliged to her from seeing it was contrary to her inclination. I was sorry, but I could not compliment at the expense of putting myself again into a situation I had been so earnest to change. Miss Planta bore it very well, and only wished the maid farther for never finding us out till we began to be comfortable without her.

"THE EQUERRIES WANT THE LADIES."

Here we remained about two hours, unsummoned, unnoticed, unoccupied,-except in forcing open a box which Mrs. Thielky had lent me for my wardrobe, and of which I had left the key, ingeniously, at Windsor. At ten o'clock a maid caine to the door, and said supper was ready.

"Who sent you?" I called out.

"Who do you come from?" cried Miss Planta.

She was gone;—we could get no answer. About a quarter of an hour after, one of those gentlemen footmen, for whom you must already have discovered my partiality, called out, from the stairs, without troubling himself to come to the door, "The supper waits."

He was already gone; but Miss Planta darted after him, calling out, "Who sent you?—who did you come to?"

She was not heard by this gentleman, but what she said was echoed after him by some other, and the answer that reached our ears was, "The equerries want the ladies."

This was enough; Miss Planta returned quite indignant, after hastily replying, "We don't choose any supper."

We were now precisely of an opinion. Miss Planta, indeed, was much more angry than myself; for I was very sure the equerries had sent a very different message, and therefore thought nothing of the words used by the servant, but confined all my dissatisfaction to its first origin,—the incivility of the ladies of the house, that they came not themselves, or some one from them, to invite us in a manner that might be accepted. From this time, however, we became more comfortable, as absconding was our mutual desire; and we were flung, by this means, into a style of sociability we might else never have arrived at.

We continued together till Miss Planta thought it right to go and see if Mhaughendorf had prepared every thing for the princesses; and then I was left to myself-the very companion I just at that time most wished a t`ete-`a-t`ete with—till I was summoned to the queen. In this t`ete-`a-t`ete, I determined very concisely upon my plan of procedure: which was to quietly keep my own counsel, unless I found my conduct disapproved - and, in that case, to run all risks in openly declaring that I must always prefer solitude to society upon terms to which I was unaccustomed.

SUMMONED TO THE QUEEN.

A LITTLE after the scenes I have described, I was surprised when, late at night, my summons was brought me by Lady Harcourt, who tapped gently at my door, and made me 'a little visit, previously to telling me her errand. She informed me, also, that the queen had given her command, for Miss Planta 'and me to belong to the suite the next day, in the visit to Oxford; and that a carriage was accordingly ordered for us.

The queen said not a word to me of the day's adventures and I was glad to have them passed over, especially as Lady Harcourt's visit, and the civility which accompanied it, appeared a little conscious of remissness. But when, in speaking of Oxford, her majesty condescended to ask what gown I had brought with me, how did I rejoice to answer, a new chamberry gauze, instead of only that which I have on, according to my Cerbera's advice.

My next difficulty was for a hair-dresser. Nuneham is three or four miles from Oxford; and I had neither maid to dress nor man to seek a dresser. I could only apply to Mrs. Thielky, and she made it her business to prevail with one of the royal footmen to get me a messenger, to order a hair-dresser from Oxford at six o'clock in the morning. The queen, with most gracious consideration, told me, over night, that she should not want me till eight o'clock.

Thus ended the first night of this excursion.

Aug. 13.-At six o'clock my hair-dresser, to my great satisfaction, arrived. Full two hours was he at work, yet was I not finished, when Swarthy, the queen's hair-dresser, came rapping at my door to tell me her majesty's hair was done, and she was waiting for me. I hurried as fast as I could, and ran down without any cap. She smiled at sight of my hasty attire, and said I should not be distressed about a hair-dresser the next day, but employ Swarthy's assistant, as soon as he had done with the princesses: "You should have had him," she added, "to-day, if I had known you wanted him."

When her majesty was dressed, all but the hat, she sent for the three princesses - and the king came also. I felt very foolish with my uncovered head; but it was somewhat the less awkward from its being very much a custom, in the royal family, to go without caps ; though none that appear before them use such a freedom. As soon as the hat was OD, "Now, Miss Burney," said the queen, "I won't keep you; you had better go and dress too."

While I was dressing, a footman came to my door, with a formal message that Miss Vernons begged I would come to breakfast. I immediately promised to make haste, glad to find something more resembling civility at length coming round to me. Presently after entered Miss Planta, in high spirits and great enjoyment. She told me she had been acquainting the queen with the whole affair, and that the queen quite approved of our staying upstairs. She had been also with the equerries, and had a fine laugh with them about their " wanting the ladies they declared they had sent no message at all, and that the servant had simply received orders to tell us that Miss Vernons desired our company to supper.

I thought it mighty unnecessary to have acquainted the equerries with what could only furnish a laugh against ourselves : however, the thing was done, and down we went together.

A CHECK FOR THE COLONEL.

The two Miss Vernons, General Harcourt, Colonel Fairly, Major Price, and - Mr. Hagget were all at breakfast. The Miss Vernons immediately began an apology about the supper the preceding night, declaring themselves exceedingly sorry we should not have had any, which they found was entirely owing to a blunder in the message given by the servants.

The gentlemen were all dying to make a laugh about the equerries " wanting the ladies ; " and Colonel Fairly began ; but the gravity of my behaviour soon quieted him. Mr. Hagget was content to be observant of a new person ; General Harcourt scarce ever speaks but from necessity; and Major Price was as grave as myself.

The eldest Miss Vernon is plain, and a little old-maidish but I found her afterwards sensible, well read, and well bred but not quite immediately did she appear so, as you will soon see. The youngest is many years her junior, and fat and handsome, good-humoured, and pleasing in her smiles, though high and distant till they are called forth.

After breakfast, when we were all breaking up, to prepare for church, I had a short explanatory conversation with Major Price, who came to speak to me concerning the preceding evening, and to confess his extreme surprise at our shutting ourselves up from their society. He had had a great mind, he said, to have come himself to see for us, but did not know whether it would be right. They waited, he added—Miss Vernons and all of them -a quarter of an hour after the supper was upon the table, and then a servant came in from us, to tell the equerries that we would not have any supper;—"And, indeed," continued he, a little forcibly, "I must own I was rather hurt by the message."

"Hurt?" cried I,—"what a gentle word!—I am sure I think you might rather have been angry."

"Why-to own the truth—I believe I was."

I was interrupted before I could explain more fully how the matter stood ; nor have I ever found opportunity since. However, I think it very likely he suggested the truth himself. Be that as it may, Miss Vernons went for their cloaks, and Miss Planta ran to the princesses, and therefore I was obliged to be a little abrupt, and retreat also.

When Miss Planta was ready, she came to fetch me. We went downstairs, but knew not whither to proceed. In the eating-parlour we had left only the gentlemen, and they were waiting to attend the king. There was no other place to which we could turn, and we had another of those wandering distresses that had made me so comfortless the night before. My wish was to find Miss Vernons:-niy expectation was to be found by them. Neither, however, happened; and the first time we met anybody that could give us any information, we were told they had been gone some time.

Very agreeable news!

THANKSGIVING SERVICE; AT NUNEHAM.

I could not, however, bear to give Up going to church, for I knew that the thanksgiving was to be that morning for the preservation of the king from assassination : and to let pique at this unaccountable behaviour, after all the apologies just passed, prevent my hearing and joining in a prayer of such a nature, in which now I am peculiarly interested, would have been ill worth the while. I therefore - proposed to Miss Planta that we should go by ourselves, and desire one of the servants to show us at once into Mr. Hagget's pew: for that we had already heard offered to the use of Miss Vernons, as Lord Harcourt's was reserved for their majesties. She agreed; and we proceeded, following such stragglers as shewed us our way : the servant to whom we applied having soon deserted us.

The church is in a very beautiful situation in the park, and built in the form of a Grecian temple. I admired it very much for its plainness and elegance. When we got to it, the very first step we took in it shewed us the Miss Vernons, very composedly seated in a large pew at the entrance. I now led the way, and took a place next to Miss Vernons, as much without apology as without invitation.

Mr. Hagget both read and preached. I was a good deal touched by the occasional thanksgiving, chiefly from knowing how much it must affect the queen and the princesses. Cause enough, indeed, is there for thanksgiving and rejoicing the safety of so mild and exemplary a sovereign.

When the service was over, and the royal family were gone, I thought it but right, in such a place, to subdue my proud feelings so far as to say to the Miss Vernons, I hoped we had not disturbed them.

I was very glad I took this little step down, for Miss Vernon, colouring, apologised for not waiting for us, which she said was owing to the fear of not getting into the chapel before the royal family. And then she asked if we should like to look at the altar-piece, which was the work of Mr. Mason.

ROYAL VISIT TO OXFORD: RECEPTION BY THE UNIVERSITY.

And now for the Oxford expedition.

How many carriages there were, and how they were arranged, I observed not sufficiently to recollect; but the party consisted of their majesties, the Princesses Royal, Augusta, and Elizabeth, the Duchess of Ancaster, Lord and Lady Harcourt, Lady Charlotte Bertie, and the two Miss Vernons. These last ladies are daughters of the late Lord Vernon, and sisters of Lady Harcourt.

General Harcourt, Colonel Fairly, and Major Price and Mr. Hagget, with Miss Planta and myself, completed the group. Miss Planta and I, of course, as the only undignified persons, brought up the rear. We were in a chaise of Lord Harcourt.

The city of Oxford afforded us a very noble view on the road, and its spires, towers, and domes soon made me forget all the little objects of minor spleen that had been crossing me

as I journeyed towards them ; and indeed, by the time I arrived in the midst of them, their grandeur, nobility, antiquity, and elevation impressed my mind so forcibly, that I felt for the first time since my new situation had taken place a rushing in of ideas that had no connection with it whatever.

The roads were lined with decently dressed people, and the high street was so crowded we were obliged to drive gently and carefully, to avoid trampling the people to death. Yet their behaviour was perfectly respectful and proper. Nothing could possibly be better conducted than the whole of this expedition.

We all drove straight to the theatre[211] in procession. Here, in alightingfrom the carriages, there was some difficulty, on account of the pressure of the people to see the king and queen, and princesses : however, even then, it was still the genteelest and most decent crowd I ever saw.

Here it was that Major Price signalised that part of his character I have so strongly marked, of his being truly a gentleman. It was his business to attend and guard the king. but he was determined to take almost equal care of some of his majesty's subjects: he was everybody's equerry during the whole expedition, assisting and looking after every creature, seeing us all out of our carriages and into them, and addressing the people, when they pressed too forward, with a steadiness and authority that made them quicker in retreat than all the staves of all the constables, who were attending by dozens at the entrance of every college.

At the outward gate of the theatre, the vice-chancellor, Dr. Chapman, received their majesties. All the professors, doctors, etc., then in Oxford, arrayed in their professional robes, attended him.—How I wished my dear father amongst them

The vice-chancellor then conducted their majesties along the inner court, to the door of the theatre, all the rest following ; and there, waiting their arrival, stood the Duke and Duchess of Marlborough, the Marquis of Blandford, in a nobleman's Oxford robe, and Lady Caroline and Lady Elizabeth Spencer.

After they had all paid their duties, a regular procession followed, which I should have thought very pretty, and much have liked to have seen, had I been a mere looker on; but was frequently at a loss, what to do with myself, and uncertain whether I ought to proceed in the suite, or stand by as a spectator ; and Miss Planta was still, if possible, more fearful.

The theatre was filled with company, all well dressed, and arranged in rows around it. The area below them was entirely empty, so that there was not the least confusion. The chancellor's chair, at the head of about a dozen steps, was prepared for the king ; and just below him, to his left, a form for the queen and the princesses.

The king walked foremost from the area, conducted by the University's vice-chancellor. The queen followed, handed by her own vice-chamberlain. The Princess royal followed, led by the king's aide-de-camp, General Harcourt; and Princess Augusta, leaning on Major Price. Princess Elizabeth walked alone, no other servant of the king being present, and no rank authorising such a conduct, without office.

Next followed the Duke and Duchess of Marlborough ; then the Duchess of Ancaster, and Marquis of Blandford - next, Lord and Lady Harcourt, then the two Lady Spencers and Lady Charlotte Bertie, then the Miss Vernons, and then Miss Planta and a certain F. B. .

We were no sooner arranged, and the door of the theatre shut, than the king, his head covered, sat down ; the queen did the same, and then the three princesses. All the rest, throughout the theatre, stood.

THE ROYAL FAMILY ARE MUCH AFFECTED.

The vice-chancellor then made a low obeisance to the king, and producing a written paper, began the address of the University, to thank his majesty for this second visit, and to congratulate him and the nation on his late escape from assassination. He read it in an audible and distinct voice; and in its CODclusion, an address was suddenly made to the queen, expressive of much concern for her late distress, and the highest and most profound veneration for her amiable and exalted character.

An address, to me so unexpected, and on a subject so recent and of so near concern, in presence of the person preserved, his wife, and his children, was infinitely touching.

The queen could scarcely bear it, though she had already, I doubt not, heard it at Nuneham, as these addresses niust be first read in private, to have the answers prepared. Nevertheless, this public tribute of loyalty to the king, and of respect to herself, went gratefully to her heart, and filled her eyes with tears- which she would not, however, encourage, but smiling through them, dispersed them with her fan, with which she was repeatedly obliged to stop their Course down her cheeks.

The princesses, less guarded, the moment their father's danger was mentioned, wept with but little control; and no wonder, for I question if there was one dry eye in the theatre. The tribute, so just, so honourable, so elegant, paid to the exalted character of the queen, affected everybody, with joy for her escape from affliction, and with delight at the reward and the avowal of her virtues.

When the address was ended, the king took a paper from Lord Harcourt, and read his answer. The king reads admirably; with ease, feeling, and force, and without any hesitation. His voice is particularly full and fine. I was very much surprised by its effect. When he had done, he took off his hat, and bowed to the chancellor and professors, and delivered the answer to Lord Harcourt, who, walking backwards, descended the stairs, and presented it to the vice chancellor.

All this ceremony was so perfectly new to me, that I rejoiced extremely in not missing it. Indeed I would not have given up the pleasure of seeing the queen on this occasion for any sort of sight that could have been exhibited to me.

Next followed music: a good organ, very well played, anthem-ed and voluntary-ed us for some time.

THE PRESENTATIONS : RETIRING BACKWARDS.

After this, the vice-chancellor and professors begged for the honour of kissing the king's hand. Lord Harcourt was again the backward messenger ; and here followed a great mark of goodness in the king: he saw that nothing less than a thoroughbred old courtier, such as Lord Harcourt, could walk backwards down these steps, before himself, and in sight of so full a hall of spectators - and he therefore dispensed with being approached to his seat, and walked down himself into the area, where the vice-chancellor kissed his hand, and was imitated by every professor and doctor in the room.

Notwithstanding this considerate good-nature in his majesty, the sight, at times, was very ridiculous. Some of the worthy collegiates, unused to such ceremonies, and unaccustomed to such a presence, the moment they had kissed the king,'s hand, turned their backs to him, and walked away as in any common room ; others, attempting to do better, did still worse, by tottering and stumbling, and falling foul of those behind them some, ashamed to kneel, took the king's hand straight up to their mouths; others, equally off their guard, plumped down on both knees, and could hardly get up again; and many, in their confusion, fairly arose by pulling his majesty's hand to raise them.

As the king spoke to every one, upon Lord Harcourt's presenting them, this ceremonial took up a good deal of time but it was too new and diverting to appear long.

It was vacation time; there were therefore none of the students present.

When the whole was over, we left the theatre in the same form we had entered it. The Duke and Duchess of Marlborough, the Marquis and the Ladies Spencer, attended the king and queen to their carriages, and then went back to the theatre, to wait for their own.

I cannot now go on with our progress regularly, for I do not remember it. I will only, therefore, in general, say, that I was quite delighted with the city, and so entertained and so pleased with such noble buildings as it presented to me, that I felt, as I have told you, a consciousness to pleasure revived in me, which had long lain nearly dormant.

THE COLLEGES VISITED: A STEALTHY COLLATION.

We went to all the colleges in the same order that we came to the theatre. I shall attempt no descriptions ; I shall only mention a few little personal circumstances, and some of those court etiquettes which, from their novelty to me, will, I judge, be new also to my Susan ; and what is new in customs or manners is always worth knowing.

At Christ-church college, when we arrived at about three o'clock, in a large hall there was a cold collation prepared for their majesties and the princesses. It was at the upper end of the hall. I could not see of what it consisted, though it would have been very agreeable, after so much standing and sauntering, to have given my opinion of it in an experimental way.

Their majesties and the princesses sat down to this table - as well satisfied, I believe, as any of their subjects so to do.

Duchess of Ancaster and Lady Harcourt stood behind the chairs of the queen and the princess royal. There were 11, other ladies of sufficient rank to officiate for Princesses Augusta and Elizabeth. Lord Harcourt stood behind the king's chair and the vice-chancellor, and the head master of Christ-church' with salvers in their hands, stood near the table, and ready to hand, to the three noble waiters, whatever was wanted : while the other reverend doctors and learned professors stood aloof, equally ready to present to the chancellor and the master whatever they were to forward.

We, meanwhile, untitled attendants, stood at the other end of the room, forming a semi-circle, and all strictly facing the royal collationers. We consisted of the Miss Vernons, thrown out here as much as their humble guests-Colonel Fairly, Major Price, General Harcourt, and,-though I know not why,—Lady Charlotte Bertie;—with all the inferior professors, in their gowns, and some, too much frightened to advance, of the upper degrees. These, with Miss Planta, Mr. Hagget, and myself, formed this attendant semi-circle.

The time of this collation was spent very pleasantly-to me, at least, to whom the novelty of the scene rendered it entertaining. It was agreed that we must all be absolutely famished unless we could partake of some refreshment, as we had breakfasted early, and had no chance of dining before six or seven o'clock. A whisper was soon buzzed through the semi-circle, of the deplorable state of our appetite apprehensions ; and presently it reached the ears of some of the worthy doctors. Immediately a new whisper was circulated, which made its progress with great vivacity, to offer us whatever we would wish, and to beg us to name what we chose.

Tea, coffee, and chocolate, were whispered back.

The method of producing, and the means of swallowing them, were much more difficult to settle than the choice of what was acceptable. Major Price and Colonel Fairly, however, seeing a very large table close to the wainscot behind us, desired our refreshments might be privately conveyed there, behind the semi-circle, and that, while all the group backed very near it, one at a time might feed, screened by all the rest from observation.

I suppose I need not inform you, my dear Susan, that to eat in presence of any of the royal family is as much hors d'usage as to be seated. This plan had speedy success, and the very good doctors soon, by sly degrees and with watchful caution, covered the whole table with tea, coffee, chocolate, cakes, and bread and butter.

The further plan, however, of one at a time feasting and the rest fasting and standing sentinels, was not equally approved; there was too much eagerness to seize the present moment, and too much fear of a sudden retreat, to give patience for so slow proceeding. We could do no more, therefore, than stand in double row, with one to screen one throughout the troop ; and, in this manner, we were all very plentifully and very pleasantly served.

The Duchess of Ancaster and Lady Harcourt, as soon as the first serving attendance was over, were dismissed from the royal chairs, and most happy to join our group, and partake of our repast. The duchess, extremely fatigued with standing, drew a small body of troops before her, that she might take a few minutes' rest on a form by one of the doors ; and Lady Charlotte Bertie did the same, to relieve an ankle which she had unfortunately sprained.

"Poor Miss Burney," cried the good-natured duchess, "I wish she could sit down, for she is unused to this work. She does not know yet what it is to stand for five hours following, as we do."

The beautiful window of Sir Joshua Reynolds and Mr. Jervis, in New college, would alone have recovered me, had my fatigue been infinitely more serious.

In one of the colleges I stayed so long in an old chapel, lingering over antique monuments, that all the party were vanished before I missed them, except doctors and professors ; for we had a train of those everywhere ; and I was then a little surprised by the approach of one of them, saying, "You seem inclined to abide with us, Miss Burney?"—and then another, in an accent of facetious gallantry, cried, "No, no, don't let us shut up Miss Burney among old tombs!—No, no!"

After this, many of the good doctors occasionally spoke to me, when there happened to be opportunity. How often did I wish my dear father amongst them! They considered me as a doctor's daughter, and were all most excessively courteous, handing, and pointing, and showing me about as much as possible.

In another college, while Miss Planta and myself were hanging a little back, at the entrance into a small cedar chapel, that would not much more than hold the royal family and their immediate suite, the Duchess of Ancaster, who took every opportunity to show me civilities, and distinguish me, came down the steps, and made me ascend them, to turn with her, when she called to her daughter, and in the most obliging terms introduced me to her, with many kind speeches of her wish that we should cultivate much acquaintance. Lady Charlotte is very handsome, and has a very good figure: she unfortunately lisps very much, which, at first, never prejudices in favour of the understanding; but I have conversed with her too little to know anything more of her than that she is well bred, and seems to have a large portion internally, of the good-natured and obliging disposition of her mother.

At the Town-hall, an address was presented by the mayor and corporation of the city of Oxford to the king, which the mayor read, while the same ceremony of the sitting and standing was practised that I have described at the theatre. The king took off his hat, and bowed, and received the address, after hearing it, but returned no answer. Nor has his majesty made any except to the Oxford University, though they have, since, poured in upon him from every part of the kingdom. The mayor was then knighted.

I think it was in Trinity college that we saw the noblest library I have ever happened to enter. For 'tis but little, my dear Susan, I have seen of sights. Here we had new court scenery, in which I acted but an uncourtier-like part. The queen and princess had seats prepared for them, which, after a stroll up and down the library, they were glad, I believe, to occupy. The ladies of their suite were then graciously ordered by her majesty to be seated, as there was not here the state or public appearance that was observed at the theatre, and in the college where the refreshments were given. As to the poor men, they never must sit in the presence of the queen, be they whom they will, or what they will: so they were fain to stand it out.

Miss Planta glided away, behind a pillar, and, being there unseen, was able to lounge a little. She was dreadfully tired. So was everybody but myself. For me, my curiosity was so awake to every thing, that I seemed insensible to all inconvenience. I could not, in such a library, prevail with myself to so nodest a retirement as Miss Planta's: I considered that the queen had herself ordered my attendance in this expedition, and I thought myself very well privileged to make it as pleasant as I could. I therefore stole softly down the room, to the further end, and there amused myself with examining what books were within reach of my eyes, and with taking down and looking into all such as were also within reach of my understanding. This was very pleasant sport to me, and had we stayed there till midnight would have kept me from weariness.

RETREATING FROM THE ROYAL PRESENCE.

In another college (we saw so many, and in such quick succession, that I recollect not any by name, though all by situation) I saw a performance of courtly etiquette, by Lady Charlotte Bertie, that seemed to me as difficult as any feat I ever beheld, even at Astley's or Hughes's. It was in an extremely large, long, spacious apartment. The king always led the way out, as well as in, upon all entrances and exits : but here, for some reason that I know not, the queen was handed out first ; and the princesses, and the aide-de-camp, and equerry followed. The king was very earnest in conversation with some professor ; the attendants hesitated whether to wait or follow the queen ; but presently the Duchess of Ancaster, being near the door, slipped out, and Lady Harcourt after her. The Miss Vernons, who were but a few steps from them, went next. But Lady Charlotte, by chance, happened to be very high up the room, and near to the king. Had I been in her situation, I had surely waited till his majesty went first - but that would not, I saw, upon this occasion, have been etiquette she therefore faced the king, and began a march backwards, -her ankle already sprained, and to walk forward, and even leaning upon an arm, was painful to her: nevertheless, back she went, perfectly upright, without one stumble, without ever looking once behind to see what she might encounter ; and with as graceful a motion, and as easy an air, as I ever saw anybody enter a long room, she retreated, I am sure, full twenty yards backwards out of one.

For me, I was also, unluckily, at the upper end of the room, looking at some portraits of founders, and one of Henry VIII. in particular, from Holbein. However, as soon as I perceived what was going forward,-backward, rather,-I glided near the wainscot, (Lady Charlotte, I should mention, made her retreat along the very middle of the room,) and having paced a few steps backwards, stopped short to recover, and, while I seemed examining some other portrait, disentangled my train from the heels of my shoes, and then proceeded a few steps only more .- and then, observing the king turn another way, I slipped a yard or two at a time forwards - and hastily looked back, and then was able to go again according to rule, and in this manner, by slow and varying means, I at length made my escape. Miss Planta stood upon less ceremony, and fairly ran off.

Since that time, however, I have come on prodigiously, by constant practice, in the power and skill of walking backwards, without tripping up my own heels, feeling my head giddy, or treading my train out of the plaits—accidents very frequent among novices in that business; and I have no doubt but that, in the course of a few months, I shall arrive at all possible perfection in the true Court retrograde motion.

In another college, in an old chapter house, I had the opportunity to see another Court-scene. It was nearly round in shape, and had various old images and ornaments. We were all taken in by the doctors attendant, and the party, with doctors and all, nearly filled it ; but, finding it crowded, everybody stood upon the less ceremony, and we all made our examinations of the various contents of the room quite at our ease: till suddenly the king and queen, perceiving two very heavy old-fashioned chairs were placed at the head of the room for their reception, graciously accepted them, and sat down. Nothing could exceed the celerity with which all confusion instantly was over, and the most solemn order succeeded to it. Chairs were presented to the three princesses by the side of the queen, and the Duchess of Ancaster anc Lady Harcourt planted themselves at their backs ; while Lady Charlotte instantly retreated close to the wall, and so did every creature else in the room, all according to their rank or station, and the royal family remained conspicuous and alone, all crowd dispersed, and the space of almost the whole room unoccupied before them, so close to the walls did every body respectfully stand.

SURPRISED BY THE QUEEN.

The last college we visited was Cardinal Wolsey's—an immense fabric. While roving about a very spacious apartment, Mr. Fairly[212]came behind me, and whispered that I might easily slip out into a small parlour, to rest a little while ; almost everybody having taken some opportunity to contrive themselves a little sitting but myself. I assured him, very truly, I was too little tired to make it worth while ; but poor Miss Planta was so woefully fatigued that I could not, upon her account, refuse to be of the party. He conducted us into a very neat little parlour, belonging to the master of the college, and Miss Planta flung herself on a chair, half dead with weariness.

Mr. Fairly was glad of the opportunity to sit for a moment also; for 'my part, I was quite alert. Alas! my dear Susan, 'tis my mind that is so weak, and so open to disorder;- my body, I really find, when it is an independent person, very strong, and capable of much exertion without suffering from it.

Mr. Fairly now produced, from a paper repository concealed in his coat pocket, some apricots and bread, and insisted upon my eating ;-but I was not inclined to the repast, and saw he was half famished himself;-so was poor Miss Planta : however, he was so persuaded I must both be as hungry and as tired as himself, that I was forced to eat an apricot to appease him.

Presently, while we were in the midst of this regale, the door suddenly opened, and the queen came in!—followed by as many attendants as the room would contain. Up we all started, myself alone not discountenanced ; for I really think it quite respect sufficient never to sit down in the royal presence, without aiming at having it supposed I have stood bolt upright ever since I have been admitted to it. Quick into our pockets was crammed our bread, and close into our hands was squeezed our fruit; by which I discovered that our appetites were to be supposed annihilated, at the same time that our strength was to be invincible.

Very soon after this we were joined by the king, and in a few minutes we all paraded forth to the carriages, and drove back to Nuneham.

I have been very minute in this Oxford account, because it presented scenes so new to me, and because I concluded that, after you have had a month or two of general journal, you will have nothing more to be new to either of us.

This Oxford expedition was, altogether, highly entertaining to me; but I ought not to close it without telling you the sweetness of all the princesses, who each made a point of speaking to, Miss Planta and to me upon entering or quitting every college, as we stood in the ranks, while they passed.

AT NUNEHAM AGAIN.

I stayed in my own room till a message from the miss Vernons brought me down to dinner; and from this time forward those ladies exerted themselves to the utmost in being attentive, sociable, and civil. I found the major, Mr. Fairly Mr. Hagget, Miss Planta, and themselves ; and we had a very pleasant dinner, talking over the sights just seen. All the afternoon was spent in the same party. We went into Lord Harcourt's library to tea and coffee, and there we had short visits from his lordship and the Duchess of Ancaster.

In the evening Lady Harcourt came also, and was amazingly courteous. The queen then sent for the Miss Vernons into the drawing-room, and Miss Planta and myself left the gentlemen to take care of themselves, and retired for the evening to our own rooms.

You must know, wherever the king and queen are, nobody comes into their sight unsent for, not even the master and mistress of the house, unless they are publicly acquainted that their majesties are coming, and mean to see them.

A LIVELY BREAKFAST INCIDENT.

Monday, Aug. 14.-I come now to introduce to you a new acquaintance.

I did not get down to breakfast till it was almost over, as I was detained with the queen, and as everybody was obliged to make what haste they could, in order to insure a meal before a summons. I found Miss Planta, and the aide-de-camp, vice chamberlain, and equerry; Lady Harcourt had already breakfasted with them, but made off as soon as the queen was visible, to wait upon her majesty. Miss Vernons lay in bed from yesterday's fatigues.

The extreme silence and gravity of the aide-de-camp threw a reserve and constraint on all the party, and we were all nearly dumb, when a new lady suddenly rushed into the room. This was Mrs. Harcourt, the aide-de-camp's wife, who had been ill the preceding day, and therefore had not ventured to Oxford. She is a showy, handsome woman, extremely talkative, with quick parts, high spirits, and a rattling vein of humour.

Miss Planta, who had taken Lady Harcourt's place, in order to pour out the tea, instantly moved to another. Mrs. Harcourt hurried into that just vacated, without ceremony, calling out, "How monstrous late you all are!—though I need not talk, for I hate getting up early. I was so vastly ill yesterday I could not stir, but I am vastly well to-day, so I am going to Blenheim."

This day had been previously dedicated to seeing Blenheim.

"To Blenheim?" repeated General Harcourt, in a low voice.

"Yes, sir, to Blenheim! So no grave faces, for my plan is fixed."

He half articulated a fear of her being ill again, but she stopped him with "O, no matter, leave that to the Fates;—the queen has been so gracious as to say I may go, and therefore go I shall : so say nothing about it, for that's settled and unalterable."

"After being so ill yesterday," said Mr. Fairly, "I think it will be rather too much for you."

"Not at all !-and what's more, you must carry me."

"I am very glad to hear it," cried he, " if go you will."

"Yes, that I will, certainly; and some of you must take me. I have no coach ordered,-and there is not one to spare : so, amongst you, you equerries, You must carry me. I have never been to Blenheim since I married."

"Were you before ? " said the general.

"Yes, sir, and you took me."

"Did I?

" Yes, sir, you had that honour ; and I think you have never taken that trouble since."

All this, though uttered in a voice as peremptory as the language, was spoken with very becoming smiles, and an air of saucy good humour.

The breakfast all this while had stood quite still: indeed there was nobody but myself that had not nearly done. Major Price handed me roll and butter and bread across the table, by way of hint, I believe ; all which I declined: at last Mr. Fairly said, "Miss Burney, which is your cup?"

Upon this, Mrs. Harcourt, abruptly turning to me, exclaimed "O dear, you've got no tea!" Then pouring out a dish of slop, added, "Can you drink it? It looks very melancholy."

"No," I said, "I have had enough."

Have not you also, my Susan, had enough of this scene ?

The Blenheim visit being considered as a private one, nobody went but of the Marlborough acquaintance: though in all royal parties, the whole company is always named by the royals, and the lords and ladies of the mansions have no more right to invite a guest than a guest has to come uninvited.

I spent this day very pleasantly, in walking over the grounds which are extremely pretty, seeing a flower-garden planned by Mr. Mason, and the pictures in the house. The two MISS Vernons, Miss Planta, and Mr. Hagget, were all that remained at Nuneham. And it was now I wholly made peace with those two ladies; especially the eldest, as I found her, the moment she was removed from rays so bright that they had dazzled her, a rational, composed, obliging woman. She took infinite and unwearied pains to make amends for the cold and strange opening of our acquaintance, by the most assiduous endeavours to give me pleasure and amusement. And she succeeded very well. I could blame nobody but the countess' sister for our reception ; I plainly saw these ladies had been unprepared to look upon us as any charge to themselves.

The royal excursioners did not return till between six and seven o'clock, when we dined with the same party as the preceding day. The evening, too, had just the same visitors, and passed in just the same manner.

---

211   i.e. the University theatre.-ED.

212   Colonel Digby, who from this time is always called Mr. Fairly instead of Colonel Fairly, in the "Diary,"-ED,

SECTION 9 (17867)

COURT DUTIES AT WINDSOR AND KEW.

[THE following section and the two sections which succeed it, relate, almost exclusively, to Fanny's dreary prison-life in the royal household. Of the world without the palace, of the friends whom she had left, we hear next to nothing. The change for her was complete ; the rare visits of her father, her sister, and the Lockes, one hasty excursion to Chesington, and one delightful evening at Mrs. Ord's, form nearly the sum total of her personal intercourse, during these eighteen months, with those whose kindness and sympathy had brightened her past years. She complained seldom, and only to her best-beloved Susan, but there is something truly pathetic in these occasional evidences of the struggle which she was making to conquer her repugnance, and to be happy, if that were possible, in her new situation. Dazzled by the royal condescension Fanny may have been ; blinded she was not. It was her father who, possessed by a strange infatuation, remained blind to the incongruity, charmed by the fancied honour, of his daughter's position; and she, tender-hearted as she was, could not bear to inflict upon one so dear the pain which she knew must be the consequence of his enlightenment. Meanwhile, her best comfort was still in the friendship of Mrs. Delany, and this, in the course of nature, could not be of long duration.

But dreary as this life of routine was to the unfortunate victim, we venture to assure the reader that he will find the victim's account of it very far from dreary. Indeed, these pages might almost be instanced to show from what unpromising materials a person endowed with humour and observation can construct a singularly entertaining narrative. Our wonder is that neither the monotony of her official duties, nor the insipidity of her associates, nor even *the odious tyranny of her colleague, could wholly subdue in the author of "Evelina" and "Cecilia" that bright and humorous disposition to which the following pages bear frequent testimony.-ED.]

THE MISCHIFF-MAKING KEEPER OF THE ROBES.

Tuesday, Aug. 15.-This morning we all breakfasted together, and at about twelve o'clock we set off again for Windsor.

Lord Harcourt came into the breakfast room with abundance of civil speeches upon his pleasure in renewing our acquaintance, and the Miss Vernons parted with me like wholly different people from those I met.

As soon as I returned to the queen's Lodge at Windsor, I called upon Mrs. Schwellenberg. I found her still occupied concerning the newspaper business about Mrs. Hastings. She was more than ever irritated against Mr. Fairly for his information, and told me she was sure he must have said it to her on purpose, and that she wished people might hold their tongue: but that she was bent upon having satisfaction, and therefore she had sent for Mrs. Hastings, and informed her of the whole business.

I was not only sorry, but frightened, lest any mischief should arise through misrepresentations and blunders, between Mr. Fairly and Mr. Hastings: however, this imprudent step was taken already, and not to be called back.

She protested she was determined to insist that Mr. Fairly should produce the very paper that had mentioned the queen, which she should show, and have properly noticed.

I, on the other side, instantly resolved to speak myself to Mr. Fairly, to caution him by no means to be led into seeking any such paper, or into keeping such a search awake; for, with the best intentions in the world, I saw him on the point of being made the object of vindictive resentment to Mr. Hastings, or of indignant displeasure to the queen herself,-so wide-spreading is the power of misapprehension over the most innocent conversation.

I saw, however, nothing of Mr. Fairly till tea-time; indeed, except by very rare chance, I never see any of the king's people but at that meeting. Mrs. Schwellenberg was then present, and nothing could I do. Major Price and Mr. Fisher were of the party. Mr. Fairly fortunately had letters to write, and hastily left us, after taking one dish of tea. The moment he was gone Mrs. Schwellenberg said she had forgot to speak

to him about the newspaper, and told Major Price to ask him for it. Major Price assented with a bow only, and the matter dropped.

I, however, who best knew the danger of its going any farther, now determined upon speaking to Major Price, and making him contrive to hush it up. Utterly impossible, nevertheless, proved this scheme; Major Price was too great a favourite to be an instant disengaged. I was obliged, therefore, to be quiet.

A TERRACE PARTY.

Wednesday, Aug. 16-Was the birthday of Prince Frederick, Duke of York. The queen sent me in the morning to my dear Mrs. Delany, whom I had but just found a moment to fly to the preceding day, and I was commanded to brin- her, if well enough, just as she was, in her home morning dress, to her majesty. This I did with great delight ; and that most venerable of women accepted the invitation with all the alacrity of pleasure she could have felt at fifteen. The queen, in the late excursion, had made many purchases at Woodstock : and she now made some little presents from them to this dear lady.

In the evening, as it was again a birthday, I resolved upon going to the Terrace, as did Mrs. Delany, and with her and Miss Mawer, and Miss Port, I sallied forth. To avoid the high steps leading to the Terrace from the Lodge, we went through a part of the Castle.

The Terrace was much crowded, though so windy we could hardly keep our feet ; but I had an agreeable surprise in meeting there with Dr. Warton. [213]He joined Mrs. Delany instantly, and kept with us during the whole walk. He congratulated me upon my appointment, in terms of rapture; his ecstacies are excited so readily, from the excessive warmth of his disposition, and its proneness to admire and wonder, that my new situation was a subject to awaken an enthusiasm the most high-flown.

Presently after we were joined by a goodly priest, fat, jovial, breathing plenty, ease, and good living. I soon heard him whisper Mrs. Delany to introduce him to me. It was Dr. Roberts, provost of Eton: I had already seen him at Mrs. Delany's last winter, but no introduction had then passed. He is a distant relation of Mr. Cambridge. His wife was with him, and introduced also.

These also joined us; and in a few minutes more a thin, little, wizen old gentleman, with eyes that scarce seemed to see, and a rather tottering gait, came up to Mrs. Delany, and after talking with her some time, said in a half whisper, "Is that Miss Burney?" and then desired a presentation. It was Mr. Bryant, the mythologist. [214]I was very glad to see him, as he bears a very high character, and lives much in this neighbourhood. He talks a great deal, and with the utmost good humour and ease, casting entirely aside his learning, which I am, nevertheless, assured is that of one of the most eminent scholars of the age.

We had now a very good party, and seated ourselves in a sort of alcove, to be sheltered from the wind; but it was so ,ery violent that it deterred the royal family from walking. They merely came on the Terrace to show themselves to those who were eager to pay their compliments upon the day, and then returned to the Castle.

Dr. Warton insisted upon accompanying me home as far as the iron rails, to see me enter my re,,al premises. I did not dare invite him in, without previous knowledge whether I had any such privilege; otherwise, with all his parts, and all his experience, I question whether there is one boy in his school at Winchester who would more have delighted in feeling himself under the roof of a sovereign.

A NERVOUS READER.

Aug. 17.-From the time that the queen condescended to desire to place me in immediate attendance upon her own person, I had always secretly concluded she meant me for her English reader; since the real duties of my office would have had a far greater promise of being fulfilled by thousands of others than by myself. This idea had made the prospect of reading to her extremely awful to me: an exhibition, at any rate, is painful to me, but one in which I considered her majesty as a judge, interested for herself in the sentence she should pronounce, and gratified or disappointed according to its tenor-this was an exhibition formidable indeed, and must have been considered as such by anybody in similar circumstances.

Not a book, not a pamphlet, not a newspaper, had I ever seen near the queen, for the first week, without feeling a panic ; I always expected to be called upon. She frequently bid me give her the papers ; I felt that they would be the worst reading I could have, because full of danger, in matter as well as manner: however, she always read them herself.

To-day, after she was dressed, Mrs. Schwellenberg went to her own room; and the queen, instead of leaving mee, as usual, to go to mine, desired me to follow her to her sitting dressing-room. She then employed me in helping her to arrange her work, which is chair covers done in ribbon; and then told me to fetch her a volume of the "Spectator." I obeyed with perfect tranquillity. She let me stand by her a little while without speaking, and then, suddenly, but very gently, said, "Will you read a paper while I work?"

I was quite "consternated!" I had not then the smallest expectation of such a request. I said nothing, and held the book unopened.

She took it from me, and pointed out the place where I should begin. She is reading them regularly through, for the first time. I had no choice: I was forced to obey; but my voice was less obedient than my will, and it became so husky, and so unmanageable, that nothing more unpleasant could be heard. The paper was a curious one enough—all concerning a Court favourite. I could hardly rejoice when my task was over, from my consciousness how ill it was performed. The queen talked of the paper, but forbore saying anything of any sort about the reader. I am sorry, however, to have done so ill.

Miss BURNEY REPINES AT HER POSITION.

(Fanny Burney to Mrs. Philips. August 20.

. . . . .O my beloved Susan, 'tis a refractory heart I have to deal with!—it struggles so hard to be sad—and silent—and fly from you entirely, since it cannot fly entirely to you. I do all I can to conquer it, to content it, to give it a taste and enjoyment for what is still attainable: but at times I cannot manage it, and it seems absolutely indispensable to my peace to occupy myself in anything rather than in writing to the person most dear to me upon earth! . . . If to you alone I show myself in these dark colours, can you blame the plan that I have intentionally been forming, namely, to wean myself from myself—to lessen all my affections—to curb all my wishes—to deaden all my sensations? This design, my Susan, I formed so long ago as the first day my dear father accepted my offered appointment: I thought that what demanded a complete new system of life, required, if attainable, a new set of feelings for all enjoyment of new prospects, and for lessening regrets at what were quitted, or lost. Such being my primitive idea, merely from my grief of separation, imagine but how it was strengthened and confirmed when the interior of my position became known to me!—when I saw myself expected by Mrs. Schwellenberg, not to be her colleague, but her dependent deputy! not to be her visitor at my own option, but her companion, her humble companion, at her own command! This has given so new a character to the place I had accepted under such different auspices, that nothing but my horror of disappointing, perhaps displeasing, my dearest father, has deterred me,from the moment that I made this mortifying discovery, from soliciting his leave to resign.

But oh my Susan,—kind, good, indulgent as he is to me, I have not the heart so cruelly to thwart his hopes—his views—his happiness, in the honours he conceived awaiting my so unsolicited appointment. The queen, too, is all sweetness, encouragement, and gracious goodness to me, and I cannot endure to complain to her of her old servant. You see, then, my situation; here I must remain!—The die is cast, and that struggle is no more.—To keep off every other, to support the loss of the dearest friends, and best society, and bear, in exchange, the tyranny, the exigeance, the ennui, and attempted indignities of their greatest contrast,- -this must be my constant endeavour.

Amongst my sources of unhappiness in this extraordinary case is, the very favour that, in any other, might counteract it—namely, that of the queen: for while, in a manner the most attractive, she seems inviting my confidence, and deigning to wish my happiness, she redoubles my conflicts never to shock her with murmurs against one who, however to me noxious and persecuting, is to her a faithful and truly devoted old servant. This will prevent my ever having my distress and disturbance redressed ; for they can never be disclosed. Could I have, as my dear father conceived, all the time to myself, my friends, my leisure, or my own occupations, that is not devoted to my official duties, how different would be my feelings, how far more easily accommodated to my privations and sacrifices! Little does the queen know the slavery I must either resist or endure. And so frightful is hostility, that I know not which part is hardest to perform.

MADAME DE GENLIs DISCUSSED.

Windsor, Monday Evening.-Madame de la Fite, who calls upon me daily, though I am commonly so much engaged I can scarce speak to her for a moment, came to desire I would let her bring me M. Argant, [215]who was come to Windsor to show some experiment to the king.

Madame de la Fite has long pressed me with great earnestness to write to Madame de Genlis, whose very elegant little note to me I never have answered. Alas! what can I do? I think of her as of one of the first among women—I see her full of talents and of charms—I am willing to believe her good, virtuous, and dignified;—yet, with all this, the cry against her is so violent and so universal, and my belief in her innocence is wholly unsupported by proof in its favour, or any other argument than internal conviction, from what I observed of her conduct and manners and conversation when I saw her in London, that I know not how to risk a correspondence with her, till better able to satisfy others, as well as I am satisfied Myself: most especially, I dare not enter into such an intercourse through Madame de la Fite, whose indiscreet zeal for us both would lead her to tell her successful mediation to everybody she could make hear her. Already she has greatly distressed me upon this subject. Not content with continual importunity to me to write, ever since my arrival, which I have evaded as gently as possible, to avoid giving her my bumiliating reasons, she has now written Madame de Genlis word that I am here, belonging to the same royal household as herself; and then came to tell me, that as we were now so closely connected, she proposed our writing jointly, in the same letter.

All this, with infinite difficulty, I passed over,—pleading my little time; which indeed she sees is true. But when M. Argant was here, she said to me, in French, "M. Argant will immediately wait upon Madame de Genlis, for he is going to Paris; he will tell her he saw us together, and he will carry her a letter' from me; and surely Miss Burney will not refuse M. Argant the happiness of carrying two lines from one lady so celebrated to another?" I was quite vexed; a few lines answer the same purpose as a few sheets; since, once her correspondent, all that I am hesitating about is as completely over, right or wrong, as if I wrote to her weekly.

As soon as they left me, I hastened to my dear Mrs. Delany, to consult with her what to do. "By all means," cried she, "tell the affair of your difficulties whether to write to her or not, to the queen : it will unavoidably spread, if you enter into such a correspondence, and the properest step you can take, the safest and the happiest, is to have her opinion, and be guided by it. Madame de Genlis is so public a character, you can hardly correspond with her in private, and it would be better the queen should hear of such an intercourse from yourself than from any other."

I entirely agreed in the wisdom of her advice, though I very much doubted my power to exert sufficient courage to speak, unasked, upon any affair of my own. You may be sure I resolved to spare poor Madame de la Fite, in my application, if I made it: "to write, or not to write," was all I wanted to determine; for the rest, I must run any risk rather than complain of a friend who always means well. . . .

An opportunity offered the next morning, for the queen again commanded me to follow her into her saloon ; and there she was so gentle, and so gracious, that I ventured to speak of Madame de Genlis.

It was very fearfully that I took this liberty. I dreaded lest she should imagine I meant to put myself under her direction, as if presuming she would be pleased to direct me. Something, I told her, I had to say, by the advice of Mrs. Delany, which I begged her permission to communicate. She assented in silence, but with a look of the utmost softness, and yet mixed with strong surprise. I felt my voice faltering, and I was with difficulty able to go on,-so new to me was it to beg to be heard, who, hitherto, have always been begged to speak. There is no absolutely accounting for the forcible emotions which every totally new situation and new effort will excite in a mind enfeebled, like mine, by a long succession of struggling agitations. I got behind her chair, that she might not see a distress she might wonder at: for it was not this application

itself that affected me ; it was the novelty of my own situation, the new power I was calling forth over my proceedings, and the—O my Susan!—the all that I was changing from—relinquishing-of the past—and hazarding for the future!

With many pauses, and continual hesitation, I then told her that I had been earnestly pressed by Madame de Genlis to correspond with her; that I admired her with all my heart, and, with all my heart, believed all good of her; but that, nevertheless, my personal knowledge of her was too slight to make me wish so intimate an intercourse, which I had carefully shunned upon all occasions but those where my affection as well as my admiration had been interested ; though I felt such a request from such a woman as Madame de Genlis as an honour, and therefore not to be declined without some reason stronger than my own general reluctance to proposals of that sort ; and I found her unhappily, and I really and sincerely believed undeservedly, encircled with such powerful enemies, and accused with so much confidence of having voluntarily provoked them, that I could not, even in my own mind, settle if it were right to connect myself with her so closely, till I could procure information more positive in her favour, in order to answer the attacks of those who asperse her, [216]and who would highly blame me for entering into a correspondence with a character not more unquestionably known to me. I had been desirous to wait, suspended, till this fuller knowledge might be brought about; but I was now solicited into a decision, by M. Argant, who was immediately going to her, and who must either take her a letter from me or show her, by taking none, that I was bent upon refusing her request.

The queen heard me with the greatest attention, and then said, "Have you yet writ to her?"

No, I said; I had had a little letter from her, but I received it just as the Duchess of Portland died, when my whole mind was so much occupied by Mrs. Delany, that I could not answer it. \ "I will speak to you then," cried she, "very honestly; if you have not yet writ, I think it better you should not write. If you had begun, it would be best to go on; but as you have not, it will be the safest way to let it alone. You may easily say, without giving her any offence, that you are now too much engaged to find time for entering into any new correspondence."

I thanked her for this open advice as well as I was able, and I felt the honour its reliance upon my prudence did me, as well as the kindness of permitting such an excuse to be made.

The queen talked on, then, of Madame de Genlis with the utmost frankness; she admired her as much as I had done myself, but had been so assaulted with tales to her disadvantage, that she thought it unsafe and indiscreet to form any connection with her. Against her own judgment, she had herself been almost tormented into granting her a private audience, from the imprudent vehemence of one of Madame de G.'s friends here, with whom she felt herself but little pleased for what she had done, and who, I plainly saw, from that unfortunate injudiciousness, would lose all power of exerting any influence in future. Having thus unreservedly explained herself, she finished the subject, and has never started it since. But she looked the whole time with a marked approbation of my applying to her.

Poor Madame de Genlis! how I grieve at the cloud which hovers over so much merit, too bright to be bid but not to be obscured.

A DISTINGUISHED ASTRONOMER.

In the evening Mr. Herschel[217]came to tea. I had once seen that very extraordinary man at Mrs. de Luc's, but was happy to see him again, for he has not more fame to awaken curiosity, than sense and modesty to gratify it. He is perfectly unassuming, yet openly happy; and happy in the success of those studies which would render a mind less excellently formed presumptuous and arrogant. The king has not a happier subject than this man, who owes wholly to his majesty that he is not wretched : for such was his eagerness to quit all other pursuits to follow astronomy solely, that he was in danger of ruin, when his talents, and great and uncommon genius, attracted the king's patronage. He has now not only his pension, which gives him the felicity of devoting all his time to his darling study, but he is indulged in licence from the king to make a telescope according to his new ideas and discoveries, that is to have no cost spared in its construction, and is wholly to be paid for by his majesty.

This seems to have made him happier even than the pension, as it enables him to put in execution all his wonderful projects, from which his expectations of future discoveries are so sanguine as to make his present existence a state of almost perfect enjoyment. Mr. Locke himself would be quite charmed with him. He seems a man without a wish that has its object in the terrestrial globe.

At night, Mr. Herschel, by the king's command, came to exhibit to his majesty and the royal family the new comet lately discovered by his sister, Miss Herschel; and while I was playing at piquet with Mrs. Schwellenberg, the Princess Augusta came into the room, and asked her if she chose to go into the garden and look at it. She declined the offer, and the princess then made it to me. I was glad to accept it, for all Sorts Of reasons.

We found him at his telescope, and I mounted some steps to look through it. The comet was very small, and had nothing grand or striking in its appearance ; but it is the first lady's comet, and I was very desirous to see it. Mr. Herschel then showed me some of his new-discovered universes, with all the good humour with which he would have taken the same trouble for a brother or a sister-astronomer : there is no possibility of admiring his genius more than his gentleness.

EFFUSIVE MADAMF DE LA ROCHE.

I come now to introduce to you, with a new character, some new perplexities from my situation. Madame de la Fite called the next morning, to tell me she must take no denial to forming me a new acquaintance—Madarne de la Roche, a German by birth, but married to a Frenchman;—an authoress, a woman of talents and distinction, a character highly celebrated, and unjustly suffering from an adherence to the Protestant religion. [218]

"She dies with eagerness to see you," she added, in French, ".and I have invited her to Windsor, where I have told her I have no other feast prepared for her but to show her Dr. Herschel and Miss Burney."

I leave you to imagine if I felt competent to fulfil such a promise : openly, on the contrary, I assured her I was quite unequal to it. She had already, she said, written to Madame de la Roche, to come the next day, and if I would not meet her she must be covered with disgrace. Expostulation was now vain; I could only say that to answer for myself was quite, out of my own power.

"And why?—and wherefore?—and what for?—and surely to me!—and surely for Madame de la Roche!—une femme d'esPrit—mon amie— l'amie de Madame de Genlis," etc., etc., filled up a hurried conference in the midst of my dressing for the queen, till a summons interrupted her, and forced me, half dressed, and all too late, to run away from her, with an extorted promise to wait upon her if I possibly could.

Accordingly I went, and arrived before Madame de la Roche. Poor Madame de la Fite received me in transport; and I soon witnessed another transport, at least equal, to Madame de la Roche, which happily was returned with the same warmth; and it was not till after a thousand embraces, and the most ardent professions—"Ma digne amie!—est il possible?—te vois-je?" etc.—that I discovered they had never before met in their lives!—they had corresponded, but, no more! [219]

This somewhat lessened my surprise, however, when my turn arrived; for no sooner was I named than all the embrassades were transferred to me—"La digne Miss Borni!—l'auteur de C'ecile?- -d'Evelina?—non, ce n'est pas possible!-suis-je siheureuse!—oui, je le vois `a ses yeux!—Ah! que de bonheur!" etc. . . .

Madame de la Roche, had I met her in any other way, might have pleased me in no common degree; for could I have conceived her character to be unaffected, her manners have a softness that would render her excessively engaging. She is now bien pass`ee— no doubt fifty—yet has a voice of touching sweetness, eyes of dove-like gentleness, looks supplicating for favour, and an air and demeanour the most tenderly caressing. I can suppose she has thought herself all her life the model of the favourite heroine of her own favourite romance, and I can readily believe that she has had attractions in her youth nothing short of fascinating. Had I not been present, and so deeply engaged in this interview, I had certainly been caught by her myself; for in her presence I constantly felt myself forgiving and excusing what in her absence I as constantly found past defence or apology.

Poor Madame de la Fite has no chance in her presence for though their singular enthusiasm upon " the people of the literature," as Pacchierotti called them, is equal, Madame de la Fite almost subdues by her vehemence, while Madame de la Roche almost melts by her softness. Yet I fairly believe they are both very good women, and both believe themselves sincere.

I returned still time enough to find Mrs. Schwellenberg with her tea-party ; and she was very desirous to hear something of Madame de la Roche. I was led by this to give a short account of her : not such a one as you have heard, because I kept it quite independent of all reference to poor Madame de la Fite; but there was still enough to make a little narration. Madame de Ja Roche had told me that she had been only three days in England, and had yet made but a beginning of seeing les spectacles and les gens c'el`ebres;—and what do you think was the first, and, as yet, sole spectacle to which she had been carried?— Bedlam!—And who the first, and, as yet, only homme c'el`ebre she had seen— Lord George Gordon!—whom she called le fameux George Gordon, and with whom she had dined, in company with Count Cagliostro.

Sunday, Sept. 17-At the chapel this morning, Madame de la Fite placed Madame de la Roche between herself and me, and proposed bringing her to the Lodge, "to return my visit." This being precisely what I had tried to avoid, and to avoid without shocking Madame de la Fite, by meeting her correspondent at her own house, I was much chagrined at such a proposal, but had no means to decline it, as it was made across Madame de la Roche herself.

Accordingly, at about two o'clock, when I came from the queen, I found them both in full possession of my room, and Madame de la Fite occupied in examining my books. The thing thus being done, and the risk of consequences inevitable, I had only to receive them with as little display of disapprobation of their measures as I could help ; but one of the most curious scenes followed I have ever yet been engaged in or witnessed.

As soon as we were seated, Madame de la Fite began with assuring me, aloud, of the "conquest" I had made of Madaine de la Roche, and appealed to that lady for the truth of what she said. Madame de la Roche answered her by rising, and throwing her arms about me, and kissing my cheeks from side to side repeatedly.

Madame de la Fite, as soon as this was over, and we had resumed our seats, opened the next subject, by saying Madame de la Roche had read and adored "Cecilia:" again appealing to her for confirmation of her assertion.

"O, oui, oui!" cried her friend, "mais la vraie C`ecile, est Miss Borni! charmante Miss Borni! digne, douce, et aimable—com to me arms! que je vous embrasse millefois!"

Again we were all deranged, and again the same ceremony being performed, we all sat ourselves down. "Cecilia" was hen talked over throughout, in defiance of every obstacle I could put in its way. After this, Madame de la Fite said, in French, that Madame de la Roche had had the most extraordinary life and adventures that had fallen to anybody's lot; and finished with saying, "Eh! ma ch`ere amie, contez-nous un peu."

They were so connected, she answered, in their early part with M. Wieland, the famous author, that they would not be ietligible without his story.

Madame de la Roche, looking down upon her fan, began then the recital. She related their first interview, the gradations of their mutual attachment, his extraordinary talents, his literary fame and name; the breach of their union from motives of prudence in their friends; his change of character from piety to voluptuousness, in consoling himself for her loss with an actress; his various adventures, and various transformations from good to bad, in life and conduct; her own marriage with M. de]a Roche, their subsequent meeting when she was mother of three children, and all the attendant circumstances.

This narrative was told in so touching and pathetic a manner, and interspersed with so many sentiments of tenderness and of heroism, that I could scarcely believe I was not actually listening to a Clelia, or a Cassandra, recounting the stories of her youth. [220]

When she had done, and I had thanked her, Madame de la Fite demanded of me what I thought of her, and if she was not delightful ? I assented, and Madame de la Roche then, rising, and fixing her eyes, filled with tears, in my face, while she held both my hands, in the most melting accents, exclaimed, "Miss Borni! la plus ch`ere, la plus digne des Angloises! dites-moi-m'aimez-vous!"

I answered as well as I could, but what I said was not very positive. Madame de la Fite came up to us, and desired we might make a trio of friendship, which should bind us to oneanother for life. And then they both embraced me, and both wept for joyful fondness! I fear I seemed very hard-hearted; but no spring was opened whence one tear of mine could flow.

A DINNER DIFFICULTY.

The clock had struck four some time, and Madame de la Fite said she feared they kept me from dinner. I knew it must soon be ready, and therefore made but a slight negative. She then, with an anxious look at her watch, said she feared she was already too late for her own little dinner. I was shocked at a hint I had no power to notice, and heard it in silence—silence unrepressing! for she presently added, "You dine alone, don't you?"

"Y-e-s,—if Mrs. Schwellenberg is not well enough to come down stairs to dinner."

"And can you dine, ma ch`ere mademoiselle—can you dine at that great table alone?"

"I must !—the table is not mine."

"Yes, in Mrs. Schwellenberg's absence it is."

"It has never been made over to me, and I take no power that is not given to me."

"But the queen, my dearest ma'am—the queen, if she knew such a person as Madame de la Roche was here."

She stopped, and I was quite disconcerted. An attack so explicit, and in presence of Madame de la Roche, was beyond all my expectations. She then went to the window, and exclaimed, "It rains!—Mon Dieu! que ferons-nous?—My poor littel dinner!—it will be all spoilt!—La pauvre Madame de la Roche! une telle femme!"

I was now really distressed, and wished much to invite them both to stay; but I was totally helpless ; and could only look, as I felt, in the utmost embarrassment.

The rain continued. Madame de la Roche could understand but imperfectly what passed, and waited its result with an air of smiling patience. I endeavoured to talk of other things - but Madame de la Fite was restless in returning to this charge. She had several times given me very open hints of her desire to dine at Mrs. Schwellenberg's table ; but I had hitherto appeared not to comprehend them: she was now determined to come home to the point; and the more I saw her determination, the less liable I became to being overpowered by it. At length John came to announce dinner.

Madame de la Fite looked at me in a most expressive manner, as she rose and walked towards the window, exclaiming that the rain would not cease; and Madame de la Roche cast upon me a most tender smile, while she lamented that some accident must have prevented her carriage from coming for her. I felt excessively ashamed, and could only beg them not to be in haste, faithfully assuring them I was by no means disposed for eating.

Poor Madame de la Fite now lost all command of herself, and desiring to speak to me in my own room, said, pretty explicitly, that certainly I might keep anybody to dinner, at so great a table, and all alone, if I wished it.

I was obliged to be equally frank. I acknowledged that I had reason to believe I might have had that power, from the custom of my predecessor, Mrs. Haggerdorn, upon my first succeeding to her ; but that I was then too uncertain of any Of my privileges to assume a single one of them unauthorised by the queen. Madame de la Fite was not at all satisfied, and significantly said,

"But you have sometimes Miss Planta?"

"And M. de Luc, too,-he may dine with you

" He also comes to Mrs. Schwellenberg. Mrs. Delany alone, and her niece, come to me; and they have had the sanction of the queen's own desire."

"Mais, enfin, ma ch`ere Miss Burney,—when it rains,—and when it is so late,—and when it is for such a woman as Madame de la Roche!"

So hard pressed, I was quite shocked to resist her ; but I assured her that when my own sisters, Phillips and Francis, came to Windsor purposely to see me, they had never dined at the Lodge but by the express invitation of Mrs. Schwellenberg; and that when my father himself was here, I had not ventured to ask him. This, though it surprised, somewhat appeased her; and we were called into the other room to Miss Planta, who was to dine with me, and who, unluckily, said the dinner would be quite cold.

They begged us both to go, and leave them till the rain was over, or till Madame de la Roche's carriage arrived. I could not bear to do this, but entreated Miss Planta, who was in haste, to go and dine by herself. This, at last, was agreed to, and I tried once again to enter into discourse upon other matters. But how greatly did my disturbance at all this urgency increase, when Madame de la Fite said she was so hungry she must beg a bit of bread and a glass of water!

I was now, indeed, upon the point of giving way; but when I considered, while I hesitated, what must follow-my own necessary apology, which would involve Madame de la Fite in much blame, or my own concealing silence, which would reverse all my plans of openness with the queen, and acquiesced with my own situation-I grew firm again, and having assured her a thousand times of my concern for my little power, I went into the next room : but I sent her the roll and water by John; I was too much ashamed to carry them.

When I returned to them again, Madame de la Fite requested rne to go at once to the queen, and tell her the case. Ah, poor Madame de la Fite Fi to see so little a way for herself, and to suppose me also so every way short-sighted ! I informed her that I never entered the presence of the queen unsummoned. . . .

Again she desired to speak to me in my own room ; and then she told me that Madame de la Roche had a most earnest wish, to see all the royal family; she hoped, therefore, the queen would go to early prayers at the chapel, where, at least she might be beheld : but she gave me sundry hints, not to be misunderstood, that she thought I might so represent the merits of Madame de la Roche as to induce the honour of a private audience.

I could give her no hope of this, as I had none to give for I well knew that the queen has a settled aversion to almost all novels, and something very near it to almost all novelwriters.

She then told me she had herself requested an interview for her with the princess royal, and had told her that if it was too much to grant it in the royal apartments, at least it might take place in Miss Burney's room ! Her royal highness coldly answered that she saw nobody without the queen's commands. . . .

In the end, the carriage of Madame de la Roche arrived, about tea-time, and Madame de la Fite finished with making me promise to relate my difficulties to the queen, that she might give me such orders as to enable me to keep them any other time. To give you the result at once, Miss Planta, of her own accord, briefly related the affair to the queen, dwelling upon my extreme embarrassment, with the most good-natured applause of its motives. The queen graciously joined in commendation of my steadiness, expressed her disapprobation of the indelicacy of poor Madame de la Fite, and added that if I had been overcome, it would have been an encouragement to her to bring foreigners for ever to the Lodge, wholly contrary to the pleasure of the king.

AN ECCENTRIC LADY.

Sept. 25.-Mrs. Delany came to me to dinner, and we promised ourselves the whole afternoon t`ete-`a-t`ete, with no other interruption than what we were well contented to allow to Major Price and General Bud`e. But before we were well settled in my room, after our late dinner in the next, a visitor appeared,-Miss Finch.

We were both sadly vexed at this disappointment ; but you will wonder to hear that I became, in a few minutes, as averse to her going as I had been to her coming : for the Princess Amelia was brought in, by Mrs. Cheveley, to carry away Mrs. Delany to the queen. I had now, therefore, no one, but this chance-comer, to assist me in doing the honours to my two beaus; and well as I like their company, I by no means enjoyed the prospect of receiving them alone: not, I protest, and am sure, from any prudery, but simply from thinking that a single female, in a party, either large or small, of men, unless very much used to the world, appears to be in a situation awkward and unbecoming.

I was quite concerned, therefore, to hear from Miss Finch that she meant but a short visit, for some reasons belonging to her carriage ; and when she rose to go, I felt my distaste to this new mode of proceeding so strong, that I hastily related to her my embarrassment, and frankly begged her to stay and help to recreate my guests. She was very much diverted with this distress, which she declared she could not comprehend, but frankly agreed to remain with me; and promised, at my earnest desire, not to publish what I had confessed to her, lest I should gain, around Windsor, the character of a prude.

I had every reason to be glad that I detained her, for she not only made my meeting with the equerries easy and pleasant, but was full of odd entertainment herself. She has a large portion of whimsical humour, which, at times, is original and amusing, though always eccentric, and frequently, from uttering whatever comes uppermost, accidental.

Among many other flights, she very solemnly declared that she could never keep any body's face in her mind when they were out of her sight. "I have quite forgot," cried she, "the Duke of York already, though I used to see him so continually. Really, it's quite terrible, but I cannot recollect a single trait of anybody when they are the shortest time out of my sight; especially if they are dead;—it's quite shocking, but really i can never remember the face of a person the least in the world when once they are dead!" '

The major, who knows her very well, and who first had introduced her to me on my settling here, was much amused with her rattle; and General Bud`e is always pleased with anything bordering upon the ridiculous. Our evening therefore turned out very well.

THE WRONG GUEST INVITED.

I have something to relate now that both my dearest friends will take great pleasure in hearing, because it appertains to my dignity and consequence. The queen, in the most gracious manner, desired me this morning to send an invitation to M.

Mithoff, a German clergyman, to come to dinner; and she added, "I assure you he is a very worthy man, of very excellent character, or I would not ask you to invite him."

Was not this a very sweet manner of making over to me the presidency of the table in Mrs. Schwellenberg's absence?

It was for the next day, and I sent John to him immediately ;-rather awkward, though, to send my compliments to a man I had never seen, and invite him to dine with me. But there was no other mode —I could not name the queen. I knew Miss Port would be happy to make us a trio, and I begged her not to fail me.

But alas!—If awkwardness was removed, something worse was substituted in its place ; my presidency was abolished on the very day it was to be declared, by the sudden return of its rightful superseder. I acquainted her with the invitation I had been desired to send, and I told her I bad also engaged Miss Port. I told of both as humbly as possible, that I might raise no alarms of any intention of rivalry in power.

Mr. Mithoff was not yet come when dinner was announced, nor yet Miss Port; we sat down t`ete-`a-t`ete, myself in some pain for my invitations, my companion well content to shew she would wait for none of my making,

At length came Miss Port, and presently after a tall German clergyman entered the room. I was a little confused by his immediately making up to me, and thanking me in the strongest terms for the honour of my invitation, and assuring me it was the most flattering one he had ever received.

I answered as short as I could, for I was quite confounded by the looks of Mrs. Schwellenberg. Towards me they were directed with reproach, and towards the poor visitor with astonishment: why I could not imagine, as I had frequently heard her speak of M. Mithoff with praise.

Finding nothing was said to him, I was obliged to ask him to take a place at the table myself, which he did; still, and with great glee of manner, addressing himself wholly to me, and never finishing his warm expressions of gratitude for my invitation. I quite longed to tell him I had her majesty's orders for what I had done, that he might cease his most unmerited acknowledgments; but I could not at that time. The dinner went off very ill . nobody said a word but this gentleman, and he spoke only to do himself mischief.

When we all adjourned to Mrs. Schwellenberg's room up stairs, for coffee, my new guest again poured forth such a torrent of thanks, that I could not resist taking the first opportunity to inform him he owed me no such strong obligation, as I had simply obeyed the commands of the queen.

"The queen!" he exclaimed, with yet greater enchantment; "then I am very happy indeed, madam; I had been afraid at first there was some mistake in the honour you did me."

"It might have seemed a mistake indeed, sir," cried I, "if you supposed I had taken the liberty of making you such an invitation, without the pleasure of knowing you myself."

Mrs. Schwellenberg, just after, calling me aside, said, "For what have you brought me this man?"

I could make no answer, lest he should hear me, for I saw him look uneasily towards us ; and therefore, to end such interrogations, I turned to him, and asked how many days he should continue at Windsor. He looked Surprised, and said he had no thought of leaving it.

It was my turn to look surprised now; I had heard he only came upon her majesty's commands, and was to stay but a day or two. I now began to suspect some mistake, and that my message had gone to a wrong person. I hastened, therefore, to pronounce the name of Mithoff, and my suspicion was changed into certainty, by his telling me, with a stare, that it was not his.

Imagine but my confusion at this information !-the queen's commission so ill executed, M. Mithoff neglected, and some one else invited whose very name I knew not!—nor did he, though my mistake now was visible, tell it me. Yet he looked so much disappointed, that I thought it incumbent upon me, since the blunder must have been my servant's, to do what I could to comfort him. I therefore forced myself forward to talk to him, and pass over the embarrassment but he was modest, and consequently overset, and soon after took his leave.

I then cleared myself to Mrs. Schwellenberg of any voluntary deed in " bringing her this man," and inquired of John how it happened. He told me he had forgot the gentleman's name, but as I had said he was a German clergyman, he had asked for him as such, and thought this must be the right person. I heard afterwards that this is a M. Schrawder, one of the masters of the German language to the princesses. I jDacle all the apologies in my power to him for the error. . . .

The queen, at night, with great good humour, laughed at the mistake, and only desired it might be rectified for the next day. Accordingly it was ; and M. Mithoff had an invitation for the next day, in proper order: that is, from Mrs. Schwellenberg,

THE PRINCEss ROYAL's BIRTHDAY.

Friday, Sept. 29-This day the princess royal entered her twenty-first year. I had the pleasure of being in the room with the queen when she sent for her, early in the morning. Her majesty bid me stop, while she went into another apartment to fetch her birthday gifts. The charming princess entered with so modest, so composed an air, that it seemed as if the day, with all its preparations for splendour, was rather solemn than elevating to her. I had no difficulty, thus alone with her, in offering my best wishes to her. She received them most gracefully, and told me, with the most sensible pleasure, that the King had just been with her, and presented to her a magnificent diamond necklace.

The queen then returned, holding in her hands two very pretty portfolios for her drawings, and a very fine gold etui. The princess, in receiving them with the lowest curtsey, kissed her hand repeatedly, while the queen gave back her kisses upon her cheeks.

The king came in soon after, and the three youngest princesses. They all flew to kiss the princess royal, who is affectionately fond of them all. Princess Amelia shewed how fine she was, and made the queen admire her new coat and frock ; she then examined all the new dresses of her sisters, and then looking towards me with some surprise, exclaimed, " And won't Miss Burney be fine, too?"

I shall not easily forget this little innocent lesson. It seems all the household dress twice on these birthdays—for their first appearance, and for dinner-and always in something distinguished. I knew it not, and had simply prepared for my second attire only, wearing in the morning my usual white dimity great coat. I was a little out of countenance ; and the queen, probably perceiving it, said—

" Come hither, Amelia; who do you think is here-in Miss Burney's room?"

"Lany," answered the quick little creature ; for so she calls Mrs. Delany, who had already exerted herself to come to the Lodge with her congratulations.

The king, taking the hand of the little princess, said they would go and see her ; and turning to the queen as they left the room, called out,

What shall we do with Mrs. Delany?"

"What the king pleases," was her answer.

I followed them to my room, where his majesty stayed some time, giving that dear old lady a history of the concert of the preceding evening, and that he had ordered for this day for the princess royal. It is rather unfortunate her royal highness should have her birth-day celebrated by an art which she even professes to have no taste for, and to hear almost with pain.

The king took Mrs. Delany to breakfast with himself and family.

I wore my memorable present-gown this day in honour of the princess royal. It is a lilac tabby. I saw the king for a minute at night, as he returned from the Castle, and he graciously admired it, calling out "Emily should see Miss Burney's gown now, and she would think her fine enough."

ARRIVAL OF A NEw EQUERRY.

The following evening I first saw the newly-arrived equerry, Colonel Goldsworthy. Mrs. Schwellenberg was ill, and sent for Mr. de Luc, and told me to go into the eating-roorn, and make the tea for her. I instantly wrote to Miss

Port, to beg she would come to assist me : she did, and Mrs. Schwellenberg, changing her plan, came downstairs at the same time. The party was Major Price, General Bud'e, Mr. Fisher, and the colonel. Major Price immediately presented us to each other.

"Upon my word!" cried Mrs. Schwellenberg, "you do the honour here in my room!—you might leave that to me, Major Price!"

"What! my brother equerry?" cried he; "No, ma'am, I think I have a right there."

Colonel Goldsworthy's character stands very high for worth and honour, and he is warmly attached to the king, both for his own sake, and from the tie that binds him to all the royal family, of regard for a sister extremely dear to him, Miss Goldsworthy, whose residence here brings him frequently to the palace. He seems to me a man of but little cultivation or literature, but delighting in a species of dry humour, in which he shines most successfully, in giving up himself for its favourite butt.

He brought me a great many compliments, he said, from Dr. Warton, of Winchester, where he had lately been quartered with his regiment. He rattled away very amusingly upon the balls and the belles he had seen there, laughing at his own gallantry, and pitying and praising himself alternately for venturing to exert it.

CUSTODIAN OF THE QUEEN'S JEWEL Box.

Od. 2-The next day we were all to go to Kew : but Mrs, Schwellenberg was taken ill, and went by herself to town.

The queen sent for me after breakfast, and delivered to me a long box, called here the jewel box, in which her jewels are carried to and from town that are worn on the Drawing-room days. The great bulk of them remain in town all the winter, and remove to Windsor for all the summer, with the rest of the family. She told me, as she delivered the key into my hands, that as there was always much more room in the box than her travelling jewels occupied, I might make what use I pleased of the remaining part ; adding, with a very expressive smile, "I dare say you have books and letters that you may be glad to carry backwards and forwards with you."

I owned that nothing was more true, and thankfully accepted the offer. It has proved to me since a comfort of the first magnitude, in conveying all my choice papers and letters safely in the carriage with me, as well as books in present reading, and numerous odd things. . . .

Friday, Oct. 6. - We returned to Windsor without Mrs. Schwellenberg, who stayed in town for her physician's advice. The queen went immediately to Mrs. Delany, and the princess royal came into my room.

"I beg pardon," she cried, "for what I am going to say: I hope you will excuse my taking such a liberty with you—but, has nobody told you that the queen is always used to have the jewel-box carried into her bedroom?"

"No, ma'am, nobody mentioned it to me. I brought it here because I have other things in it."

"I thought, when I did not see it in mamma's room," cried she, "that nobody had told you of that custom, and so I thought I would come to you myself: I hope you will excuse it?"

You may believe how I thanked her, while I promised to take out my own goods and chattels, and have it conveyed to its proper place immediately. I saw that she imagined the queen might be displeased; and though I could never myself imagine that, for an omission of ignorance, I felt the benevolence of her intention, and received it with great gratitude.

"My dear ma'am," cried she, "I am sure I should be most happy to do anything for you that should be in my power, always; and really Mrs. Schwellenberg ought to have told you this."

Afterwards I happened to be alone with this charming princess, and her sister Elizabeth, in the queen's dressing-room. She then came up to me and said,

"Now will you excuse me, Miss Burney, if I ask you the truth of something I have heard about you?"

"Certainly, ma'am."

"It's such an odd thing, I don't know how to mention it; but I have wished to ask you about it this great while. Pray is it really true that, in your illness last year, you coughed so violently that you broke the whalebone of your stays in two?"

"As nearly true as possible, ma'am;it actually split with the force of the almost convulsive motion of a cough that seemed loud and powerful enough for a giant. I could hardly myself believe it was little I that made so formidable a noise."

"Well, I could not have given credit to it if I had not heard it from yourself! I wanted so much to know the truth, that I determined, at last, to take courage and ask you."

"And pray, Miss Burney," cried the Princess Elizabeth, "had you not a blister that gave you great torture?"

"Yes, ma'am,—in another illness."

"O!—I know how to pity you!—I have one on at this moment!

"And pray, Miss Burney," cried the princess royal, "were not you carried out of town, when you were in such a weak condition that you could not walk?"

"Where could your royal highness hear all this?"

"And were you not almost starved by Sir Richard jebb?" cried Princess Elizabeth.

"And did you not receive great benefit from asses' rnilk?" exclaimed the princess royal.

Again I begged to know their means of hearing all this; but the queen's entrance silenced us all,

A LAUDATORY ESTIMATE OF THE QUEEN.

The queen was unremittingly sweet and gracious, never making me sensible of any insufficiency from My single attendance; which, to me, was an opportunity the most favourable in the world for becoming more intimately acquainted with her mind and understanding. For the excellency of her mind I was fully prepared ; the testimony of the nation at large could not be unfaithful ; but the depth and soundness of her understanding surprised me : good sense I expected - to that alone she could owe the even tenor of her conduct, universally approved, though examined and judged by the watchful eye of multitudes. But I had not imagined that, shut up in the confined limits of a Court, she could have acquired any but the most superficial knowledge of the world, and the most partial insight into character. But I find, now, I have only done justice to her disposition, not to her parts, which are truly of that superior order that makes sagacity intuitively supply the place of experience. In the course of this month I spent much time quite alone with her, and never once quitted her presence without fresh admiration of her talents.

There are few points I have observed with more pleasure in her than all that concerns the office which brings me to her in this private and confidential manner. All that breaks from her, in our t`ete-`a-t`etes, upon the subject of dress, is both edifying and amiable. She equips herself for the drawing-room with all the attention in her power; she neglects nothing that she thinks becoming to her appearance upon those occasions, and is sensibly conscious that her high station makes her attire in public a matter of business. As such, she submits to it without murmuring; but a yet stronger consciousness of the real futility of such mere outward grandeur bursts from her, involuntarily, the moment the sacrifice is paid, and she can never refuse herself the satisfaction of expressing her contentment to put on a quiet undress. The great coats are so highly in her favour, from the quickness with which they enable her to finish her toilette, that she sings their praise with fresh warmth every time she is allowed to wear them, archly saying to me, with most expressive eyes, "If I could write—if I could but write!—how I would compose upon a great coat! I wish I were a poetess, that I might make a song upon it—I do think something very pretty might be said about it."

These hints she has given me continually ; but the Muse was not so kind as ever to make me think of the matter again when out of her sight-till, at last, she one day, in putting on this favourite dress, half gravely, said, "I really take it a little ill you won't write something upon these great coats!"

I only laughed, yet, when I left her, I scribbled a few stanzas, copied them very fairly, and took them, as soon as they were finished, into her room ; and there kept them safely in my pocket-book, for I knew not how to produce them, and she, by odd accident, forbore from that time to ask for them, though her repeated suggestion had, at last, conquered my literary indolence.

I cannot here help mentioning a very interesting little scene at which I was present, about this time. The queen had nobody but myself with her, one morning, when the king hastily entered the room, with some letters in his hand, and addressing her in German, which he spoke very fast, and with much apparent interest in what he said, he brought the letters up to her, and put them into her hand. She received them with much agitation, but evidently of a much pleased sort, and endeavoured to kiss his hand as he held them. He would not let her, but made an effort, with a countenance of the highest satisfaction, to kiss hers. I saw instantly in her eyes a forgetfulness, at the moment, that any one was present, while, drawing away her hand, she presented him her cheek. He accepted her kindness with the same frank affection that she offered it; and the next moment they both spoke English, and talked upon common and general subjects.

What they said I am far enough from knowing; but the whole was too rapid to give me time to quit the room ; and I could not but see with pleasure that the queen had received some favour with which she was sensibly delighted, and that the king, in her acknowledgments, was happily and amply paid.

TABLE DIFFICULTIES.

No sooner did I find that my coadjutrix ceased to speak of returning to Windsor, [222] and that I became, by that means, the presidentess of the dinner and teatable, than I formed a grand design—no other than to obtain to my own use the disposal of my evenings.

From the time of my entrance into this Court, to that of which I am writing, I had never been informed that it was incumbent upon me to receive the king's equerries at the teatable ; yet I observed that they always came to Mrs. Schwellenberg, and that she expected them so entirely as never to make tea till their arrival. Nevertheless, nothing of that sort had ever been intimated to me, and I saw no necessity of falling into all her ways, without commands to that purpose : nor could I conclude that the king's gentlemen would expect from me either the same confinement, or readiness of reception, as had belonged to two invalid old ladies, glad of company, and without a single connection to draw them from home. . . .

I could not, however, but be struck with a circumstance that shewed me, in a rather singular manner, my tea-making seemed at once to be regarded as indispensable : this was no other than a constant summons, which John regularly brought me every evening, from these gentlemen, to acquaint me they were come upstairs to the tea-room, and waiting for me.

I determined not to notice this: and consequently, the first time Mrs. Delany was not well enough to give me her valuable society at the Lodge, I went to her house, and spent the evening there; without sending any message to the equerries, as any apology must imply a right on their part that must involve me in future confinement.

This I did three or four times, always with so much success as to gain my point for the moment, but never with such happy consequences as to ensure it me for the time to come; since every next meeting shewed an air of pique, and since every evening had still, unremittingly, the same message for John.

I concluded this would wear away by use, and therefore resolved to give it that chance. One evening, however, when, being quite alone, I was going to my loved resource, John, ere I could get out, hurried to me, "Ma'am, the gentlemen are come up, and they send their compliments, and they wait tea for you."

"Very well," was my answer to this rather cavalier summons, which I did not wholly admire; and I put on my hat and cloak, when I was called to the queen. She asked me whether I thought Mrs. Delany could come to her, as she wished to see her? I offered to go instantly, and inquire.

"But don't tell her I sent you," cried the most considerate queen, "lest that should make her come when it may hurt her: find out how she is, before you mention me."

As I now knew I must return myself, at any rate, I slipped into the tea-room before I set off. I found there Colonel Goldsworthy, looking quite glum, General Bud`e, Mr. Fisher, Mr. - Fisher, his brother, and Mr. Blomberg, chaplain to the Prince of Wales.

The moment I opened the door, General Bud`e presented Mr. Blomberg to me, and Mr. Fisher his brother; I told them, hastily, that I was running away to Mrs. Delany, but meant to return in a quarter of an hour, when I should be happy to have their company, if they could wait so long ; but if they were hurried, my man should bring their tea.

They all turned to Colonel Goldsworthy, who, as equerry in waiting, was considered as head of the party; but he seemed so choked with surprise and displeasure, that he could only mutter something too indistinct to be heard, and bowed low and distantly.

"If Colonel Goldsworthy can command his time, ma'am," cried Mr. Fisher, "we shall be most happy to wait yours."

General Bud6 said the same : the colonel again silently and solemnly bowed, and I curtsied in the same manner, and burried away.

Mrs. Delany was not well ; and I would not vex her with the queen's kind wish for her. I returned, and sent in, by the page in waiting, my account : for the queen was in the concertroom, and I could not go to her. Neither would I seduce away Miss Port from her duty ; I came back, therefore, alone, and was fain to make my part as good as I was able among my beaus.

I found them all waiting. Colonel Goldsworthy received me with the same stately bow, and a look so glum and disconcerted, that I instantly turned from him to meet the soft countenance of the good Mr. Fisher, who took a chair next mine, and entered into conversation with his usual intelligence and mildness. General Bud`e was chatty and well bred, and the two strangers wholly silent.

I could not, however, but see that Colonel Goldsworthy grew less and less pleased. Yet what had I done ?-I had never been commanded to devote my evenings to him, and, if excused officially, surely there could be no private claim from either his situation or mine. His displeasure therefore appeared to me so unjust, that I resolved to take not the smallest notice of it. He never once opened his mouth, neither to me nor to any one else. In this strange manner we drank our tea. When it was over, he still sat dumb - and still I conversed with Mr. Fisher and General Bud`e.

At length a prodigious hemming showed a preparation in the colonel for a speech : it came forth with great difficulty, and most considerable hesitation.

"I am afraid, ma'am,—I am afraid you—you—that is—that we are intruders upon you."

"N-o," answered I, faintly, "why so?"

"I am sure, ma'am, if we are—if you think—if we take too much liberty—I am sure I would not for the world!—I only—your commands—nothing else—"

"Sir!" cried I, not understanding a word.

"I see, ma'am, we only intrude upon you: however, you must excuse my just saying we would not for the world have taken such a liberty, though very sensible of the happiness of being allowed to come in for half an hour,—which is the best half-hour of the whole day; but yet, if it was not for your own commands—"

"What commands, sir?"

He grew still more perplexed, and made at least a dozen speeches to the same no purpose, before I could draw from him anything explicit ; all of them listening silently the whole time, and myself invariably staring. At last, a few words escaped him more intelligible.

"Your messages, ma'am, were what encouraged us to come."

"And pray, sir, do tell me what messages?—I am very happy to see you, but I never sent any messages at all?"

"Indeed, ma'am!" cried he, staring in his turn; "why your servant, little John there, came rapping at our door, at the equerry room, before we had well swallowed our dinner, and said, 'My lady is waiting tea, sir.'"

I was quite confounded. I assured him it was an entire fabrication of my servant's, as I had never sent, nor even thought of sending him, for I was going Out.

"Why to own the truth, ma'am," cried he, brightening up, "I did really think it a little odd to send for us in that hurry, for we got up directly from table, and said, if the lady is waiting, to be sure we must not keep her; and then-when we came-to just peep in, and say you were going out!"

How intolerable an impertinence in John !-it was really no wonder the poor colonel was so glum.

Again I repeated my ignorance of this step ; and he then said "Why, ma'am, he comes to us regularly every afternoon, and says his lady is waiting; and we are very glad to come, poor souls that we are, with no rest all the livelong day but what we get in this good room !-but then-to come, and see ourselves only intruders-and to find you going out, after sending for us!"

I could scarce find words to express my amazement at this communication. I cleared myself instantly from having any the smallest knowledge of John's proceedings, and Colonel Goldsworthy soon recovered all his spirits and good humour, when he was satisfied he had not designedly been treated with such strange and unmeaning inconsistency. He rejoiced exceedingly that he had spoke out, and I thanked him for his frankness, and the evening concluded very amicably. . . .

The evening after, I invited Miss Port, determined to spend it entirely with my beaus, in order to wholly explain away this impertinence. Colonel Goldsworthy now made me a thousand apologies for having named the matter to me at all. I assured him I was extremely glad he had afforded me an opportunity of clearing it. In the course of the discussion, I mentioned the constant summons brought me by John every afternoon. He lifted up his hands and eyes, and protested most solemnly he had never sent a single one.

"I vow, ma'am," cried the colonel, "I would not have taken such a liberty on any account; though all the comfort of my life in this house, is one half-hour in a day spent in this room. After all one's labours, riding, and walking, and standing, and bowing-what a life it is! Well! it's honour ! that's one comfort ; it's all honour ! royal honour !-one has the honour to stand till one has not a foot left ; and to ride till one's stiff, and to walk till one's ready to drop,-and then one makes one's lowest bow, d'ye see, and blesses one's self with joy for the honour!"

AN EQUERRY'S DUTIES AND DISCOMFORTS.

His account of his own hardships and sufferings here, in the discharge of his duty, is truly comic. "How do you like it, ma'am?" he says to me, "though it's hardly fair to ask you yet, because you know almost nothing of the joys of this sort of life. But wait till November and December, and then you'll get a pretty taste of them! Running along in these cold passages, then bursting into rooms fit to bake you, then back again into all these agreeable puffs !-Bless us ! I believe in my heart there's wind enough in these passages to carry a man of war! And there you'll have your share, ma'am, I promise you that! you'll get knocked up in three days, take my word for that."

I begged him not to prognosticate so much evil for me.

"O ma'am, there's no help for it!" cried he; "you won't have the hunting, to be sure, nor amusing yourself with wading a foot and a-half through the dirt, by way of a little pleasant walk, as we poor equerries do!, It's a wonder to me we outlive the first month. But the agreeable puffs of the passages you will have just as completely as any of us. Let's see, how many blasts must you have every time you go to the queen? First, one upon your opening your door; then another, as you get down the three steps from it, which are exposed to the wind from the garden door downstairs; then a third, as you turn the corner to enter the passage; then you come plump upon another from the hall door; then comes another, fit to knock you down, as You turn to the upper passage ; then, just as You turn towards the queen's room, comes another; and last, a whiff from the king's stairs, enough to blow you half a mile off!"

"Mere healthy breezes," I cried, and assured him I did not fear them.

"Stay till Christmas," cried he, with a threatening air, "only stay till then, and let's see what you'll say to them; you'll be laid up as sure as fate! you may take my word for that. One thing, however, pray let me caution you about—don't go to early prayers in November; if you do, that will completely kill you! Oh, ma'am, you know nothing yet of all these matters! only pray, joking apart, let me have the honour just to advise you this one thing, or else it's all over with you, I do assure you!"

It was in vain I begged him to be more merciful in his prophecies; he failed not, every night, to administer to me the same pleasant anticipations.

"Why the princesses," cried he, "used to it as they are, get regularly knocked up before this business is over; off they drop, one by one:—first the queen deserts us; then Princess Elizabeth is done for; then princess royal begins coughing; then Princess Augusta gets the snuffles; and all the poor attendants, my poor sister at their head, drop off, one after another, like so many snuffs of candles: till at last, dwindle, dwindle, dwindle—not a soul goes to the chapel but the king, the parson, and myself; and there we three freeze it out together!"

One evening, when he had been out very late hunting with the king, he assumed so doleful an air of weariness, that had not Miss Port exerted her utmost powers to revive him, he would not have uttered a word the whole night; but when once brought forward, he gave us more entertainment than ever, by relating his hardships.

"After all the labours," cried he, "of the chase, all the riding, the trotting, the galloping, the leaping, the—with your favour, ladies, I beg pardon, I was going to say a strange word, but the—the perspiration—and—and all that—after being wet through over head, and soused through under feet, and popped into ditches, and jerked over gates, what lives we do lead! Well, it's all honour! that's my only comfort! Well, after all this, fagging away like mad from eight in the morning to five or six in the afternoon, home we come, looking like so many drowned rats, with not a dry thread about us, nor a morsel within us—sore to the very bone, and forced to smile all the time! and then after all this what do you think follows?—'Here, Goldsworthy,' cries his majesty: so up I comes to him, bowing profoundly, and my hair dripping down to my shoes; 'Goldsworthy,' cries his majesty. 'Sir,' says I, smiling agreeably, with the rheumatism just creeping all over me ! but still, expecting something a little comfortable, I wait patiently to know his gracious pleasure, and then, 'Here, Goldsworthy, say !' he cries, 'will you have a little barley water?' Barley water in such a plight as that! Fine compensation for a wet jacket, truly!—barley water! I never heard of such a tiling in my life! barley water after a whole day's hard hunting!"

"And pray did you drink it?"

"I drink it?—Drink barley water? no, no; not come to that neither. But there it was, sure enough!—in a jug fit for a sick room, just such a thing as you put upon a hob in a chimney, for some poor miserable soul that keeps his bed! just such a thing as that!—And, 'Here, Goldsworthy,' says his majesty, 'here's the barley water,'"

"And did the king drink it himself?"

"Yes, God bless his majesty! but I was too humble a subject to do the same as the king!—Barley water, quoth I!—Ha! ha!—a fine treat truly! Heaven defend me! I'm not come to that, neither!—bad enough too, but not so bad as that."

ROYAL CAUTIONS AND CONFIDENCES.

Nov. 1.-We began this month by steadily settling ourselves at Kew. A very pleasant circumstance happened to me on this day, in venturing to present the petition of an unfortunate man who had been shipwrecked; whose petition was graciously attended to,'and the money he solicited was granted him. I had taken a great interest in the poor man, from the simplicity and distress of his narration, and took him into one of the parlours to assist him in drawing Up his memorial.

The queen, when, with equal sweetness and humanity, she had delivered the sum to one of her pages to give to him, said to me, "Now, though your account of this poor man makes him seem to be a real object, I must give you one caution : there are so many impostors about, who will try to speak to you, that, if you are not upon your guard, you may be robbed yourself before you can get any help : I think, therefore, you had better never trust yourself in a room alone with anybody you don't know."

I thanked her for her gracious counsel, and promised, for the future, to have my man always at hand.

I was afterwards much touched with a sort of unconscious confidence with which she relieved her mind. She asked me my opinion of a paper in the "Tatler," which I did not recollect; and when she was dressed, and seated in her sitting-room, she made me give her the book, and read to me this paper. It is an account of a young man of a good heart and sweet disposition, who is allured by pleasure into a libertine life, which he pursues by habit, but with constant remorse, and ceaseless shame and unhappiness. It was impossible for me to miss her object: all the mother was in her voice while she read it, and her glistening eyes told the application made throughout. [223]My mind sympathised sincerely, though my tongue did not dare allude to her feelings. She looked pensively down when she had finished it, and before she broke silence, a page came to announce the Duchess of Ancaster.

THE QUEEN TIRED OF HER GEWGAWS.

Nov. 3.-In the morning I had the honour of a conversation with the queen, the most delightful, on her part, I had ever yet been indulged with. It was all upon dress, and she said so nearly what I had just imputed to her in my little stanzas, that I could scarce refrain producing them ; yet could not muster courage. She told me, with the sweetest grace imaginable, how well she had liked at first her jewels and ornaments as queen,—"But how soon," cried she, "was that over! Believe me, Miss Burney, it is a pleasure of a week,—a fortnight, at most,—and to return no more! I thought, at first, I should always choose to wear them, but the fatigue, and trouble of putting them on, and the care they required, and the fear of losing them,—believe me, ma'am, in a fortnight's time I longed again for my own earlier dress, and wished never to see them more!"

She then still more opened her opinions and feelings. She told me she had never, in her most juvenile years, loved dress and shew, nor received the smallest pleasure from any thing in her external appearance beyond neatness and comfort : yet did not disavow that the first week or fortnight of being a queen, when only in her seventeenth year, she thought splendour sufficiently becoming her station to believe she should thenceforth choose constantly to support it. But her eyes alone were dazzled, not her mind ; and therefore the delusion speedily vanished, and her understanding was too strong to give it any chance of returning,

A HOLIDAY AT LAST.

NOV. 4.-This morning, when I attended the queen, she asked me if I should like to go and see my father at Chesington ? and then gave orders immediately for a chaise to be ready without delay— "And there is no need you should hurry yourself," she added, "for it will do perfectly well if you are back to dinner; when I dress, I will send for Miss Planta."

I thanked her very much, and she seemed quite delighted to give me this gratification. "The first thing I thought of this morning, when I woke," said she, "and when I saw the sun shining in upon the bed, was that this would be a fine morning for Miss Burney to go and see her father."

And soon after, to make me yet more comfortable she found a deputy for my man as well as for myself, condescending to give orders herself that another person might lay the cloth, lest I should be hurried home on that account.

I need not tell my two dear readers how sensibly I felt her goodness, when I acquaint them of its effect upon me ; which was no less than to induce, to impel me to trust her with my performance of her request. just as she was quitting her dressing-room, I got behind her, and suddenly blurted out—

"Your majesty's goodness to me, ma'am, makes me venture to own that there is a command which I received some time ago, and which I have made some attempt to execute."

She turned round with great quickness,—"The great coat?" she cried, "is it that?"

I was glad to be so soon understood, and took it from my pocket book— but holding it a little back, as she offered to take it.

"For your majesty alone," I cried; "I must entreat that it may meet no other eyes, and I hope it will not be looked at when any one else is even in sight!"

She gave me a ready promise, and took it with an alacrity and walked off with a vivacity that assured me she would not be very long before she examined it; though, when I added another little request, almost a condition, that it might not be read till I was far away, she put it into her pocket unopened, and, Wishing me a pleasant ride, and that I might find my father well, she proceeded towards the breakfast parlour.

My dear friends will, I know, wish to see it,-and so they shall; though not this moment, as I have it not about me, and do not remember it completely. 224

My breakfast was short, the chaise was soon ready, and forth I sallied for dear—once how dear!—old Chesington! Every step of the road brought back to my mind the first and most loved and honoured friend of my earliest years, and I felt a melancholy almost like my first regret for him, when I considered what joy, what happiness I lost, in missing his congratulations on a situation so much what he would have chosen for me— congratulations which, flowing from a mind such as his, so wise, so zealous, so sincere, might almost have reconciled me to it myself—I mean even then—for now the struggle is over, and I am content enough.

John rode on, to open the gates ; the gardener met him and I believe surprise was never greater than he carried into the house with my name. Out ran dear Kitty Cooke, whose honestly affectionate reception touched me very much,—"O,"

cried she, "had our best friend lived to see this day when you came to poor old Chesington from Court!"

Her grief, ever fresh, then overflowed in a torrent and I could hardly either comfort her, or keep down the sad regretful recollections rising in my own memory. O my dear Susan, with what unmixed satisfaction, till that fatal period when I paid him my last visit, had I ever entered those gates-where passed the scenes of the greatest ease, gaiety, and native mirth that have fallen to my lot!

Mrs. James Burney next, all astonishment, and our dear James himself, all incredulity, at the report carried before me, came out. [225]Their hearty welcome and more pleasant surprise recovered me from the species of consternation with which I had approached their dwelling, and the visit, from that time, turned out perfectly gay and happy.

My dearest father was already gone to town; but I had had much reason to expect I should miss him, and therefore I could not be surprised. . . .

I left them all with great reluctance: I had no time to walk in the garden,-no heart to ascend the little mount, and see how Norbury hills and woods looked from it!

I set out a little the sooner, to enable me to make another visit, which I had also much at heart,-it was to our aunts at Kingston. I can never tell you their astonishment at sight of me; they took me for my own ghost, I believe, at first, but they soon put my substance to the proof, and nothing could better answer my motives than my welcome, which I need not paint to my Susan, who never sees them without experiencingit. To my great satisfaction, also, my nieces Fanny and Sophy happened to be there at that time.

My return was just in time for my company, which I found increased by the arrival of two more gentlemen, Mr. Fisher and Mr. Turbulent. Mr. Fisher had been ordered to come, that he might read prayers the next day, Sunday. Mr. Turbulent[226]was summoned, I suppose, for his usual occupations; reading with the princesses, or to the queen. Shall I introduce to you this gentleman such as I now think him at once? or wait to let his character open itself to you by degrees, and in the same manner that it did to me? So capital a part as you will find him destined to play, hereafter, in my concerns, I mean, sooner or later, to the best of my power, to make you fully acquainted with him. . . .

He took his seat next mine at the table, and assisted me, while Mr. Fisher sat as chaplain at the bottom. The dinner went off extremely well, though from no help of mine. . . . The three men and the three females were all intimately acquainted with one another, and the conversation, altogether, was equal, open, and agreeable.

You may a little judge of this, when I tell you a short speech that escaped Miss Planta. Mr. Turbulent said he must go early to town the next morning, and added, he should call to see Mrs. Schwellenberg, by order of the queen, "Now for heaven's sake, Mr. Turbulent," she cried, eagerly, "don't you begin talking to her of how comfortable we are here !-it will bring her back directly!"

This was said in a half whisper; and I hope no one else heard it. I leave you, my dear friends, to your own comments.

TEA Room GAMBOLS.

Mr. and Mrs. Smelt and Mrs. Delany came to us at teatime. Then, and in their society, I grew more easy and disengaged.

The sweet little Princess Amelia, who had promised me a visit, came during tea, brought by Mrs. Cheveley. I left every body to play with her, and Mr. Smelt joined in our gambols. We pretended to put her in a phaeton, and to drive about and make visits with her. She entered into the scheme with great spirit and delight, and we waited upon Mrs. Delany and Mrs. Smelt alternately. Children are never tired of playing at being women; and women there are who are never tired, in return, of playing at being children!

In the midst of this frolicking, which at times was rather noisy, by Mr. Smelt's choosing to represent a restive horse, the king entered! We all stopped short, guests, hosts, and horses ; and all, with equal celerity, retreated, making the usual circle for his majesty to move in. The little princess bore this interruption to her sport only while surprised into quiet by the general respect inspired by the king. The instant that wore off, she grew extremely impatient for the renewal of our gambols, and distressed me most ridiculously by her innocent appeals.

"Miss Burney!—come!—why don't you play?—Come, Miss Burney, I say, play with me!—come into the phaeton again!—why don't you, Miss Burney?"

After a thousand vain efforts to quiet her by signs, I was forced to whisper her that I really could play no longer.

" But why? why, Miss Burney?—do! do come and play with me!—You must, Miss Burney!"

This petition growing still more and more urgent, I was obliged to declare my reason, in hopes of appeasing her, as she kept pulling me by the hand and gown, so entirely with all her little strength, that I had the greatest difficulty to save myself from being suddenly jerked into the middle of the room: at length, therefore, I whispered, "We shall disturb the king, ma'am!"

This was enough ; she flew instantly to his majesty, who was in earnest discourse with Mr. Smelt, and called out, "Papa, go!"

"What?" cried the king.

"Go! papa,—you must go!" repeated she eagerly.

The king took her up in his arms, and began kissing and playing with her; she strove with all her might to disengage herself, calling aloud "Miss Burney! Miss Burney! take me—come, I say, Miss Burney!—O Miss Burney, come!"

You may imagine what a general smile went round the room at this appeal: the king took not any notice of it, but set her down, and went on with his discourse. She was not, however, a moment quiet till he retired: and then we renewed our diversions, which lasted to her bed-time.

A DREADFUL MISHAP.

Nov. 6.-This morning happened my first disgrace of being too late for the queen-this noon, rather; for in a morning 'tis a disaster that has never arrived to this moment.

The affair thus came to pass. I walked for some time early in Kew gardens, and then called upon Mrs. Smelt. I there heard that the king and queen were gone, privately, to Windsor, to the Lodge : probably for some papers they could not intrust with a messenger. Mr. Smelt, therefore, proposed taking this opportunity of shewing me Richmond gardens, offering to be my security that I should have full time. I accepted the proposal with pleasure, and we set out upon our expedition. Our talk was almost all of the queen. Mr. Smelt wishes me to draw up her character. I owned to him that should it appear to me, on nearer and closer inspection, what it seemed to me then, the task could not be an unpleasant one.

He saw me safe to the Lodge, and there took his leave : and I was going leisurely upstairs, when I met the Princess Amelia and Mrs. Cheveley; and while I was playing with the little princess, Mrs. Cheveley announced to me that the queen had been returned some time, and that I had been sent for immediately.

Thunderstruck at this intelligence, I hastened to her dressing-room; when I opened the door, I saw she was having her hair dressed. To add to my confusion, the Princess Augusta, Lady Effingham, and Lady Frances Howard were all in the room. I stood still at the door, not knowing whether to advance, or wait a new summons. In what a new situation did I feel myself!-and how did I long to give way to my first impulse, and run back to my own room.

In a minute or two, the queen not a little drily said, "Where have you been, Miss Burney?"

I told her my tale,-that hearing she was gone to Windsor, I had been walking in Richmond gardens with Mr. Smelt. She said no more, and I stood behind her chair. The princess and two ladies were seated.

What republican feelings were rising in my breast, till she softened them down again, when presently, in a voice changed from that dryness which had wholly disconcerted me, to its natural tone, she condescended to ask me to look at Lady Frances Howard's gown, and see if it was not very pretty.

This made a dutiful subject of me again in a moment. Yet I felt a discomposure all day, that determined me upon using the severest caution to avoid such a surprise for the future. The Windsor journey having been merely upon business, had been more brief than was believed possible.

When I left the queen, I was told that Mrs. Delany was waiting for me in the parlour. What a pleasure and relief to me to run to that dear lady, and relate to her my mischance, and its circumstances! Mr. Smelt soon joined us there; he was shocked at the accident ; and I saw strongly by his manner how much more seriously such a matter was regarded, than any one, unused to the inside of a Court, could possibly imagine.

"IS IT PERMITTED?"

Nov. 8.-This was the birth-day of the Princess Augusta, now eighteen. I could not resist this opportunity of presenting her one of my fairings, though I had some little fear she might think herself past the age for receiving birth-day gifts, except from the royal family: however they had arrived so seemingly `a propos, and had been so much approved by the queen, that I determined to make the attempt. I took one of the work-boxes, and wrote with a pencil, round the middle ornament, "Est-il permis?"—and then I sent for Miss Makentomb, the princess's wardrobe woman, and begged her to place the box upon her royal highness's table.

At the queen's dressing-time, as I opened the door, her majesty said, " "O, here she is!—Est-il permis?—Come, come in to Augusta!" and made me follow her into the next room, the door of which was open, where the princess was seated at a writing-desk, probably answering some congratulatory letters.

Immediately, in a manner the most pleasing, she thanked me for the little cadeau, saying, "Only one thing I must beg, that you will write the motto with a pen."

The queen seconded this motion, smilingly repeating "Est-il permis?"

And afterwards, in the evening, the Princess Augusta came to the parlour, to fetch Mrs. Delany and Mrs. Smelt, and again said, "Now, will you, Miss Burney—will you write that for me with a pen?"

THE PLUMP PROVOST AND His LADY.

Nov. 23.-In the evening I had a large party of new acquaintance; the provost of Eton, Dr, Roberts, his lady, Mr. Dewes, Miss Port, the Duke of Montagu, General Bud`e, Colonel Goldsworthy, and Madame de la Fite. The party had the royal sanction, I need not tell you. The king and queen are always well disposed to shew civility to the people of Eton and Windsor, and were therefore even pleased at the visit.

The provost is very fat, with a large paunch and gouty legs. He is good-humoured, loquacious, gay, civil, and parading. I am told, nevertheless, he is a poet, and a very good one. This, indeed, appears not, neither in a person such as I have described, nor in manners such as have drawn from me the character just given.

Mrs. Roberts is a fine woman, though no longer very young; she is his second wife, and very kind to all his family. She seems good-natured and sensible.

The evening turned out very well: they were so delighted with making a visit under the royal roof, that everything that passed pleased them: and the sight of that disposition helped me to a little more spirit than usual in receiving them.

The king came into the room to fetch Mrs. Delany, and looked much disappointed at missing her; nevertheless, he came forward, and entered into conversation with the provost, upon Eton, the present state of the school, and all that belongs to its establishment. His majestytakes a great interest in the welfare and prosperity of that seminary.

The provost was enchanted by this opportunity of a long and private conference, and his lady was in raptures in witnessing it. She concluded, from that time, that the door would never open, but for the entrance of some of the royal family; and when the equerries came, she whispered me, " Who are they ? " And again, on the appearance of a star on the Duke of Montagu., she said, "Who can that be, Miss Burney?"

THE EQUERRIES VIOLATE THE RULES.

Dec. 10.-Mrs. Delany, upon her recovery, [227]had invited the general and colonel to come to tea any evening. For them to be absent from the Lodge was contrary to all known rules ; but the colonel vowed he would let the matter be tried, and take its course. Mrs. Delany hoped by this means to bring the colonel into better humour with my desertion of the teatable, and to reconcile him to an innovation of which he then must become a partaker.

On the day when this grand experiment was to be made, that we might not seem all to have eloped clandestinely, in case of inquiry, I previously made known to the queen my own intention, and had her permission for my visit. But the gentlemen, determining to build upon the chance of returning before they were missed, gave no notice of their scheme, but followed me to Mrs. Delany's as soon as they quitted their own table. I had sent to speak with General Bud`e in the morning, and then arranged the party: he proposed that the colonel andhimself should esquire me, but I did not dare march forth in such bold defiance ; I told him, therefore, I must go in a chair.

Mrs. Delany received us with her usual sweetness. We then began amusing ourselves with surmises of the manner in which we should all be missed, if our rooms were visited in our absence ; and the colonel, in particular, drew several scenes, highly diverting, of what he supposed would pass,-of the king's surprise and incredulity, of the hunting up and down of the house in search of him, and of the orders issued throughout the house to examine to what bed-post he had hanged himself,-for nothing less than such an act of desperation could give courage to an equerry to be absent without leave!

Further conjectures were still starting, and all were engaged in aiding them and enjoying them, when suddenly a violent knocking at the door was followed by the most unexpected entrance of the queen and the Princess Amelia!

Universal was the start, and most instantaneous and solemn the silence ! I felt almost guilty, though not for myself: my own invariable method of avowing all my proceedings saved me from the smallest embarrassment on my own account in this meeting; but I was ashamed to appear the leader in a walk so new as that of leaving the Lodge in an evening, and to have induced any others to follow my example. The queen looked extremely surprised, but not at me, whom she knew she should encounter; and the two gentlemen hardly could settle whether to make humble explanations, or frank ridicule, of the situation in which they were caught. The queen, however, immediately put them at their ease, speaking to them with marked civility, and evidently desirous not to mar what she found intended as a private frolic, by any fears of her disapprobation.

She did not stay long, and they soon followed her to the Lodge. I also returned, and at night the queen owned to me, but very good-humouredly, that she had never been more astonished than at sight of the equerries that evening, and asked me how it came to pass.

"Mrs. Delany, ma'am," I answered, "as she had taken away their tea-maker, thought she could do no less than offer them tea for once at her own table."

And here the matter rested. But the enterprise has never been repeated. .

MR. TURBULENT ON COURT ROUTINE.

Dec. 13.-Our dinner was as usual, the Smelts, Messrs. de Luc and Turbulent, and Miss Planta; and the last only was gone when Mr. and Mrs. Hayes arrived. Mrs. Hayes is a really pretty as well as a pretty sort of woman, [228]and modest, well-bred, and sensible - and the afternoon, with the assistance of Mr. Smelt, did very well. They went early home, and both the Smelts were called to the queen's rooms; M. de Luc said he must retire to write down " some thoughts upon an experiment in his head," and only Mr. Turbulent remained.

I found the partner of my confinement a man of uncommon capacity, but something there was hung about him, or hung about me, that prevented my assimilating-with him in anything. I saw he was endowed with great powers of agreeability; but I thought him obtrusive ; and that alone is a drawback to all merit, that I know not how to pass over. He spoke his opinions with great openness, equally upon people and things ; but it seemed rather from carelessness than confidence, and I 'know him too little to feel obliged in his trust.

The talk was chiefly upon mere general subjects, till by 'some accident the approaching birth-day of the queen was mentioned. He then inquired of me how I should like the state business of that day?

I told him I knew nothing of what I had to expect from it. He undertook readily to inform me. He said I was to be sumptuously arrayed, to sit in one of the best rooms at St. James's, and there to receive all the ladies of the queen in particular, and to do the honours to all the gentlemen also, belonging to the establishment.

I laughed, and told him he had painted to me a scene of happiness peculiarly adapted to my taste!

He did not concern himself to examine whether or not I was serious, but said he supposed, of course, the dignity of such a matter of state could not be disagreeable to me, and added, he should take the liberty to wish me joy of the day, among the rest, when it arrived, and to see me in my glory. After this he said, "You have now nearly seen the whole of everything that will come before you: in a very short time you will have passed six months here, and then you will know your life for as many, and twice and thrice as many years.

You will have seen everybody and everything, and the same round will still be the same, year after year, without intermission or alteration."

AN EQUERRY ON THE COURT CONCERT.

Dec. 26-Colonel Goldsworthy ran on, till General Bud`e reminded him it was time they should appear in the concertroom.

"Ay," cried he, reluctantly, "now for the fiddlers! There I go, plant myself against the side of the chimney, stand first on one foot, then on the other, hear over and over again all that fine squeaking, and then fall fast asleep, and escape by mere miracle from flouncing down plump in all their faces."

"What would the queen say if you did that?"

"O, ma'am, the queen would know nothing of the matter; she'd only suppose it some old double bass that tumbled."

" Why, could not she see what it was?"

"O no! ma'am, we are never in the room with the queen! that's the drawing-room, beyond, where the queen sits; we go no farther than the fiddling-room. As to the queen, we don't see her week after week sometimes. The king, indeed, comes there to us, between whiles, though that's all as it happens, now Price is gone. He used to play at backgammon with Price."

"Then what do you do there?"

"Just what I tell you—nothing at all, but stand as furniture. But the worst is, sometimes, when my poor eye-peepers are not quite closed, I look to the music-books to see what's coming; and there I read 'Chorus of Virgins:' so then, when they begin, I look about me. A chorus of virgins, indeed! why, there's nothing but ten or a dozen fiddlers! not a soul beside! it's as true as I'm alive ! So then, when we've stood supporting the chimney-piece about two hours, why then, if I'm not called upon, I shuffle back out of the room, make a profound bow to the harpsichord, and I'm off."

DR. HERSCHFL's LARGE TELESCOPE.

Dec. 3o.-This morning my dear father carried me to Dr. Herschel. That great and very extraordinary man received us with almost open arms, He is very fond of my father, who is one of the Council of the Royal Society this year, as well as himself, and he has much invited me when we have met at the Lodge or at Mr. de Luc's.

At this time of day there was nothing to see but his instruments: those, however, are curiosities sufficient. His immense new telescope, the largest ever constructed, will still, I fear, require a year or two more for finishing, but I hope it will then reward his labour and ingenuity by the new views of the heavenly bodies, and their motions, which he flatters himself will be procured by it. Already, with that he has now in use, he has discovered fifteen hundred universes ! How many more he can find who can conjecture? The moon, too, which seems his favourite object, has already afforded him two volcanoes ; and his own planet, the Georgium sidus, [229]has now shewn two satellites. From such a man what may not astronomy expect, when an instrument superior in magnitude to any ever yet made, and constructed wholly by himself or under his own eye, is the vehicle of his observation?

I wished very much to have seen his sister, whose knowledge in his own science is so extraordinary, and who herself was the first discoverer of the last comet ; but she had been up all night, and was then in bed.

Mr. Smelt joined us by appointment ; and the Bishop of Worcester came afterwards, with Dr. Douglas, to whom I was then introduced. He is the famous editor, who has published and revised and corrected so many works: among them the last voyage round the world.

By the invitation of Mr. Herschel, I now took a walk which will sound to you rather strange : it was through his telescope and it held me quite upright, and without the least inconvenience ; so would it have done had I been dressed in feathers and a bell hoop—such is its circumference. Mr. Smelt led the way, walking also upright ; and my father followed. After we were gone, the bishop and Dr. Douglas were tempted, for its oddity, to make the same promenade.

ILLNESS, AND SOME REFLECTIONS IT GAVE RISE TO.

Wednesday, Jan. 10, 1787.-This morning, when I was hurrying to the queen, I met Mr. Fairly, who said he was waiting to see me. Very melancholy he looked-very much changed from what I had seen him. His lady, to whom he is much attached, is suffering death by inches, from the most painful of all complaints, a cancer. His eldest son, who seems about twelve years old, was with him. He was going, he said, to place him at Eton.

The day following I was taken very ill myself; a'bilious fever, long lurking, suddenly seized me, and a rheumatism in my head at the same time. I was forced to send to Mr. Battiscombe for advice, and to Miss Planta to officiate for me at night with the queen.

Early the next morning Miss Planta came to me from the queen, to desire I would not be uneasy in missing my attendance, and that I would think of nothing but how to take care of myself. This, however, was not all, for soon after she came herself, not only to my room, but to my bedside, and, after many enquiries, desired me to say sincerely what I should do if I had been so attacked at home.

A blister, I said, was all I could devise; and I had one accordingly, which cured the head, and set me at ease. But the fever had been long gathering, and would not so rapidly be dismissed. I kept my bed this day and the next. The third day I was sufficiently better to quit my bed and bedroom ; and then I had not only another visit from the queen, but also from the two eldest princesses.

Tuesday, Jan. 16-Was the day appointed for removing to town for the winter; from which time we were only to come to Windsor for an occasional day or two every week.

I received a visit, just before I set out, from the king. He came in alone, and made most gracious enquiries into my health, and whether I was sufficiently recovered for the journey.

The four days of my confinement, from the fever after the pain, were days of meditation the most useful: I reflected upon all my mental sufferings in the last year; their cause seemed inadequate to their poignancy. In the hour of sickness and confinement, the world, in losing its attractions, forfeits its regrets :-a new train of thinking, a new set of ideas, took possession of all my faculties ; a steady plan, calm, yet no longer sad, deliberately formed itself in my mind; my affliction was already subsided; I now banished, also, discontent. I found myself as well off, upon reflection, as I could possibly merit, and better, by comparison, than most of those around me. The beloved friends of my own heart had joined me unalterably, inviolably to theirs —who, in number, who, in kindness, has more?

Now, therefore, I took shame to myself, and resolved to be And my success has shown me how far less chimerical than it appears is such a resolution. To be patient under two disappointments now no longer recent;—to relinquish, without repining, frequent intercourse with those I love;—to settle myself in my monastery, without one idea of ever quitting it; to study for the approbation of my lady abbess, and make it a principal source of content, as well as spring of action; -and to associate more cheerily with my surrounding nuns and monks;— these were the articles which were to support my resolution.

I thank God I can tell my dearest friends I have observed them all; and, from the date of this illness to the time in which I am now drawing out my memorandums, I can safely affirm I know not that I have made one break with myself in a single promise here projected.

And now, I thank God, the task is at an end;-what I began from principle, and pursued from resolution, is now a mere natural conduct. My destiny is fixed, and my mind is at ease; nay, I even think, upon the whole, that my lot Is, altogether, the best that can betide me, except for one flaw in its very vitals, which subjects me at times, to a tyranny wholly subversive of all power of tranquillity.

---

213   Dr. Joseph Warton, author of the "Essay on the Genius and Writings of Pope." He was headmaster of Winchester school-ED.

214   Jacob Bryant, the distinguished classical scholar and author; born 1715; died 1804. His principal work was "A New System or an Analysis of Ancient Mythology," published in 1774. During the last part of his life he resided at Cypenham, in Farnham Royal, near Windsor. One of Bryant's friends said of him that "he was a very good scholar, and knew all things up to Noah, but not a single thing in the world beyond the Deluge!"-ED.

215   Aim`e Argand, inventor of the argand lamp.-ED.

216   Madame de Genlis was governess to the children of the Duke D'Orl`eans (Philippe `egalit`e), and, there is no doubt, his mistress. The beautiful Pamela, who married Lord Edward Fitzgerald, was generally supposed to be her daughter by the duke, but this appears to be questionable.-ED.

217   William Herschel, the famous astronomer. He was the son of a German musician, and in early life followed his father's profession, which he afterwards abandoned for the study of astronomy. He received much encouragement from George III., was knighted in 1816, and died at Slough, near Windsor, in 1822. His monster telescope, mentioned in the text, was completed in 1787, and was forty feet in length.-ED.

218Maria Sophie de la Roche was a German authoress of sentimental novels, of some distinction in her day, but now chiefly remembered as the friend of Wieland and Goethe. The history of the attachment between her andWieland is very pretty, very idyllic, and very German. Sophie was born in 1731, and the idyll commenced when she was nineteen, and Wieland only seventeen years old. it lasted some time, too, for a passion so very tender and tearful; but the fate;, and, more particularly, the parents, were unpropitious, and after about three years it came to an end, the heart-broken Sophie consoling herself by marrying M. de la Roche shortly afterwards. Her friendship with Wieland, however was maintained to the end of her days, he editing the first and last productions of her pen—the "History of Fr`aulein von Sternheim," published 1771, and "Melusinens Sommerabende," 1806. Madame de la Roche died in 1807-ED.

219   Madame de la Fite had, however, translated her friend's "History of Fr`aulein von Sternheim" into French, and the translation had been published in 1773.-ED.

220   "Clelia" and "Cassandra" were celebrated heroic romances of the seventeenth century, the former (in ten volumeswritten by Mdlle Scud`eri, the latter by the Sieur de la Calprende. One of the most constant and tiresome characteristics of the heroes and heroines of the romances of this school, is the readiness with which they seize every opportunity of recounting, or causing their confidential attendants to recount, their adventures, usually with the utmost minuteness of detail-ED.

221   See P. 434.-ED.

222   Mrs. Schwellenberg found her health better in London, and was prolonging her stay there in consequence. -ED,

223   The reader will scarcely need to be told that allusion is made here to the Prince of Wales, afterwards George 1V.-ED.

224   It is hardly worth remembering, except for Fanny's sake; however, it has the merit of brevity, and here it is.

     "THE GREAT COAT.

     "Thrice honour'd Robe! couldst thou espy The form that deigns to show thy worth; Hear the mild voice, view the arch eye, That call thy panegyric forth;

     "Wouldst thou not swell with vain delight? With proud expansion sail along? And deem thyself more grand and bright Than aught that lives in ancient song,

     "Than Venus' cestus, Dian's crest, Minerva's helmet, fierce and bold, Or all of emblem gay that dress'd Capricious goddesses of old? "Thee higher honours yet await:- Haste, then, thy triumphs quick prepare, Thy trophies spread in haughty state, Sweep o'ei the earth, and scoff the air.

     "Ah no!—retract!—retreat!—oh stay! Learn, wiser, whence so well thou'st sped; She whose behest produced this lay By no false colours is misled.

"Suffice it for the buskin'd race Plaudits by pomp and shew to win; Those seek simplicity and grace Whose dignity is from within.

"The cares, or joys, she soars above That to the toilette's duties cleave; Far other cares her bosom move, Far other joys those cares relieve.

"The garb of state she inly scorn'd, Glad from its trappings to be freed, She saw thee humble, unadorn'd, Quick of attire,—a child of speed.

"Still, then, thrice honour'd Robe! retain Thy modest guise, thy decent ease; Nor let thy favour prove thy bane By turning from its fostering breeze.

"She views thee with a mental eye, And from thee draws this moral end:— Since hours are register'd on high, The friend of Time is Virtue's friend."

For this precious production Fanny received quite as much as it was worth,—the thanks of the queen, who added, "Indeed it is very pretty—only! I don't deserve it." -ED.

225   Captain James Burney had married, on the 6th of September, 1785, Miss Sally Payne, daughter of Mr. Thomas Payne, bookseller.-ED.

226   "Mr. Turbulent" is the name given in the "Diary" to the Rev. Charles de Guiffardiere, a French Protestant minister, who filled the office of French reader to the queen and princesses.-ED.

227   Mrs. Delany had been for a short time indisposed.-ED.

228   The queen had spoken of Mrs. Hayes as a "very pretty kind of woman," and desired Fanny to invite her to tea.-ED.

229   Herschel had discovered this planet in 1781, and named it in honour of the king.-ED.

Printed in the United States
84149LV00004B/93/A

9 781406 800920